# Thinking with Water

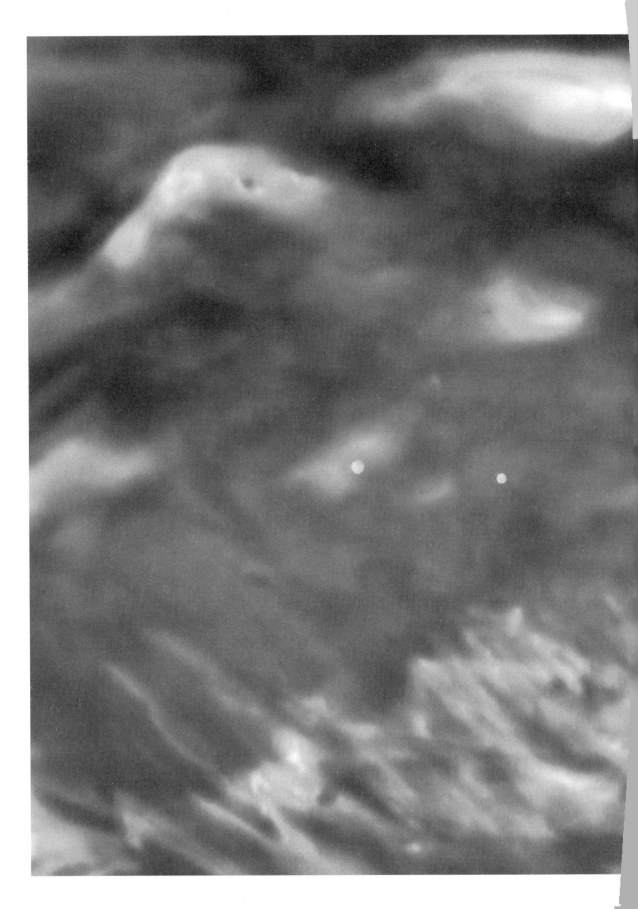

# Thinking with Water

Edited by

**Cecilia Chen, Janine MacLeod, and Astrida Neimanis**

McGill-Queen's University Press

Montreal & Kingston • London • Ithaca

ISBN 978-0-7735-4179-5 (cloth)
ISBN 978-0-7735-4180-1 (paper)
ISBN 978-0-7735-8933-9 (ePDF)
ISBN 978-0-7735-8934-6 (ePUB)

Legal deposit third quarter 2013
Bibliothèque nationale du Québec

Printed in Canada on acid-free paper

This book has been published with the help of a grant from the Canadian Federation for the Humanities and Social Sciences, through the Awards to Scholarly Publications Program, using funds provided by the Social Sciences and Humanities Research Council of Canada. Funding has also been received from Concordia University's ARRE program, administered by the Office of the Vice-President for Research and Graduate Studies.

McGill-Queen's University Press acknowledges the support of the Canada Council for the Arts for our publishing program. We also acknowledge the financial support of the Government of Canada through the Canada Book Fund for our publishing activities.

Library and Archives Canada Cataloguing in Publication

Thinking with water / Cecilia Chen, Janine MacLeod, and Astrida Neimanis.

Includes bibliographical references and index.
Issued in print and electronic formats.
ISBN 978-0-7735-4179-5 (bound).–ISBN 978-0-7735-4180-1 (pbk.).–
ISBN 978-0-7735-8933-9 (ePDF).–ISBN 978-0-7735-8934-6 (ePUB)

1. Water. 2. Water–Social aspects. 3. Water--Environmental aspects. I. Chen, Cecilia, 1970–, editor of compilation III. MacLeod, Janine, 1979–, editor of compilation III. Neimanis, Astrida G. (Astrida Gundega), 1972–, editor of compilation

GB665.T55 2013          553.7          C2013-903960-0
C2013-903961-9

This book was designed and typeset by studio oneonone in Sabon 10.2/13.5

# Contents

*Handwritten annotations:*

— capitalism + flow
— memory + water: metaphor + material memory
— counter-hegemonic space of modernism (comp.
ecopoetics according to Bate: space outside)
— multi-generational memory: contra fragmented time of capital!
Benjamin etc. vs. Bergson: priviledged experience - Latour - actor-network

sociality

Levinas: thinking of Proceedures - non-human stakeholders? — non-essentialist
generative ethics: litigacy. fluidity
ethics / ontology  agency in non-human: new democracy.
72 - Partial dissolution of boundedness of bounded subjects. gestational. Water proto-ethical.

Trans - corporeal flows +
alterity. Politics of visibility + flows of
images w/in context of capital, media etc.
Theatricality + disrupting logic of capital. Logic of capital / alterity of water

Truax: soundscapes,
spread of sound in ocean, speciesism in
ursound - acoustic ecology — acoustic ecology  thought concerning sound + protection.
contemplation of the arctic  Accoustic horizons, acoustic communities.
Acoustic dimension of conservation  Sound / noise - cultural component of these. Sound + modernity

*Handwritten annotations:*

Latour – political collective + the non-human value of aestheticised and mediated life forms.

Rancière - political act disrupts what people can see.

connection between hearing voices - Rancière, p.156 + whale song. Jellyfish beyond understanding of sensible - what an animal might be. Make insensible sensible. Fluidity, world view, inside/outside posthumanism

Group size - socio-spatial understanding, national (or other) identity, limits and resource use.

Abundance vs. scarcity. Water control, domination of nature and capitalism / bureaucratic state. Who controls + how do we manage? Small operation over large. Scarcity deployed politically

Different world views - Aus. Ab. dream time + temporal cycles. Contrast w/ Western dualism + damming/resisting time → loss of faith in god, fear of antagonistic nature "water both represents and constitutes power" 200.

The ideological coherence of texts + the megadam as icon of modernity's control of nature - conquer causality. Marxist/psychoanalytic reading of blockbuster

Western individualism vs. Indigenous embedded, concentric perspective

Water body bobs up again - in indigenous thinking

## List of Poems and Credits

Armstrong, Jeannette. "Water is Siwlkw," in *Water and Indigenous Peoples*. Edited by R. Boelens, M. Chiba, and D. Nakashima. *Knowledge of Nature 2*. Paris: UNESCO, 2006.

Dickinson, Adam. "Erratics." In *Cartography and Walking*, 51. London, Ontario: Brick Books, 2002.

Marlatt, Daphne. "generation, generations at the mouth." In *Steveston*, 3rd Edition, 61–2. Vancouver: Ronsdale Press, 2001.

McKay, Don. "Pond." In *Strike/Slip*. Toronto: McClelland & Stewart, 2006.

Siebert, Melanie. "Alsek Lake." In *Deepwater Vee*, 16. Toronto: McClelland & Stewart, 2010.

*...ed to ...pened property framework (p. 237) – as well as Western Individualism.*

# Plates and Figures

## Plates

1–2 Selected images from *Water Drawing (version 1.0)* (2010), video and sound installation by Rae Staseson. All photos printed courtesy Rae Staseson. Photographer: Darren Ell / 23–7

3–11 Selected images from *light, sweet, cold, dark, crude* (2006–ongoing), a series of micro-events performed by Ælab (Gisèle Trudel and Stéphane Claude). Photos: 3–7 by Jacques Perron; 8 by Jonathan Gröger; 9 by Keith Armstrong; 10–11 by Gisèle Trudel. Produced with the financial assistance of the Canada Council for the Arts, Media Arts, and PAFARC-UQÀM (Programme d'aide financière à la recherche et à la création de l'Université du Québec à Montréal). Equipment and software support from Hexagram (Centre for Research/Creation in Media Arts and Technologies) and Sennheiser Canada. / 29–37

12–13 Selected images from *Frozen Refractions: Text and Image Projections on Ice* (2010), artwork by Sarah T. Renshaw. All photos courtesy S.T. Renshaw, except for the image in the middle row at far right of plate 13, courtesy James Renshaw. / 129–31

14 Evolving base map of the Lachine rapids by Cecilia Chen. / 132–3

15–17 Selected images from *Taste the $ource (while supplies last)* (2006–present), installation and performance by Emily Rose Michaud. Plate 15: Photograph © 2012 Emily Rose Michaud, emilyrosemichaud.com. Plates 16 and 17: Photographs © 2006 Melissa Campbell. / 134–7

18 "Discomedusae." Colour engraving by Ernst Heinrich Haeckel, previously published as Plate 8 in Haeckel, *Art Forms in Nature*, 1904 (in Alaimo's "Jellyfish Science"). / 142

# Acknowledgments

The *Thinking with Water* project began in October 2007. A panel about water brought the three editors of this volume together for the first time at an environmental cultural studies conference entitled "Nature Matters." Thanks are due to Cate Sandilands, Meghan Salhus, and all those who helped organize that extraordinary event. During the robust collaboration that followed, we organized a workshop at Concordia University in Montreal in June 2010, at which we shared and discussed the original scholarly and artistic works in this volume with the support of that university's Department of Communication Studies. We would like to acknowledge the Kanien'kehá:ka of the Haudenosaunee Confederacy, on whose territory the workshop took place.

From workshop through to final publication, Peter van Wyck has been unflagging in his support. Cate Sandilands and Andrew Biro brought both encouragement and financial contributions to the project through their Canada Research Chairs, in Sustainability and Culture and in Political Ecology and Environmental Political Theory, respectively. Rae Staseson's support as chair of Concordia's Department of Communication Studies has been greatly appreciated, as has Michele Kaplan's expert shepherding through various applications for project funding.

This book has been published with the help of a grant from the Canadian Federation of Humanities and Social Sciences, through the Awards to Scholarly Publications Program, using funds provided by the Social Sciences and Humanities Research Council of Canada (SSHRC). Its distribution is further supported by an award from Concordia University's Aid to Research Related Events, Exhibition, Publication and Dissemination Activities Program (ARRE), through its Office of the Vice-President, Research and Graduate Studies (VPRGS). Moreover, this project would not have been possible without financial support from SSHRC's Aid to Research Workshops and Conferences in Canada and an earlier award from Concordia University's ARRE Program. The institutional and financial generosity of the Department of Communication Studies at Concordia University and Hexagram-Concordia: Institute for Research/Creation in Media Arts and Technologies were also invaluable to the workshop. From an early stage, Jonathan Crago of McGill-Queen's University Press offered encouragement, sound advice, and a sharp editorial eye. Many thanks as well to the staff at MQUP, and especially to Jane McWhinney for her careful copyediting of the manuscript.

This book has benefited greatly from two anonymous peer reviews of the manuscript, and we extend our gratitude to the reviewers for their careful comments and constructive criticism. During the workshop, Claire Kenway demonstrated excellent competence, spirits and DJ skills in her role as assistant coordinator. Darren Douglas Lee helped Cecilia Chen to create a beautiful website for our project. Liz Groeneveld copyedited the first draft of the manuscript and offered helpful comments on the chapters. Our website was skillfully translated into French by Raphaël Beaulieu.

A heartfelt thank you to the contributors to this volume. In the process of refining the manuscript, authors generously commented on each other's developing chapters. *Thinking with Water* has flourished thanks to the goodwill, enthusiasm, and patience of its artists and authors. We also extend our gratitude to our good friends and families for all of their encouragement and advice. And, finally, we would like to thank the many waters – sweet and salty, tangible and imaginary – which have animated all of these contributions.

Thinking with Water

# Introduction: Toward a Hydrological Turn?

*Cecilia Chen, Janine MacLeod, and Astrida Neimanis*

The act of reading this page is enabled by a confluence of literacy, focused intent, and opportunity – but underlying this privileged and human practice is a necessary balance of waters. If a sense of well-being accompanies this act, it rests on a frequently assumed, but always precarious, equilibrium. As the reader draws in breath, the relative humidity of the air is neither too wet nor scorchingly dry. And while these words (this page or this screen) are dry enough to be legible, the reader is neither distracted by thirst or dehydration, nor by an urgent need to pee. In all likelihood, both reader and book are sheltered from the extremes of inclement weather. An environmental and somatic balance of waters, this quiet background condition of healthy hydration and safety, is easy to forget. In fact, it may need to be forgotten to sustain the focus necessary to reading, to writing, and to thinking. And, yet, our intent with this book is to bring water forward for conscious and careful consideration, and to explore the possibilities and limits of thinking with water.

When dominant cultures are undergirded by anthropocentric logics of efficiency, profit, and progress, waters are all too often made nearly invisible, relegated to a passive role as a "resource," and subjected to containment, commodification, and instrumentalization. Where they are not being immediately managed or contested, when they are not unexpectedly flooding or washing away human lives and livelihoods, waters are often conveniently forgotten and assumed to be malleable resources. For these reasons, the diverse conceptual and artistic contributions in this volume are offered in remembrance and recognition of the watery relations without which we could not live.

There are certainly times when water is at front and centre stage: a steady stream of popular books and documentaries herald the arrival of a world water crisis, while scholarly and political debates contest whether water should be understood as a common public good or a commodified private resource. Important bodies of scholarship address the urgent need to manage water scarcities, negotiate political and military conflicts over water, mitigate the impacts of climate change on watersheds, and oppose the appropriation, diversion, and contamination of water. Thinking *of* or *about* water in these ways may nonetheless repeat the assumption that water is a resource needing to be managed and organized. While engaging in conversation with these literatures that think *about* water, this collection attempts to enter into a more collaborative relationship with the aqueous, (actively questioning habitual instrumentalizations of water. )We propose that waters enable lively possibility even as they exceed current understandings.

In questioning habitual ways of understanding, representing, and forgetting waters, this volume responds to a series of everyday assaults on the hydrosphere. Consider, for instance, the widespread industrial and agricultural practices that deplete and contaminate ancient aquifers, or the reductive rechoreography of vital waterways with dams, canals, and diversions. Once-vigorous rivers are exhausted before they reach the sea.[1] Emerging markets in water rights, bulk exports, and bottled water attempt to profit from socially produced pollution and scarcity. In the context of Canada, where many of this book's authors and artists live, a significant number of Indigenous communities suffer from chronically unsafe drinking water and witness widespread appropriation and pollution of their waters. All is not well with the waters of the world – nor with the social relations mediated by their flows.

While compiling this volume, we have also been acutely aware of the many troubled ways in which water intersects with the production of energy. In northern Alberta, tar sands operations are tearing up the boreal forest and transforming the waters of the Athabasca River into precarious "holding ponds." These manufactured water bodies leak deadly toxins back into the groundwater and the river to flow into Cree, Chipewyan, and Métis territories downstream.[2] The explosion of the British Petroleum Deepwater Horizon oil rig in April 2010 led to the still-unfolding devastation of coastlines and aquatic dwelling places in the Gulf of Mexico.[3] In the Niger Delta, ongoing oil spills from deteriorating pipelines, terminals, pumping stations, and platforms are contaminating lands and waters at a scale comparable to the Deepwater Horizon disaster.[4] In March 2011 an earthquake and tsunami flattened Japan's northeast coast, drowning tens of thousands and exposing adjacent lands and waters to both active and spent nuclear fuel from the Fukushima Daiichi power plant. A year later, communities along the Pacific coast of North America are finding flotsam from this deadly event washing up on their shores. As we attempt to imagine the invisible dispersal of toxic and radioactive materials into oceans, rivers, clouds, and aquifers, no human response feels quite sufficient.

These are merely some of the more spectacular instances of catastrophic aquatic contamination within the larger progress of what is often referred to as the "global water crisis" – a series of interconnected practices, institutions, and attitudes that transform water bodies in cumulative and seemingly inexorable ways. In each case, specific ecopolitical contexts fundamentally shape the way we conceive of these events and processes. So too, the locations and positions from which we regard these troubled waters are radically important – whether we are upstream or downstream, distant or immersed. Our relation to any specific water body affects our way of knowing its waters. For this reason, addressing these ongoing dilemmas requires that we deepen awareness of our material connections within the very particular watersheds in which we live, and that we recognize their continuing and multiform exchanges with other places and times.

Given our entanglements with the lively materiality that we inhabit, we may, here, address why we insist on thinking with *water* – and not, for instance, with air, with plastics, with rare earths, or with any of the other articulable categories of matter that we experience. First, we love water. Water attracts us: rivers, ponds, rainstorms, coastlines – even puddles – have an undeniable sensual charisma. Waters hold great spiritual meaning across cultures; they gather stories, identities, and memories. For many of us, water possesses spirit. And of course, water is a material substance essential to our life. As so many of us (plant and animal) are largely made up of water, we cannot help but be moved by this shared relation. Furthermore, among the many elements that come together to materialize life, water offers a visceral experience of the transformations that all biota sense, both internally and in their surrounding environments. Unlike other kinds of elemental matter (earth, fire, air, metal, stone, and wood, for example), water moves from solid to liquid to vapour with acute environmental responsiveness. We experience circadian and seasonal rhythms most prominently through water's phase changes: from rain to snow, from morning dew to afternoon humidity. Even otherwise "invisible" phenomena like climate change become immediately tangible through the volatility of weather patterns and the intensity of floods, hurricanes, tsunamis, and droughts. At the slower but epochal scale of acidifying oceans, changed currents, wetland encroachment, and desertification, we are also part of watery transformations. Water's responsiveness to particular places – its ability to interact with the permeability, chemistry, and temperature of a particular environment – offers radical insight into any ecocultural context.

Although the works collected here diverge widely in their disciplinary backgrounds, modes of expression, and sites of inquiry, they share five currents of thought. First, in bringing water to the forefront, the authors and artists in this volume are driven by ecopolitical concerns; they explore what it might mean to practise politics in more aqueous modes. Next, they resist the tendency to approach water as an abstract idea – waters are carefully placed or embodied in specific materialities and spacetimes. Third, this collection underlines the continuity of watery materiality (for example, its capacity to gestate life, transform, or destroy) with discursive practices and ways of knowing. In addition, the contributions emphasize water's relationality, and its ability to generate unexpected or unrecognized communities. Finally, the works gathered here demonstrate water's capacity to challenge our ways of knowing, both by crossing conventional disciplinary boundaries and by revealing the ways in which "nature" and "culture" are always co-constituted. Throughout, our aim is to demonstrate how a recognition of water's critical presence in all aspects of our lives can encourage a radically inclusive politics and an invigorated practice of cultural theory.

## An Aqueous Ecopolitics

We – in the broadest of senses – all have water in common. If we think of politics as the practice of speaking and acting together on matters of common concern,[5] then water may be the most exemplary of political substances; it is an intimately and continuously shared "matter," in both senses of the term. This political commons includes not only those of us living here now, but also all life that is past and all life that is still to come.[6] And, although it may be argued that politics is a distinctly human facility, thinking with water continues to raise the question of politics as concerned also with the (imperfectly surmised) interests of a squeaking, humming, chirping, and pheromone-exuding non-human multitude.[7] Accordingly, more aqueous ecopolitics might above all encourage further expansion of the sphere of political "stakeholders," and shift our focus toward those multiple others – human and otherwise, past, present and future – with whom these watery matters are shared.

Moreover, given water's capacity to connect and combine, thinking the political with water might help us bring together issues and concerns too often addressed in isolation. When we take common waters into account, environmental actions against species extinction or ecological degradation become more difficult to separate from alter-globalization efforts, anticolonial struggles, or social justice activism more broadly. We more clearly see, for example, how in the Athabasca watershed, human and wildlife health, the preservation of wetlands, geographies of colonization, petropolitics, gendered labour-related mobility, and the flows of multinational capital are all intricately bound to the waters of the river. Similarly, water plays a central role in multi-dimensional issues such as climate change, which urgently demand conversation across arenas of political engagement.

Water-related concerns are not the only sites where greater attention to such inter-connection is needed. However, as a substance essential for life and for the generation of wealth and well-being, water is a crucial term in struggles for environmental justice. As Donald Worster argues, water has a particularly intimate relationship with political and social power. In many cases, the achievement of domination over watercourses (however temporary) coincides with an intensification of social domination.[8] The construction of the Sardar Sarovar mega-dam in India's Narmada Valley, for example, has displaced and disenfranchised approximately half a million people.[9] It has done so in order to provide water to large-scale growers of sugar and other cash crops, as well as to numerous politically powerful urban centres and industrial interests. In spite of discourses promising a fair distribution of benefits, the imposition of managerial control over the Narmada River has brought more water (and, therefore, economic wealth) to already-privileged constituencies, while radically dispossessing the mostly tribal populations of the region.[10] In contexts like these, efforts to protect and restore the integrity of rivers become inseparable from efforts to bring about conditions of social justice and diffused political power.

Even as water joins us in a political commons, it hardly follows that the political stakes are evenly distributed across this wide community. As outlined in more detail below, each body is oriented toward water and other watery bodies in specific ways – ways specific to our species, our biome, our watershed, our culture, our singular desires, and our fears. In such a political community, we are both common and different. We are called to the difficult but necessary work of holding tensions – even of cultivating dissent – rather than ceding to the impulse toward neat resolution. This is equally true in negotiating the concepts and frameworks of ecopolitics itself. We debate: Can ethics apply to the more-than-human world? Can political agency be attributed to the work of water? Upon what exclusions might the right to water be based? Attention to water as a matter of concern shared across our differences might invite more humility and careful listening – while annulling neither solidarity nor decisive action.

Perhaps the need to resist the erasure or avoidance of dissent is nowhere greater than in relationships between water and colonization; historically, "resolution" has too often been synonymous with conquest. "Indigeneity" is another contested term (within these pages as well) that demands an open attitude toward dialogue, and spaces need to be created where Indigenous and Western knowledges can meet on a more equitable footing.[11] Our open call for papers, as it was originally formulated, did not attract proposals from Indigenous writers and artists. Further, when we sent out specific invitations to Indigenous thinkers, the absence of a prior relationship with these scholars resulted in some initial interest but an ultimate lack of participation in this project. Whether this was due to the overcommitment of established Indigenous scholars or to an understandable wariness to engage with projects framed primarily from settler perspectives, it became clear that meaningful intercultural collaboration on water issues could not be simply conjured by our good will as editors.

In this volume, Dorothy Christian and Rita Wong explicitly critique the ways in which some approaches to knowledge marginalize Indigenous and minority voices. As Christian points out, "we are not in that place of equality yet." To decolonize water, they suggest, it is also necessary to decolonize our relationships with one another. During the workshop that preceded this volume, Christian expressed great discomfort at being the only Indigenous person in the room. Both she and Wong subsequently challenged us, as curators of the contributions gathered here, to consider the ways in which normative knowledge infrastructures are still strongly tied to colonial ways of thinking that construct Indigeneity as other. What responsibility might we have to proactively counter such tendencies? If we set out to generate interdisciplinary conversation on water, how can we also engage in intercultural conversation? If we want to practise theory in a way that invites meaningful exchange between Indigenous and settler perspectives, what changes do we need to make in our scholarly networks, discourses, and institutionalized practices to do this effectively? As Wong has pointed out, decolonizing habitual and too-often-invisible academic conventions may require extraordinary measures. We (editors, contributors, readers) may need to venture outside comfortable epistemic communities.

The political commons we create together must allow ample room for consonance and disagreement, and for patient cultivation of long-term relationships that are respectful of difference. It may be precisely through the discomfort of dissonance that we come to learn new ways of thinking our obligations to water.

## Situating Waters

Water does not exist in the abstract. It must take up a body or place (a hedgehog, a weather front, a turn of phrase) somewhere, sometime, somehow. All water is situated. Moreover, we are all situated in relation to water. We may live by a particular stream, along an ocean front, in a drought-prone landscape, or above an aquifer, and we certainly live in a specific watershed (whether healthy or polluted). We come to identify with, or are touched and moved in different ways, by the waters that we experience. Situating water therefore requires that we become more aware of the daily practices and repeated encounters through which we locate ourselves in relation to water. And, in turn, we need to acknowledge the wealth and complexity of these watery relations, including *how* we share these relations with many others.

Consider, for example, a mayfly, whose day-long existence is premised upon the good health and spring temperatures of a freshwater river or lake. It emerges from the water and its winter larval form for a brief day of aerial mating before falling, mortally exhausted, back to the surface of the water to lay its eggs (if it is female) and certainly to feed hungry fish. In some sense, we all emerge from and return to waters.[12] There is incalculable diversity in how we (the many life forms within a given watershed) relate to the waters that are integral to the places we inhabit. However, for humans, place is often strongly associated with landed locations; situating waters may thus be quite tricky. Water can evoke an uncanny space-time in many human myths – a place of others, or an *other* place.[13] Our spatial and temporal relations to water may seem unintelligible, unruly, and vague, but they are also full of disturbing potential.[14] By drawing upon the reservoir of unknowability carried within all waters, we may situate ourselves in ways that challenge land-based preconceptions of fixity.

Every attempt to situate common waters is inevitably partial. Our understanding of unfolding water crises such as the Deepwater Horizon oil spill, changes in the world's oceans, or the degradation caused by the Canadian tar sands is constituted, for instance, by news stories, reports from scientists and local activists, and, increasingly, by satellite images and underwater cameras. We must therefore consider how our relations to these near or distant waters are affected and shaped by various forms of mediation. Andrew Biro, in this volume, suggests that certain kinds of media enable us to form communities and political identities in relation to waters that we may never have touched. However, can these mediated and long-distance relationships with shared waters lead to lasting political commitments? Veronica Strang's contribution to this book, for instance, argues that physical proximity may be a necessary precondition for such loyalties. Questions of scale and location thus open another arena of productive tension in situating watery place.

Whether by means of local or international media, the manipulation of resource management discourses, or traditional wisdom passed down through oral histories, we are also reminded that storytelling is a powerful way to bring a community together into articulations of place. We situate both waters and ourselves by narrating our relations. Thinking with water demands that we move beyond simply asking, "Where are these waters located?" and "How can they be useful (to humans)?" to also ask, "By whom and how are these waters situated?" and "How do they bring us together into community?" As Cecilia Chen suggests, alternative ways of "story-ing" and mapping waters can give voice to inclusive and evolving vocabularies of watery place, thereby transforming collective ways of thinking.

Different ways of situating water may serve to acknowledge or deny our participation in and our obligations to the communities enabled by these same waters. For example, many urbanites forget (or little recognize) how the health of a city and its inhabitants is premised upon the well-being of the surrounding waters – a situation that parallels that of the mayfly. Indeed, the way we choose to build our cities can severely limit our understanding of water and may even encourage its forgetting. Urban water infrastructures channel our watery relations through taps and plumbing, chlorinated pools and drinking fountains, and the tightly controlled shores of harbours or waterside parks. The ways in which we situate water have the potential to alter its presence and change its discursive representations in cultural and political contexts.

If we are to be responsible to water – if we are to respond to its unknowability, its articulations of kinship, and its radical importance in the places we inhabit – then we are obliged to recognize, and to deliberately iterate and reiterate, the diverse situations of water. Given that water is a transformative and transforming element, its situation can only be understood dynamically – as a materially complex intersection with a participant-observer in space and time. In articulating the situations of water, we shape the relations between our watery selves and our watery others.

## Water as Language and Material Metaphor

When we turn our attention to matters of language, a commitment to materially situated scholarship remains crucial. Whether in the form of Hegelian idealism or Marxist materialism, cultural and intellectual worlds have often been conceptualized as territories distinct from the realm of material history, either preceding or following more "concrete" economic or political developments.[15] In our thinking with water against the habitual divides between "nature" and "culture," the material relations of language become very important. The co-constitution of water as a substance and water as poetics is particularly critical. How do waters, as subjects of continuous sensory encounters – from bathing to street-cleaning to puddle-hopping to drinking – shape the emergence of language and ideas?

In his book *Water and Dreams: An Essay on the Imagination of Matter*, Gaston Bachelard asserts that our concepts always depend on material metaphors for their expression. As abstract as they sometimes may seem, ideas cannot thrive without some reference to embodied experience.[16] Similarly, George Lakoff and Mark Johnson argue that we cannot avoid thinking in metaphor, and that our thoughts are always structured by our bodily experiences.[17] We situate ourselves spatially as "ahead" or "behind" in our work and debate the merits of ideas using metaphors of weight – "on the one hand," "on the other hand." Language emerges from corporeal experience.

Similarly, the intimate involvement of waters with every aspect of our lives has made it a primary constituent of our conceptual worlds as well. Many fundamental concepts and ideas would be unthinkable without a language of flow, circulation, and depth. In everyday speech, emotions "flood," "bubble up," and "surge"; a "dry" text is one that lacks feeling and passion. We "freeze up" with stage fright, join or diverge from "mainstream" populations. Money "circulates"; commodities "flood" the market. The past is a "depth" and time "evaporates." Neither is the realm of theory immune to inspiration from the liquid world: aqueous dynamics of "flux" and "flow" characterize qualities of indeterminacy and continuous change within many contemporary epistemologies, while feminist concepts of "leakiness" and "seepage" have been mobilized to identify crucial porosities in bodies and theories alike. We already think with water, both physiologically and in this use of watery language and metaphor. Just as water animates our bodies and economies, so it also permeates the ways we think.

Waters add very particular nuances and associations to the concepts they help to signify, and symbolic meanings of waters accumulate from both personal and collective experiences. When I say I am "flooded" with grief, for example, the quality of my sadness gets mingled with the sensual and associative resonances of a submerged dike, levee, or coastline – or perhaps the messiness and mould of an inundated basement. The tangible forms of water – gentle rain, immovable ice, crashing wave – mingle their qualities with our ideas of generosity, emotional paralysis, or overwhelming power, even as they accumulate new connotations on their transit through paragraphs or paintings.

As a substance that carries strong associations, then, water can be understood as a particularly potent linguistic ingredient. However, not all water-inspired language is helpful or desirable from an ecopolitical perspective. As Janine MacLeod argues in her contribution to this volume, watery symbols and metaphors can be mobilized both to legitimate and to challenge operations of power. The "flow of capital" metaphor, for example, in its persistent evocation of "liquidity," and "trickle down effect," tends to naturalize patterns of ecological and social exploitation, while positioning investment as an essential substance of life and health.[18] In structuring our thoughts, metaphors shape vital interactions with the world. They focus our attention in particular ways, dictating what is perceived and what remains invisible.[19] In this case, the metaphor highlights ways in which capital is like water – in its ability to generate abundance for investors, for example – while hiding the ways in which capital is decidedly *unlike* water. For example, capital is necessary for life only within very particular social and historical contexts. In celebrating the possibilities of thinking with water in this volume, we recognize that the political implications of water metaphors are not universally benign.

Further, while the sounds, smells, textures, and visual repertoires of water can inspire us to rethink a broad spectrum of critical questions – from temporality and ethics to identity and mapping – scholarly water metaphors can sometimes slip into a naïve or universalizing deployment of "fluidity" in the abstract. An excess of water can threaten the integrity of living bodies; similarly, an over-emphasis on fluid concepts can obliterate important theoretical and material distinctions. For example, even as migrating bodies and global capital "flow" across state borders, excessive recourse to such languages elides the important ways in which such borders still regulate this traffic. As editors and authors, we use and enjoy water metaphors in our own writing – indeed, they are difficult to avoid. In doing so, however, we have tried to be attentive to the specific work they accomplish.

Metaphor is a key form through which words and ideas come to be shaped by waters. To recognize the materiality of metaphor, therefore, is to acknowledge language as a more-than-human collaboration.[20] At the same time, our vital ways of knowing also exceed language. Corporeal sensibility, too, shapes and is shaped by water – in ways that are inseparable from language. Throughout this collection, we think with water in more-than-metaphorical ways, as well.

## Relational Waters

As Dorothy Christian reminds us within these pages, "from an Indigenous perspective, everything within Creation is sacred and interrelated."[21] Such cosmologies of essential connectivity have deep roots and remain integral to Indigenous communities across our shared planet.[22] The relationship of Western knowledge and theory to Indigenous cosmologies has too often been characterized by ignorance or gross appropriation. However, alongside – and resonant with – worldviews of interrelation, thinkers across a variety of traditions continue to question the atomistic ontologies of Western liberal individualism. More relational ways of knowing are emerging from feminist, postcolonial, posthumanist, and phenomenological perspectives, among others.[23] While they do not share a single philosophical genealogy, and are certainly subject to critiques on their own terms, these perspectives together signal a developing ontological and epistemological shift in contemporary cultural theory and practice.

Thinking with water encourages relational thinking, as theories based on notions of fluidity, viscosity, and porosity reveal. But if water is deployed as a potent metaphor in such thinking, as described above, we must recall that these theories are inspired by relations that are decidedly material. Water is a *matter* of relation and connection. Waters literally flow between and within bodies, across space and through time, in a planetary circulation system that challenges pretensions to discrete individuality. Watery places and bodies are connected to other places and bodies in relations of gift, transfer, theft, and debt. Such relationality inaugurates new life, and also the infinite possibility of new communities. Human wombs, evolutionary theories of hypersea, the impressive biodiversity of marine ecosystems – all testify to water's creative-connective capacity, or what Astrida Neimanis and Mielle Chandler describe as the "gestational milieu." In these senses, water is a deep source of plurality and potential, as bodies share and connect through their common waters.

But water also reminds us that relationality is more than a romanticized confluence of bodies. Water also circulates contamination and disease. Pollutants travelling through rainclouds and groundwaters, or pieces of plastic carried by ocean currents underscore other, more difficult communications. It is clear that the relationality of water cannot be considered without critical attention to anthropogenic intervention, as human bodies are the cause of much of this toxic transit. And ongoing industrial pollution, megadam construction, massive groundwater extractions, and large-scale irrigation schemes re-choreograph relations in harmful ways. A consideration of relational waters brings us back to ecopolitics and the need for more accountability to the waters we all share.

These examples illustrate the inescapable materiality of relational waters. But, as noted, the substance and the semiotics of water are deeply entangled. Specific articulations of water are also "events"[24] whereby aqueous interactions of bodies, space, and time transform not only the matter of these phenomena but also the ways in which they are rendered meaningful. For example, when the water supply of Walkerton, Ontario, became contaminated by E. coli bacteria in May 2000, not only were waters and human bodies transformed, but the meaning of "safe tap water" was radically reconfigured as well.[25] As noted above, language is a primary means through which we know things, but corporeal sensibility draws us back to the rootedness of language in our material entanglements with the watery world. Thinking with water amplifies these complex ways of both knowing and relating, as well as their inextricability.

At the same time, an attunement to the varied and sometimes vague relations of the aqueous reminds us that there are limits to human knowledge, perception, and power. Despite the responsibility we must assume for certain communications, as humans, with our specifically human motivations, we can never fully direct water's relational reach. Water has a remarkable capacity to resist containments of all kinds – be they the language we use to capture water's materiality, or the dams and dikes we deploy to keep its surges at bay. This is what Max Haiven in this volume calls water's "unimaginable causality," or what Jennifer Spiegel cites as "planetarity" – Gayatri Spivak's term for an incalculable and ineradicable alterity. Knowledge born out of corporeal relationality necessarily includes a certain *un*knowability. Or, as Wong notes, "water has a syntax   i am still learning."[26] Even as, on the one hand, we must become more attuned to all the ways in which "the babble of water" (as Chen here calls it) is a language we need to learn, we must also recognize that not all speech can be captured by human ears or usurped by human voices.

By engaging the specific qualities of water, then, we can begin to think relationality in increasingly sophisticated ways. We can (cautiously) voice the subtleties of relations that may previously have been ignored, invisible, under-articulated, or unintelligible, at the same time as we realize that full fluency in these languages is beyond our grasp. And we can continue to refine our understanding of the complex and inextricable relation of matter and meaning in both our theoretical and our political engagements with water.

## Watering Cultural Theory (Rethinking the *oikos*)

Given that its contributors hail from a wide range of backgrounds and disciplines, *Thinking with Water* is best described as a collection of cultural theory. Perhaps it should be enough to leave it at that – to accept that analyses of watery bodies and aqueous actors "properly" belong within cultural studies. Yet, as some cultural studies scholars remind us,[27] environmental and ecological approaches within cultural studies are still marginalized as a sub-category of the discipline, when they are included at all. While the reasons for this separation are too numerous to rehearse comprehensively here, they are not only a product of the history of the discipline itself, but – more broadly, and most significantly for this particular collection of work – they are also closely connected to a pervasive and long-standing worldview within Western cultures. This is what Strang refers to as "a conceptual bifurcation between culture and nature" that results in both highly gendered and colonial modes of understanding the world.[28] Despite longstanding alternatives to such views and mounting critiques thereof, cultural studies – like most, if not all, other academic disciplines in the West – has not escaped the influence of this persistent bifurcation. In line with this dichotomous way of ordering the world, objects of academic study tend to be similarly delineated; and hence the "eco" struggles to assert its radical relation to the "cultural."

In response to this marginalization, Jennifer Slack asserts that the "eco" in ecocultural must not be merely prepositional; it must be transformative for cultural theory as a whole.[29] Given that nature and culture are engaged in a perpetual dance of co-constitution, and that, in fact, no decisive boundary could ever separate the two, ignoring the "eco" in cultural studies has "profound political and ethical effects."[30] Thus, Slack suggests that we do away with the term "ecocultural" altogether, and work instead to radicalize the whole of the discipline, such that – as suggested above – a focus on the "eco" would demand no further explanation. Cultural theory would have taken an "ecological turn."

We certainly take Slack's point. At the same time, perhaps we should hold onto the "eco" just a little bit longer. With its etymological root in the Greek *oikos*, meaning "home" or "dwelling," the prefix "eco-" indicates *where we live*. In this sense, ecocultural studies implies a recontextualizing of critical cultural thinking, a way of bringing it home – we might even be tempted to say, to where it "belongs." In other words, we suggest that this prefix be read not as a specializing manoeuvre, but rather as a way of remembering that "eco" is far more inclusive, expansive, *and* quotidian than conventional views of the "natural" or the "biological" suggest. "Eco" is also culture, technology, representation, identity, poetry. Yet, at the same time, homes can be radically uncanny,[31] and "coming home" can be fraught with risk, uncertainty, and ghosts. In this specific case, there is the risk that assuming the "eco" within the cultural will result in the further forgetting of this *oikos* that makes the cultural possible in the first place. For these reasons, we also hold onto the "eco" as a means of making our position visible: ecological and environmental perspectives are crucial to a full understanding of what "cultural studies" entail – even if such markers *should* be unnecessary.

*Thinking with Water* emphasizes that this home (this place, this body, this time, this planet) is composed largely of water. Our use of the word "with" in the title of this collection thus signifies a dual recognition. First, we bring waters into the foreground, noticing how they already animate key ways of knowing – including practices of politics and language, metaphor, corporeal relation, and theory. Second, we invite waters to further inform our concepts, consciously and strategically engaging their potential to transform ecocultural theory. Thus, not only do we acknowledge waters' ubiquity and potency within the more-than-human production of knowledge; we also assert that waters themselves have their own intelligences[32] – that they can and should be approached as collaborators in our theoretical endeavours.

## Charting these Particular Waters

An explicit goal of this collection is to demonstrate how water brings different ways of thinking into productive conversation. Its chapters engage in diverse and unconventional disciplinary crossings, responding to the growing need in humanities scholarship for enacting generative transdisciplinary inquiry. It is also for this reason that we have included poems by Jeannette Armstrong, Melanie Siebert, Don McKay, Adam Dickinson, and Daphne Marlatt,[33] and artworks by Ælab, Emily Rose Michaud, Sarah Renshaw, and Rae Staseson. These poetic and artistic approaches to thinking with water are integral to the multivocal spirit that animates this project. Given the multivalent relations between the individual works of this book, the selection of one physical ordering for this volume was not easy. We have charted one possible passage through, although we hope and expect that readers will find their own ways of moving in and among the concepts, texts, and images of *Thinking with Water*.

○

We begin with an excerpt from Rae Staseson's *Water Drawing (version 1)*, an intense meditation in video and sound on the uncanny surface of water. Between and beyond the frames of this diptych, beneath the glinting and restless surface of water, we sense unseen movements. Like the play of light, opacity, and transparency on its surface, this articulation of water challenges the conventional bounds of perception and representation. *Water Drawing* documents Staseson's relationship with Lake Katepwa in Saskatchewan, a body of water close to her home. In a more urban context, Ælab investigates waste-waters as a viscerally important way that we participate in (or "give back" to) waters. In *light, sweet, cold, dark, crude (LSCDC)*, the municipal wastewater infrastructures of Montreal, usually hidden from view, are juxtaposed with the innovative Eco-Machines designed by John Todd – wetland-mimicking systems that engage a community of plants and animals to treat sewage and other waters. Through an on-going series of micro-events using image, sound, and installation-performance, *LSCDC* reveals wastewater as an active force of change and transformation.

Water and the cycling of life appear in yet another register in Daphne Marlatt's poem "generation, generations at the mouth" (2006). Lingering at the mouth of the Staľəw (the Fraser River), Marlatt considers how our interactions affect salmon, bears, eagles, and other non-human kin. She describes the river mouth as a "bardo" where the un-born, the dead, and the "clans of the possible" are gathering. In this, her poem antici-pates the concerns of other authors in this volume who engage water as a material reservoir of the past and the future.

In "Water and the Material Imagination," Janine MacLeod contrasts two powerful water metaphors: the "flows of capital" and the "depths of the past." She articulates how these pervasive metaphorical waters can either drain or animate the dimension of memory that dwells in the "wet hearts of everyday objects." In an ecopolitical reading of novels by Virginia Woolf and Marcel Proust, MacLeod suggests ways in which the waters of memory might help us to resist the amnesiac effects of the commodity form, and thus recover both the well-being of the hydrocommons and a consciousness of multi-generational time.

Where MacLeod focuses on the presence of the past in everyday waters, Mielle Chan-dler and Astrida Neimanis, in "Water and Gestationality: What Flows Beneath Ethics," consider water as a site of material sociality for the cultivation of a plural future. By engaging with Emmanuel Levinas, Gilles Deleuze, and the Deepwater Horizon oil spill, the authors observe that water makes possible the conditions for human ethics by "be-coming-milieu" for all life. As such, they invite feminist understandings of gestational ethics to be recast in posthumanist terms. Chandler and Neimanis, with Marlatt and others in this book, call on us to protect and nourish the waters to which we are all so indebted.

With its focus on frequently ignored waters, Jennifer Spiegel's "Subterranean Flows: Water Contamination and the Politics of Invisibility after the Bhopal Disaster" shares concerns with Ælab's performative work. In her exploration of the aftermath of the 1984 industrial tragedy in Bhopal, India, Spiegel draws our attention to the toxic subterranean waters that still inform life in Bhopal. The denial of responsibility for Bhopal's contaminated groundwaters by multi-national corporation Union Carbide (now Dow Chemical) makes past deaths and present illnesses invisible. Spiegel examines how this evasion is being countered by local and global activists who simultaneously perform and protest these toxic waters in a complex bid for recognition. Like Chandler and Neimanis, Spiegel looks towards watery futures, but futures that also harbour the anxiety of denied and unknown contaminations.

Jeannette Armstrong's poem "Water is Siwlkw" offers a legato catalogue of water's movements between animals and plants, earth and sky, poles, savannas, and deserts. The syntax of the poem invites a flow of words without pause for breath, mimicking the movement of water in its fluid form. This extended rhythm, along with the poem's long list of creatures, places, and phase states, evokes water's inexhaustible repertoires. Armstrong effectively decentres the human in her poem, drawing her readers' attention, often minutely, to water's intimacy with other species.

Water's more-than-human dimensions also come to the fore in Shirley Roburn's "Sounding a Sea-Change: Acoustic Ecology and Arctic Ocean Governance." This chapter invites us to consider the proximity of humans and whales through an examination of the pervasive impacts of sound pollution. The empathy she proposes requires that we listen otherwise – that we relinquish our habitual human environs and venture into the oceans, where sound becomes far more important than it is on land. Roburn approaches the whale-human relationship through soundscape studies, ototoxicity in cetaceans, the cultural impacts of whale-song recordings, and Indigenous ways of knowing and communicating about and with whales. She explores how diverse representational practices are also practices that make the world.

Sarah Renshaw brings words, images, and frozen waters together in a painting performance, *Frozen Refractions*. Excerpts from Henri Bergson's *Matter and Memory* are layered with shifting light patterns on a melting slab of ice against the dark of an autumn night, to visceral effect. Renshaw's piece materializes the ambiguous relationship between memory and briefly frozen water, as ice is at once retentive (a glacial seizing of material memory) and ephemeral (as it melts and easily evokes forgetting). In Emily Rose Michaud's performance, *Taste the $ource (while supplies last)*, often-forgotten local waters are brought playfully to the attention of passersby in Montreal. A lovely but strange merwoman dares us to taste seemingly raw waters from nearby sources. How do we recognize, care for, and accept into our very selves the waters that we live with?

Where Roburn draws attention to the striking similarities between humans and whales, Stacy Alaimo asks how we might cultivate an ethics toward animal bodies utterly unlike us. In "Jellyfish Science, Jellyfish Aesthetics, or Posthumanism at Sea," she challenges humanism from an aqueous perspective. Alaimo responds to Jacques Rancière's call to examine the relation of politics to "the visible, the sayable and the thinkable." Like Spiegel, Alaimo grapples with the ethics and politics of making certain watery bodies visible, but Alaimo's focus is the "non-descript goo" of the jellyfish. Through historical and contemporary representations of gelata, Alaimo considers the ambiguous aesthetics of these creatures without faces. Barely distinguishable from their ocean habitat, the jellies "captured" and framed by human photographers and artists disrupt conventional modes of knowing.

Like Alaimo, Melanie Siebert highlights the otherness encountered in and through water, this time through the thundering, creaking, and spitting speech of ancient glaciers. In Siebert's "Alsek Lake," we witness glacial phenomena that far exceed the scale of our short lives. Water's deep time becomes tangible as "glacial ages roll over, become drinkable." The Tatshenshini River, in contrast to the passivity so often ascribed to waters, manifests as a "thunder-flask," "rough-tongued, relentless." In its presence, the poet is "ice-kicked"; her "chest caves open." Siebert, like Roburn, demands that her readers listen actively in the presence of these waters.

The next chapter, Andrew Biro's "River-Adaptiveness in a Globalized World," takes up questions relating to mobility, community, and identity. Biro notes the frequent privileging of the "local" in environmental discourses, and asks how we might cultivate "river-adaptiveness" at overlapping scales of social and political organization. He also interrogates the production of water's scarcity and abundance, as these relate to patterns of social and ecological domination. In his concluding case study of Anglo-Canadian national identity, Biro investigates an "imagined community" of water convened at scales that may reconfigure or challenge definitions of the "local."

Water and identity serve as a hinge between Biro's study and the Australian context of Veronica Strang's chapter, "Conceptual Relations: Water, Ideologies, and Theoretical Subversions." Water bodies are important to both Aboriginal and settler communities – albeit in quite different ways. In considering these differences, Strang examines how inequitable impoundments of water are enabled by a conceptual separation of nature and culture. She is critical of the human arrogance that attempts to contain and control "nature" in general, and water in particular. Linking theoretical and cosmological approaches to current political-economic containments of water, Strang argues that our ways of conceiving of water and our ways of interacting with it are significantly and radically related. She further narrates ways in which people seek to transform water into what they desire (food, capital, places, and identity).

In his poem "Erratics," Adam Dickinson also evokes water's ability to shift and mutate. He brings us quietly into the transformations of water at the shore of a town, as it becomes dog, dress, cloud, window. Dickinson's words recall Chandler and Neimanis's descriptions of water's infinitely variable becoming (as cloud and raindrop, as girl and woman). Sketching moments of light, sky, and beach, Dickinson reminds us that water's metamorphoses are always with us, cycling through different entities, washing up at the edges of everyday perception.

With its focus on the metaphoric and material hauntings of the mega-dam, Max Haiven's chapter, "The Dammed of the Earth: Reading the Mega-Dam for the Political Unconscious of Globalization," is strongly critical of large-scale water impoundments that attempt to fix water's lively transformations. Haiven reveals the technological colonialisms and – echoing the concerns of Strang – the modernist hubris that enable a mega-dam to be constructed in the first place. He examines the role of the mega-dam in the political unconscious, analysing climactic dam-bursting scences in Hollywood blockbusters.

The anticolonial politics of Haiven's chapter are amplified in Dorothy Christian and Rita Wong's collaborative piece "Untapping Watershed Mind." With a conscious nod to the principles of the Two-Row Wampum,[34] each author speaks in her own voice to weave together sympathies, respectful differences, and lived experiences in a narrative of enspirited watery place. Christian and Wong convey a deep respect for the often-unseen generative forces of water. While, as both Biro and Strang have pointed out, water already informs our collective identities, Christian and Wong gesture toward radically different relations with water – relations conducted with greater humility, in which prayer and poetry both play important roles.

With the initially unassuming "Pond," Don McKay suggests that a modest but murkily alive body of water could have altered myth: Narcissus may have become a limnologist and lived to become a wrinkled old man. Against the singular and homogenous abstraction "water," MacKay draws our attention to the particularity of different water bodies, "for pond is not pool." Like Staseson's *Water Drawing*, the poem draws us into phenomenological awareness of details – the play of light, reflection, responses to wind. However, the humble pond is also an active subject as it "gathers," "ponders" (!), "puckers," and even experiences "momentary ecstasy."

No less inventive is "Footbridge at Atwater: A Chorographic Inventory of Effects," Peter van Wyck's study of the Lachine Canal in Montreal. This meditation considers fluid and mud, perception, memory, and situation – a "river in slow motion." Author, reader, and other spectres that haunt the site are complicit as we stand with van Wyck on the footbridge. Like MacLeod, who finds in deep waters a transformative archive of multigenerational memories, van Wyck sifts the sediments of the canal to reveal its multiple pasts. In a chorography of thirty-two gestures, the canal waters are suggestively triangulated with the narrator-listener on the footbridge, and with stories of transport and industry, the park-like banks of a national heritage site, a discarded mitten, oligochaetes, and zones of bureaucratic jurisdiction.

This canal was built to bypass Iohná:wate', or the Lachine Rapids, the catalyst for Cecilia Chen's chapter "Mapping Waters: Thinking with Watery Places." Whereas maps may facilitate colonial appropriations and strategic attempts to fix the meaning of watery places, Chen proposes that we move mapping practices toward more collaborative processes that better represent the more-than-human communities of water. She is critical of how water is narrowly and instrumentally framed as a "resource" and notes that the excesses of water escape conventional conceptual and material containments in generative and risky ways. By proposing a heuristic approach to the mapping of watery places, Chen seeks to enable a more inclusive way of "knowing" and negotiating our relations with shared waters.

○

As the many works collected here demonstrate, water teaches us about an ethics of care and response; about the need for all bodies to be sustained by good water, good nourishment, good words; about patience and resilience; about the way theory, activism, and art overlap and blur; about the need to listen to voices that are too often silenced or deemed mere "babble." While it is certainly fraught with conflicts and crises, the eco-political moment of this project also yields numerous attempts to give back to waters, to cultivate other ways of relating with water, and to resist practices of contamination and appropriation. In many rural and urban communities, people become "keepers" or "friends" of a body of water to which they feel strongly connected. They gather to plant native vegetation along watercourses, remove debris, and block developments harmful to the health of watersheds.

On almost every continent, Indigenous peoples are engaging in land-based struggles that not only assert sovereignty but often also defend the integrity of the waters flowing through their territories. Turtle Island (also known as North America) is no exception. In 2010, the Tsilhqot'in Nation, with help from allied non-governmental organizations, successfully protected Teztan Biny (Fish Lake) from becoming a dump site for mine tailings.[35] Each spring since 2003, Anishinawbe grandmothers have led a Mother Earth Water Walk, carrying water for long distances and offering prayers to rivers, streams, and coastlines as they go.[36] With the understanding that our theoretical and artistic interventions have political implications, we would like to offer the thoughts, phrases, and images here in solidarity with such actions initiated in protection of the waters we share.

As bodies of water – which we all inescapably are – we are all (perhaps unwittingly) collaborating, all of the time. In fact, a collaborative dynamic runs through this project at many levels: from co-authored work, to the animated flow of ideas among artists, authors, and poets, to the generous hours that participants spent providing detailed responses and commentaries to one another's work. Not least, the organization of the project and the editing of the work you now hold in your hands were the offspring of a gentle but suitably monstrous three-headed hydra. We do not idealize collaboration.

It is sweaty work replete with tense negotiations. Thinking with water, however, asks that we attend to the way we collaborate – whether in our scholarly and creative pursuits or in our ecopolitical endeavours.

We live in a world where millions of people lack access to adequate drinking water, where the depths of the oceans remain less charted than the surface of the moon, where farmers in Australia and Gujarat are being driven to suicide by drought, where the world's disenfranchised from New Orleans to Bangladesh are swept away in raging overflows, and where the fluid that bathes your brain may once have stroked the gills of fish, or dripped from the stairs of a South Indian stepwell. In such a context, thinking with water is much more than a theoretical meander. Our wish is that this collaboration in ecocultural scholarship may respond to urgent questions concerning where and how we dwell, articulations with our more-than-human watery others, the flows of power caught up in the currents of our planetary watercourses, and the possibility of a watershed moment – a sea change, a hydrological turn – in all of our ecocultural relations. May the works in this collection encourage full immersion.

NOTES

1 Among the major rivers that no longer reach the sea are the Colorado, the Amu Darya, the Syr Darya, the Nile, the Yellow River, and the Indus.

2 According to the Indigenous Environment Network, "toxic wastewater is discharged in holding or tailing ponds that now leak 11 million liters of toxic waste per day into the Athabasca and seep into the ground water." See "Canadian Tar Sands: Impacts to US and Canadian Indigenous Communities." Some of the holding "ponds" have areas as large as fifteen square kilometres. See "Water Depletion."

3 During the worst of the BP oil spill, some sources estimated that oil was haemorrhaging into the deep ocean at a rate of approximately 2,520,000 gallons per day. See Garcia, "Flow Rate Technical Group estimate of oil for June 20, 2010."

4 The United Nations Environmental Program has completed an environmental assessment of oil contamination in Ogoniland, one part of the Niger Delta. This assessment was requested by the Nigerian State and, according to UNEP, is funded by Shell on the basis of "polluters pay" principles. Nnimmo Bassey, chairman of Friends of the Earth International, has criticized the independence of the data and analysis of this report. See: Bassey, UNEP, and Vidal.

5 Here, we refer to Hannah Arendt's definition of the term "politics" as outlined in *The Human Condition*, and as might be reappropriated from a posthumanist perspective.

6 As conceived by Arendt, the common world (with which politics is concerned) is shared by the living, the dead, and the unborn. While Arendt insists that the common world is built of durable *human* creations, we might extend an Arendtian concept of politics to include such apparently "natural" and mutable entities as rivers and springs. That is, if we think of creeks and oceans as collaborative projects – produced

as much by freshwater molluscs as by urban planners, altered by shared cultural understandings as much as by the root systems of alder and the hungers of algae – then the waters we share in common might be indeed considered artifacts, albeit of a decidely more-than-human kind.

7   See, for example, Latour, *We Have Never Been Modern* and *Politics of Nature*; Lingis, "The Murmur of the World"; and Braun and Whatmore (editors), *Political Matter: Technoscience, Democracy and Public Life*.

8   Worster, *Rivers of Empire*.

9   This is a contested figure. The estimate of half a million comes from the Narmada Bachao Andolan. See Roy, "The Greater Common Good."

10   Roy, "The Greater Common Good."

11   *Downstream*, a cultural-scholarly gathering organized by Rita Wong in March 2012, is an inspiring example of this sort of work. See *Downstream*.

12   See Strang's description of the hydrotheology of the Rainbow Serpent, this volume.

13   See, for instance, the sense of other places engaged by Michel Foucault's writing on heterotopia ("Des Espaces Autres," 47–8).

14   Water and vagueness are semantically and etymologically linked. Vincent Miller (2006) offers an interesting exploration of "vagueness" as an approach to multivalent social space and complex intersubjective relations.

15   Williams, *Marxism and Literature*, 19.

16   Bachelard, *Water and Dreams*, 134.

17   Lakoff and Johnson, *Metaphors We Live By*.

18   See MacLeod in this volume, page 42.

19   Lakoff and Johnson, *Metaphors We Live By*, 10, 145.

20   Karen Barad writes: "There is an important sense in which practices of knowing cannot fully be claimed as human practices, not simply because we use nonhuman elements in our practices but because knowing is a matter of part of the world making itself intelligible to another part. Practices of knowing and being are not isolable; they are mutually implicated. We don't obtain knowledge by standing outside the world; we know because we are *of* the world." Barad, *Meeting the Universe*, 185.

21   See Christian and Wong in this volume, page 238.

22   See also, for example, the chapters by Roburn and Strang in this volume.

23   Such innovations range from the corporeal feminisms of Luce Irigaray to the material semiotics of Michel Serres or Bruno Latour; from the intersubjectivity of Merleau-Ponty to the ecological imaginations of Rachel Carson, Aldo Leopold, and Félix Guattari; from the symbioses of Donna Haraway, Lynn Margulis, and Karen Barad to the interconnections and alterities of Rebecca Belmore, Henry Lickers, and Jeannette Armstrong.

24   Deleuze posits the "event" as a transformative process that results from a synthesis of forces (see Deleuze, *Logic of Sense*). For Derrida, moreover, the "result" of an event is never finalized or knowable in advance, but rather always still "to come" (see Derrida, "The Future of the Profession"). In other words, the communication circuits

of water are neither mechanistic nor fully predictable, and aqueous contact continually opens to something new.

25 On this tragic series of events in the spring of 2000, see Berland, "Walkerton: The Memory of Matter."

26 Christian and Wong, this volume, page 249.

27 See, for example, Ivakhiv, "Ecocultural Theory and Ecocultural Studies"; Berland, "What is Environmental Cultural Studies?"; Slack, "Resisting Ecocultural Studies"; Pezzullo, "The Most Complicated Word"; or Mortimer-Sandilands, "Nature Matters."

28 See Strang in this volume, page 185.

29 Slack, *Resisting Ecocultural Studies*, 493.

30 As Slack puts it, "as cultural theorists, we ought to wrestle with the knowledge that it is impossible to contextualize culture without considering the co-evolution of all [the] significant articulating vectors," in which the "eco" is a major player. Thus, all cultural studies would have to acknowledge the "eco" without which any cultural inquiry would be impossible.

31 The "uncanny" has a long modern history. Among many writings, Anthony Vidler offers a short introduction to this history in *The Architectural Uncanny* (wherein he discusses the uncanny in terms of Freud, Heidegger, Bachelard, and many others).

32 See Serres, *Angels: A Modern Myth*, 30. "If winds, currents, glaciers, volcanoes etc. carry subtle messages that are so difficult to read that it takes us absolutely ages to decipher them, wouldn't it be appropriate to call them intelligent? ... How would it be if it turned out that we were only the slowest and least intelligent beings in the world?"

33 Unlike the text chapters and the artworks in this volume, the poems of Dickinson, Marlatt, McKay, and Siebert were selected only subsequent to a workshop, held in 2010, where the authors and artists collected in this volume first shared their contributions.

34 A treaty made in 1613 between Holland and the Onkwehonwe (Five Nations of the Iroquois). The wampum belt consists of two rows of purple beads on a white background, signifying the courses of two vessels travelling down the river of life together. The treaty states: "In our canoe we have all our laws, culture, and beliefs and in your vessel you shall have all your laws, culture, and beliefs, traveling side by side through life as equals never enforcing or interfering in each other's affairs as long as the sun shall shine the grass shall grow and the rivers shall flow this will be everlasting." Some hold up the two-row wampum as a model for respectful Indigenous-settler relationships.

35 Unfortunately, this victory was short-lived. Taseko Mines Ltd. has since submitted a new mining proposal that affects Teztan Biny (or Fish Lake): See Tetzan Biny and RAVEN.

36 This walk has taken place every spring since 2003, with the exception of 2010, when a non-walking prayer for waters was initiated. See Mother Earth Water Walk.

# Water Drawing (version 1.0) (2010)

*Rae Staseson*

## DESCRIPTION/ARTIST'S TEXT

Staseson makes strange water's un-still surface. *Water Drawing* is a video and sound installation that explores water's materiality. Through long and intense close-ups, and seamlessly looped studies, we experience the vulnerability and mutability of this substance. Reflected light continually morphs and transforms on water's enigmatic surface. This light becomes unrecognizable, abstract, appearing to be drawn by hand. Multi-layered sound design combines manipulated water phrases with ambient source sound collected near Lake Katepwa, Saskatchewan. The familiar mixes with the unfamiliar, to encourage reflection, introspection, and imagination. We are invited to be mesmerized by the play between water's surface and camera lens, our eyes and the installation, our ears and the hypnotic sound of this uncanny study. *Water Drawing* challenges and dissolves lingering modernist boundaries that still exist between video, film, painting, and drawing through its formal and technical deceptions.

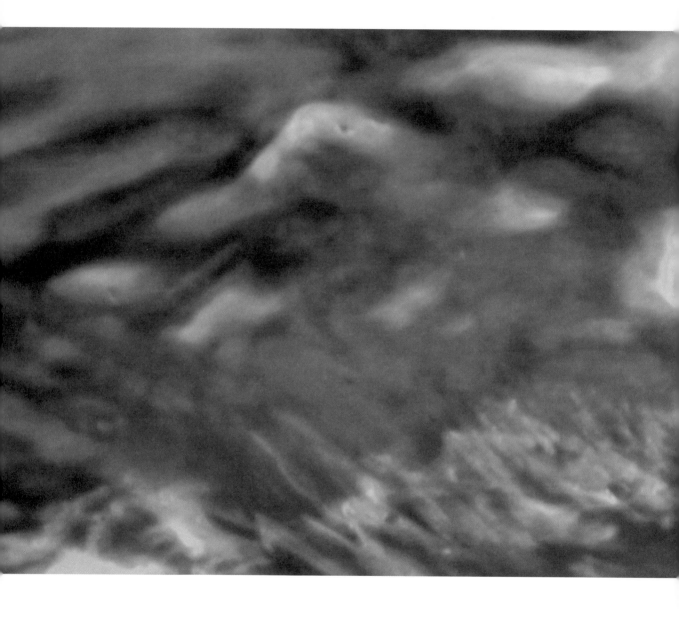

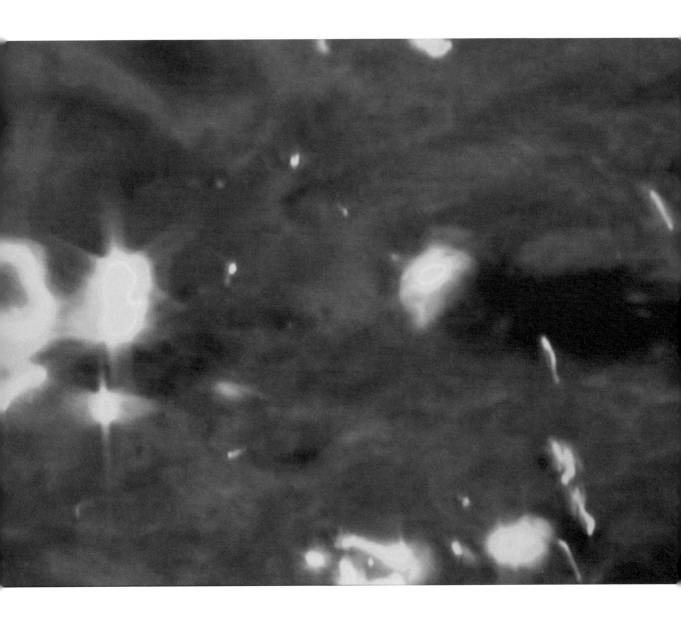

Plate 1
Untitled image, *Water Drawing (version 1.0)* (2010) video and sound installation by Rae Staseson.

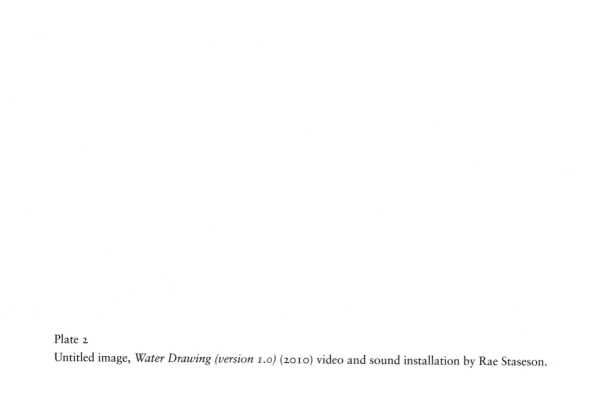

Plate 2
Untitled image, *Water Drawing (version 1.0)* (2010) video and sound installation by Rae Staseson.

# light, sweet, cold, dark, crude (LSCDC)
# a cycle of audiovisual micro-events (2006–ongoing)

*Ælab (Gisèle Trudel and Stéphane Claude)*

DESCRIPTION/ARTIST'S TEXT

The work references the processes of two waste water treatment systems: the Eco-Machines pioneered by Dr John Todd, located at the Vietnam Veterans' Memorial on Interstate 89 in Vermont and the industrial scale facility in Montreal, the Station d'épuration des eaux usées. Eco-Machines comprised distinct basins and their lodgers (fish, algae, plants) that treat grey and black waters through interconnectivity and photosynthesis. Other sources include the desert and Ælab's documentary about the Todds, *These organisms have the ability to self-organize* (2009, 12 min).

We are inspired by the desert (the etymological root of *wastum*, or waste), which is incredibly creative with very little water. Thus, desert footage collected from southern California and Arizona offers an "in-between" that engages the treatment of waste water into zones of indiscernibility. Gilbert Simondon's concepts of transduction, metastable environments, and the successive co-evolutionary relations between humans, nature, and technology have strongly influenced how we accentuate the "carrying over" and "spilling into each other" of systems, images, sounds, light, and other sensory information with the unfolding of each micro-event.

The performances were initially presented in a transformed room in our Montreal home with only fifteen people at a time. These events disrupted the typical household (the *oikos*) – the living room isn't a living room. Always positioning participants in the centre, the setup is reconfigured for each performative micro-event (seven in total), creating new relations between ourselves and the audience, multiple video and audio channels, the projection screens, and diverse venues in Montreal (2008–10), Berlin, Germany (2009), and New Plymouth, New Zealand (2011).

Plate 3
1st micro-event, 9 June 2008, Flevoland, Montreal

These images are drawn from a variable series of performative micro-events begun in June 2008. Each micro-event involves the live mixing of drawing, text, moving images (1-2-3 "streams"), LED lighting system, custom software, and immersive sound (up to 6.2 speakers, subwoofers).

Plate 4
2nd micro-event, 29 June 2008, Flevoland, Montreal

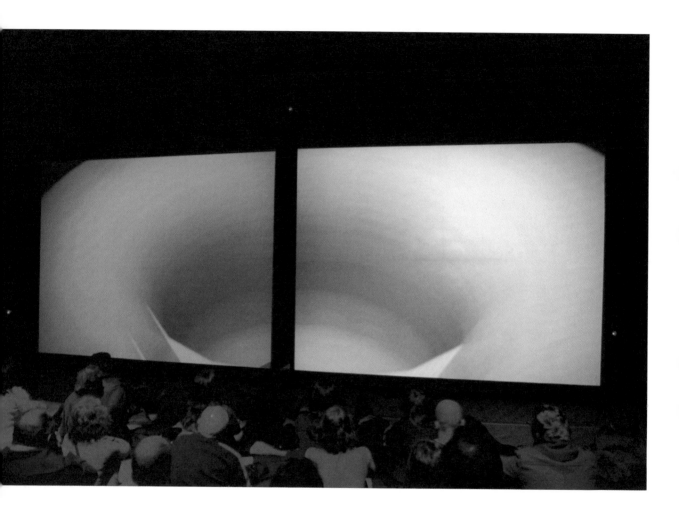

Plates 5 and 6
*Festival Temps d'Images*, 19–21 February 2009, Usine C, Montreal

Plate 7
*Station d'épuration des eaux usées*, July 2008, Montreal

Plate 8
Deep North, *Festival transmediale*, 30–31 January 2009, Berlin, Germany

Plate 9
Fernery House 1, Pukekura Park Botanical Gardens, 27 January 2011,
International thematic residency *EcoSapiens* (Intercreate.org),
New Plymouth, New Zealand

Plate 10
Joshua Tree National Park, July 2007, California, USA

Plate 11 *Opposite*
Eco-Machines (John Todd Ecological Design, toddecological.com), July 2007, Sharon, Vermont, USA

# generation, generations at the mouth

*Daphne Marlatt*

clans of salmon, chinook, coho, gathering just off shore, backbones no longer
intact, steam-pressured in millions of cans, picked clean barbecue leavings in a
thousand garbage bags ripped open by cats, rats, they can't find their way back

what is the body's blueprint?

return what is solid to water, the first peoples said –
returned, every bone intact
generates the giving back of race, kind, kin

choked in urban outfalls, fished as they aim for rivers sediment-thick with runoff,
*tamahnous* of the wild they hover, sonar streaks, impossible vision-glitches,
outside pens where farmed lookalikes grow pale & drugged

kin, wild skin, wild & electric at the mouth where rivers disappear in the that
that is not that, the chinook can't find their way back

come out of the blue: this flow, these energy rivers & wheels, radiant giving
unlocked. & not this frozen, this canned product eagles once stripped, eagles,
bears going, gone, hungry & wild outside shut doors where light pools & we
pore over stock market news, refuse, refuse our interrelation, refuse to pour
back

what *is* the body's blueprint? impermanent, shifting energy blocks in its own
becoming, a stream & streaming out to the void where rivers lose themselves

in the bardo as many beings as waves gather at any opening, those in-between
and not-yet ones that race a river of sperm to be here now, light-pour, each cell
in its dying turn returns

what is the mouth of the river now? a toxic O of emptiness? teeming hole of ever-becoming we create? re-entry. re-turn. verbing the noun out of its stuck edges into an occurrence, currents, *curre-* . . . we've lost the verb in our currency, a frozen exchange streaming emptiness

                                    (they're fishing in London now)

at the mouth of the river, clans of the possible are gathering, the chinook, the coho rivering just offshore are us

# Water and the Material Imagination:
# Reading the Sea of Memory against the Flows of Capital

*Janine MacLeod*

This is a chapter about two very large metaphoric seas. The first of these encompasses the movements of capital. It is the invisible current we refer to when we say the word "currency" – literally, "the condition of flowing."[1] It circles the globe in an instant, pours through stock exchanges and tattered wallets alike. It pauses when assets are frozen and accelerates when investors achieve greater liquidity. Some say that it trickles down to the poor like inconstant rain. Its rising tide is supposed to lift all boats. We survey an economic landscape dotted with pools of resources, poling our little rafts of consumption up greater or lesser tributaries of cash flow, always striving to tap new sources of funding.

The second ocean emerges in literary figures, religious traditions, mythologies, and everyday language. It is an infinite water in which everything is retained, and where all times mingle together. This is the body of water we refer to whenever we talk about the past as a watery depth.[2] Those who have passed on rise up from its fathomless reaches to speak with us. It is the final outlet of those rivers that so many cultures entrust with the task of receiving and carrying away the dead. It is the dimension of memory lingering in the wet hearts of everyday objects. The novels of Virginia Woolf and Marcel Proust give us a particularly compelling view of these waters of memory, and will act as our places of entry into this liquid substance of time.

As an important component of what Gaston Bachelard calls "the material imagination," water brings a powerful and varied repertoire of emotional, cultural, and sensual associations to its role as metaphor. This symbolic potency can be engaged both to confirm and to challenge current systems of exploitation, domination, and ecological devastation. When water appears in a metaphor, its material properties inform our understandings of the concepts it helps to signify. The material and sensual qualities of water, in turn, are always mingling with individual and collective associations – all of a reader's own experiences of rain, for example, come together with her cultural understandings of the purity carried by water, and with all the ways she may have seen the rain associated with erotic scenes in films. Water metaphors can be understood as active and transformative encounters in which ideas about fundamental concepts like health and morality come to be shaped by waters and the meanings they carry. Reciprocally, in these more-than-linguistic associations, the meanings of water may be subtly altered, given different emphases, concealed or brought into the foreground. The understandings that emerge – of wealth, for example, or of time, or of water itself – may have very particular effects on collective responses to environmental threats.

This chapter explores the tensions between these two very different metaphoric waters, and traces some of their relationships to the more tangible waters from which they derive their symbolic and affective resonance. There are different modes of temporal experience associated with the realm of commodity exchange on the one hand, and with the material memory of water on the other. From the disposability and built-in obsolescence of consumer goods, to the intensified mobility of populations, to the effects of commodity fetishism itself, current historical conditions tend to obliterate the habitat in which multi-generational memories thrive. Late capitalist modes of production and consumption alienate the living from the dead and from the unborn, even as they exhaust and contaminate aquifers and rivers. The "flows of capital" metaphor contributes to the aura of naturalness surrounding such conditions.

By contrast, I suggest that "the sea of memory" metaphor, as it appears in the novels of Woolf and Proust, can offer us access to an alternative – and potentially counter-hegemonic – temporal experience. Literary depictions of the watery "depths" of memory can help to cultivate a sensual awareness of multi-generational time, and can gesture toward the meaningful integration of personal and collective histories. They can also draw our attention to the simultaneous age and newness of water, and to its capacity to communicate between the living, the dead, and the unborn. In exploring the friction between these two metaphors, the commodity form and water emerge as very different global media of communication, radically opposite in their relationships to ecological diversity.

Interesting difficulties emerge in the attempt to draw upon high modernist novels within an ecopolitical project. Woolf and Proust are often seen as novelists who write for a privileged readership, crafting rarified spaces of refuge from the effects of capitalist alienation. Indeed, writers from their period often characterize the "depths" of the past as spaces *prior to* or *outside of* the historical conditions of modernity. Further, in these works, a fascination with memory unfolds in relation to emotional and psychological dimensions of experience, in ways that might seem to resist translation into a collective or overtly political register. However, I argue that we can read these works *toward* the materiality of waters, in ways that engage with, rather than escape from, the particular difficulties of our historical moment. An ecopolitical reading can approach the "sea of memory" as something immanent and alive, a substance that saturates everyday life.

○

Watery language naturalizes the movements of capital. To the degree that it is carried by aqueous imagery, capital is figured as a necessity, no less a biospheric feature than an ocean or a raincloud. Everyday metaphors imply that the "circulation" of wealth is as fundamental to the maintenance of life as the blood flowing through the veins of vascularized creatures, or the arterial branchings of river deltas. However, water is more than fundamental, essential, and "natural"; these aquatic images carry other powerful associations, as well. The ocean has long been regarded as a place of uncertainty and risk; it can be navigated more or less bravely, but never controlled. Like the unruly floodwaters feared by early civilizations, the movements of capital can, at any moment, crush a nascent economy, dispense or withdraw prosperity.[3] "Flows" of investment can also blast the top off of a local mountain, poison air and water, and displace communities. Cloaked in a watery guise, the devastations wrought by floods or droughts of capital may be more readily interpreted as unfortunate inevitabilities.

Further, as Veronica Strang has observed, water can also function as a powerful symbol of prosperity, health, and agency.[4] In various times and places, particular rivers, wells, shores, and streams have been approached as places of healing and regeneration,[5] or even, in folklore, as sources of immortality and eternal youth. Fountains have often signified wealth and power, whether their gushing and burbling echo through a square in ancient Rome,[6] a gated garden in Peru, or the forecourt of a downtown Toronto banking headquarters. Thinkers from Karl Wittfogel and Donald Worster to, in this volume, Andrew Biro and Max Haiven have argued that technical control over the flow of large rivers has often coincided with intensified social domination; the construction of mega-dams and other large-scale waterworks has both required and facilitated more pronounced social hierarchy and a greater concentration of power.[7] There is thus a significant overlap between the meanings of capital and water's capacity to symbolize agency. Within current systems of social organization, the ease of one's "cash flow" does to a greater or lesser degree determine one's access to political influence, healthy food, housing, and unpolluted air, land, and water. And, to the extent that shorelines, watercourses, and wells come to be regarded as commodities, the blessings and potencies of water appear less often as qualities distinct from the mobilization of wealth. Where water is commodified outright, in fact, it quite literally flows as capital.[8]

Water metaphors help to figure a wide range of concepts and experiences, including time, emotional life, and collective identity.[9] However, the "flows of capital" metaphor is exceptional in that it not only borrows water's meanings, but appropriates them directly. That is, as investment comes to be regarded as an essential source of health, good livelihood, and agency, water's more fundamental association with these qualities falls into the background. An operation like the Alberta tar sands, which is rapidly and catastrophically contaminating the world's third-largest watershed in the pursuit of short-term monetary gain, is one among far too many examples of this (il)logic at work.[10] The conversion of healthy watercourses and ocean ecosystems into profit often obliterates the real material foundations of wealth and well-being. Such substitutions could only seem politically palatable, or acceptable within what Antonio Gramsci would call "common sense,"[11] if capital had to some degree usurped water's place in the dominant cultural imaginary as an unquestionable and irrefutable source of life.

The displacement of actual waters by the "waters of capital" in dominant cultural imaginaries can be understood as one manifestation of contemporary processes of reification. Reification here refers to the process by which a quasi-abstraction like capital comes to seem as real as a river. The term also describes a displacement from context, in which the origins of a thing, its production by labour and by ecological processes, get forgotten. As a particularly pervasive form of reification, commodity fetishism strips objects or experiences of any trace of the relations through which they were produced, and through which they will be broken down. That is, the act of assigning exchange value to an object either effaces or instrumentalizes its history. In the first case, the object appears "new," like the bottle of water whose origins become unreadable in its seemingly spontaneous genesis by the convenience store refrigerator. In the second instance, the past of the object is itself commodified, as when the bottle's brand image harnesses the water's supposed connection to a pristine Fijian aquifer. Richard Terdiman writes that "essentially, 'reification' is a memory disturbance: the enigma of the commodity is a memory disorder."[12] He emphasizes the significance of this process to our capacity for remembrance – since so many of our memories dwell within objects, sounds, smells, and the like, the hollowing out of these last by processes of commodification could be seen as a relentless destruction of the habitat for human memory.

On a significant and devastating scale, the penetration of capital evicts the past from objects and landscapes. The forest that I played in as a child has been completely obliterated by a subdivision, along with all the memories I might have rediscovered in walking through it as an adult. The rapid turnover of everyday objects and built environments limits the depth of association that these can accumulate, and provides scant material habitat for multi-generational memories. As the movements of globalized capital impose conditions of accelerated mobility on so many of us, the likelihood of sharing particular woods, streets, or shorelines with our own ancestors and descendants diminishes even further. The forest that preceded the subdivision was familiar to me for only a short time, as my family moved to the area shortly after my second birthday, and moved away again when I was seven. Even before the removal of the forest, my relations with this place were radically tenuous in comparison with those cultivated by the Chonnonton and other peoples prior to European settlement of the area in the late-eighteenth century. As Victoria Freeman notes in her meditations on these matters, many North Americans of English, Irish, or Scottish descent seem to lack a connection to the histories of their own families. She writes: "I was struck by the amnesia of each generation: our family memories often went back only as far as our grandparents ... I have come to realize how much immigrants lose of their family memory because it is tied to physical places – to houses, farms, towns, landmarks, battlefields and graves."[13] These amnesiac effects of mobility are further intensified when the effects of capital strip and colonize the terrain of remembrance, transforming lands and waters beyond recognition.

And yet, even as such conditions inhibit certain kinds of memory in very tangible ways, the erasure of the past by the commodity form itself is actually illusory. The sub-division is not "new" at all – its vinyl siding was once fossilized carbon and chlorinated salt. Water's hydrogen bonds introduced vinyl chloride monomers to other chemicals in a reactive slurry. Some of the factory workers who watched over this process may have died from lung cancer, lymphoma, leukemia, liver cirrhosis, or angiosarcoma, condi-tions strongly associated with exposure to these substances.[14] The wooden frames in the houses of the subdivision were held by labouring hands and run through sawmills, and may once have helped to raise epiphytic ferns closer to the sun in some British Columbian valley.

The occlusion of social and ecological relations by the commodity form is accelerated by related changes in temporal experience under conditions of advanced capitalism. In his 1939 essay "On Some Motifs in Baudelaire," Walter Benjamin describes a condition he calls *Erlebnis*, or "the passing moment," in which a fragmentation of life into a series of discrete events segregates the present continuously from the moments that precede it. Benjamin traces the genesis of this temporal condition to modern modes of production. Particularly, he notes how the rhythms of factory work pervade life and leisure, segre-gating individual moments from meaningful connection with one another. In similar fashion, Benjamin argues, individual articles within newspapers are disconnected from one another, such that the paper as a whole lacks cohesive structure or meaning.[15] Ben-jamin distinguishes the resulting "information" from "stories," arguing that the latter call for assimilation into the experience of the individual, while also integrating indi-vidual and collective pasts. Unlike stories, which bind together generations of tellers and listeners, "the value of information does not survive the moment in which it was new."[16] As such, modern modes of communication tend to disconnect individual events from one another and allow the links between generations to atrophy.[17] In fragmenting and decontextualizing events, this mode of temporal experience also hinders our abil-ity to perceive and understand environmental threats, which often occur over long spans of time and whose effects may be deferred in time and space.

Writing more then fifty years later, Fredric Jameson points out that the postmodern flood of information allows no space for distance or reflection. He laments the "wan-ing of historicity," and with it, the possibility of achieving a critical distance from the present.[18] Jean Baudrillard, too, notes the oppressive immediacy of communication and information. Figuring this condition through images of fluidity, he characterizes con-temporary communication networks as places "of superficial saturation, of an inces-sant solicitation, of an extermination of interstitial and protective spaces."[19] The expulsion of the past from everyday objects, accompanied by the simultaneous satura-tion with and disassociation between discrete pieces of information, may be understood as integral to the operation of capital: these characteristics of temporal experience arise as effects of reification and, in turn, help to facilitate the continuing expansion of markets into new watersheds and areas of life.

○

As inhabitants of a globe dominated by capital, supposedly drifting like helpless flotsam on vast waves of investment, is it possible for us to envision and understand a radically different relationship to time, memory, and collective material relationships? Among the many counterhegemonic visions in circulation, I would like to draw attention to an obscure imaginative waterway sparkling between the pages of a handful of modernist novels and their critical commentary.[20] Unlike the lakes and rivers of myth and fable, which emerge fully formed with names like "Mnemosyne," "Oceanus," and "The Lake at the End of the World," this waterway only becomes visible here and there, in intermittent but persistent springs of metaphor. In writing about the works of Marcel Proust, Benjamin called this figural body of water the "sea of the *temps perdu*."[21] Although my reading of Proust may differ somewhat from Benjamin's, and while the "sea" I describe may vary among literary works and authors, I will borrow Benjamin's phrase to refer to a collection of water metaphors that to me seem to provide a kind of imaginative antidote to the amnesiac floods of reification.

The metaphors I will be exploring emerge from the late nineteenth- and early twentieth- century literary moment known as "high modernism." While this period has been retrospectively defined and characterized in many ways, commentators have widely noted that high-modernist authors such as Woolf, Proust, Mann, and Eliot tend to share a fascination with time and temporality, memory and the persistence of the past.[22] These authors were writing at a time when Freud was beginning to probe the retentive depths of the unconscious, asserting that nothing from one's past is ever entirely lost – every experience is stored away and in theory accessible to retrieval. It was also in this period that Henri Bergson sought to replace a chronological conception of time with an awareness of what he called *la durée*, a flux of human experience in which the past and the present mingle together.[23] As Bergson conceived it, the role of the artist was to dive into the depths of the unconscious, or of the past, which were frequently figured as bodies of water.[24]

As titles like *The Waves*, *To the Lighthouse*, and *The Voyage Out* suggest, Virginia Woolf's novels tend to draw their readers away from solid ground into a distinctly aqueous literary universe. Her characters exhibit a remarkable fondness for leaning against bridge railings and looking down over the sides of boats; emotions, madness, music, sociability, and time all turn to liquids that drip, surge, and saturate. Within this prolific figural hydrology, Woolf's engagement with the "depths" of time communicates the immanence of the past in a profoundly tangible way. Distinguishing this mode of temporal experience from one based on surfaces, Woolf writes: "the past only comes back when the present runs ever so smoothly that it is like the sliding surface of a deep river. Then one sees through the surface to the depths ... For the present when backed by the past is a thousand times deeper than the present when it presses so close that you can feel nothing else, when the film on the camera reaches only the eye."[25]

Woolf's description of the shallowness of a present without the backing of the past recalls Baudrillard's observations on the oppressive immediacy of postmodern communication and information, in which there is "too great a proximity of everything," and a "superficial saturation."[26] It also calls to mind more recent critiques of contemporary cyberculture, such as Nicholas Carr's popular 2010 publication, *The Shallows*. Writing about the neurological effects of heavy Internet use, Carr argues that surfing the Web discourages states of deep concentration and reflection. His choice of metaphors highlights the extent to which images of surface and depth continue to inform cultural critique: "once I was a scuba diver in the sea of words," Carr writes; "now I zip along the surface like a guy on a Jet Ski."[27] By contrast, the depths of time evoked in Woolf's novels endow the present with its own inner distance, one that brings it into meaningful unity with the past.

The depths of the past absorb everything that happens. One of Woolf's characters, upon stepping out from a luncheon at the home of an old widow named Lady Bruton, succumbs to forgetfulness: "But there are tides in the body. Morning meets afternoon. Borne like a frail shallop on deep, deep floods, Lady Bruton's great-grandfather and his memoir and his campaigns were whelmed and sunk. And Millicent Bruton too, she went under."[28] The luncheon conversation, like so many other incidental and fleeting experiences, disappears below the surface of conscious remembrance. However, everyday events like these persist within the sea of memory, accessible to artistic retrieval.

For Bergson, the stream of consciousness style employed by Woolf and many other modernists permits access to the aqueous *durée*. Bergson comments that such writers "delve yet deeper still. Beneath these joys and sorrows ... they grasp ... certain rhythms of life and breath that are closer to man than his inmost feelings."[29] By employing fluid forms of language, Woolf is able to communicate not only what is conscious in the minds of her characters, but all that has been felt and experienced and forgotten. As Woolf's character Lily Briscoe tackles an incomplete canvas toward the end of *To the Lighthouse*, her act of creation is described as an externalization of this inner water: "Her mind kept throwing up from its depths, scenes, and names, and sayings, and memories and ideas, like a fountain spurting over that glaring, hideously difficult white space, while she modelled it with greens and blues."[30] For Woolf, as for Bergson, the role of the artist is to reach into the invisible domain beneath the surface of the psyche and make its contents visible.

In some of Woolf's passages, the depths seem to correspond not only to the individual psyche but also to collective histories. Standing in front of her canvas, Lily describes a feeling of being immersed in the waters of the past: "She seemed to be standing up to the lips in some substance, to move and float and sink in it, yes, for these waters were unfathomably deep. Into them had spilled so many lives. The Ramsays', the children's; and all sort of waifs and strays of things besides. A washerwoman with her basket; a rook; a red-hot poker; the purples and grey-greens of flowers: some common feeling which held the whole together."[31] The depths accumulate everything, retain everyone. A particular artistic attitude or posture seems to permit access to the limitless memory of water, which is at once the resting place of every forgotten event and the dwelling place of the dead. Elsewhere in the same novel, Woolf describes the sea as an "underworld": "Her hand cut a trail in the sea, as her mind made the green swirls and streaks into patterns and, numbed and shrouded, wandered in imagination in that underworld of waters."[32] After having "spilled" (suggesting that lives themselves are fluid) into the receptive ocean of memory, the lives of the departed remain. Within this aqueous underworld, individual lives have not lost their identity; they may still be distinguished from one another ("the Ramsays', the children's"). This is also true of particular objects and moments ("the washerwoman with her basket, a rook, a red-hot poker"). The creation that springs from this densely populated memory-well happens in a space of contiguity not only with the artist's own past, but with the lives and histories of others.

Bergson, in elaborating his thoughts on stream of consciousness writing, observes that consciousness cannot be "chopped up in bits … it flows. A river or a stream are metaphors by which it is most naturally described."[33] Similarly, one of Woolf's characters observes, "how life, from being made up of little separate incidents which one lived one by one, became curled and whole like a wave which bore one up with it and threw one down with it, there, with a dash on the beach."[34] In descending into the depths, the artist does not encounter a meaningless collection of trash, but rather a multiplicity held together by "some common feeling." The waters of the past seem to give cohesiveness to their suspended content. Water quite literally binds together the "little separate incidents" of life – the lunchtime feast of a freshwater mussel and the fluid-bathed neural connections that drive my typing fingers; the extraction of bitumen in Northern Alberta; and the cancers of teenagers downstream.

Marcel Proust's *À la recherche du temps perdu*, in its tenacious and brilliant preoccupation with memory, ties the notion of the retentive depths of the past to everyday materiality. Proust revels in the way smells and songs and objects can connect us to the past through the associative power of memory. In reading Proust, one becomes aware that the material world is saturated with the past, and that it is possible to engage with the world in a way that reveals its latent histories: "still, alone, more fragile, but with more vitality, more unsubstantial, more persistent, more faithful, the smell and taste of things remain poised a long time, like souls, ready to remind us, waiting and hoping for their moment, amid the ruins of all the rest; and bear unfaltering, in the tiny and almost impalpable drop of their essence, the vast structure of recollection."[35] The immense "structure of recollection" is here figured as something that inhabits an "impalpable drop," that is, a vital liquid that is at once "tiny" and "vast."

Like Woolf, Proust approaches the past as a watery depth out of which he must pull submerged memories: "I feel something start within me, something that leaves its resting place and attempts to rise, something that has been embedded like an anchor at a great depth."[36] In another passage, the retrieval of a lost memory takes the form of a "reclamation" from Lethe, the waters of forgetfulness: "The passer-by … would see me … standing still on the spot, before that steeple, for hours on end, motionless, trying to remember, feeling deep within myself a tract of soil reclaimed from the waters of Lethe slowly drying."[37] This passage brings out an important dual quality of the waters of the past. In them, Lethe, the waters of forgetfulness that consign histories to oblivion, and Mnemosyne, the waters of remembrance, seem to form the same substance. The histories that Lethe washes away are always retained. They are thus potentially accessible to recovery.[38]

Figured in this way as a watery depth, time no longer follows a chronological progression. In describing the memories triggered involuntarily by smells and tastes and sounds, Proust writes: "these sudden returns of disinterested memory [make] us float between the present and the past in their common essence."[39] In these images, the substance of the present is made up of the accumulated depth of the past; moments do not move in a linear sequence. Our own past colours our perceptions of the present through the associations called up by the things around us. Further, everything we know and touch has been generated by collective histories – the words and actions of the dead, the past expressions of multiple human and more-than-human others. The world is heavy with immanent, tangible pasts, both personal and collective, associative and material.

○

Why does water serve as such a recurrent figure for this concept of time? In his book *Water and Dreams: An Essay on the Imagination of Matter*, Bachelard speculates that it may be impossible to describe the past without drawing on images of deep water.[40] Observing that "elementary matter receives and preserves and exalts our dreams," he argues that fundamental ideas cannot be truly felt and understood in the abstract; they need to be animated by the substance of the world.[41] That is, it is our everyday sensual experience of water that allows us to imagine the temporality described by Woolf and Proust. Reciprocally, the metaphors elaborated by these authors might unintentionally, but no less profoundly, alter their readers' perception of a sink full of dirty dishwater.

The immanence of the past evoked by Woolf and Proust draws on the simultaneous age and newness of water. In *The Voyage Out*, one of Woolf's characters reflects: "the water was very calm … So it had been at the birth of the world, and so it had remained ever since."[42] Aside from occasional supplements brought in on comets, the water we drink and touch is the same water that erupted as steam at the origins of the earth. All of the moments of the past have had this same water as their witness. The promiscuous waters that have bathed me and irrigated my cells have been everywhere, animating

Amazonian centipedes, Antarctic jellyfish, depression-era schoolteachers, and Xia-dynasty farmers. They are the moisture we exhale with our breath, the blood, sweat, urine, and breastmilk that flows or evaporates from openings in our bodies. At the same time, these waters have the capacity to make things new, to act as agents of birth, rebirth, purification, and germination. All matter is ultimately shared across generations. However, as the medium that carries away the dead and nurtures the unborn, water is uniquely capable of symbolizing multi-generational time. In some sense, it actually *is* multi-generational time.

The material memory of water can be thought of as a function of its great solvent capacity. This "memory" is not only retentive; it is also communicative. Water is the ultimate medium for the conversations that continually create the world. It introduces sperm to eggs, carries nutrients to tree roots, rushes chemical messages between different parts of the body. Water molecules weaken the electromagnetic forces holding atoms together, loosening up shy solutes that might otherwise refuse to speak to one another. Sodium meets chlorine, calcium meets coral, giardia meets thirsty hiker. Water tells the coast of Brittany all about the heat of the tropics and describes the flavours of peppermint and cinnamon to my tongue. Smells travel in moisture. More eagerly than air, water transmits the voices of whales, machines, and cracking rocks. Rivers, one-molecule thick, thread their way into the interior of cellular proteins, bearing the hydrogen ions necessary for vital chemical reactions.[43] Sugar-daddy fertilizers sneak downstream to woo tender estuarine algae. When water appears in metaphor as the substance through which we encounter other times and places, the reader's imagination, however unconsciously, recognizes the way this substance acts forever as a meeting place and medium.

Returning, then, to the contrast between the sea of the *temps perdu* and the "flows of capital" we see that two opposing temporal frameworks are at stake and, simultaneously, two very different global mediums of communication. As Baudrillard observes: "the commodity … is the formal place of transcription of all possible objects; through it, objects communicate. Hence, the commodity form is the first great medium of the modern world. But the message that the objects deliver through it is already extremely simplified, and it is always the same: their exchange value."[44] In situating economic exchange as a system of global circulation analogous to the hydrological cycle, the "flows of capital" metaphor exposes the commodity form's ambitions as a universal medium. As we have seen, exchange value strips objects of their histories as they enter into price-mediated relationship with other objects. Unlike water, which nurtures into being a fantastic complexity of life forms and modes of interaction, the commodity form reduces all objects to a single quantified abstraction. In this process of simplification, the commodity form diminishes the complexity of every ecosystem it touches.

○

Modernist literary texts might seem to be unlikely places to look for a counterhege-monic, ecologically oriented consciousness of time and materiality. Both Woolf and Proust wrote from positions of relative privilege within the urban capitals of large European colonial powers. Proust's characters lounge on the grass outside luxurious homes in the French countryside and attend parties with dukes and duchesses, counts and countesses. Woolf's novels tend to feature the thoughts and feelings of middle- and ruling-class British characters, as they plan and attend elegant social events, or travel to and fro between England and the colonies.[45] Further, the modernist passage into memory was generally a movement inward, into emotional and psychological dimensions of experience. Surely there are social and artistic movements more obviously oriented toward goals of political transformation.

However, modernist writing may be regarded as an imaginative, if not always overtly political, mode of resistance.[46] Modernist yearnings for the deep waters of the past can be understood as attempts to access memories or histories untouched by capitalism. Anticolonial writer Aimé Césaire, for example, describes how a poetic "plunge" into the "depths" of memory and into the unconscious allowed him to access an Africa that preceded the imposition of French culture, philosophy, and rhetoric.[47] For Césaire, the pre-colonial African culture accessible through such poetic immersion was "not only ante-capitalist … but also anti-capitalist."[48] Fredric Jameson suggests that opposition to the market is actually a defining characteristic of modernism. He argues that the shift from modernism to postmodernism, with its accompanying decline of "depth models" in favour of "surfaces," is marked by a new surrender to, and celebration of, the com-modification of culture.[49] Whether implicitly or explicitly, the sea of the *temps perdu* emerges from the benthic cradle of modernism as an entity anterior to, and in conflict with, the "floodwaters" of capital.

In contrast to the evaporation of history effected by reification, the sea of memory serves as a reminder of the pervasive immanence of the past, its potency, and accessibility to retrieval. Where the effects of the commodity form disconnect fragments of information from one another, the integrative waters of memory provide a sense of continuity and coherence to what might otherwise seem to be separate events. When the commodity form empties objects of their histories, it is precisely the sea of the *temps perdu*, that "impalpable drop of their essence," which is being drained. Reification does not inhibit water's memory of where it has been. It does, however, quite profoundly suppress our ability to notice and to know the persistence of the past. As a metaphoric antithesis of the "flows of capital," the waters of memory are threatened by, but also perhaps threatening to, the continuing penetration of the commodity form.

○

If novels such as *Swann's Way* and *To the Lighthouse* immerse their readers in an aqueous temporality otherwise obliterated by the conditions of late capitalism, could they be understood as refugia within the landscape of the imagination? Ecocritic Jonathan Bate suggests that under the right circumstances, poems can act as "imaginary parks in which we may breathe an air that is not toxic and accommodate ourselves to a mode of dwelling that is not alienated."[50] He sees ecopoetics as "not a description of dwelling with the earth, not a disengaged thinking about it, but an experiencing of it."[51] As such, he says, ecopoetry cannot be relied upon to yield particular political outcomes, but rather has the ability to effect change at the level of consciousness and feeling. Bate describes this work of ecopoetry as "pre-political."[52]

For Bate, the high modernist was "the very antithesis of the bioregionally grounded poet," a figure altogether too "cosmopolitan" to create ecopoetry.[53] However, as other ecocritics have pointed out, literary works can stimulate reflection on issues of ecological concern without taking "nature" or its degradation as explicit points of focus.[54] Woolf and Proust are primarily concerned with subjective experience. They use water metaphors to describe personal remembrance, artistic visions, and emotional states; real waters merely provide the material model or the metaphoric language for speaking about the inner lives of their characters. In using such metaphors, however, these authors not only give their readers access to a mode of temporal experience otherwise difficult to describe but they also, inadvertently, generate a powerful affective awareness of water's material memory. In drawing on water to communicate inner states of feeling, these writers help us to know water's great age and fathomless receptivity. When the fluid paths of their sentences wash us into the sea of the *temps perdu*, we are given a glimpse of the way that water is profoundly shared among the living, the dead, and the unborn – a vision that is embellished with all the beauty and emotional resonance of the writer's craft.

This feeling for the continued presence of the dead throughout the world around us echoes, however distantly, the living traditions of peoples indigenous to the places where I am writing this chapter.[55] Whenever I have heard Indigenous speakers discuss the importance of cultivating relationships with ancestors – and fulfilling responsibilities toward them – I have been inspired to seek out tributaries within my own cultural heritage that might lead toward some sense of communication and reciprocity between the living and the dead.[56] In speaking and writing about these novels by Proust and Woolf, in addition to connecting to readers from other times and places, I feel that I am also, in some way, sharing vital questions with their dead authors, reaching out to them collaboratively on matters of environmental concern. While Woolf and Proust may not be my ancestors in a literal sense, they are certainly people with whom I share a common world.[57]

There is an undeniable tension between the solidity of a book and the wetness of water's memory, the abstraction of the printed word and the materiality of water. However, books and waters, in their different ways, both enable communication between the living and the dead. And they do so even for diasporic subjects who may lack an ancestral connection to the lands and waters where they live. For those of us who dwell continuously in one place, specific hills and rocks and rivers connect the living to the ancestors, and bind together communities and cultures. However, in these novels by Proust and Woolf, the water that connects the living and the dead – the substance in which we "float between the present and the past in their common essence," or in which Lily stands "up to the lips" with her dead friends – is not a particular lake or spring. For those of us who are more migratory, perhaps water itself (which is always moving), rather than the banks or shores it flows against, can constitute a place of memory wherever we happen to find ourselves. In this way, it is precisely as "antithes(es) of the bioregionally grounded poet" that Woolf and Proust are able to speak so meaningfully to the contemporary condition of subjects affected by intensified mobility and other amnesiac effects of capital.

○

In bringing us to imaginative waters that seem to be situated prior to or outside of capitalist alienation, an ecopoetic text, as conceived by Bate, would potentially inspire its readers with a sense of alternative possibilities, an upwelling of desire for social transformation. However, what if such texts merely act as hiding places from the ugliness of alienation, social injustice, and ecocide? In his *Critique of Everyday Life*, Henri Lefebvre problematizes the desire to seek aesthetic refuge from the disappointments and horrors of the everyday. To the extent that artists and thinkers strive to situate their works outside or above the inauthenticity of existing social relations, he argues, they risk making the possibility of meaningful social change more remote. Lefebvre contends that in the attempt to generate "another, truer life" in the realms of art and thought, works of literature and philosophy inadvertently affirm the notion that actual social realities cannot be changed. They thus neglect the pressing tasks of illuminating alternative possibilities and rehabilitating the everyday through social transformation.[58]

Like Lefebvre, Benjamin is critical of the artistic or philosophical impulse to "lay hold of the 'true' experience" by ignoring or neglecting the realities of what he calls "the inhospitable, blinding age of big-scale industrialism."[59] Benjamin regards poetic and philosophical attempts to hide in lyricism, nature, and myth as aesthetically flawed because they fail to engage with the realities of their historical moment. The poetry that Benjamin admires grapples with the indifference of crowds, the breakdown of traditional forms of experience, and the decline of the "aura" of mutual regard and recognition.[60] His critique targets Bergson in particular, asserting that a philosophy of time and memory must acknowledge the production of these phenomena by historical conditions. For Benjamin, Bergson's work is counterproductive to the extent that "he leads us to believe that turning to the contemplative actualization of the stream of life is a matter of free choice."[61] A factory worker completing one disconnected task after another cannot simply think her way into a coherent and flowing relationship to time. The fragmentation of temporal experience has its origins in material conditions, and thus cannot be overcome by a simple act of individual will or imagination.

Modernist writers in general, and Woolf and Proust in particular, could certainly be considered prime candidates for such critiques. As stated previously, the "depths" prized by this literary movement have often been construed as spaces beneath, or prior to, capitalist alienation. Like many of his contemporaries, Proust quite explicitly attempts to separate the aesthetic realm from the realm of everyday life, so that art can flourish independent of the burdens of politics, habit, or practical considerations.[62] If nothing else, these novelists' experiments with form establish their works as rarefied cultural spaces, set apart from everyday language. Bate's characterization of ecopoetic works as "imaginary parks" is apt in this context. Do we visit literary works the way we might visit a national park? If so, what cultural or economic privilege is required for us to visit these literary or geographic preserves? Significant problems are connected with both of these spaces, such as the elitism of the literary text, the explosion of recreation in parks, and the prohibition of traditional uses and customs in some protected areas.

The experimental language favoured by the modernists, and the legal frameworks accompanying the creation of parks, both discourage certain kinds of commercial activity. Woolf and Proust do not have mass-market appeal; parks, in theory, are not sites of active logging, mining, real estate development, or hydroelectric power generation. In both cases, the act of protection appears to sever its object – book, mountain, desert, or body of water – from everyday life. In a North American context, among others, rivers, lakes, and ocean shores (whether legally protected or not) often appear as places of recreation or aesthetic appreciation, set apart from everyday activities of washing, bathing, flushing, boiling, and drinking. The meanings attributed to a northern lake (bearing, perhaps, a single, silent canoe) and domestic tap water might be even more distinct. How many North Americans would consider a bucket full of mop-water to be a place of deep and abiding personal or collective history? As rarefied spaces, the wilderness area and the modernist novel might, as Lefebvre suggests, simply function as elite spaces of refuge, rather than nurseries of transformation. Indeed, the meanings and properties associated with water in texts like *To the Lighthouse* might easily conform to such unspoken distinctions, attaching themselves more readily to the "wild" waters of relatively unpolluted rivers or lakes than to the tainted ones carrying layers of frothy scum through industrial parks.[63]

However, as Lefebvre himself might be quick to point out, any escape from everyday life is actually illusory.[64] Reading novels, for many of us, is an essential part of everyday life. The park, too, is not as separate as it might seem. Its forests exhale rainclouds that drift over park boundaries to rain on urban reservoirs. Its relatively unmolested rocks shelter crustaceans that will crawl into contiguous waters. Further, I would argue that both the protected area and the novel have inherent value, independent of whether they inspire more widespread political engagement. Respectively, they shelter the lives of particular fish and seaweeds and forest fungi which might not otherwise flourish, and generate precious moments of beauty in the minds of readers. However, for such literal or literary spaces to have broader political impacts, there need to be significant tributaries of meaning and affect linking them with other everyday places and states of mind. We cannot be content with their rarefied status. To actually function as pre-political spaces, they somehow need to inspire a sense of possibility, a sense that places of work and domesticity might also be places of biodiversity and deep memory. The water in the toilet bowl, while certainly different from the water in the forest spring, has also lubricated the sex of slugs and sea squirts, and fallen as tears on the faces of the dead.

○

To the extent that the sea of the *temps perdu* is understood as a space external to everyday lived experience, then, it cannot exercise its capacity to challenge the penetration of the commodity form, and may even function as a deleterious place of escape. To this critique, Jameson might add that memory itself has been so thoroughly colonized by stereotypes and simulacra that it can no longer serve as a source of "genuine" and "authentic" perception. Against Proust's imperative to cultivate involuntary memory, Jameson contends that a host of commodified images now come between the subject and reality, and between the subject and her memories. He argues that we can no longer access a past that is prior to, or outside of, capital.[65] In tracking this loss of critical and creative distance, Jameson notes that "the prodigious new expansion of multinational capital ends up penetrating and colonizing those very precapitalist enclaves (Nature and the Unconscious) which offered extraterritorial and Archimedean footholds for critical effectivity on the left."[66] With the advent of the postmodern, then, according to Jameson, art loses its potential to offer the sort of unalienated experience that is central to Jonathan Bate's ecopoetics. The waters of memory have themselves been mingled with an unceasing outflow of commodified images, sounds, and identities.

The waters of memory are certainly not untouched by the effects of capital, just as the material waters on which we model our metaphoric understanding of them have likely been laced, to one degree or another, with traces of petrochemicals, anthropogenic radioactive isotopes, and the like. As Jameson points out, the realm of memory is saturated with oft-repeated advertising slogans and images, and is thus unlikely to offer a point of access to a precapitalist existence. The symbolic meanings of water, however deeply embedded in collective cultural memory, are themselves regularly bound not only to capital itself, but also to consumer products and identities. As they are exploited, for instance, to sell bottled water, real estate, and package tours, water's symbolic resonances of well-being, prosperity, serenity, or power may be associatively linked to the markets in which they circulate.

At the same time, water is by no means entirely commodified. Some of us, sometimes, can still encounter waters without being confronted by their exchange value. To drink freely from a public tap, dip a cup into a wild creek, or draw water from a cistern – where such experiences are possible – may be to internalize the possibility of an uncommodified material existence. Although many of these experiences may be fetishized in various ways,[67] they can provide everyday sensual proof that the world is larger than the market. Even in areas where domestic water is highly commodified, contact with the rain, frost, or dew may still be available free of charge. Against Jameson, I would argue that the reach of the market is not yet total. While material and imaginative relationships to water are certainly influenced by market forces, they are not entirely encompassed by processes of commodification and reification. And to the extent that water remains uncommodified, it can provide sensual knowledge of the market as limited, inessential, and contingent.

Even as we struggle to increase access to relatively uncommodified waters and literary experiences alike, it is crucial to remember that even the most commodified objects and places conceal infinite histories. While the effects of reification might seem to condemn us to the shallows, the deep memory of a wall of vinyl siding or a pile of seemingly generic two-by-four wooden planks is real and materially present, somewhere. Jameson characterizes modernist nostalgia as a pain directed at "a past beyond all but aesthetic retrieval."[68] However, if we are truly inhabiting the nonlinear temporality of the sea of the *temps perdu*, despite the nostalgia suggested by its name, we have not "lost" the past at all.

Animated by the waters of memory, the world is made of the compost of the dead, inhabited by living languages and institutions that were secreted by earlier ages. The dead whom I have loved are with me not only in the coffee mugs they used to hold, in photographs and letters, but in all the gestures of thought and activity I have knowingly or unknowingly inherited from them. Woolf's Mrs. Dalloway, musing on her own death and dissolution into the world around her, reflects that: "somehow in the streets of London, on the ebb and flow of things, here, there, she survived, Peter survived, lived in each other, she being part, she was positive, of the trees at home; of the house there, ugly, rambling all to bits and pieces as it was; part of people she had never met; being laid out like a mist between the people she knew best, who lifted her on their branches as she had seen the trees lift the mist, but it spread ever so far, her life, herself."[69]

In this fluid concept of immortality, we persist in "the ebb and flow of things," or "like a mist" that spreads something of ourselves into the world without our intent, and without our signature. As such, to recognize the mnemonic depths of everyday objects and experiences could be quite different from nostalgia. It is not necessarily to mourn what is past, or to retreat from the present. Rather, to communicate with the sea of memory is to cultivate an awareness that the past itself is "current" and alive.

The figure of the sea of the *temps perdu* invites us to challenge capital from a place of immersion rather than a position of distance. How this might be accomplished remains a critical question. In thinking my way further into what such an immersive temporal condition might entail, I'd like to turn again briefly to Benjamin's discussion of Proust's perception of memory. Reflecting on the recovery of involuntary memories so central to the novelist's project, Benjamin struggles to imagine how such moments of spontaneous recollection might be transformed from an individual aesthetic experience into a collective revolutionary "innervation."[70] On reading *Swann's Way* for the first time, I walked delightedly through my East Vancouver neighbourhood, rediscovering bits of my childhood in the sounds made by dry leaves and in the texture of the shiny chestnuts gathering against the curbs. I remembered using the fallen chestnuts to outline the floor plan of a house on a bed of brown cedar twigs, when I was six. The transformation of my everyday perception was wondrous; but it was not political.[71] It linked my personal history to the world around me, but did not tie my own memories to the broader social or ecological pasts embedded in the dry leaves, the chestnuts, the stop signs. The collective material histories of objects – the violations and displacements associated with the hydroelectricity powering the streetlights or the mining of metals for the stop signs, the colonial histories implied by the presence of streets and chestnuts (an introduced species) on this south shore of "Burrard Inlet" – continued to feel distant and impersonal.

My Proust-inspired revelation about the chestnuts on the sidewalk was small and private. At the same time, it gave me a feeling for the mysterious closeness between thoughts and things, and helped to erode my sense of alienation from the world around me. As Benjamin points out, a cognitive awareness of social conditions is, on its own, not sufficient; to be effective, a rupture of the current social formation must operate simultaneously on intellectual, libidinal, emotional, unconscious, and somatic levels.[72] If the landscape of the imagination is understood to share a messy intimacy with everyday reality, and if the stark division between art and life is itself understood to have arisen from capitalist social relations, then pre-political works of art and literature may, in actuality, be inseparable from more obvious forms of resistance.

As he muses on Proustian memory and politics, I'd like to invite Benjamin to step, with Woolf's Lily Briscoe, "up to the lips" in the waters of memory. The particular dis-alienation from matter pursued by Proust can, through the medium of shared aqueous metaphor, be combined with the sense of watery connectivity between disparate selves and moments evoked by Woolf. Our moments of discovering our own histories throughout the world around us might then be linked to a discovery of material connection with others, both human and non-human. The effects of the commodity form on culture and material life limit the possibilities for revealing the way personal and collective histories mingle together. However, water continues to record these shared pasts in its molecular archive. Read together not only as comments on the human psyche, but as intuitions of the real memory of matter, these novels can provide a feeling for the intimate intermingling of personal, ecological, and social histories.

○

Water is arguably as essential to our self-understandings as it is to the vitality of ecosystems. Although the landscape of the imagination can be neither quantified nor mapped, I think it very likely holds a ratio of water comparable to the human body, or to the planet's surface. As such, figurative and symbolic uses of water can be assumed to carry a great deal of political significance. I doubt that hegemony could function without them. It follows that struggles to evoke alternative modes of experience can only be made more fertile by their immersion in water. Water metaphors such as "the trickle down effect" and the "circulation" of wealth help to naturalize the movements of capital. In appropriating water's symbolic associations with health, vitality and power, "flows of capital" metaphors encourage a forgetting of water itself as an essential source of these conditions. While literary evocations of the sea of the *temps perdu* may not on their own wash capitalism into the storm sewer of history, they do suggest that other relationships to time, to the past, to water, and to one another may be possible. Reading literature towards – rather than as an escape from – the fraught historical conditions of the present may help us both to remember water, and to remember *with* water.

The vitality of multi-generational memory and the well-being of the water commons are threatened by the same operations of capital. The decline of the former reinforces the despoliation of the latter, as a collective amnesia about the shared substance of the world helps to generate political consent for, or inattention to, the violation of glaciers, watercourses, and ocean ecosystems. Water, being everywhere, is an ideal mnemonic device. It is possible that the memory of water might seep into our emotional and political lives, through capillaries of art and literature and thought, to recall us to an integrity that is not lost, but only hidden.

NOTES

1 This sort of language has been prevalent in common usage for the last two or three centuries. The use of the word "currency" to describe the movement of money is first attributed to John Locke in the year 1699, while "circulation" began to describe the movement of money sometime around 1750. See Illich, *H2O and the Waters of Forgetfulness*, 43.

2 Some examples: "Like a pearl-diver who descends to the bottom of the sea … this thinking delves into the depths of the past." See Arendt, Introduction, 50–1. "Deep is the well of the past. Should we not call it bottomless?" See Mann, *Joseph and His Brothers*, 2.

3 Adorno and Horkheimer point out that for self-preserving heroes like Odysseus and Robinson Crusoe, the sea helps to constitute an atomized subjectivity, separated from the collective by the uncertainty of the waves. Without assistance from a society based on mutual aid, the enlightenment heroes "are forced … into a ruthless pursuit of their atomistic interest." Further, the threatening power of the sea justifies taking advantage of the weaknesses of others: "the possibility of foundering is seen as a moral justification for profit." As a symbol of threatening uncertainty, the sea of Homer's *Odyssey* not only invokes self-denial and a repudiation of pleasure but also legitimates exploitation. See Adorno and Horkheimer, *Dialectic of Enlightenment*, 48.

4 Strang, *The Meaning of Water*, 124–6 and 131–2.

5 See Porter, *The Medical History of Waters and Spas*.

6 Schama, *Landscape and Memory*, 305 and 337–46.

7 See, among others, Worster, *Rivers of Empire*.

8 Many thanks to Stefan Kipfer for this last observation.

9 See Strang, *The Meaning of Water*; and Bachelard, *Water and Dreams*.

10 See Nikiforuk, *Tar Sands*, 57–76.

11 "Common sense," in this usage, refers to the mass of assumptions, beliefs, and attitudes taken for granted by a large majority of people in a given society. Despite their particularity to a given time, place, and culture, common sense beliefs come to seem "natural" to those who share them, and help to generate consent for the ruling social order. Gramsci, *Prison Notebooks*, 323–34.

12 Terdiman, *Present Past*, 12.

13 Freeman, *Distant Relations*, xvi–xvii.

14 Steingraber, *Update*, 8–10.

15 Benjamin, *Illuminations*, 158–9.

16 Ibid., 90.

17 Elaborating on Benjamin's critique, Terdiman observes that what he calls an "archival consciousness" has come to replace the associative structures of memory. Here, archives attempt to compensate for the decline of remembrance by gathering and storing "the individual *item* of information, to the detriment of its relation to any whole." Terdiman, *Present Past*, 37.

18 Jameson, *Postmodernism*, 21, 284.

19 Baudrillard, "The Ecstasy of Communication," 131.

20 The commonalities between these authors' water figures have inspired me to bring them together in my own imaginary "sea of memory." I find it helpful to conceive of the ecocultural dialectic at work here with my own material metaphor – one that allows me to trace the relations between the "waters of the imagination" (mental images of water evoked by the written word) and "material waters" (which would get the reader's book wet if they came too close).

21 Benjamin, *Illuminations*, 214.

22 Jameson, "The End of Temporality," 695–6.

23 Kumar, *Bergson and the Stream of Consciousness Novel*, 8–10 and 26; and McIntire, *Modernism, Memory, and Desire*, 5, 8.

24 Kumar, *Bergson and the Stream of Consciousness Novel*, 12.

25 Quoted in McIntire, *Modernism, Memory, and Desire*, 170.

26 Baudrillard, "The Ecstasy of Communication," 131–2.

27 Carr, "Is Google Making Us Stupid?"

28 Woolf, *Mrs. Dalloway*, 124.

29 Kumar, *Bergson and the Stream of Consciousness Novel*, 24.

30 Woolf, *To the Lighthouse*, 132.

31 Ibid., 157.

32 Ibid., 150.

33 Kumar, *Bergson and the Stream of Consciousness Novel*, 14.

34 Woolf, *To the Lighthouse*, 41.

35 Proust, *Swann's Way*, 45.

36 Ibid., 44.

37 Ibid., 65.

38 Lincoln, "Waters of Memory, Waters of Forgetfulness," 21–3.

39 Quoted in Terdiman, *Present Past*, 209.

40 Bachelard, *Water and Dreams*, 52.

41 Ibid., 134.

42 Woolf, *The Voyage Out*, 238.

43 Ball, *Life's Matrix*, 266–7.

44 Baudrillard, "The Ecstasy of Communication," 131.

45 This is not to diminish the political force of Virginia Woolf's writing: *Mrs. Dalloway*, among other novels, is a powerful feminist text that also explores the psychological after-effects of the First World War and engages in overt criticism of the hollowness and superficiality of high society.

46 Jameson, *Postmodernism*, 304–5.

47 Césaire, *Discourse on Colonialism*, 84.

48 Quoted in Kelley, "A Poetics of Anticolonialism," 21.

49 Ibid., 12, 16, and 304–5.

50 Bate, *The Song of the Earth*, 64.

51 Ibid., 42 and 266.

52 Ibid., 266.

53 Ibid., 234.

54 See, for example, Buell, *The Future of Environmental Criticism*, 12–25.

55 Anishinaabe scholar Darlene Johnston writes that "in Anishinaabeg culture, there is an ongoing relationship between the Dead and the Living; between Ancestors and Descendants." Quoted in McGregor, "Honouring Our Relations," 30.

56 As Polish and Russian Jews living in conditions of migration and exile, my mother's ancestors found intergenerational continuity not only in the cyclical repetition of rituals and traditions, but also in texts. They carried on millennial conversations (unfortunately, without much direct input from women until very recently) about the meaning and interpretation of Torah. Although few texts exhibit the longevity of a book like the Old Testament, the practice of discussing literary works can still constitute a form of multi-generational dialogue, if only over the span of a few decades or, more rarely, a century or two.

57 As Hannah Arendt defines it, the common world is built of durable human creations that are shared among the living, the dead, and the unborn (see *The Human Condition*, 55). Drawing inspiration from Arendt, ecocritical thinker Catriona Sandilands

suggests that literary works can act as sites where we form and discuss opinions about matters of environmental concern. She writes that "literature is an exemplary world-making process in which a meaningful story *about* life is brought into being, given rest, and allowed to appear as *something common among us*." Sandilands, "Acts of Nature: Literature, Excess and Environmental Politics."

58  Lefebvre, *Critique of Everyday Life*, 127.

59  Benjamin, *Illuminations*, 156–7.

60  Ibid., 165, 181, and 188.

61  Ibid., 157–8.

62  Terdiman, *Present Past*, 160–74.

63  My thanks to Cate Sandilands for prompting me, repeatedly, to recognize the particularity of different waters in discussing their symbolic meanings.

64  Lefebvre, *Critique of Everyday Life*, 40.

65  Jameson, *Postmodernism*, 123–4.

66  Ibid., 49. Although we may argue that the exteriority of these "Archimedean footholds" was always illusory.

67  Maria Kaika and Erik Swyngedouw have explored the ways in which tap water systems, among other infrastructures, conceal the socioecological contexts of drinking waters. See Kaika and Swyngedouw, "Fetishizing the Modern City."

68  Jameson, *Postmodernism*, 19.

69  Woolf, *Mrs. Dalloway*, 9.

70  Benjamin, *Illuminations*, 261; Gunster, *Capitalizing on Culture*, 123 and 128.

71  Here, following Hannah Arendt, I am defining the realm of the political as a space where we speak and act together on matters of common concern (see Arendt, *The Human Condition*).

72  Gunster, *Capitalizing on Culture*, 129.

# Water and Gestationality: What Flows beneath Ethics

*Mielle Chandler and Astrida Neimanis*

*Operating at a depth of 1,260 metres below the surface of the Gulf of Mexico, the semisubmersible oil rig known as* Deepwater Horizon *made history in 2009 by drilling the deepest oil well to date: the rig had penetrated ten kilometres beneath the sea floor to unearth a major petroleum find. The plan was to contain the sticky mix of hydrocarbons and organic compounds in pipes and to pump it up through the sea to be carried away to become something else: oil that becomes speed and motion; oil that becomes multinational profits; oil that becomes pharmaceuticals, solvents, fertilizers, pesticides, plastics; oil that becomes ...*

*But on 20 April 2010 an explosion on the rig brought us new headlines, and soon these waters that flooded over the Triassic rock 150 million years ago, spawning sponges and siphonophores, copepods and crustaceans, cetaceans and sirenians, were aswim in sixty thousand barrels a day.*

*From the surface, observers watched as the slicks snaked around mangrove roots, choking out the vegetation that establishes a critical ecotone between aquatic and terrestrial life.*
*Birds grounded in puddles of crude.*

*As terrestrial mammals, few humans could witness the slow smother beneath the surface. Divers describe a red toxic soup, billowing plumes of oil washing over them at 5 metres, 10 metres, 20 metres deep. The underwater ochre stream carrying nothing but the bloated bodies of a few dead jellyfish.*

Water, the condition of all possibility, has become the unheeded recipient of the material wastes and toxins of late-capitalist production and consumption. Even as its continual movement between bodies and across borders defies the economic mechanics of quantification and instrumentalization, water is commodified, turned into measurable

units, and sold for profit. As it changes forms and cycles through various manifestations of bodies, societies, and polities, diffusing, spreading, and bringing back to us the
very matter we cast away, water shows us that at every level we are of water. But to
harm water is not simply to harm ourselves; it is, as so many ecologists have shown, to
harm the conditions for the proliferation of life itself. If Western imperialism has muted
the plurality of voices that would contest the worldview undergirding late capitalism's
treatment of water, this chapter suggests that water itself provides a starting point from
which to rethink this worldview.

The facilitative capacity of water – that is, water's facilitation of the inception, repetition, and proliferation of life in its potentially infinite plurality – throws into question
Western thought's construction of "being."[1] A particular but pervasive trajectory of
being that runs through Western cosmology and underpins its legal, political, and economic institutions is predicated on ontological frameworks that denigrate facilitative
modes of existence. Within the binary logic of these frameworks, facilitation denotes
"means" rather than "ends," passivity in contrast to activity; and it lacks the bounded
self-determination essential for sovereignty. Water gives us material evidence of an alternative mode of being that seeks to problematize this hierarchical binary logic. We term
this mode of being "gestationality." Gestationality defies the either/or structure of activity and passivity; it is neither active nor passive, and yet both active and passive. Gestation provides material evidence of the integration of what logic separates. Whereas
sovereign subjects (ideally) recognize the agency of other already-existent sovereign subjects, a gestational orientation turns toward bringing into existence that which is "not
yet." Gestationality thus challenges the dominant mode of being which we could call
"sovereign ontology." A gestational approach does not immediately lend itself to mutual
recognition or exchange but is, rather, oriented toward providing the conditions for an
unpredictable plurality to flourish.

The present chapter unfolds this proposition, and further explores the thesis that, in
its gestational mode, and as the facilitative milieu for all life, water constitutes a proto-
ethical material phenomenon. Water makes ethics possible. Water's gestational aspect
is repeated, although *differently*, at the level of interhuman ethical engagement. Water
both responds to a limited number of already-existent others and proliferates plurality
in and beyond the human. We suggest that, in this capacity, water *models* a mode of
sociality that we, as human sovereign subjects, repeat – dissolving the sovereign self in
a becoming-responsive to others, both human and more-than-human. We also propose,
in a critical materialist vein, that watery gestationality *constitutes* a proto-ethical possibility that circulates through our material selves. As beings composed mostly of water,
we all – each of us within this more-than-human community of watery bodies – carry
this capacity for facilitative responsivity, for nourishing an other, for proliferating life
in the plural, in our own aqueous flesh. This material phenomenon is iterated, at a different stratum, in human sociality and interhuman ethics.

The connection we draw between a corporeal logic of gestation and ethics is not new in Western philosophy, and it enjoys prominence in feminist embodied phenomenological thought. Luce Irigaray, while she does not use the precise term "gestationality," develops concepts of the maternal, the placental, and the intrauterine to underline the feminine materiality that allows another to be.[2] Similarly, the *écriture féminine* of Hélène Cixous and Catherine Clément describes the giving, diffuse, and overflowing feminine body as evidencing a challenge to phallogocentrism. Irigaray and Cixous and Clément all invoke the material amniotic waters of the maternal body to speak for corporeal sensibility as a source of ethical relation.[3] Our aim is to contribute to such articulations of facilitative and relational modes of being, and our own understanding of gestationality is indebted to these feminist accounts.

At the same time, we insist on untying a gestational mode of being from human, female, reprosexual experience. Taking the lineaments of gestation as paradigmatic need not be a "biologically essentialist" or heteronormative move.[4] All living bodies of water owe their corporeal existence to gestation in a watery milieu, which is evidenced in a plurality of processes that extend beyond human wombs. Making this claim requires challenging the notions that ethics originates and ends with the human. Our project is to recuperate the gestational aspect of water in order to articulate a posthumanist account of gestationality. By taking water's facilitative properties as our epistemic point of departure we move beyond biological essentialism and heteronormativity, and suggest a more inclusive understanding of gestationality. Our normative aim: to endorse the proliferation of gestational modes of engagement and response within all humans, irrespective of their biological proclivities.

Our posthumanist conceptualization of gestationality thus seeks to unsettle, in a feminist orientation, the denigration of facilitative modes of being. We see this denigration of facilitation all around us, in the trampling of generosity by greed and exchange, in the usurpation of hospitality by imperialism, and in the exploitation of those who care for others. Our motivation is further fuelled by the urgent and precarious state of our planetary bodies of water. A concept of gestationality that decentres the human is also our response to water-related environmental crisis, the concomitant harm to life-in-the-plural to which this crisis contributes, and our human disregard for more-than-human bodies as worthy of our gestational efforts and care. Here, we join scholars in Science and Technology Studies and the area of scholarship referred to as the post-humanities and "new" or "critical materialisms,"[5] who call into question the long and entrenched history of privileging the human (unencumbered, monadic, rational, and so on) in Western modes of thought and action.

A leading thinker in this field, Bruno Latour, makes the case for a radically revised civilization in which both human and non-human "actants" – entities that modify other entities – are integrated as legitimated agents in an expanded political collective.[6] Latour's actor-network theory interrogates and dismantles the "person/thing" distinction on ontological, epistemological, and ethical grounds, illustrating that conventional separations between "person" and "thing" – subject and object, being and its material preconditions, citizen and property, active agent and passive matter – are provisional and shifting. In contesting democracy's denial of agency, and thus political legitimacy, to non-human entities, Latour opens up for critical analysis the ways in which current capitalist processes are predicated on maintaining the very subject-object structure we find so abhorrent, and which we term "slavery" when it is human beings that are relegated to object status.[7]

Yet, while Latour's scholarship disrupts the ontological paradigm of Western anthropocentrism in important and exciting ways, it also simultaneously underlines the tenacity of these same ontological paradigms. In other words, his challenge to anthropocentrism retains central tenets of Western androcentrism. Even as Latour's project expands the realm of a political sphere once reserved for male citizens and property owners to a potentially limitless number of entities, by retaining one of Western philosophy's central ontological tenets – that it is the active, rather than the facilitative, capacity of the entity that renders it worthy of political voice – this iteration of political entities nonetheless retains a vestige of a troubling pedigree.[8] We are concerned that an overreliance on action might unwittingly perpetuate an age-old chauvinism denigrating the "passivity" previously attributed to nature, women, and inanimate objects, thereby upholding the deep structure of the very androcentric and anthropocentric binaristic ontologies that these theories aim to subvert. It is perhaps not surprising that Latour's model for a posthumanist democracy brings the more-than-human world under the purview of human Western social, political, and economic institutional structures, magnanimously extending politics to the material world. Our aim is to break free from this lingering anthropocentrism, to search instead for something more-than-human (even as this "something" is the stuff of human bodies, too) upon which to ground a posthumanist mode of responsiveness. We seek to articulate a new conceptual starting point – one that *flows beneath the human* as its condition of possibility.

> *I am suspicious of sedimented logics of "beneath" – what is less than, lower than, subservience or inadequacy.*
> *Water has its own logic we are still trying to learn.*[9]
> *"Beneath" is neither inferiority,*
> *nor foundation. "Beneath" is not a solid and delimited bedrock whose density and strength we can measure, calculate, know. "Beneath" is the well of potential from which new possibilities spring. "Beneath" is the precondition of what is, what will be, what will become.*

Latour's location of agency within the material world resonates in other contributions within the emerging field of critical material feminisms. Elizabeth A. Wilson, for example, critiques feminist accounts that have been "brokered" through a repudiation of the agency, intelligence, and sociality of the material world.[10] Like Latour's actor-network theory, such feminist accounts are concerned with the ontological distinction between the human and the more-than-human. Unlike Latour, however, feminist contributions such as Wilson's also explicitly seek to challenge androcentrism in ways that other new materialist accounts do not, as the distinction between (more-than-human) matter and (human) culture is directly linked to other forms of binaristic thinking, widely accepted as anathema to feminist liberation. As Stacy Alaimo argues, "rather than fleeing from [a] debased nature, associated with corporeality, mindlessness, and passivity" and thereby reinforcing the very dualisms endemic to women's oppression, "it would be more productive for feminist theory to undertake the transformation of gendered dualisms."[11] The difficulty nonetheless lies in enacting this feminist transformation without maintaining a reliance on terms like "active" and "passive";[12] the task remains to refuse a denigration of "nature," but without imbuing all nature and matter with a valorized activeness. A posthumanist conception of gestationality, as both "active" and "passive," or agential and facilitative, contributes in no small part to the conceptual transformation of this tenacious dualism.

Inspired, then, by feminist corporeal phenomenologies as well as by the growing chorus of scholars whose investigations of "nature" and matter resonate and overlap with this feminist dissatisfaction with dominant Western ontological frameworks, our objective is to contribute to feminist critical materialisms that are *both* carefully attuned to corporeal sensibility *and* interested in challenging the denigration of matter, while cautiously negotiating the traps of biological essentialism and the unwitting retention of hierarchized dualisms. In order to forward this proposal, we develop it through the philosophical thought and conceptual tools of two key twentieth-century precursors to contemporary corporeal ethics and new materialisms: Emmanuel Lévinas and Gilles Deleuze.

Before turning to Lévinas and Deleuze, a final important qualification is needed. The starting point for our position is water's materiality; our thesis is indebted to close and careful attunement to water's material capacities. Our claim, however, is not that water is *only* gestational. The logics of water are many: gestation is joined by communication, contamination, dissolution, and destruction.[13] In other words, even if water is a proto-ethical mode of being, it is more than that. Our claim, rather, is that as the primary facilitative substance, and the condition of possibility for all life on our planet, water's proliferation of life-in-the-plural must be foregrounded in the project of recalibrating Western cosmology. As a gestational milieu, water exemplifies a proto-ethical mode of being that we humans must attune ourselves to if a plural and abundant world is our aim. Water calls upon us, as human sovereign subjects, to amplify our own facilitative capacity as watery milieux in our interactions with all bodies of water.

Thinking beneath Ontology with Water: Infinity in Immanence

Emmanuel Lévinas's work gives us a phenomenology of an ethical sensibility responsive to and facilitative of others. It thereby provides an important starting point for developing a theoretical understanding of how water, in its facilitative mode, might also challenge the violence of political ontology. Lévinas's search for alternatives to the central problematic tenets he sees in Western philosophical renditions of being entails distinguishing the *ontological* (the entity as in-and-for-itself) and the *ethical* (the entity as for-another) as different modes of significance and existence. In Lévinas's framework, ontological being, or the being of the sovereign subject (the self-interested cognizing self), displaces other possibilities and is thus fundamentally violent and violating.[14] Concerned to perpetuate its own being in an enduring time, the sovereign subject issues from a milieu of contest, mutual recognition, exchange, contract, and war. The subject engages with its surroundings in ways that reinforce and perpetuate the allergic milieu termed the "political realm" by Lévinas.[15]

Ontological being, or what Lévinas simply terms "ontology," is for him the form of being that political agents enact. It orients and structures political relations between sovereign subjects, entities that are in-and-for-themselves. In Lévinas's analysis, our political systems and modes of engagement do not create peace among citizens so much as they curb the blatancy of ontological violence by proceduralizing it. Politics proceduralizes or institutionalizes the antagonism and exploitation endemic to this kind of self by adapting its fundamental violence to forms endorsable by the body politic. In such a political mode, for example, we justify a violent gash in the sea floor to remove its ancient fossilized liquids as a fair, economic exchange between human buyer and human seller – the only legitimate "subjects" in this interaction, despite the risks to the watery milieu.[16]

> *The quantification of harm: Over 200 million gallons spilled.*
> *Over six thousand bodies of fish, turtles, birds and dolphins dead*
> *in the spill zone. Forty thousand square miles of fisheries closed*
> *off.*
> *The oil leak poisons the primordial sphere, the milieu of possibility,*
> *but this harm to the gestational biosphere is unquantifiable.*

Lévinas maintains that there is far more depth to human existence than this sovereign ontology allows for, and that this depth provides for possibilities beyond the generalized antagonism permeating the current order. While at one level human existence is self-interested, at another level – well-hidden by the dominance of the ontological stratum – the human exists as non-ontological, giving and responding to the needs of others. At this level beneath the realm of the ontological, the human is motivated not by concern for its own identity or perpetuation, but by a sense of responsibility for the well-being of the other people with whom contact is made. Distinguished from the level of sovereign ontology, this "otherwise-than-being" is, for Lévinas, the realm of ethics and sociality. Ethics entails a certain self-erasure in the facilitation of the flourishing and well-being of others. It is found in the compulsion to come to the aid of another person (a compulsion often revealed most clearly in kinship relations) and, in the instant of that compulsion, to let go of one's own concerns. This, for Lévinas, is the foundation of sociality and plurality.[17] The social self is compelled as responsible for other people who are insurmountably different and other – ungraspably so. This social responsivity at the level of ethics is different from political engagement and from the ontological level at which we label and instrumentalize each other, reducing and circumscribing plurality, even when we refer to this instrumentalization using hallowed terms such as "mutual recognition," "contract," "self-determination," and, in its most recent incarnation, "human rights."[18]

Lévinas characterizes the ontological or political approach to another person as allergic – a response of irritation to another, an attempt not to let the other get underneath one's skin. One suffers the other as an incursion that one attempts to reject. An ethical or otherwise-than-ontological response is no less uncomfortable, but rather than rejecting an other, one offers what one has to this other. Expulsion and aversion are the movements of politics, but the movement of ethics is gift. One nourishes the other within one's own body the way the maternal body nourishes a foetus. Lévinas posits maternity not *as* ethics, but as paradigmatic of the ethical relation.[19] The maternal body facilitates the well-being of the other-within, before and independently of the control of mind; one is oriented toward the well-being of the other before one has even thought about it.

In the economic sphere, an ontological-political approach takes the form of exploitation or exchange. I either take from another in self-interest or, if the proceduralization of equality prevails, I exchange with another person, offering something of value in return for something else of equal value. The economics of gestation and ethics are quite different. The maternal body does not ask for an exchange with the foetus. This maternal response takes place at another register, in the kinship of sociality. In interhuman kinship, I am motivated not by self-interest but by my social proximity to others. Ethics, in other words, follows, at another level, the lineaments, or pattern of biological gestation, birth, lactation. I feel a pull within me, within my body and sensibilities, to respond to the needs of the others with whom I am faced in ways that ease their suffering, fill their needs, and provide the material conditions for their flourishing.

*I also feel a pull*
*toward that body of water that lies between Florida and Mexico,*
*toward the bodies of water therein and along its shore.*
*I feel the oil leak in the Gulf of Mexico as a painful incursion, calling for response, –*
*how to respond?*

While Lévinas inspires our conception that sociality iterates the gestational elements of water, his anthropocentrism disallows the possibility. Lévinas explicitly posits human reproduction as paradigmatic of ethical relations; however, he stops short of evoking reproduction broadly conceived, or, as we are suggesting, the material more-than-human preconditions of reproduction, as also paradigmatic of ethics. Among the features of Lévinas's conceptualization of ethics that we wish to retain, is the location of ethics in the body, in corporeal sensibility, in feeling rather than in thought and decision.[20] Although Lévinas insists that ethical compulsion is only experienced by anatomically human entities, and only felt when faced with suffering tied to human morphology, if ethics is fundamentally a *bodily* compulsion, it follows that similar compulsions are potentially shared by other, non-human, bodies – potentially by any material entity with a capacity for corporeal response.

Lévinas ascribes to ethics a morphological requirement – a human face. This ascription has fostered much discussion about what constitutes a face, cross-species facial experiences, and so on.[21] Delving beneath Lévinas's morphological requirement exposes that the ethically privileged position of the human face issues out of a monotheistic conceptualization of creation. For Lévinas the human differs from animals and all other matter in that the human is called forth into existence by the divine; when one human looks into the face of another, she or he feels the call of God.[22] Although felt in the body, and fundamentally sensorial, Lévinas's ethics originates *beyond* manifestation, in divine interpellation. Our analysis seeks to posit the (proto-)origins of ethics *beneath* manifestation, in the cycling of water through all processes of life. What we see (or otherwise sense) in the body of another is also water. Water, in its gestational and facilitative capacity, is not *beyond*; it is not a divine creator itself unfettered by corporeal existence. Water is rather *beneath*, the very material precondition of infinite biological life. In its capacity to gestate others into corporeal existence, water is evidenced as the matter of potential *par excellence*.

*beneath the seemingly stagnant surface, entire worlds are teeming*

Here it is also important to underscore the distinction that Lévinas draws between ontology, which is tied to self-interested sovereign identity, and ethics as other-orientation. In Lévinas's understanding (which runs counter to modernist conceptions of the "political" decidedly breaking from the "natural"), "nature" is ontological – that is, fundamentally at war.[23] But is war what we really encounter when we turn to the natural world that Lévinas so readily excludes from the realm of ethics? Yes, we find violence, quite plentifully. Bound up in this violence we also find a material world replete with sociality and responsivity – with assistance, facilitation, and gestation that give rise to plurality. By emptying the material world of divinity, by desacralizing matter, Lévinas forecloses the possibility of thinking the ethical or proto-ethical significance of the material world. This poses a problem for the development of a Lévinasian ecological or biosphere ethics.

*The oil, I am told, is mostly gone – this means we no longer see it at the surface. Particulate matter, sinking in slow motion, now blankets the broken seafloor.*

Lévinas offers us a way of thinking about modes of relation that are not predicated on instrumentalization and the forms of exploitation that instrumentalization makes possible, if not probable. His conviction that the natural world is necessarily both instrumentalizable and driven by an all-pervading self-interest reinvokes, however, a dangerous and destructive privileging of the interhuman over all other interactions in the living world. Lévinas's theorization can only recognize ethics in the self-erasing-for-the-other as elicited in face-to-face interhuman contact. This thinking precludes him from paying heed to facilitative sociality at the level of matter. On the other hand, critical theories that attempt to undo the person/thing hierarchy, such as Latour's, reinvoke the privileging of the ontological characteristics of personhood (that is, acting, rather than facilitating) that Lévinas's ethics contests. The gestational capacity of water manifests Lévinas's depriviliging of action: by effecting possibility through modes of responsivity and facilitation, water disrupts a privileging of political action and agency. And, as we shall explain, as milieu, rather than as Latourian "actor" in a "network," water defies the confines of Latour's conceptual apparatus as well. Water asks us to contemplate modes of existence beyond the binary paradigms of person/thing, subject/object, active/passive. We return to these points below. Water, in a sense, flows between Lévinas and Latour, suggesting a proto-ethics at the material level that also challenges what it can mean to be a material entity.

Leaving ontology to the realm of politics, and instead approaching the real through water's material capacities, the next two sections of this chapter locate the precondition of ethics in watery gestationality. If we, as human subjects, can cultivate corporeally felt ethical sensibilities toward bodies of water (human, animal, geophysical, and other), we do so *as* bodies of water. This is not to say, *contra* Lévinas, that we are responsive only to those beings that are "like" us. It is, rather, to recognize the fundamental alterity of other bodies to whom we are nonetheless connected, in and as watery milieux. If what we feel in response to the oil leak in the Gulf cannot be properly termed "ethics," it can certainly be understood as belonging to a more broadly shared compulsion to respond which flows beneath ethics – to sociality broadly understood. This conceptual reorientation allows us to see the ethical gestures that ground environmental and social justice, including our relations to our watery others, as made possible by gestational sociality in the material realm. Water's gestational capacity – that is, a more-than-human proto-ethics – is repeated both in and as ethics in the interhuman realm.

Thinking the Real with Water: Material Sociality

The work of philosopher Gilles Deleuze (often in conjunction with Félix Guattari) also presents a significant break from dominant Western ontological schemata. Like Lévinas, Deleuze rejects sovereign ontology. But Deleuze does not posit an "otherwise-than-being." Rather, he eschews the term "ontology" in favour of reconceptualizing the "real." The resulting schema provides helpful conceptual tools for unfolding a theory of material sociality. At the same time, even Deleuze's work cannot quite accommodate the logic of gestationality that water evidences. Careful phenomenological attunement to water itself helps us to nuance Deleuze's conceptual categories, and develop our understanding of water as the material prototype for the phenomenology of ethics that Lévinas describes.

The real, or "what is," in Deleuze's view, is inseparable from how it is, how it might have been, and how it might be. Deleuze sets up a tripartite schema here: (1) "the actual" – or "what is," at least provisionally; (2) "the virtual" – what might be or could have been, or what he calls an immaterial cloud of potentiality out of which "actuals" emerge; and (3) "the intensive" – "how" something is, or the morphogenetic processes of becoming and the movements of relation that continually compose "what is." Deleuze's "real" is *both* what is already assembled or stratified *and* the cloud of indeterminate potentiality that hovers around this stratification,[24] *as well as* operations of relation that enact these sedimentations or manifestations.[25] For Deleuze, the actual, the virtual, and the intensive are all *real*.

This schema echoes Lévinas's distinction between ontology and ethics in some subtle and surprising ways. Both philosophers seek to elucidate modes of existence that facilitate the being of entities. Lévinas, as we have seen, associates this facilitative engagement with ethics; for Deleuze, the key term is "becoming." Processes of becoming – schematized as the intensive – are what allow one being to affect another, and through such affecting, to bring about a transformation.[26] Through the work of the intensive, new beings come into being. Yet, despite their shared concern for the proliferation of plurality, there is also a significant divergence between Lévinas and Deleuze. Being and the facilitation of becoming are not, for Deleuze, distinct planes, as is the case in Lévinas's formulation of the realms of ontology and ethics. Nor does Deleuze separate the human from the more-than-human world. The capacity to affect and be affected, and to bring other bodies into being, belongs to all bodies. Hence, Deleuze implicitly challenges not only Lévinas's separation of ethics from ontology (and Lévinas's placement of ethics as prior to and the precondition of ontology), but also his privileging of the interhuman.

> *Perhaps the oil is a distraction: this watery body has been casually assaulted for generations. A critical mass of mangrove swamps and wetlands in the Mississippi Delta was destroyed long ago to facilitate wider and straighter*

*shipping lanes. The deadzone off the coast of Louisiana caused by fertilizer run-off was the size of Labrador last year.*

*Water, a universal solvent. They say oil is "like butter" to hungry, crude-munching oceanic bacteria. Recovery will come. As an erudite philosopher optimistically quipped over three centuries ago, we do not yet know what a body can do.*

*Nor do we know what a body can take.*

"Sociality" refers to qualities of relating, or modes of existence, that are neither active nor passive, neither purely intentional nor mechanical, but rather fundamentally responsive. While "sociality" may connote a particularly interhuman mode of being – and this is Lévinas's conceptualization of sociality – Deleuze's refusal to hierarchize human and more-than-human entities enables us to understand sociality as more-than-human, which in turn enables a reconceptualization of our own human modes of sociality. We are responsive as part of a much broader lifeworld of responsivity between material phenomena. *Material sociality* thus refers to the ways in which bodies are necessarily materially implicated in one another's corporeal existence. Processes of porosity, fluidity, and absorption evidence water as the medium of material sociality *par excellence.* Indeed, we might say that all bodies – human, other animal, vegetable, meteorological, geophysical, or otherwise – necessarily "water" one another in key co-constitutive ways. Human bodies ingest reservoir bodies to keep themselves alive, while reservoir bodies are slaked by rain bodies, rain bodies absorb ocean bodies, ocean bodies permeate fish bodies, fish bodies are consumed by whale bodies, and so forth. To borrow the terminology of Nancy Tuana, these flows and exchanges are best understood as "viscous."[27] Viscosity as a mode of sociality highlights the fact that bodies also have their own thresholds of resistance. We do not all melt into an amorphous mass of aqueous materiality, but rather we differentiate ourselves. The membranes that distinguish and separate us make us multiple and, as plural, imbricate us in social relations. As these various operations of material sociality make evident, our aqueous gifts and debts to one another are an intrinsic and inextricable dimension of our existence.

Recent scholarship under the broad rubric of new materialism challenges human ontological privilege, while also seeking to extend a version of relationality or sociality into the more-than-human world. Latour, for example, argues that entities only come into being through their relations within actor-networks. To reiterate our concern with such a project, a privileging of action ties material sociality to a framework of sovereign ontology that privileges self-sustaining action. The concept of "network" does not wholly undo the prerequisite for a bounded entity whose political standing is tied to influencing an other while retaining its own perdurance.

*BP assures the public that it remains committed to paying all necessary cleanup costs and any other legitimate claims for loss and damages caused by the spill – a liability estimated to run to $14 billion. Earning $17 billion in 2010, BP can certainly withstand the hit.*

The challenge, then, is to conceptualize material sociality as untied from the framework of sovereign ontology and "political entities." Our aim is *not* to make water an actant or political entity; we are troubled by the "outside" that inevitably remains when the oppressed are brought into the space of the privileged (here, the actors). Nor are we calling for a complete relinquishment of intentionality or orientation – for a dissolving, or a washing away of one's boundedness as an entity. One cannot "de-commit" entirely. Rather, the challenge here is to discern *what flows beneath* a commitment to ourselves as sovereign, acting individuals, to bring to the fore the modes of sociality that make such commitments possible in the first place. In other words, we are seeking a conceptual schema that recognizes that even as a bounded subject, one can engage in a partial dissolution of this boundedness. Such a mode of subjectivity would eschew the instrumentalization of slavery or servitude, and be better understood in terms of a generative generosity.

Deleuze's schema of the real provides, in part, a conceptual corrective to the tendency to preserve the sovereignty of the entity or the actant. For even though Deleuze offers a tripartite schema whereby "the actual" is seemingly distinct from the "intensive," his insistence that *becomings* are *real* suggests that no decisive distinction between these two categories of the real can be made. Responsivity, a process of affecting and being affected, must be intrinsically part of any entity, human or more-than-human. For example, the concept of the "actual" could be applied to bodies of water themselves – aquifer, storm cloud, booklice, magnolia – and the "intensive" to the various morphogenetic processes that bring watery bodies into co-constitutive relation. Our planet's hydrological cycles of precipitation, transpiration, evaporation, and condensation can be understood as examples of water's intensive operations.[28]

Yet close attention to water's materiality reveals that all kinds of aqueous "actuals" literally incorporate these hydrological cycles into their own inter- and intra-corporeal operations. A puddle is becoming cloud, while a raindrop is becoming river. We might think, also, of water's metamorphosis in and through our human bodies: our bodies of water transport nutrients, cushion our organs so that they may safely stretch and expand, bring about a flushing of blood in menstruation, or produce the amniotic fluid that gestates another. Water facilitates our transformation as subjects, as our infant-body becomes our child-body, our girl-body becomes our woman-body, and so on. Our changing bodies are still watery, but water also facilitates these changes. Water's materiality thus also nuances Deleuze's schematization of the real. The double articulation of water here as *both* "the transformed" – that is, the actualized, the "what" – *and* the process of transformation – that is, the intensive, the "how" – reveals a mode of existence whereby water is not "thing" *or* "force," "cause" *or* "effect," "the doer" *or* "the deed" but rather both actual *and* intensive. As such, water blurs the discrete compartmentalization of "entity" and "responsiveness." Such facilitation is not coextensive with sovereign subjectivity, as it requires a de-commitment to sovereign ontology. But nor is it a third term, distinct from our relative coherence as a subject. Watery sociality flows beneath our subjectivity, facilitating it but also dissolving it.

## Thinking Futurity with Water: Repetition and Milieu

Thinking along with Deleuze allows us to conceptualize material sociality as a mode of relation and response in both the human and more-than-human realms. We, like all other entities, leak into and siphon from one another in response to our environment – that is, in response to all the other bodies that affect us. As corporeal entities, we manifest in forms that are provisionally sedimented – as nodes of pattern in development.[29] But thinking with water suggests a particular kind of material sociality whereby we not only respond to others but also in turn comprise the fluid social gestational condition of possibilities beyond ourselves. We respond *as* entities, at the same time de-committing to our sovereign subjectivity *as* entity. In its provision of conditions for new possibilities, watery sociality is gestational, and this gestationality entails the facilitation of futurity, the plurality of the "not yet," through becoming-milieu. Again, this is true not only of maternal bodies but of all living entities, which are all mostly water. Unfolding the question of how we become – and must become – watery milieu is the task to which we now turn.

Deleuze's theorization of difference and repetition offers a theoretical support for this unfolding. In Deleuze's schema, repetition can only manifest difference; only difference – or the manifestation of the unknowable – can repeat. This proposition may seem counter-intuitive, in that unknowability suggests something that has never been before, while repetition suggests the return of the same. Similarly, repetition is commonly understood in terms of the identical, suggesting that what repeats is the "same," only at a different time, perhaps in a different place. Deleuze insists, however, that logic of this sort subordinates everything to the realm of identity, unjustifiably privileging some "original" – which itself must have originated somewhere, at some inconceivably distant time. Alternatively, Deleuze posits the force of differentiation.[30] Differentiation, he says, is a compulsion or desire to differ from oneself.[31] He calls this desire "different/*c*iation" – to highlight that he is speaking of an internal, intensive force of differing. Repetition is not *re*-presentation, but rather an affirmation of and a selection from the virtual potential that already exists. Freed from the insistence that a repetition must be only the return of the "same," repetition *necessitates* a new articulation, a new configuration, a new proliferation, a new intersectional node instantiated within the real. What repeats, in other words, is pure difference.

Deleuze's conception of difference and repetition provides a theoretical frame that helps conceptualize what water, cycling through our lifeworld, already evidences: any watery entity is, in both its inception and its ontogenetic manifestations, always already constituting and constituted by overlapping and interconnected cycles of repetition. It is here that we find infinity in immanence. The finite quantity of water on our earth has given rise, and will continue to give rise, to an unfathomable plurality of life forms. Except for perhaps some minute amounts of vapour that may enter our atmosphere from the cosmos, all the water that is here, on, in, and hovering above our planet, has been here since our planet's inception.[32] *The watery materiality of each watery entity has been somewhere, sometime before*, cycling through its various articulations for millennia. Yet, while this repeating water is always "the same," it is by no means undifferent/ciated. Each repetition of a biological vessel of water is iterated anew. As much as it may repeat the morphological blueprint, genomic pattern, or chemical structure of its "parent," it is a unique iteration – and this difference implies the radical unknowability of the "not yet."

*The duck repeats. Exxon Valdez. Syncrude.* BP. *But sometimes it is a brown pelican, a least tern, a reddish egret.*

Deleuze's third category of the real, the "virtual," offers another way of conceptualizing the difference and repetition instantiated in water's overlapping hydrological cyclings. In Deleuze's conception, virtuality is the zone of potentiality from which actualities are extracted. The virtual is like an infinitive verb (for example, "to be"), rather than an actualized declination thereof (such as "is"). "To be" holds all the potentiality out of which materializations emerge into actuality. The watery cycles of difference and repetition give Deleuze's theory a grounding in the material lifeworld, but the materiality of water also challenges a conceptualization of the virtual (suggested by Deleuze and confirmed in various commentaries on his work[33]) which posits virtuality as an "immaterial" and abstract (albeit real) field of potential that surrounds an actualized entity. This challenge is accentuated if we consider the hydrological cycle. Because the earth does not produce its planetary water but only recycles it, we might think of this as a "closed system" of knowable material entities. But because water is always becoming (drawing on its latent virtual potential), it is always repeating, but differently. In this sense, then, these cycles manifest an "open system." In our watery world of hydrological cycles, the unbounded virtuality that repeats is water itself. The latent potentiality of the virtual is thus hardly immaterial, as it inheres in water's very material capacity to repeat itself as new watery bodies. It is water's compulsion to do so. So, while Deleuze turns to the metaphor of an "indeterminate cloud" that surrounds and hovers around one's actuality as a way of explaining the virtual, water's virtuality is no metaphor. Watery virtuality may be "indeterminate," but it does more than hover around a body like an immaterial idea; it materially invests that body.[34]

*[handwritten margin notes: material / virtual – water is matter, also is becoming]*

We might understand the impulse to conceptualize the virtual as immaterial as being theoretically overdetermined by sovereign ontology. This paradigm encourages us to conceive of materiality only in terms of sovereign entities – that is, in terms of entities that are in-and-for-themselves, committed to their own perdurance. Under the influence of sovereign ontology, it is difficult to conceptualize material entities that might also *de*-commit to their self-preservation in order to become embodied in others, as others. Yet, this is what we encounter in watery virtuality: the materiality of water is a well of unknown futurity and facilitative capacity. To think watery virtuality as *both* material *and* virtual not only challenges a reading of virtuality as immaterial but also moves us into the domain of sociality and responsivity. Watery virtuality reveals a specific aspect of material sociality in its gestational mode: futurity, and the becoming-plural of the lifeworld.[35]

> *Even after the invasion of land by adventurous amphibians, the survival of terrestrial life was still dependent on finding ways of bringing the oceanic surround ashore. We enfolded our watery habitats inside of ourselves, absorbed what we could from the water saturated air and soil. We dug interconnective channels through one another's bodies. We devised an interconnected system of terrestrial life that extended and (literally) incorporated the sea.*
> *Survival, yes. But also: multiplication. "The land biota represents not simply life from the sea, but a variation of the sea itself."*[36]

And becoming plural, as water, is a potential available to us all. Recall that we live as watery bodies *in a watery world*. Our milieu – in the ocean, in the water-drenched soil, in the water-saturated air – is always more or less watery. We are not only of water, but *in* water. A key aspect of watery gestationality is thus this notion of milieu. Milieu, however, is not only an indeterminate environment we inhabit. This environment is ingested and incorporated both by our individualized selves and by our evolutionary lineages. Our watery milieux are enfolded into our bodies, repeating our ancestors differently. By considering the watery milieux that all living bodies not only inhabit but also ingest, become, and pass on, we come to see the virtual as a mode of sociality and responsiveness to others. Becoming milieu for an other demands a radical reorientation of oneself as existing in part for the purpose of what is beyond oneself, and thus a (partial) dissolution of oneself as a sovereign subject. The aqueous virtuality that we enfold within our own actualized bodies is the gift we offer to unknowable futures; our virtuality thus *becomes a material milieu* that facilitates the becoming of others.

Again, this concept fundamentally challenges the idea that future potentiality is an immaterial cloud, and also the idea that material entities must be necessarily self-preserving. And again, while this self-dissolving subjectivity is certainly evidenced in maternity, we all carry this water with us, a well of unknown futurity enfolded in our flesh; we all have the possibility of reorienting toward bathing other lives into existence. Seen in this way, gestationality is fundamentally expanded beyond female reprosexual bodies. We might be milieu as womb – but we are also milieu as symbiote, milieu as host, and milieu as watery matter that can be bequeathed to all kinds of others, as our bodies fragment and dissolve back into water. At the same time, we can also be milieu as neighbour, milieu as interlocutor, milieu as voter, consumer, passerby on the street. In each of these interactions, we have the possibility of depriveleging our own self-preservation and instead creating the conditions for the flourishing of an other. We propose that this sociality is conditioned by a material mode of responsivity that flows beneath our sovereign subjectivity. In any of these interactions, it is not our "selves" that we are reproducing differently. Rather, in becoming milieu and the condition of possibilities beyond ourselves, we are, in part, undoing these "selves."

> *In the Gulf of Mexico, sailfish becomes dolphin and larval crab becomes turtle.*
> *Once upon a time, perhaps plesiosaur became sea snake, or swan.*
> *But water becomes them all.*

Such a view of watery milieu clearly challenges common views of sociality. "Milieu" is usually read as separate from the entities that dwell or interact therein.[37] "Milieu" in this sense is but the passive backdrop upon which actants play out their social dramas.[38] Yet, water teaches us that milieu is both *of* us (as part of our material virtuality) and also that which responds to the call of the "not yet," providing the conditions for its emergence. Water, here, is neither active nor passive, and yet it is both active and passive, revealing itself as a mode of sociality that is transformative, facilitative, responsive. In the previous section, water, as both actual and intensive, was shown to blur any discrete separation between *what* becomes (an "actual") and *how* one becomes (an "intensive" process). Thinking with water also challenges a conception of the virtual as necessarily immaterial – for water constitutes virtual materiality. Finally, here, we see that milieu is both a subject and a "backdrop," an entity and a potential response.

Watery milieu thus embodies a sociality in which one can be bounded, intentional, and animated while at the same time partially dissolving oneself and being oriented in one's capacity as milieu for an other. This orientation flows beneath our sovereign subjectivity, but it is suppressed in self-protection when generosity is exploited, gifts are stolen, and self-interest is the *modus operandi* encoded into political and economic structures. *Becoming-milieu* does not entail total desubjectification (as Deleuze notes, to desubjectivize oneself completely only results in annihilation[39]), but it does require that we loosen our commitments to our own sovereign instantiations. In being both an actual entity and also a responsive milieu, forged out of a material virtual potential, water reveals that such nuanced and multi-layered modes of subjectivity are possible. In fact, not only are they possible, but they are the very condition of possibility – of life – in the material world.

> *Beneath everything that I can name, that I can speak, there is something more. We might call these depths "water," but even "water," the word, is already contained; it has taken up residence in a body to which I have given a name: gulf, pelican, mangrove, human.*
> *I can trace it back as far, as deep, as an elemental oceanic milieu, but I know it flows even deeper. At these depths, my own lungs give out, the pressure too much for this human to withstand. "Water," in its most elemental gestational body, is the conceptual threshold beyond which I cannot dive. I can only live it as my material condition of possibility, as the reservoir of potential to be gifted to an unknowable future.*

### Repeating Water: The Matter of Ethics, the Ethics of Matter

Sociality, plurality, kinship, being-for-the-other, maternity, fraternity – these are terms Lévinas uses to indicate response to the needs of an other. A shorthand for the pull or compulsion that motivates this beneficent response is "ethics." For Lévinas, these modes of being entail giving up one's ontological sedimentation, softening one's self-fortification in order to move beyond oneself. Lévinas thus asks us to imagine the future before us as conceived in our sociality, and as a foetal becoming, a becoming that requires response, nourishment, and the greatest of care. In this sense, he sketches for us a mode of being beyond what we have termed sovereign ontology. In a social and ethical mode of existence we feel compelled from within to offer a facilitative response – a response that entails a transformation of the self into the conditions of possibility for the other, into a *reciprocal?* nourishing environment for the flourishing of people and possibilities beyond the self.

Such facilitation is what water effects at the material level. Water infuses us. It is materialized as our various bodies, thus losing its "own" morphology. If in ethics the "I" dissolves and begins to flow, in water we see the effacement and reconstitution of radically different and multiple morphologies. Water takes provisional shape as manatee or sea grass. But as such, it does more than subsist only in and for itself; it also subsists as and for the other, which it also is, and which it also nourishes. As sea grass water is "invisible." When we look at sea grass, we see the manifestation we call sea grass; we do not see the water. The water is hidden, covered over, forgotten, in the shape and manifestation of the other. This self-effacement in sociality as responsivity to others, openness to the "not yet," and becoming-milieu is a mode of being that politics and ontology – grounded in action and *telos* – can accommodate only by attempting to relegate it to object status, thereby robbing it of its significance and radical potential. Gestationality as becoming-milieu is a mode of sociality that eschews not only a commitment to self-preservation *at all costs*, but also the requirement for one to be *either* (active) entity *or* (passive) backdrop. It is a gift to a "not yet" other, a gift that is not predictable, calculable, or symmetrically exchangeable.

Watery gestationality is a form of sociality beyond quantification and measurement – that is, beyond the forms of engagement upon which Western economic and political structures are predicated. While sovereign ontological relations make demands that anticipate calculable responses, gestationality is a mode of sociality that acknowledges the unknown, and does so by gifting its own materiality as milieu to the facilitation of unknowable plurality. Moreover, the watery virtuality of all bodies as material milieu for an unknowable future illuminates the way in which watery bodies themselves enact the very difference and repetition that we have described above: bodies are repeating other bodies, always (unknowably) differently.

> *Some 4,200,000 litres of chemical dispersants were sprayed at the wellhead five thousand feet under the sea. Because the dispersants were applied at such depths, much of the oil never rose to the surface. Sixty to a hundred million gallons of oil still remain unaccounted for. Where and how will it all repeat?*
> *Bluefin tuna.*
> *Phytoplankton.*
> *Portuguese man-o-war.*

But it is not only bodies that repeat. In ethics, the lineaments of watery gestation are repeated in the ontological letting-go that takes place when one feels compelled to respond to the call of another. Ethics, then, is not something that we need to magnanimously bequeath to the more-than-human world. Material, more-than-human entities do not require that this mode of sociality be "extended" to them. Rather, it is gestationality, in its capacity as responsivity, milieu, and facilitation of the "not yet," that is repeated by ethics. In other words, if we recast *ethics as watery gestationality, repeated differently*, water becomes the material condition and precondition of infinity in immanence, of the "not yet" – not only of all possible forms of biological life, but also of our human social modes of existence. We are ethical because we are first, beneath our social and political commitments, watery.

The gestational imperative today is to respond when the gestational substance itself cries out. What does water want? What does water need? How can we transform our modes of sociality with all of our multitudinous others into something that repeats the gestationality of water, and as something that could respond to the watery bodies that we continue to exchange, commodify, instrumentalize – enslave? Such a transformation would require a commitment to becoming milieu. *for water*

*Perhaps the winds had mercy on the wetlands. Perhaps the currents co-operated. By the time autumn rolls around, we heave a collective sigh, another bullet dodged. As I write these words, on October 13, 2010, news comes in that the moratorium on deepwater drilling in the Gulf of Mexico, imposed by the U.S. government after the disaster, has now been lifted.*

The ethical imperative that Lévinas outlines, the imperative to respond only to humans who have human subjectivity, those with whom I am immediately faced, is insufficient in the global economic context, in which we are not immediately faced with those disrupted by our patterns of life. We, residents of the Western middle class, are not faced with the nomadic Khoi San driven from the Kalahari and forcefully corralled within the borders of reservations in order to make way for oil company exploits. We fill up the car, or eat imported produce, without facing the Khoi San. Lévinas's ethics is also insufficient when faced with the destruction of the ancient baobab trees of Madagascar – faceless but each uniquely etched with age and deeply rooted in place. And it is insufficient in order to respond to the oil gushing forth from a puncture on the bottom of the sea, the habitat within which life first flourished. Becoming gestational for the gestational requires that we respond to the needs of habitats, the ecological dwelling places and sources of nourishment that give rise to and support life as plural. But becoming gestational for the gestational, becoming milieu for our watery milieux, also requires certain refusals. Refusals to collude with, and to continue to feed and shore up the systems that violate the plurality that still abounds and which excessively foreclose the "not yet." What is required of us is to take upon ourselves the labour of providing the resources necessary for nurturing the interhuman and lifeworld possibilities currently under erasure. An ethical response to water requires becoming more watery, becoming for pluralities beyond oneself. Participating in material infinity.

*What else lies beneath the surface, quiet, inquisitive?*
*Through the sinking "sea snot," through the underwater plumes of undissolved crude, between the schools of oil-fed microbes, the clouds of chemical dispersant, across the stretch of federal waters still closed to fishing boats, in the deepwater of Ewing Bank, a whale shark, forty years old, but sixty million years old too, is buoyed by the underwater current. Even in top form, she is not an efficient swimmer. She sucks in a mouthful of water, closes her mouth and expels the water through her gills. Anything larger than a small pea must be swallowed.*
*Eating.*
*Water continually passes across her filters, then across her gill slits.*
*Breathing.*
*While her sight is poor, her sense of smell is exquisite, if selective. In her*

*twinned uteri swim 300 fetal specimens. She too feels a pull, along her*
*customary migration route,*
*toward the Florida panhandle,*
*through the epicentre of the rupture.*

NOTES

1  Here we borrow Emmanuel Lévinas's understanding and elaboration of "being."
Lévinas explains the underlying conceptual structure of being as issuing from a gener-
alizable Hellenic trajectory influenced by Judeo-Christian theology. In his phenomenology, Lévinas characterizes our conceptualization of "being" as influenced by the
cult of an imperialist heroism that privileges action, rendering invisible a primordial
compulsion to give freely and occluding modes of relating that are other-oriented.
Lévinas, *Otherwise*.

2  For Irigaray, gestationality is an explicit rejection of Socratic maieutics, whereby new
ideas are purportedly born with the help of an "intellectual midwife" who assists the
birth but does not materially contribute to it. Irigaray, *Speculum*.

3  Irigaray, *Marine Lover*; Cixous and Clement, *Newly Born*. See also Neimanis, "Bodies of Water." For further explorations of maternal bodies and corporeal sensibility,
see Minh-ha on women's creative waters in *Woman, Native, Other*, 38; Diprose
on corporeal generosity in "What is (Feminist) Philosophy?"; Hird's extension of
corporeal generosity in a posthumanist vein in "Corporeal Generosity"; Bigwood on
physical cultivation in *Earth Muse*; Simms on placental ethics in "Eating."

4  The "biological essentialism" of Irigaray has been challenged by numerous commentators. Some suggest that her invocation of feminine morphology is a "strategic essentialism." See Whitford, *Luce Irigaray*; Braidotti, "Becoming-Woman"; and Butler,
*Bodies*. Lorraine reads Irigaray's more "sloganistic" proclamations on feminine bodies as tactical interventions. Lorraine, *Visceral*. Stone's reading of Irigaray privileges
a materialist but non-essentialist reading. Stone, *Sex*. See also Kirby, *Telling Flesh*;
Weiss, *Body Images*; Fielding, "The Sum of What She Is Saying"; Shildrick, *Leaky
Bodies*; and Grosz, *Nick of Time*. This discussion of the materiality of bodies in
Irigaray is found in Neimanis, "Bodies of Water."

5  See Alaimo and Hekman, eds., *Material Feminisms*; Frost and Coole, eds., *New Materialisms*; Braun and Whatmore, eds., *Political Matter*; Åsberg, Koobak, and Johnson,
eds, NORA, special issue on post-humanities.

6  Latour, *Politics of Nature*.

7  Latour's work to create political agents out of so-called natural entities is importantly
linked to the work of Michel Serres. See Serres, *The Natural Contract*.

8  Latour's invocation of Kant displays for us the sentiments of moral reprehensibility
tied, in Western thought, to passivity (nature, women, and so forth). In Latour, that
passivity is usurped as the "means" for the "ends" of an active agent: "no entity –

whale, river, climate, earthworm, tree, calf, cow, pig, brood – agrees any longer to be treated 'simply as means' but insists on being treated 'always also as an end.'" Latour, *Politics of Nature*, 156.

9  We are grateful to Rita Wong, this volume, for inspiring this formulation.

10  Wilson, "Gut Feminism," 70.

11  Alaimo, "Trans-Corporeal," 239, 240.

12  As Alaimo notes, feminists have too often "diminish[ed] the significance of materiality," (Alaimo, "Trans-corporeal," 237). Yet, posthumanisms have too often diminished the significance of facilitation, relegating it to mere passivity. For example, by prioritizing the intra-actional relationship, Karen Barad's project of reformulating and extending agency beyond the human is very close to our own project of prioritizing responsivity. In Barad's theory of agential realism, matter is constituted through "intra-action." Action, in other words, precedes the actor. However, Barad's liberation of matter, a task that requires recognizing its activity, is accomplished by excising its passivity: "Matter **is not** little bits of nature ... surface, or site **passively** awaiting signification ... Matter **is not** immutable or **passive** ... Rather *matter is substance in its intra-**active** becoming – not a thing, but a doing, a congealing of **agency***." Barad, "Post-humanist Performativity," 821, 822 (italics in original; authors' bolding). Our goal in this paper is not to reprioritize passivity, but to point out the difficulties inherent in resisting this dualistic structure, and to suggest a mode of being that destabilizes and transforms them.

13  For a discussion of water's more destructive logics, see Haiven, this volume; Spiegel, this volume; and Berland, "Walkerton." In the context of the repeating lineaments of matter, we recognize – although do not discuss in depth here – that water's life-proliferative mode cannot be severed from its logics of destruction, and the reclaiming of entities back to matter in interconnected cycles of repetition. For a provisional inventory of water's various logics, see Neimanis, "Feminist Subjectivity."

14  Lévinas, *Otherwise*.

15  Ibid.

16  This formulation of all non-human matter as properly instrumentalized is exemplified in Coase, "The Problem of Social Cost" – a foundational text for economic theory and property law.

17  Lévinas's concern here is part of a broader concern shared more widely among French Continental thinkers following the Second World War: to resist totalization. For Lévinas, it is of utmost importance that persons are distinct entities. Jean-Luc Nancy's discussion of "being in common," although in some respects radically divergent from Lévinas's ethics, displays a similar concern with effecting plurality and resisting totality. Nancy, *The Inoperative Community*.

18  Frédérique Apffel-Marglin and Loyda Sanchez do a wonderful job of explaining the way human rights are embedded in a Western cosmology incommensurable with how indigenous women in an Andean community understand themselves, their kinship and

community relations, and their relations to, in, with, and as water. Apffel-Marglin and Sanchez, "Developmentalist Feminism."

19  This is embedded in the terminology Lévinas draws upon throughout *Otherwise than Being* in which "maternity," as well as the physicality of gestation, labour, and birth, is repeated in descriptors of the ethical experience.

20  The intention here is not to reinstate a mind-body dualism, but to draw attention to feeling and cognition as distinct (albeit intertwined) modes of embodied being. See Merleau-Ponty, *Phenomenology*. Mallin's exegetical work on Merleau-Ponty identifies four intertwined modes of embodied being: cognition, affectivity-sociality, perception, and motility. Mallin, *Merleau-Ponty's Phenomenology*.

21  See Wright, Hughes, and Ainley, "The Paradox of Morality."

22  See Chandler, "Creation, Sovereignty, Ethics."

23  This point requires a bit of explanation. In his later work, *Otherwise than Being: Or Beyond Essence*, Lévinas tells us he has set himself the task of philosophically extracting "humanity" from "being" in order to conceive of humanity beyond being – in order to "de-essentialize" the human. The human subject, Lévinas explains, overflows being. It is neither "an avatar of nature [n]or a moment of the concept." Lévinas, *Otherwise*, 8. In extracting the subject from a notion of being issuing from the Greeks and fleshed out in a certain historical trajectory of "Western" philosophy, Lévinas nonetheless leaves the lifeworld entirely in the clutches of being, the realm of the pursuit of self-interest, one's own endurance in time, and thus also of war. The idea of gestationality calls for a wresting not only of the human but also of the non-human lifeworld from entrapment within a structure of sovereignty predicated on private property. In illustrating how the instantiation of sovereign subjectivity is predicated on usurping all that is gestational, and thereby radically curtailing the potential of the "not yet" to the replication of the same, this work does not so much critique Lévinas's thought as seek to extend it.

24  Deleuze and Parnet, "The Actual and the Virtual": Deleuze, *Difference and Repetition*, 208–14.

25  De Landa, *Intensive Science*.

26  For Deleuze, beings are neither static nor perduring. All entities are continuously becomings, yet temporarily stabilize in "actual" bodies. Deleuze and Parnet, "The Actual and the Virtual."

27  Tuana, "Viscous Porosity," 194.

28  Protevi, "Water."

29  Oyama, *Ontogeny*.

30  Deleuze's conceptual apparatus here is indebted to his reading of Nietzsche's eternal return. Deleuze, *Nietzsche;* Deleuze, *Difference and Repetition*.

31  Deleuze, *Difference and Repetition*, 20.

32  Our planet's originary wateriness is not only found in modern Western scientific accounts but also comprises accounts of creation across many cultures.

33  For example, Boundas, "What Difference?"; Colebrook, "On Not Becoming Man." Despite this, one could also read Deleuze's writing on larval subjects and the embryo/egg as opening to a conception of material, rather than immaterial, virtuality. See Neimanis, "Strange Kinship." For our purposes here, we emphasize the dominant reading of virtuality in order to read these commentaries against watery virtuality as an instance of material sociality.

34  Water as virtuality could also be understood as "proto-body" for, to be recognized by us, water must already have taken form as an actualized body to which we give a name – a river, a raincloud, a sunfish, a poplar. Prior to its embodiment in an intelligible form, "water" escapes our human powers of articulation. Even vague bodies of water such as "vapour" are contained by a name.

35  See MacLeod, this volume for a discussion of the materiality of the present-past in similar terms; see also Spiegel, this volume, on the futurity of water.

36  McMenamin and McMenamin, *Hypersea*, 25.

37  We could recall here various new materialist theories such as Latour's.

38  We recognize that much work in environmental theory and ecological ethics is oriented toward challenging this view. See, for example, Evernden, *The Natural Alien*; Ingold, *Being Alive*.

39  Deleuze and Guattari, *A Thousand Plateaus*, 161, 270.

# Subterranean Flows: Water Contamination and the Politics of Visibility after the Bhopal Disaster

*Jennifer Beth Spiegel*

In 2010 the British Petroleum (BP) oil spill in the Gulf of Mexico shocked and enraged the world. Suddenly, the high stakes of water contamination, usually ignored, were brought into full view. However, despite the environmental devastation it signalled and the widespread media coverage it received, this was hardly the first time an environmental disaster of devastating proportions had occurred. As American president Barack Obama made speeches about corporate accountability, victims of corporate crime elsewhere wondered why the water in their territories continued to be contaminated by American companies with impunity. Shortly after the BP oil spill, survivors of the 1984 Bhopal Gas Disaster – widely considered to be the most devastating industrial disaster of the twentieth century – and their supporters around the world, began asking why *their* efforts to render visible the ongoing problem of water contamination and its consequences for the future continued to be ignored, and why the flows of contamination themselves remained shrouded in mystery.[1] How, then, are such subterranean flows of water and chemicals rendered visible, and what is at stake in this rendering? In addressing this question, I follow various political protest events aimed at increasing the visibility of water contamination and at altering sensibilities about what is considered important on the local, national, and international stage.

Those who are most affected by material flows of water and contaminants are frequently the silent backdrop against which political decisions are made. They are also those whose conditions and activities are to be managed by those in charge. Thinking with their interventions, however, demands that the materiality of water and the encounters that take place in watery flows alter the manner in which social and political networks are conceived. The challenge that remains is to think with the alterity of water, and the unknown futures that gestate within its flows, even as they pervade and traverse the various human and non-human bodies they encounter.

I begin with the story of the iconic "Bhopal Tragedy": an event that made international headlines on 3 December 1984 when, in the capital city of the Indian state of Madhya Pradesh, a valve broke in the American-owned Union Carbide factory, releasing forty tons of methyl isocyanate into the air. Thousands of people were killed on the spot, and thousands more died in the days, years, and decades that followed. More than twenty-eight years later, with Union Carbide long since sold to Dow Chemical, questions of liability, remediation, and rehabilitation remain unresolved. Moreover, in the intervening years, another crisis has arisen, as contaminants from the factory leach into the soil and groundwater. Whereas the gas leak received extensive media coverage in its immediate aftermath, the contemporary implications of the secondary repercussions of the gas leak and the ongoing groundwater contamination from the now-abandoned factory remain largely invisible within global networks of political decision-making. Much of the work that I observed, chronicled, and participated in with local and international survivor and solidarity organizations was oriented toward making these flows more visible. I was especially interested in the power of symbolic action to effect change in perceptions of water contamination and the responses to which changed perceptions give rise. I also studied the power of the politics of representation and participation to generate symbolic action, and the ability of these dynamics to alter the global flow of information, economic currency, and, ultimately, toxic hazards. What symbolism do these dynamics generate? Who benefits? And what impact do they have in redressing the damages caused by the ongoing contamination of groundwater?

Two key concepts are useful in examining how these flows are rendered visible. The first is Gayatri Spivak's (2003) concept of "planetarity," developed in response to the new image of the globe imposed by the engines of globalization. Spivak writes: "Globalization is the imposition of the same system of exchange everywhere … To talk planet-talk by way of an unexamined environmentalism, referring to undivided 'natural' space rather than a differentiated political space, can work in the interest of this globalization in the mode of the abstract as such … The globe is on our computers. No one lives there. It allows us to think that we can aim to control it. The planet is in the species of alterity, belonging to another system; and yet we inhabit it on loan."[2]

Spivak's concept of planetarity highlights the differential logics at work in understanding planetary processes, and the fact that these processes can never be fully contained by a single discourse. The concept of planetarity is a way of gesturing to the alterity of the water that circulates around the planet. The water that an "unexamined environmentalism" might render in an abstract, undifferentiated mode is always, in fact, situated, and it has particular meaning for the bodies through which it flows most directly. Whether the water flows beneath the ground or through the bodies of those who populate the area around the now-abandoned factory, it is always contained and characterized by political dynamics related to who and what is at risk, or to differing sensibilities about what is at stake. This is the case whether watery flows are characterized in light of capital production, or medical concerns for the health of humans living in the region.

In thinking through the stakes of water contamination and the politics of visibility in light of the alterity of water and its passage through differentiated political spaces and bodies, I also make use of Stacy Alaimo's concept of "trans-corporeality." Alaimo writes: "the term 'trans-corporeality,' rather than inter-corporeality, suggests that the humans are not only interconnected with each other but with the material flows of substances and places."[3]

Trans-corporeality of this sort suggests that matter flows through bodies, substantially recomposing them in the process. The bodies of individual humans living around the factory are not only linked to one another, to the soil, and to the industrial complex of the factory by the flows of water, chemicals, and gases; their bodies are also in some sense indistinguishable from the ground water and the chemicals produced in the factory: the same flow of substances passes through all these bodies.

The conjoining of the concept of planetarity as a gesture toward the alterity of the planet with the concept of a pervasive trans-corporeality might strike the reader as somewhat paradoxical. How can these flows at once be constitutive of human bodies and yet retain a species of radical alterity? In order to address the alterity of water[4] as it encounters and pervades various bodies, chemicals, and systems of exchange, I consider three interrelated flows – biochemical, representational, and capital – and the ways in which each of them orients the others.

I look first at ethical appeals to take seriously the trajectories of biochemical flows and allow these flows to influence political decision-making. These ethical appeals are the focus of acts of protest that highlight material conditions, and function by gesturing toward the unknown biochemical potential of the fluids that pervade the bodies of those living in contaminated (or potentially contaminated) areas to affect the horizon of the future.

In the second section I focus on the political logics suggested by thinking about the trajectories of fluids and contaminants as they pass through human bodies in the form of urine. Political networks of science, academia, corporations, and media can be appropriated and challenged by symbolic actions that make the material excesses and effects of these production networks visible. Locating the present inquiry within these networks, I propose that the challenge of thinking with water and water contamination, here, is that of allowing the unknowns that gestate within water and its potential articulations to themselves change the way the politics of visibility are addressed – not only in terms of what is represented and how, but also in terms of the way the collective act of making the situation visible itself alters the circulation of information and affects.

In the third section, I discuss how the logic of capital exchange dominates the manner in which matter, images, and thought circulate. The totalizing logic of globality, as directed by the dynamics of capital exchange, masks the stakes at issue in planetary flows, and this politics of globality particularly occludes the trans-corporeal relationships that form as a result of specific material compositions, as well as the trajectories of water and contaminants in places like Bhopal. At the same time, the specificity and material realities of particular waters suggest other ways of articulating what is at stake and organizing systems of exchange.[5] As those with access to global networks participate in representing the situation, the dynamic of transnational movements pervades local attempts to render visible the stakes of water contamination.

In taking seriously the material specificity of watery compositions and the politics of their actual trajectories, ways of utilizing these global networks are suggested, not to contain and explain away the unknown effects and experiences of water contamination, but to highlight their importance in shaping future thought and policies concerning the politics of planetary water.

## Trans-Corporeal Flows: Permeable Wombs and the Terror of Futurity

The issue of biochemical mixtures of chemicals and fluids that run through the earth and the human body ushers in the matter of the future, as it is of course water that gestates all life. What will be born in contexts where unknown mixtures are present is, however, characterized by uncanny uncertainty. In Bhopal, years after the fatal gas leak, questions about the actual nature of these mixtures still linger. These questions are, for many, framed most hauntingly in terms of what these uncertain biochemical flows signal for future generations, beginning in the wombs of the mothers that birth them.

The future birthed in the womb, from the moment of the gas leak onward, is intricately tied to the social and environmental ecosystems of the region. These relations between bodies and ecologies have been, and continue to be, rendered visible largely through the actions of those affected by the material trajectories of gases and flows. As recalled by Satineth Sarangi, a solidarity activist and clinic founder, survivors launched a number of events to ascertain the nature of this relationship and to intervene in public sensibilities governing how this relationship would be seen, felt, and acted upon:

> In 1985, some among the women *padyatras* had marched to the local government hospital, holding bottles of urine. They demanded that doctors examine their bodies to see if they should carry on or terminate their pregnancies. They expected the doctors to test the amount of thiocyanate in their urine for an evaluation of the toxins circulating in their bodies. They wanted them to administer sodium thiosulphate injections so that they could excrete some of the toxins they had involuntarily inhaled on that terrible night. They were worried that they might give birth to children with defects. The women were denied medical tests and advice, and police chased them away with sticks. Ironically, this happened in March 1985 when medical researchers from the Indian Council of Medical Research were carrying on a double-blind clinical trial to test the efficacy of sodium thiosulphate as a detoxicant for the gas exposed.[6]

The reason the women were denied thiosulphate injections at that time remains a matter of debate. However, the fact that this denial took place at a moment when officials were withholding the exact composition of the gas and downplaying the potential severity of its effects has led many survivors and activists to conclude that the denial of the injection was linked to an attempt to deny the severity of the exposure: were the injection to be effective, it would prove that compounds hazardous not only to the lungs and eyes upon contact but also to the body's systems were indeed present in the gas.[7] Both the initial disaster and the response to those who made a concrete and visible demand to have their fluids tested indicate a schism at work in the logic of care and, more generally, in the politics of managing the region.

From Union Carbide Corporation's initial failure to inform authorities and its concealment of the gas contents[8] to the Indian government's curtailment of longitudinal studies to measure the gas's effects,[9] this situation has been marked by a politics that limits what can be seen and known about the effects of biochemical flows and trans-corporeal mixtures. Only years later would the chemicals in the amniotic fluids of pregnant women be shown to have the feared effect, which those concerned had to fight to make visible and have investigated. A 2003 study published in the prominent *Journal of the American Medical Association* would show that male children born to gas-affected parents had significantly stunted growth in comparison to others living elsewhere under comparable conditions.[10] This, however, was not the worst of the fears articulated. Two decades after the disaster, the Chingari Trust foundation was set up by two women survivors, Rashida Bee and Champa Devi Shula, to provide support to children in the region born with congenital malformations thought to be caused by their parents' toxic exposure to chemicals from the Union Carbide Factory. The uncertainty of the relationships between bodily fluids and the inhalation of a gas whose chemical composition remained undisclosed was brought into public view as a problem of social and political will. The march to the hospital, jars in hand, represented a demand staged by those who had hitherto remained unseen, whose bodies had been cast out of view. While the demand was real, the jar itself figured as a symbol of the neglect women had experienced from the medical profession, the government, and the global economic system that would allow such a disaster to continue uncorrected.

According to Spivak, the alterity of the planet can be encountered much as Luce Irigaray has proposed encountering the womb:[11] the planet, like the womb, is home to life, but it is an "unhomely" or uncanny home, a home that remains always somewhat unknown. The ways of articulating this home are multiple. Within the hegemonic logic of capitalism, both planet and womb are taken as backdrops for the production and reproduction of a system of exchange. And yet, as both Irigaray and Spivak point out, both planet and womb have tended to be flattened as material backdrops, viewed merely as offering fodder for the production of goods, as sites of exploitation whence the value-rich is put into circulation. In this situation, the relationship between the flows of gases and the waters of the womb is more than a metaphor. The womb, like the planet, is mostly fluid, permeable to the waters that nourish it. Indeed, water permeates the division between the planet and individualized human bodies, seeping through such binaries as inside and outside, past and future, largely via the bodies that are active as passages.

The action chronicled above enacts a particular way of bringing the ongoing relationships between environmental conditions, bodily fluids, and gestational potentials into view. To articulate the conditions of the womb – and the thought of futurity that is birthed by its flows – the womb, along with the fluid that runs through it, is galvanized as an image: the image of women carrying jars of urine to the hospital; or rather, as the image of women who, carrying jars of urine as per standard medical testing procedures, are rebuked and denied the test that is meant to verify the status of bodily fluids and the quality of the watery environment of the womb as home. Alaimo (2010) has argued that the performing body exerts an affective force by directing attention to the vulnerability of the material body, and, in so doing, "extends the parameters of the political domain by seeking an ethical recognition of vulnerable, interdependent, interwoven, human and non-human flesh."[12]

While, as Alaimo points out, flesh, even in its vulnerability and even in what it shares with the skin of all life, has a sensual appeal laden with cultural baggage, it is important to note that here the trans-corporeality of fluids functions according to a different logic. Here, the women put their bodies on display as fluid conduits, or even the conduits of fluids, bringing what is normally either inside the body or discharged into the earth (that is, urine) out into the open, and, in so doing, bringing the trans-corporeality of these fluids, and the chemical mixtures contained in them, into view. Here, the fluidity of chemical trajectories and the wateriness of the relationships between the factory milieu, the air and earth, and the bodies of those who populate the region, are highlighted. Non-human and more-than-human fluids and chemicals constitute and pervade human bodies as part of the ecosystem as a whole. As Alaimo puts it: "Humans are vulnerable because they are not in fact 'human' in some transcendent, contained sense, but are flesh, substance, matter; we are permeable and in fact, require the continual input of other forms of matter – air, water, food."[13]

To this, we could add: we also require the continual *output* of our own matter. That is, we urinate. This output not only continues the cycle of trans-corporeality but also manifests – or *visibilizes* – the trans-corporeal intakes that have already occurred. This logic of thinking with water, or thinking with fluids, as a public act, also stages an ethical appeal to take these fluids, and the trans-corporeal relations to which they gesture, into account in orienting policies. It raises the question of why so much is still unknown about these fluids, from the actual composition of this water, to the relations it traces between the bodies that consume and excrete it, and the futures that the composition of these fluids signals for all those that are nourished by this water. And this very question of the unknown, signified here in the jars of urine held by those who demand testing, becomes a political challenge. It should never be forgotten that the challenge here is not only to respond to the symbolic appeal to have the future of women's bodies, of their children, and of their environment taken into account. It is equally, and immediately, a demand to actually have their urine tested and have policies put in place that will respond to these direct and immediate needs.

While interventions generally function through containment in order to render visible what is at stake (urine, for instance, is contained in jars to be both tested and galvanized as a media image), the horror is that in this case the flows are contained in neither time nor space. Not only do the effects of gas exposure persist across generations, but the leaks themselves are not limited to the night of the gas leak in 1984. Survivors, activists, and scientists working in Bhopal now argue that chemicals have been leaking from the factory into the groundwater for the past three decades, and continue to do so, as the site has never been adequately remediated. A report released on the eve of the twenty-fifth anniversary of the gas disaster by the Center for Science and Environment (with whom the survivors' organizations had been in communication) confirmed the presence of "chlorinated benzene compounds, organochlorine and carbamate pesticides, and heavy metals – toxic chemicals that were either used as ingredients or were the wastes generated or were the products of the plant," proving the site and groundwater to be highly contaminated.[14] Other evidence suggests that areas affected by water contamination may still be increasing yearly as the factory continues to leak actively.[15]

The report directly contradicted the claims of the state government and its scientific advisors. Less than a month earlier, government officials had enraged survivors by publicly declaring the water and soil around the abandoned factory to be safe, thus seemingly absolving themselves from the need to ensure adequate remediation and drinking water supplies to those living in the region. While the women marching with their jars made visible the terrifying trans-corporeal flows between womb and groundwater, another event staged in front of the factory, less than a week before the twenty-fifth anniversary of the gas leak, drew attention to the relationship between biochemical flows and the sociopolitical dynamics of the region. In a dramatized response to the above government statement, this second event highlighted the ongoing problem of unknown, unaddressed flows affecting ecologies of the past, present, and future. Here, the alterity of the chemical flows, which can neither be entirely known nor captured and contained by those who speak for it, is highlighted in the challenge posed by offering the water itself to be consumed. This water, may, like Spivak's planet, be "inhabited" and indeed consumed on "loan," but its force will not be contained: it will affect the entire ecosystem, and will permeate all other bodies, including, eventually, the political bodies and apparatus that seek to control it.

The event staged by two survivors' organizations (Bhopal Gas Peedit Mahila Stationery Karmachari Sangh and Bhopal Gas Peedit Mahila Purush Sangharsh Morcha) and one solidarity organization (Bhopal Group for Information and Action) was ironically called "A Benign Buffet." Invitations were sent to members of the State Cabinet and the Directors of Defense Research Development Establishment and the National Environmental Engineering Research Institute, who had together certified that the water contaminated by Union Carbide's chemical wastes was safe for consumption.

The menu of the Benign Buffet parodied that of a high society dinner with which these officials would presumably be familiar, and dramatized the state of the soil and water that survivors consumed regularly. The invitation promised delicacies prepared "with extracts from Union Carbide's Factory." On the menu were:

Semi-processed Pesticides on Watercress
Naphithol Tar Fondue, Reactor Residue Quiche
Sevin Tar Soufflé
Lime Sludge Mousse
all served with a complimentary B'eau Pal Water Cocktail.

Invited officials were conspicuously absent from the banquet, though the "feast" was nonetheless served to their empty places, carefully marked by place cards bearing their names, before the watchful gaze of the media. On the table sat a large paper-mâché crow, a symbol of deceit harkening back to the Hindu proverb *Jhoot bole kauakaate* ("crow bites liars"), invoked as a part of a campaign to "nail the state government's lies."[16] While the intervention took aim at governmental policies on soil and water quality around the factory, the satiric force of the event was directed at the government's position that the water was safe for consumption. Here, the appeal draws on symbolic action to forge new public sensibilities toward the manner in which these biochemical flows are addressed, and to intervene in the political apparatus that will dictate future policies on remediation, rehabilitation, and economic and industrial development. This strategy alters the power dynamics relating to the way the biochemical flows become publicly visible. The buffet temporarily *contains* and *frames* water and soil in order to represent what is at stake in the trans-corporeal flows of water that pass through those who live in the region.

## Thinking with Urine: A Politics of Visibility

Public gestures organize what will be rendered visible to a "public," thus (re)orienting, if only temporarily, the dynamics of both psychical and material relationships among members of said public. However, it does not necessarily follow that she who presents herself for scrutiny as part of that gesture has control over the direction of that orientation. Nor, in the case of the activism responding to the Bhopal Tragedy, does it follow that meanings associated with water, chemical flows, and amniotic fluids – or the political agendas generated by such liquids – can be controlled. The process of making these flows visible is always caught up in a politics of representation. As performance theorist Peggy Phelan points out, being visible does not necessarily equate to holding any cultural power. Images of the vulnerable are proliferated for a number of reasons. Phelan

Bhopali gas survivor and president of Chingari Trust Rasida Bee with fellow protestors on the anniversary of the Union Carbide factory gas leak. Photo: Tony Millard, International Campaign for Justice for Bhopal (bhopal.net)

lists the traps of visibility as "surveillance, fetishism, voyeurism, and sometimes death," noting that the simple act of rendering a body visible may only objectify it as the object of (another's) act of representation and, potentially, their political agenda.[17]

In the context of the Bhopal Gas Tragedy, anthropologist and activist Kim Fortun writes that it is essential to consider values at work in the way one approaches the situation: "Being well versed *in* the world became much more important than having an intellectual hold *on* the world."[18] She points out that what is at stake is not only the way situations are described but also the material difference potentially made by acts of appropriation and description. As both campaigner and researcher, Fortun is aware that this duality dubiously positions her for selecting what images and information to present, and how. The question is both ethical and aesthetic: the approach affects what qualities and values will be presented and promoted. It is a question faced by all researchers, artists, and writers. And I, of course, am no exception. Here, I could detail my involvement in Bhopal: drafting documents concerning the state of healthcare and water for websites; conducting skits with children living the region; interviewing various (and always "selected") survivors, activists, artists, and so forth. Essential questions remain, however. How are the stories, the logics, and the bodies in question taken up and rendered visible? How, in this case, might the way in which a situation is rendered visible alter the material flows of contaminated water itself, and the lives of those it touches? How might the stories, logics, and bodies associated with the disaster redirect the future of these flows?

Logics of engagement re-orient choices about who participates in shaping public opinion, and how the material flows will be presented and captured by a network that disseminates and reframes these gestures to multiple viewing publics. These media systems are the ground directing how the material flows will be projected to the world, and what aspects of their materiality will be abstracted in this process. The question is: in what way do the movements, histories, and futures nascent in the material fluids themselves actually direct the processes of representation and articulation?

Launching an ethico-political appeal is not only a matter of making space for those whose concerns and stories are marginalized within the social and political arena. What is at stake, rather, is the very logic of visibility, and the politics of how the materiality of the water itself, and the material experiences of those whose own bodies are composed in large part of this water, can make a difference in directing the future trajectories of water treatment and containment. The irony is that, in articulating a challenge to this logic, the very apparatuses that entrench prevailing power dynamics will continually have to be appropriated and invoked: working with the scientific apparatuses of government, media, science, and medicine becomes core to transforming the logic of visibility, even as it is the logic of visibility of these very institutions that is often at issue.

The hegemony of scientific practices has come under much attack from theorists who rightly point to the history of domination that it has served and the reductive epistemologies that it bolsters to give legitimacy to certain voices, turning the "objects" of inquiry into mute substances to serve the explanations thrust upon them.[19] As liberation ecologists Richard Peet and Michael Watts argue, however, the point is not to therefore reject scientific practices as inherently colonialist or neocolonialist, but rather to pay heed to the manner of their actual deployments and re-appropriations.[20] Scientists render the world sensible according to particular practices, particular systems of signs, particular logics. Governmental policy-makers deploy another, corporate publicists yet another, NGOs still others, and the multitude of organized and singularized survivors still others. As Peet and Watts characterize these differences, they are differences in the "environmental imaginary [which] emerges as a site of primary contestation," adding that "critical social movements have at their core environmental imaginaries at odds with hegemonic conceptions."[21]

The major achievement of social movements is, of course, not in the realm of the "imaginary" as such, but rather in the manner in which a reconfiguration of the imaginary facilitates an intervention into the social and political networks that affect policy-making and ultimately orient material futures. As Sarangi (2010) puts it: "Survivors' organizations and their supporters have achieved much ... Most government relief and rehabilitation measures have been made possible by their legal and extralegal interventions. Credit is also due to them for introducing, in a city without any history of militancy, a culture of popular protest outside the political parties in Bhopal. It is mostly because of the persistence and grit of the survivors' organizations that the continuing disaster in Bhopal continues to receive attention."[22]

A splintering in the production of ecologic – which is to say, of the logics according to which homes and desires are rendered visible through the efforts of those who have banded together in organizations and networks – surfaces in the introduction of this culture of popular protest. Here, those who form the silent backdrop of the system of exchange, the silent subaltern woman who produces or reproduces the image of either the (disposable) worker or the tragic aid recipient, poses a challenge to the way decision-making takes place. Moreover, in the acts seen here, this challenge takes place through the insistence on making material flows primary, highlighting the role of the "silent" subterranean water that flows, moving with it the biochemical discharge from the factory, the excess of the industrial plant, and, metaphorically, the excess and unacknowledged "output" of the corporate logic that allows these flows to continue. The simple acts of marching, jars in hand, to the hospital, and of serving factory sludge to absent officials mark the representation of several unknowns (the toxicity of the groundwater, of the women's bodies, of the health of the ecosystem). These acts also highlight the denial of detoxification treatments to those in need of them, even after scientific research studies on detoxification measures. In such acts, particular social collectivities are coalesced, in which those affected deploy the imagery of scientific research (urine sample bottles, for example) as a grassroots public appeal when the "experts" refuse to put their knowledge to work. The question posed by the women marchers interrupts the logic of technological and scientific development as tied to market capitalism and its industrial engine. "Science" is here deployed against the logic that tries to keep the women – and the threat they pose to the ongoing capitalist pollution of their wombs and their water – out of sight.

The development, articulation, and reception of these logics, however, are fraught with challenges. In the Benign Buffet, the failure of the "powerful" to appear when summoned by the Bhopali activists became itself the act put on display: the state officials and state scientists were served the sludge even though they would not present themselves at their plates to eat it. As Phelan notes, there is a difference between being excluded from the realm of visibility and failing to appear when summoned.[23] Here, it is precisely the willful invisibility – the failure of those summoned to present themselves to consume what they deemed safe for consumption – that is put on display.

In both the women's presentation of their urine and the Benign Buffet, a double process of appropriation is at work. On the one hand, the protestors appropriate the practices of the officials whom they challenge: they stage a banquet, and moreover they take up the language of science and the invocation of scientific expertise. However, the banquet they stage aims to subvert the logic of governmental consumption, and their invocation of science challenges the governmental usage of science in this case. In so doing, protestors offer up their own bodies, as well as the material flows to which they gesture, as images to be appropriated by the media as well as by policy-makers, scholars, and artists, whose own bodies of thought would presumably be altered through their encounters with the protest event.

The politics of visibility thus engages not only in the production of symbolic representations but also the production of subjectivities and of collectivities more broadly, altering the nature of the activist and professional networks that form, and of the choices about who speaks to whom and in what manner. As Phelan suggests, scientific explanations about what I refer to here as trans-corporeal flows tend primarily to objectify the possessor of the womb invaded by fluids, while the possibility of re-engagement by those who seek to reinvent their futures with this knowledge is foreclosed.[24] However, while there is a politics in the way scientific practices are developed and deployed, these practices, the questions they pursue, and their means of deployment are themselves *adaptable*. Acts such as the women marching to the hospital demanding tests offer a literal or figurative "thinking with urine"; by attending to the material flows of their bodies on their own terms, these women subvert existing logics of visibility. They render visible the contamination of both material fluids and *image streams*.

To think with urine here then points to intermingled trajectories of bodily fluids, groundwater flows, and chemical flows. It means, as I have already suggested, thinking *trans-corporeally*. However, it also points to the impact of corporate image dissemination via various media channels, and the manner in which all of the above are directed, altered, and contaminated (literally and figuratively) by capital flows. Spivak has pointed out that the logic of capital exchange fixes an image of the Earth as a singular image of the globe, viewed typically as a fixed object from above. If this is the case, then thinking with the alterity of subterranean flows means thinking with the biochemical mixtures and the experiential articulations of those that live as material conduits of these flows. In other words, thinking not with the image of water as a fixed singular image, quantifiable as capital, but rather as fluid movement, means beginning by accepting that there is a sense in which the nature of these mixtures remains unknown to the outside observer. It means beginning by recognizing that the articulations and images generated are often obfuscated by the dynamic that persists among those such as artists, scholars, reporters, public relations specialists, and policy makers who orient the way bodies will be portrayed. Following the trajectory, representations, and composition of urine means following the flow that runs between all of these histories, traces, mixtures, mutations, leaks, and encounters, and taking seriously the dilemmas posed by the way the flows of water, chemicals, and representations circulate.

The logics according to which vectors of trans-corporeality "appear" are thus played out as the battleground of public appeals. For instance, in 2007 a campaign was launched by local activists against the Tata Corporation, an India-based multinational that had made a commitment to Dow to help pave the way for business by resolving "legacy issues" like the Bhopal gas disaster.[25] Tata had offered to begin a charity to clean up the abandoned factory site in an effort to curb the ongoing water contamination. According to many Bhopal activist organizations, however, while all agreed on the dire need to stop water contamination in the region, many activists felt that such a charity would hastily close the case, removing all legal liability, and would not in itself constitute a legal commitment to take on this burden. They noted the deeply flawed logic of a corporate charity – particularly from a corporation whose social and environmental track record was considered dubious at best – naming itself to "take care" of the local ecology and of all those living in the region. This proposal would only re-inscribe a distribution of power whereby Tata would choose if and how those affected would have their basic needs addressed. According to this logic, those living in the area would be regarded as passive objects to be managed by designated "experts" in accordance with corporately sanctioned interventions.

A giant effigy of the Tata logo – a smiling dog – was therefore built by the local effigy-maker, but unlike the Tata logo, this version of the dog had one leg raised in the classic canine urinating position. As it was wheeled through the streets, the paraded dog stopped at every small shop, and the shop owners were invited to throw all their Tata products for the dog to "piss on," cheered on by a procession of protestors. The symbolism at work in this action is clear: it was a collective rejection of Tata's bid, a statement that profit and sales would not be allowed to take precedence over justice, as articulated by the affected community. Tata's own symbol was thus turned against it through the symbolic act of the Tata dog urinating on Tata's own consumer products. However, while the symbolism here is potent, the actual force and threat of the gathering suggest a mutation in the circulation of power and the way the political ecology of the territory might be recoded.

The capital-driven offer of a corporate charity to clean up the abandoned Union Carbide Factory site is emblematic of contemporary approaches to "sustainably managing" regions in which alternatives would seem to have been all but obliterated by industry. At best, this offer was a techno-scientific intervention designed to further bolster the capital logic of development. Cleaning up "legacy issues like Bhopal," as negotiated between CEOs, fails categorically to take into account the socio-political transformation needed so as not only to address environmental risks but also to transform the entire social ecology, which is characterized by a lack of access to both the material means of production and the political channels required to alter these means. It is into this situation that this theatricized ritual can be seen to intervene.

Rather than simply dramatizing the issues, this protest became the harbinger of a very real threat to global capital expansion: namely, shop-owners' refusal to do business with companies that refuse to take into account the desires and needs of those living in affected areas. I am thus arguing that the threat to capital logic conjured by protestors here cultivates a political subjectivity among those who take part. In ritualistically acting out a symbolic rejection of the products they had hitherto sold, shopkeepers and community members do more than send a message to government, industry and the public. More important, perhaps, is that they rehearse their own resolve to reject complicity in processes of corporate expansionism at the expense of the health and well-being of their own communities and environment. Significantly, this is a subjectivity that emerges from trans-corporeal flows on a number of levels, and from the subversive attempt to make those flows visible.

## Logics of Exchange: Between Globality and Planetarity

The Tata effigy satire reveals the material realities behind the image: the satirized Tata dog urinates on products that are to be sold to and by those whose *own urine* is being irrevocably altered by the very capital logic that drove the production of factory expansionism, and which continues to drive corporate expansionism internationally. The material reality of urine thus becomes a force for breaking the clean image of a corporate ethic that would distance capital logic from water contamination without facing up to its historic and ongoing relationship with such contamination.

With the spread of global capitalist logic, the image of water as a resource or risk to be contained by those "in charge" is pervasive, even if it is challenged by counter-acts of representation, such as the urine protests. These interruptions, however, are not merely a matter of replacing one set of representations with another. In a globalized context, they also raise the question of how relationships between bodies and matter will form around the planet. The street theatrics by activists in Bhopal both borrow and feed an aesthetic of international activism. The interventions of the Yes Men, a New York–based satirical group, for instance, have been particularly poignant in their exposure of the convergence of capital, chemical, and environmental flows. While their satirical theatrics function on a symbolic level, making visible the international reach of corporate capitalism and the logic of exploitation that converts water, land, and labour into resources, with apparent disregard for the resulting toxic transmutations, their tactic of convincingly impersonating actual corporate figures blurs the line between symbolic and actual intervention into the material and immaterial flows of capital and the factory production it directs. Their tactics have affected international audiences as well as local activists in Bhopal. In creating an image stream that circles the planet, affecting both symbolic discourse and actual modes of networking, they raise the question: what logics and what factors permeate the flows of these images?

On the occasion of the twentieth anniversary of the Bhopal Gas Tragedy, the Yes Men, a then little-known American-based duo of anti-globalization tricksters, duped the world when they appeared on bbc claiming to represent Dow Chemical (by then the new owners of Union Carbide), announcing that Dow would finally be accepting full responsibility for the disaster and would be compensating victims and paying for remediation accordingly.[26] Of course, the company had no such intentions. The BBC had contacted the Yes Men via a website that the collective had created to mirror Dow's website – one of the virtual channels through which images, information, and affects now circulate, and which the BBC mistook as Dow's own. The stunt was described by the Yes Men as articulating the logic that Dow "should" be following, and was hugely successful in giving international exposure to the gulf between the wishes of those living around the abandoned Union Carbide factory site and actual corporate actions.

Literally speaking, the Yes Men made visible a possibility, another course of action, which *could be*. They offered a representation of what many might like to see happen. Their BBC statement embodied what activists for decades had been lobbying for – an action which, if taken, would presumably have set a massive global precedent. But the theatricality of the Yes Men intervention also mirrors the performative structures that govern capitalist logic, as actions are undertaken at an increasing distance from the actual environmental and social flows at stake, such as in Bhopal. For a short period, Dow's stock prices dropped dramatically, possibly as a result of public response to the spectacle.

Needless to say, Dow did not follow the example of the Yes Men, and once the theatricality of the gesture became evident stock prices reverted to their previous levels. The Yes Men interpret this phenomenon as an illustration of the stronghold of capitalist logic and the complicity of spectators worldwide in sustaining this logic. As they point out, when corporations are seen to "do the right thing" and take responsibility for the violence they have wreaked (even if the admission turns out to be a hoax), this gesture is nonetheless seen as "the wrong thing" within the framework of capitalist logic. Those sustaining that logic withdraw their financial support for the corporation and the stocks plummet. Rather than material biochemical flows in Bhopal orienting these virtual movements, the circulation of a capital logic becomes the prime force orienting all other flows.[27]

While the general response to the stunt indicates one stream of global response, the intervention by the Yes Men also launched a now-longstanding collaboration between this New York–based duo and the International Campaign for Justice for Bhopal (ICJB), which consists of several groups in Europe and North America, as well as several survivor-run and supporting organizations in Bhopal. This is the same network of local groups that had launched both the Benign Buffet and the Tata Dog events. The persistence of this network indicates an alternative logic. The cocktails of B'eau Pal water, for instance, which appeared on the Benign Buffet menu, were an invention born of a Yes Men collaboration in the United Kingdom. The Yes Men circulated bottles of water that claimed to be bottled at the source of the Union Carbide factory in Bhopal, with logos parodying the red triangle of the Dow logo and a small warning that read "not fit for human consumption." Here, the industry of commodifying water was used against itself to gesture toward the unknown nature of what is bottled and circulated and, more directly, toward the biochemical consistency of what some are forced to drink as a result of corporate industry. The symbolism was explicitly designed to make visible the actual product of Dow's production process – namely, water not fit for human consumption.

In fact, the bottled water was not from Bhopal, but from a London tap. Although the London tap is ultimately connected to the groundwater of Bhopal through global hydrological flows, the highlighting of water in this action was oriented less toward redressing the contamination of Bhopali water than toward altering the economy of representation, in order to make an ethical appeal to the would-be consumer and passerby in London.[28] A tension thus emerges between a global (counter)narrative that articulates the importance of water as the universal connector, and the specificity of territorial encounters, in which particular flows mix with chemicals in particular concentrations, and with differential and always somewhat elusive risks. With the global reach of corporate capitalist production, and the chemical flows that are propelled through these processes, the gulf between symbolic representation and biophysical flows represented is perpetually murky, coloured by the desires and agendas of those who frame the situation.

Clearly, there is a far different resonance when Bhopalis offer their elected officials a sip of the water they drink daily, than when the Yes Men and their volunteers offer a bottle of faux Bhopali water to pedestrians on the streets of a major world centre like London. The repetition creates, however, a kind of motif or refrain that connects overseas concerns with local interests. It provides continuity and recognizability to the tactic, linking global struggles to one another; and in addition, more potently, it provides a continuity among like-minded movements and groups of activists who, in deploying convergent modes of articulation, begin to refigure their questions, concerns, and desires pertaining to the relationship between water, capital, and human life, as a fluid and interrelated process.

It is important to note that the actual *economy of representation* and the *circulation and dissemination* of these images dance not only with the legacies of biochemical flows but also with the capital flows that direct future material, political, and aesthetic realities – transnationally, and also, of course, around the factory in Bhopal. Water is, and is imaged as, a connective fluid that connects planetary experiences and conditions, nourishing, poisoning, or otherwise altering life. The above discussion is meant to highlight, however, the uneven trajectories of water flows, whereby actual mixtures of water are distributed differently across the planet. While biochemical flows of water, as well as the representational and capital flows that turn water and images into resources, all circulate around the planet, they do not do so according to the same logic. And, water and the bodies that it permeates nonetheless retain an element of alterity, of the sort invoked by Spivak's concept of planetarity.

In a situation already marked by visibility politics, expectation, and socio-economic power dynamics, each gesture that inserts itself as an intervention in the economy of representation and the engines of aesthetic production runs the risk of being usurped at any

Activist Satinath Sarangi holds a bottle of B'eau Pal water designed by the Yes Men.
Photo: Mike Bonnano / Bhopal Medical Appeal (bhopal.org).

turn. This is not only because new subjectivities, collectivities, and inquiries can only be forged through existing practices of enunciation – thus setting the terms of intervention. It is also because there is always a pre-existing logic and a hierarchy of visibility politics directed by the flows of information and media access, as well as the ongoing pressures of economic viability. Events such as the Tata Dog demonstration and the Yes Men's impersonation of a Dow CEO gesture toward the intermingling of capital, representational, and biochemical flows. The capital flows implicated here, however, extend beyond illustrating, satirizing, or even subverting the corporate machinery.

In order to function, every social movement or collective must find ways of materially sustaining itself, and ways of appealing to those who, at any given moment, have the power to direct flows of money, resources, and toxic chemicals. In some cases, altering the distribution of money, resources, and risk is a matter of redirecting knowledge – as was earlier illustrated by acts of reorienting scientific energies and the redeployment of scientific knowledge by Bhopal survivors. However, such redistributions also often require making appeals to those who have the means, however humbly or extravagantly, to provide capital resources both for sustaining a movement and for implementing policy changes. The activities described here are part of such a process of public appeal, oriented toward influencing policy changes as well as toward sustaining and expanding the movement itself.

In appealing to those with access and currency within global networks, however, there is an ever-present risk of capital usurpation and redirection of subversive flows. *Movement building*, which includes harnessing "expert knowledge" and professionalized channels, also relies on a redirection of capital flows – and therefore must engage head-on with capital logic, if only in order to alter it. The very manner in which the "expert" economy functions – and expert knowledge circulates – is also embroiled in capital flows. This is the case not only for scientists who put the vulnerability of others on display for the sake of furthering research, knowledge, or even important policy changes. It is also, as Fortun has pointed out, as much a concern for "activist" researchers and theorists, who risk making the objects of their struggles (or their "expertise") the background objects of their own politic, bolstering careers and harnessing capital resources through the manipulation of their research.[29] In each case, as these interventions illustrate, there is a schism in the logic of exchange. Access to capital flows, control over the means of symbolic production and dissemination, and the power to assess, declare, and intervene in processes of industrial production and site remediation all act as convergent schizoid trajectories that repeatedly throw courses of action into question.

## Concluding Trajectories

To think with water in the context of water contamination means thinking with the material trajectories of water – trajectories that remain somewhat unknown even as they circulate, permeating in this case the bodies of those who live around the abandoned factory in Bhopal, and as they spread, indefinitely, to ever-larger regions. These trans-corporeal flows are contained by a stream of images. These representational streams direct the way in which the gas leak and its ongoing effects will affect social and political networks of decision-making and the ethic and ecologic that will take hold.

While the articulation of the biochemical stakes of water contamination typically falls to scientific experts, the history of scientific inquiry in this arena is thorny: thorny because scientific practices have historically tended to be forged on the basis of universalizing principles that are then imposed as explanatory devices on specific and localized situations; and because even these explanations are selectively applied, trumped by the managerial logic of market expansionism.

While the images generated by survivors, activists, and artists sensitive to the trans-corporeal nature of flows often aim to interrupt the logic of capital that currently has a hold on the politics of decision-making, casting the bodies of those who lack economic power into the background, even the circulation of these images tends to rely on an engagement with existing capital flows. If we wish to take seriously the problem posed by water contamination, it is thus not enough to look at the biochemical repercussions of industry. If the politics of visibility with respect to water contamination is to change, the challenge that lies ahead is to destabilize the capitalist managerial logic governing economies of representation which directs the ways in which images, knowledge, money, water, and chemicals interact and circulate around the planet.

As the situation in Bhopal makes evident, the alterity of water that flows indeterminately, changing the composition and the relational dynamics of and between bodies, cannot ultimately be contained by a capitalist managerial logic. To challenge this logic, then, is more than a matter of deferring to the images of water and its flows as generated from above. The trajectories and chemical composition of the water that flows through the ground and through the bodies – and the protests – of those who must drink it problematize the future of the water as well as the legitimacy and power of the global logics of exchange that purport to offer the tools to manage and contain it. As these material logics show themselves to be escaping the logics of containment that have organized the social and political narratives and the networks that form in their image, a possibility of organizations answering to trans-corporeal trajectories – and to the implications of trans-corporeal flows upon social and political networks – is now surfacing. It is ultimately in the movements of these subterranean flows, and in the ways their challenge is taken up, that the future of water will be born.

NOTES

1  Singh, "Bhopal and the bp Oil Spill: A Tale of Two Disasters."
2  Spivak, *Death of a Discipline*, 72.
3  Alaimo, "Naked Word," 23–4.
4  For further theorization on the alterity of water, please see Chandler and Neimanis, this volume.
5  See also MacLeod, this volume.
6  Sarangi, *The Hindu*, 9.
7  Sarangi, "The Thiosulphate Scandal."
8  Morehouse and Subramaniam, *Bhopal Tragedy*, 22.
9  Hanna, Morehouse and Sarangi, *The Bhopal Reader*, 126.
10  Ranjan, et al. "Methyl."
11  Spivak, *Death of a Discipline*, 75.
12  Alaimo, "Naked Word," 15.
13  Ibid., 24.
14  Johnson, et al., *Contamination*, 15.
15  Labunska and Santillo, *Bhopal Legacy*.

16  Bhopal Gas Peedit Mahila Stationery Karmachir Sangh et al., Press Release: "Benign Buffet," 28 November 2009.

17  Phelan, *Unmarked*, 11.

18  Fortun, *Advocacy*, 54.

19  See Escobar, "Constructing Nature"; Haraway, *Primate Visions*.

20  Peet and Watts, *Liberation Ecology*.

21  Ibid., 263.

22  Quoted in Mukherjee, *Surviving Bhopal*, 100.

23  Phelan, *Unmarked*, 11.

24  Ibid., 20 and 144.

25  Letter dated 9 October 2006 from Ratan Tata to Dr Montek Singh Aluwalhia of the Prime Minister's Office, obtained by International Campaign for Justice for Bhopal [ICJB] activists via a Right-to-Information request.

26  Yes Men, *The Yes Men Fix the World*.

27  See MacLeod, this volume, for a deeper discussion of these usurpations.

28  Bhopal Medical Appeal, *Activists and Yes Men at Dow Live Earth*.

29  Fortun, *Advocacy*.

# Water Is Siwlkw

*Jeannette Armstrong*

siwlkw she murmured   is an emergence   the subsequence of all else
a completeness of the design   transforming to be lapped   continuously
onto long pink tongues   in that same breathing   to be the sweet drink
coursing   to become the body   a welling spring   eternally renewing
a sacred song   of the mother   vibrating outward   from the first minute drop
formed of sky   earth   and light   bursting out of the deep quietness
siwlkw is a song she breathed   awakening cells   toward this knowing
that you   are the great River   as is   the abundant land   it brings   to carve
its banks   then spread   its fertile plains and deltas and open its basins
its great estuaries   even to where it finally   joins   once again
the grandmother ocean's vast and liquid peace   as are the headwater glaciers
of the jagged mountains   waiting   for the yearly procession of thunder beings
bearing the dark cloud's sweep   upward   as spirits released from green depths
cradling whale song   dance on wind   as are the cold ice springs feeding
rushing brooks and willow-draped creeks   meandering through teeming
wetlands to sparkling blue lakes   as are the silent   underground reservoirs
coursing   gradually up   toward roots reaching down   to draw dew upward
through countless unfurling   into the sun's full light   as much as the salmon
and sleek sturgeon   sliding through strong currents   even the tall straight
reeds   cleaning stagnant pools   equally   are the marsh bogs   swarming
multitudinous glistening flagella and wings in high country   holding dampness
for the gradual descent through loam and luxuriant life   to drink in   silkw
she said   is to remember   this song is the way   it is the storm's way   driving
new wet earth   down slippery slopes   to make fresh land   the river's way
heaving its full silt weight   crushing solid rock   the tide's way   smoothing
old plates of stone   finally deciding for all   the way of ice   piled   blue green
layer upon layer   over eons   sustaining this fragment of now   so somewhere
on her voluptuous body   the rain continues   to fall   in the right places
the mists unceasingly   float upward   to where they must   and the fog forever
ghosts across the land   in the cool desert wind   where no rain falls   and each

drop is more precious than    blood   balancing time   in the way of the silvery
hoar frost covering tundra   where iridescent ice   tinkles under the bellies of
caribou   her song   is the sky's way   holding   the gossamer filaments
of rainbow   together   guarding the silent drift of perfect white flakes   where
the moose stop momentarily to look   upward   her song in the forest ensuring
a leaf shaped   just so   captures each glistening droplet   to celebrate
the vast miles of liquid   pumping through the veins of the lion   parting
undulating savannah grasses   lifting great Condor wings soaring last circles
in the mountains of Chile   accumulating in the places it chooses   to pool
in subterranean caverns   moving through porous stone   seeping and wetting
sand   deep   inside of her   caressing   thunder eggs and smooth
pebbles at her heart

This song is the way

# Sounding a Sea-Change: Acoustic Ecology and Arctic Ocean Governance[1]

*Shirley Roburn*

On 3 February 2011, Royal Dutch Shell abruptly cancelled its summer plans to drill for oil off the Alaska coast, citing uncertainty over its ability to obtain requisite permits in time for the short ice-free season.[2] The move was one more twist in a long-running dispute.[3] As Emma Kineeveauk, the environmental program manager for the tribal government of the village of Point Hope, had explained in 2008, "Oil operations will not just hurt our community 'Tikigaq' Point Hope, but will hurt all of the hunting communities. If oil is found, there are going to be lots of ships going back and forth and this is going to interrupt the animals' migratory routes. They won't come around anymore. We hunters will have a hard time finding the food we are used to eating; it is going to hurt our way of life."[4] The village joined fourteen other native and environmental groups in a federal district court challenge of Shell and British Petroleum's authorizations for seismic surveys in the Beaufort and Chukchi seas. Foremost among petitioners' concerns were fears that bowhead, beluga, and other whale populations would suffer.

As climate change reduces the size of the polar ice cap, North American Arctic marine conditions are changing rapidly, and northern shipping, seismic mapping of the continental shelf, and underwater oil and gas exploration are experiencing rapid growth. These activities substantially increase underwater noise levels in the frequency ranges in which whales and dolphins hear and employ echolocation, and have led to political, legal, and scientific reviews across the North American Arctic. From the Bering and Chukchi seas in the west, through the oil-rich offshore zones of the Beaufort Sea, to beluga and narwhal feeding grounds in the central and eastern arctic that lie in the potential shipping corridors for large Baffin Island mineral deposits, concerns first voiced by Yu'pik, Inupiat, and Inuit subsistence whalers have evolved into complex conflicts with many stakeholders and many discourses at play. These range from national security and military concerns, to tensions between market/industrial and subsistence economies, to issues of national and international regulation and jurisdiction, to overlaps and disjunctures between Western and indigenous science practices.

This chapter uses sound studies to explore how innovative lines of legal and scientific argument, often shadowing or drawing directly from indigenous thought, have begun to shift the present impasse. The use of sound as an organizing principle opens new possibilities for interpreting contemporary debates on the future of whales and dolphins. To take increased ocean ambient noise seriously as a form of chronic environmental degradation recontextualizes threats to arctic whale survival by clearly linking such threats to the consequences of industrial development.[5] Reframing the ocean as an acoustic space both highlights the speciesism inherent in human perceptions and categorizations of space, and reclassifies ocean habitats not as wild nature but as areas differentially affected by the pollution of modernity. The industrialization of ocean spaces disrupts cetacean migration patterns and food chains, and also family and social structures.

Whale songs, believed by many researchers to offer concrete evidence not only of whale intelligence but of cetacean communication patterns, kinship ties, sharing, and culture,[6] have been instrumental in establishing this knowledge. A generation ago, when they were first widely recorded and circulated via television, radio, print media, and popular music, such songs were crucial in creating empathy and support for ending the commercial whale hunt. Today, as in the 1970s, sound forms a bridge between humans and other sentient creatures: an analysis of the shared and overlapping acoustic spaces of northern oceans underscores the continuity between human beings and other creatures, suggesting an ethics of relationship that seeks through empathy to establish greater reciprocity with the more-than-human world.

## The Acoustic Ecology of Whales: Shifting the Register of Survival

Over the past decade, prominent whale and dolphin researchers have increasingly come forward to describe chronic environmental degradation, and particularly increased ocean industrial noise, as a defining threat to cetacean survival in the twenty-first century. Because noise travels farther and much more rapidly through water than in air,[7] ocean industrial activities easily propagate noise over vast areas that is loud enough to temporarily or permanently damage hearing in fish and whales. Lindy Weilgart notes the astonishing ranges over which such industrial noise carries, giving as examples United States Navy low-frequency active sonar, which emits sound pressure of 120 dB (the level of exposure that damages human hearing) for 3.9 million km², and noise from a lone seismic survey, which may raise ocean noise levels by two orders of magnitude for days at a time for over 300,000 km².[8]

In the most dramatic cases of acoustic disturbance, mid-frequency sonar used in naval exercises has repeatedly been demonstrated to cause cetacean death. While mortality manifests through mass strandings, autopsies reveal extensive internal bleeding in cranial regions.[9] As whale researcher Ken Balcomb explains in relation to one incident from March 2000: "Envision a football squeezed to the size of a ping-pong ball by air pressure alone. Now envision this ball compressing and decompressing hundreds of times per second, between your two ears. This is what the Cuvier's beaked whales experienced as a result of the Navy's sonar testing in March 2000. Airspace resonance phenomena resulted in hemorrhaging, which caused the stranding and deaths in the Bahamas."[10] The most widely accepted hypothesis for such incidents is that disorientation and other physiological impacts interfere with whales' ability to regulate their internal pressure; they die painfully through a form of decompression sickness, similar to what human divers would refer to as "the bends."

As ocean background noise continues to rise – doubling every decade in some regions, largely as a result of increased commercial ship traffic[11] – the large-scale changes in the marine acoustic environment are affecting whale and dolphin survival through multiple, sometimes subtle mechanisms. Elevated background noise levels reduce the distances across which whales can communicate and use echolocation, from thousands of kilometres to hundreds, and from hundreds to dozens, depending on the frequency used.[12] Odontocetes (toothed whales such as narwhals and belugas) rely on high-frequency echolocation to hunt and to orient themselves.[13] In Arctic waters, which are extremely difficult to navigate because of underwater ridges and ice floe and surface ice conditions, mysticetes (filter-feeding baleen whales) such as bowheads depend heavily on systems of calls and countercalls as groups spread over many square kilometres, searching for cracks and leads in the ice in which to surface to breathe.[14] While some whales have partially adapted to shipping noise by altering the timing, loudness, frequency, and/or redundancy of their calls, these strategies have opportunity costs such as increased energy expenditure,[15] and compensate only for the masking of calls, not the masking of the other natural ocean sounds that provide important information about the local environment. Whales exposed to loud underwater noises have shown disturbance and stress responses, ranging from the physiological to the behavioural. Of particular concern are avoidance behaviours, which may cause cetaceans to lose access to feeding and calving grounds; from a conservation perspective, the balance between a population increasing, falling, or remaining stable in a given year is a fine one – a small percentage decrease in body fat of fertile females,[16] or a slightly lessened percentage of animals finding partners (in this case due to a smaller range in which to effectively locate mates) can push a population into decline.

Inuit, Inupiat, and Yup'ik whaling communities, which depend on healthy whale populations for subsistence, are particularly disturbed by threats to Arctic whales. Such communities were drastically impacted in the late nineteenth and early twentieth centuries, when commercial hunts extirpated local whale populations, causing famine. In the 1920s, while travelling through the Arctic with Knud Rasmussen, Danish ethnographer Kaj Birket-Smith noted: "In earlier days whaling gave the Eskimos that reserve of meat and blubber without which the winter would prove hard ... it was the rapid decrease in the numbers of right whales, when white whalers began their systematic butchery, which forced the government of the United States to introduce the reindeer into these regions, which had thus become almost bare of means of subsistence."[17] During the twentieth century, Inuit groups in Canada reached land claims settlements that included rights to subsistence harvesting and a say in resource management within their traditional lands. While Alaskan natives did not gain the same rights in their land claims settlements, other legislative measures ensured some access to subsistence harvesting.[18]

However, through to the present day, federal, state, and territorial governments have tended to administer and frame these rights in regional contexts, and have entered into international agreements without thinking through their obligations to local native groups. A particularly dramatic example was the Barrow Duck-in of 1961, when 138 Inupiat hunters turned themselves in, carrying dead ducks in protest of a local U.S. Fish and Wildlife officer's attempts to enforce the Migratory Bird Treaty Act, which disallowed duck-hunting during the window when the ducks migrated over Barrow.[19] The 1978 International Whaling Commission decree of a moratorium on bowhead whale hunting also provoked widespread shock and anger among Inupiat people.[20] Only when Inupiat established their own Alaska Eskimo Whaling Commission and engaged in a political struggle for recognition that included Inupiat whaling captains working with scientists and sharing their traditional knowledge to ensure more accurate whale counts (establishing a population of several thousand, not several hundred, whales) was the moratorium lifted.[21]

Successive waves of Western approaches to whaling – ranging from mass slaughter to outright ban – have been experienced by aboriginal peoples as expressions of oppressive colonial and post-colonial power relations, with outside forces disrupting subsistence harvests and challenging the validity of indigenous ethics and indigenous knowledge. A similar dynamic remains in play in the present day: the 2008 Ilulissat declaration, in which five Arctic states agreed to a set of principles for resolving overlapping continental shelf claims, excluded aboriginal groups from their deliberations. As the pan-arctic Inuit Circumpolar Conference noted in its 2009 declaration on Arctic sovereignty: "The 2008 Ilulissat Declaration on Arctic sovereignty by ministers representing the five coastal Arctic states did not go far enough in affirming the rights Inuit have gained through international law, land claims and self-government processes … Inuit inclusion as active partners is central to all national and international deliberations on Arctic sovereignty and related questions, such as who owns the Arctic, who has the right to traverse the Arctic, who has the right to develop the Arctic, and who will be responsible for the social and environmental impacts increasingly facing the Arctic."[22]

Any discussion of whale acoustic ecology enters into a history of knowledge and power relationships that has sedimented toward certain polarities – conservationist vs. hunter, subsistence economy vs. commercial – even as real conditions are changing.[23] The point of a sound studies analysis is to move beyond aspects of these relationships that are no longer productive by creating common understandings and a common vocabulary. Sound studies, and particularly a notion of acoustic ecology grounded in the work of Barry Truax and of the World Soundscape Project, provides conceptual and practical tools that speak to current gaps in ocean regulation, and enrich possibilities for dialogue between indigenous whalers and local, regional, national, and international governance bodies.

## The Acoustic Ecology of Whales: Sounding the Spaces of the Sea

The impact of ocean industrial noise on whales cannot really be understood without a further exploration of conceptions of ocean space, and in particular of how notions of acoustic space link to ecology. Whale bodies make far more sophisticated use of acoustic frequencies than do human bodies. Cetaceans employ the broadest acoustic range of any mammal group:[24] they are able to make sounds in ranges from 10 Hz to 200 kHz, as well as hear in these ranges.[25] By contrast, human hearing is in the 20 Hz–20 kHz range, and human vocal range for singing voices is roughly 80 Hz–1050 Hz.[26] For odontocetes, who feed largely below the euphotic zone, echolocation is crucial in locating and capturing prey, and in navigating the ocean environment: only about 1 percent of surface light travels to a depth of 100 m in the ocean, and at 600 m luminosity is roughly equivalent to starlight.[27] Whereas human beings use sight to orient themselves, odontocetes rely largely on sensing waves of pressure/vibrations that are outside audible sound frequencies. This sensing could be considered "hearing," an extension of the analogous sense in humans. Or, as Balcomb's description of a whale's melon (the "acoustic lens" in a whale's head) as a "football squeezed to the size of a ping-pong ball by air pressure alone" graphically suggests, this sensing of vibration could be considered feeling. In any case, it represents a type of synesthesia of what in humans are classified as discrete senses. Whales rely heavily on this extremely sensitive and well-adapted aural capacity: odontocetes to sense their immediate surroundings, and mysticetes to communicate across vast distances.

Mysticetes vocalize at very low frequencies within the ocean's deep sound channels, where such sounds may travel thousands of kilometres in the space of an hour.[28] For example, the 10-Hz sounds of fin whales can travel over 1,800 kilometres.[29] Thus, the acoustic spaces that whales occupy and draw upon may be far more extensive than the physical spaces they range over at a particular point in their migrations. In the case of wide-ranging and solitary cetacean species such as blue whales, there is evidence that very loud,[30] very low frequency calls mark patterns of populations that exist as "acoustic clans," often separated by great distances.[31]

Building on the work of R. Murray Schafer and the World Soundscape Project, Truax further developed the concept of "acoustic community ... as any soundscape in which acoustic information plays a pervasive role in the lives of the inhabitants ... sound plays a significant role in defining the community spatially, temporally in terms of daily and seasonal cycles, as well as socially and culturally in terms of shared activities, rituals, and dominant institutions."[32] Through fieldwork that included a series of case studies, Truax sought to define the parameters of acoustic communities, and especially to understand how the era of electroacoustic technologies (the modern era of industrialization as characterized through the sonic signatures of machines) was affecting acoustic communication and altering the spatial and physiological rhythms of communities. Although Truax was concerned with the acoustic design of terrestrial (human) communities, the conceptual tools he developed speak directly to cetaceans' modern plight. The definition of an acoustic community is, of itself, an environmental one: sound and space are inseparable, and Truax's description could easily be made to apply to ecological communities, for example in the case of the interrelationships between whalesongs and seasonal migration and reproductive cycles.[33] A considerable focus of Truax's field research involved creating "acoustic maps" that defined communities geographically on the basis of sound. However, this work was complicated by urban environments where acoustic definition was blurred because of industrial sound that masked keynote sounds and drowned out "acoustic" (non-mechanical) communication patterns in a wash of electroacoustic noise.[34] Truax concluded that "the acoustic profile, and hence the communicative power of a sound, is extremely vulnerable to noise and environmental change."[35]

Research on modernizing European villages suggested that increased traffic and industrial noise were radically altering the character of villages by shrinking the size and variability of local soundscapes. This impoverishment brought about a decrease in social interactions, and reduced interactions between locals and their environment.[36] Truax introduced the concept of acoustic horizon to more accurately describe these effects, which included shrinking individuals' sense of space and local connection, and creating soundscapes of modernity that were "increasingly defined by the common noise elements."[37] In Truax's communicational framework, sound creates a relationship between individuals and their environment, while noise "loosens the contact the listener has with the environment and [is] an irritant that works against effective communication."[38]

Rather than determining what constitutes noise through quantifying sound thresholds, Truax focused on behaviour effects, as demonstrated through changing relationships between individuals and their environments.[39] He concludes that "at its very basis, the electroacoustic process is not merely a simple extension of the capabilities of sound, but rather a fundamental *transformation* of how it works. The change is not only quantitative, in the sense of extending the range of a variable by some amount, but also qualitative in the way that it permits totally new concepts to operate."[40]

Drawing on a broad swath of scholarship on noise, as well as on his own fieldwork, Truax was able to sketch both a series of soundscape changes, and a series of accompanying adaptations, that have relevance cross-culturally and across the species barrier. Many of the noise effects he categorizes – reduced acoustic space and shrinking acoustic horizons, increased physiological stress, masking effects, and changing communication patterns and definitions of community – speak directly to the condition of whales in modernity. This is critical on a practical level, because most scholarship on noise is profoundly anthropocentric, leaving whales and the frequencies of echolocation and deep ocean channel communication outside even the problem definition. Models of noise regulation developed on land tend to work only with the parameter of decibels (loudness), and assume a relative uniformity of sound travel.[41] Such models are inadequate for ocean spaces, where, because of the topography of the ocean and the changing pressure and temperature of the water column, among other factors, seascapes vary dramatically: sound travels and reflects very differently in the open ocean than in the St Lawrence Seaway or the ice-covered waters of a wintry Lancaster Sound.[42] In addition, for cetaceans, decibel level is not the only noise issue: frequency, form, and periodicity are also factors, and conservation groups are pushing for regulatory measures that address all these attributes.[43]

However, as Weilgart explains,[44] the complexities of ocean acoustics and gaps in knowledge about the aural capacities of different cetacean species have long proved stumbling blocks to formulating realistic policy and regulation proposals to reduce ocean noise. Truax's framework addresses these shortfalls because it asks exactly what qualities of ocean ambient noise are problematic and for whom and how this is the case. His conception of acoustic design is flexible enough to incorporate more traditional and quantitative approaches to noise issues, such as the noise indexes and zoning measures surveyed by Karin Bijsterveld in response to the problem of airport noise. Yet, it is less speciesist, characterizing its role as achieving "an understanding of the processes of acoustic communication and seek[ing] to redirect the mediating influence of sound in relationships that are observed to be malfunctioning."[45] In other words, Truax's models are context-specific, bringing attention to the actual empirical, environmental, and bioacoustic conditions impeding communication flows.


## Song, Sentience, and Synesthesia

In recognizing that sense perception itself has a cultural component, Truax's formulations stress relationship, community, and connection – emphasizing how sound shapes lives at phenomenological and social levels. Historians of sound[46] note that the continuum between sound and noise is always shifting, because hearing/listening is a cultural as well as physiological process. As Jonathan Sterne describes, invoking the work of Pierre Bourdieu, orientations toward listening evolve from "a mix of custom, bodily technique, social outlook, style, and orientation."[47] Brian Rice, in opening his discussion of aboriginal conceptions of primal sound, is clear that "the abilities of seeing and hearing are culturally distinct and depend on a person's orientation to the cosmos."[48] The quality of a soundscape is a measure of quality of life: to suffer an excess of industrial noise is to be afflicted with the ills of modernity – stress, isolation, and the replacement of diversity with the dull, steady drone that blocks sensory experience. When beluga and other whales are exposed to steady background noise, their stress-related hormones levels rise significantly.[49] Whales in such conditions suffer psychologically as well as physiologically: with their dominant sense crippled, it is more difficult to find food, to communicate with other whales, and even to find a mate. While it may be unclear exactly how kinship groups and their calls figure in the social and physical reproduction of different whale communities, it is abundantly clear that whales engage in social learning, and that sound – for example, calls between mother and calf – is key to the communication that establishes whale kinship ties and social groups.

Drawing on his analyses of song-learning among clan-like groupings of whale pods, and on the socially acquired signature behaviours that distinguish whale pods from each other, even when they share the same habitat, Hal Whitehead makes a compelling argument for whales possessing culture. In his formulation, "the behavior that is culture has two principal elements: it is socially learned and shared … the sharing makes culture more than social learning."[50] This appeal to "culture" is a way of framing, within a Western worldview, the reason that many people feel more connected to whales than to some other non-human animals: in other words, whales are not just sentient creatures, but are creatures that live in family groups and interact in ways that we can anthropormorphize. As the hum, whir, and chronic noise stresses of modernity bleach out their vocalizations, whales are responding by falling silent – to a degree that cannot be explained as a response to masking alone.[51] Whale communities are experiencing communicational breakdowns, leaving already stressed animals increasingly atomized and separated from their kin. Such conditions are of particular concern to northern aboriginal whaling communities, where the kinship ties of whales are understood to be related to and integrated with the kinship ties of the communities themselves.

Within the context of indigenous worldviews, the utterances of whales could be considered examples of primal sound. As Rice explains in his discussion of primal sound:

> In many traditional aboriginal cultures everything that exists and is considered alive can be represented by primal sounds, and sound is more important than the name. These primal sounds exist in languages of the people and in the sounds emitted by the universe. Within these sounds is a power and energy that can be tapped by those who can access them. Aboriginal languages are based on word meaning as well as word sounds which place one in relationship to different aspects of creation. Henderson … says every indigenous language has sounds connected to the different realms that make up the cosmology. For example, to hear the Haida speak is to listen to the waves on the shore and the cry of the birds … Words derive energy and potency from the sounds that are embodied in the words. Hearing or speaking words and sounds introduces another way of hearing outside the physical realm that has far reaching implications in all aspects of daily physical and spiritual existence.[52]

In Anishnawbe, Mayan, and other indigenous creation stories, the universe emerges from primal sound, which then differentiates. Sound itself retains a vestigial primordial quality; it acts as a channel between realms, linking the physical and the spiritual. This pre-lingual power is present in all voices – human or other – and its energy is present in the calls of whales.

Rice elaborates the concept of primal sound within a much more extensive discussion of aboriginal ways of knowing that stresses connections between different realms, and human obligations to maintain balances, reciprocity, and relatedness, particularly within the earth world. While it is difficult to contextualize this knowledge in dialogue with Western worldviews, Rice suggests some elements that are particularly salient for understanding the perspectives of indigenous Arctic whalers. It is only over the last fifty years that Western science has come to recognize that whales and dolphins communicate and "sound the world," through techniques beyond the realms of our own physical senses, whether echolocating in their immediate surroundings or calling across vast ocean spaces. However, these attributes fit easily within the construct of whale cries as primal sound: if sound is a conduit between realms, if human language itself is expressed through words that resonate with the pre-lingual soundings of the world, and if faculties of hearing and seeing are culturally distinct and profoundly dependent on our orientations to the cosmos, it easily follows that whales are sentient, intelligent creatures inhabiting spaces that overlap with humans in the earth world and in other realms. The  "synesthesia" of whales' sonic sense is not exceptional, but a quality that works across species, and to which humans can become attuned. In particular, it is an important part of understanding the complex rhythms and cycles of the natural world.[53]

This synesthesia extends to forms of knowing based on different kinds of consciousness: intuition, dreams, and vision.[54] The experiences of Kupaaq/Harry Brower Sr, an Inupiat whaling captain who was instrumental in Inupiat struggles for self-determination and especially in achieving co-operation between Inupiat whalers and scientists to manage bowhead whale stocks, give a glimpse of these forms of knowledge. Toward the end of his life in 1986, when he was hospitalized for a long period of time in Anchorage, he was visited by a baby whale. "That whale took me all the way from Anchorage to Barrow. I wasn't dreaming! I was dead! He took me all the way over to Barrow where these guys were shooting at the mother whale. He talked to me; he told me all the stories about where they had all this trouble out there on the ice. And he told me which people he'd seen and what they'd done. He pointed at my boys."[55] Brower's experience gave him knowledge, including a detailed description of how the whale died, who killed him, and which ice cellar the body was in. Eugene, the son who stayed by his father's side while his brothers were in Barrow whale hunting, explained: "We thought we were losing him. It was like he went into a trance. We called his name, pinched him, and got no response. Then Dad snapped out of it and told us about the things that happened in Barrow. I called my brother, Harry Jr, who was in Barrow, and these things really happened. I don't know who all Dad told this story to. But I don't retell it much because it's like sacred. Dad really shocked us with that. I was so amazed with how close to the whale he was. He could feel the bombs going into the whale. The whale was his life, so he was this close to the whale who took him away."[56] Brower thought a lot about this episode, consulting his spiritual advisors. The incident influenced him both to suggest a deadline date for spring whale hunting (after which baby whales such as the one that came to him would be able to migrate freely) and to have conversations with various other whaling captains about the whaling incident in question and proper behaviours and protocols for hunting mother and infant whale pairs.[57]

The phrase that titles Kupaaq/Harry Brower, Sr's biography, *The Whales, They Give Themselves*, helps anchor this episode in terms of the protocols governing the whale/human relationship and the responsibilities of humans with regard to the suffering and death of whales. The belief that whales choose to give themselves to specific hunters who observe appropriate protocols, such as maintaining clean equipment and a clean ice cellar, and sharing their catch with the community, is expressed over and over in literature on the Inupiat bowhead hunt.[58] As described by Port Hope native Kirk Oviok, with specific reference to sound as a conduit between humans and whales: "Like my aunt said, the whales have ears and are more like people. The first batch of whales seen would show up to check which ones in the whaling crews would be more hospitable to be caught. Then the whales would come back to their pack and tell them about the situation stating, 'we have someone available for us' ... This is what my wife and I have heard from my aunt Negovanna. I firmly believe this is true, that whales have ears."[59]

Such beliefs arise from the direct experiences of Alaskan whalers. As Noongwook et al. describe in their research on traditional knowledge of bowhead whales around St Lawrence Island:

> Whales have been known to stay next to a whaling boat under sail for up to an hour, often positioning themselves near each "seat position" in the boat as though sizing up the crew members. While swimming alongside the boat, a whale may remain in sight even when submerged. At times, it may even touch the boat on the left side, where it is inaccessible to the harpooner ... When surfacing to breathe, these whales surface on the side of the boat opposite the harpooner, thus remaining out of reach for the whalers. This phenomenon is known as *angyi* (from the Yupik root *ang-*, which refers to giving something), meaning that the whale is considering giving itself to the whalers ... The behavior is part of the relationship between the *angyalek* ("whaling captain") and the *aghveq* ("bowhead whale"). Eventually, the whale may surface where it can be struck by the harpooner.[60]

The relationship between humans and whales is intimate, involving reciprocity and communication: hunting links the species together in cycles of birth and death that renew the world and keep it in balance:

> Animals do not only give themselves to hunters, their societies are also renewed through hunting. Hunting means rebirth, not death, in Inuit cosmology ... and the

hunt may be seen as a semi-sacred act that unites animals and human beings in webs of reciprocity. This is particularly noteworthy today among the Inupiat whalers in northern Alaska where people and whales are believed to communicate in subtle ways ... The whales are believed to be very knowledgeable and able to hear, see, and smell over long distances and can immediately tell a good and generous person from a bad and stingy one.[61]

The taking of life is one part of this ethic; respectful relationship to life is another, and is observed both through exchange/gifting, and through attention to how life is taken (not wantonly; with a purpose and without prolonging suffering).[62]

Voice and primal sound are important motifs within this worldview, calling attention to the common ancestry of whales and people. The channels and energy flows that link cycles of life must be kept open through exchange, whether of song or of life. Part of this work is enacted in hunting protocols that respect a whale's ability to hear – for example, spring hunters in Barrow use skin boats, rather than noisier aluminum ones[63] – and emphasize listening and respect.[64] Equally important, however, is that once a whale is landed, the meat must be shared – the cycles of giving and receiving meat delineate and reaffirm kinship ties between families and communities. In the words of the final amended environmental impact assessment for proposed activities for the Northeast National Petroleum Reserve Environmental Impact Statement (NNPR EIS):

> The sharing of subsistence foods is essential to the maintenance of family ties, kinship networks, and community well-being ... Bowhead whale hunting remains the center of Iñupiat spiritual and emotional life; it embodies the values of sharing, association, leadership, kinship, Arctic survival, and hunting prowess ... The importance of the whale hunt is more than emotional and spiritual. The organization of the crews does much to delineate important social and kin ties within communities and define community leadership patterns. The structured sharing of the whale harvest helps determine social relations within and between communities.[65]

When whales are not available, meat cannot be shared, and the kinship ties that quite literally nourish communities begin to break down. Also in the NNPR Environment Impact Statement, Rosemary Ahtuangaruak of Nuiqsut stated: "We had seismic activity in Camden Bay that caused us to lose two whaling boats. We did not harvest whale two seasons in a row. We went without whale those winters. Those were the deepest, darkest winters I faced as a community health aide. We saw an increase to the social ills, we saw domestic violence, we saw drug and alcohol abuse, we saw all the bad things that come when we are not able to maintain our traditional life activities (USDOI BLM 2004d)."[66] For traditional Inupiat, whales and humans are kin, and the health concerns of whale and Inupiat communities are inextricably bound together. In its most profound forms, the communication between species can be viewed as a communion in which whales make sentient, spiritual choices to give their physical bodies to nourish their human kin. Through a kind of transubstantiation, the physical and spiritual life of indigenous whaling communities is constituted through the sharing and consuming of the whale's flesh. This profound connection – in which whales are not only "others," and not only kin, but constitute one's own flesh – creates ethical, spiritual, and practical relationships with whales which are very different for indigenous whaling communities than the worldviews that guide most resource managers, governments, corporations, conservation groups, and private citizens involved in debates about whales and ocean ambient noise.

*not convinced*

However, even if we step outside a northern indigenous framework, the vocalizations of whales have the power to shift human understandings. The wide release of humpback whale songs in the 1970s was instrumental in generating a groundswell of empathy for whales as intelligent, sentient creatures. It was key in shifting popular consciousness to end their commercial slaughter.

## Whale song, Ur-Song, and the Sounding of the World

Although military and scientific research into the aural capacities of cetaceans had been ongoing since at least the mid-twentieth century, it was not until 1970s, when hydrophone recordings were made and released commercially, that the global public became aware of the sophisticated patterning of whale songs. *Songs of Humpback Whales*, released in the spring of 1970 by Capitol Records and National Geographic, became an instant smash hit.[67] It received laudatory reviews in *Time*, *Life*, and *Rolling Stone* magazines. Humpback whales, as "opera stars of the deep," became a cultural phenomenon, with popular singers such as Judy Collins and Pete Seeger either writing music about whales or actually intersplicing whale music into their own recorded songs. Roger Payne and Scott McVay, who had authored an eponymous scientific paper (which wasn't released until February 1971, in order to ensure a cover slot in the popular magazine *Science*) appeared on *Good Morning America* to discuss the recordings and the importance of whale conservation, and McVay went on a further major promotional tour to shift public opinion in Japan, the nation most strident in its support of commercial whaling. By 1971, forty-five thousand copies of the record had been sold; it went on to become the most popular nature recording of all time, with over three million units sold as of 2008. In McVay's words, "The impact of the song was huge and staggering."[68]

The release and circulation of humpback whale recordings was accompanied by a great deal of messaging aimed at shifting human understandings of whales. McVay and

Payne's scientific paper, which was read widely and popularized both by conservation groups and through mainstream journalism, meticulously analysed sonograms of humpback whale calls, establishing their sophisticated patterns and harmonics. The underlying message – consistent with the inserts in many of the recorded editions of *Songs of Humpback Whales* – was that these could only be the songs of sentient, intelligent beings.[69] The pervasiveness of this popular conviction is perhaps best demonstrated by a 1977 recording of songs of humpback whales together with greetings in fifty-four human languages, an elephant's trumpet, and the sound of a rocket launch – all amassed on a gold-plated record, and sent out on *Voyager 1* and *Voyager 2* spacecraft in case these craft were to be intercepted by extraterrestrial intelligence.

Popular literature such as Farley Mowat's *A Whale for the Killing* and Victor Sheffer's *The Year of the Whale* also fed into the cultural movement to end whaling. No longer were whales "great demons of the sea,"[70] lethal leviathans à la Moby Dick, engaged in mortal combat with hapless sailors. Instead, whales were cast as intelligent, gentle, and ancient beasts, victimized by the thousands by barbaric whalers carrying out a brutal slaughter. Part of the public appeal of these claims – a theme eerily reminiscent of constructions of native people as "noble savages" at once glorified and doomed before progress – was the threat of extinction. Equally important, however – what made the popular stake in whale survival sufficient to fuel a global campaign for a moratorium on commercial whaling – was empathy for whales as social and intelligent beings. The recognition of cetaceans' sentience caused a huge popular shift: the suffering of highly intelligent creatures was considered ethically suspect.

The booklet inserted into the original edition of *Songs of Humpback Whales* urged readers to "Listen to him singing far below the turmoil and ceaseless motion of the surface … From that profoundly peaceful place a voice calls us to Turn Back."[71] Whale song thus provides a potential point of contact between Western and indigenous worldviews: while rather overwrought, the booklet text is suggesting that through sound/song, one can channel communication between humans and whales. This channelling is used to invoke a more ancient relationship of kinship (the "Turn Back" suggests that human beings need to return to a previous more harmonious way of living with whales, a way that presumably rejects mass slaughter).

David Rothenberg's *Thousand Mile Song* – in which Rothenberg sets out on a multi-year journey to listen to and play music with whales – further explores the popular movement to end commercial whaling, attempting to tease out the resonances of whale song that provoked such public outpouring. One of the concepts he draws upon, as elaborated by composer Morton Subotnick, is "Ur-music." This concept fits closely with World Soundscape Project founder R. Murray Shafer's description, here quoted by Brandon Labelle, of acoustic ecology as reaching "for the 'primary sound,' seeking to locate the mythological beginning of sound, the *Ursound* from which the sound world itself is born. 'To find it we must return to the waters of instinct and the unshatterable unity of the unconscious, letting the long waves of Ursound sweep us beneath the surface, where, listening blindly to our ancestors and the wild creatures, we will feel it surge within us again, in our speaking and in our music.'"[72] Over and over, the composers, scientists, fishers, and conservationists that David Rothenberg interviews express versions of this sentiment. Its widespread acceptance is echoed in the *Songs of Humpback Whales* record insert. Such beliefs in a sacred connection to whales, hinting at an ancient time when human beings and animals communicated with one another, correspond closely with the concept of primal sound as elaborated in many indigenous cosmologies. In addition, categorizing the utterances of whales as "voices" draws in a complex set of Western discourses concerning the voice as presence, as marker of selfhood and of language (and, therefore, thought),[73] and as an instinctive appeal to the other;[74] "song" also brings with it a host of connotations concerning spirituality and carnality, placing whales and their vocalizations within a complex matrix of beliefs about rhythm, ritual, and the "pure connections" of music.[75] Rothenberg's analysis suggests that an emotive and intuitive response – one that operates on a spiritual level – is at work when humans listen to whales.

This phenomenological experience – which, according to Rice, is both physiologically and culturally constituted in complex, interrelated ways – has powerful purchase. More than scientific evidence (such as comparisons of spindle cells in whale and human brains[76]), such experience was able to move a critical mass of people toward recognizing whales as intelligent creatures worthy of protection from suffering. In order to save whales from commercial slaughter, it was necessary to reposition them within the social hierarchy of being. Whale song – which drew on the power of "Ur-song" or primal sound, and which could be articulated to beliefs about selfhood organized around voice – provided the necessary opening.


## Acoustic Ecology and Marine Protection


As Arctic whales face an emergent and complex set of survival challenges, including toxic chemical buildup in their blubber, starvation due to diminished ocean productivity, and the many threats of ocean ambient industrial noise, sound can again shift the tenor of debate. An acoustic contemplation of Arctic oceans opens toward a much more reciprocal, empathetic, and communicative understanding of whale-human relationships within a more-than-human world. The methods used in acoustic ecology stress relationship to the environment, asking pointed and particular questions to determine where and how individual sound sources interfere with or are productive for the sensory relationships that anchor and define aquatic communities within the spaces they occupy. These relationships have spiritual and cultural dimensions; they also have measurable and mappable physical parameters that can be defined and expressed in language compatible with global legal and scientific regimes. Within acoustic ecology, both facets coexist within a shared vocabulary and a cohesive framework, making possible a more comprehensive dialogue on ocean noise regulation.

Truax's work was decades ahead of its time in anticipating the conceptual tools required to accurately model and begin to address the harms that anthropogenic ocean noise visits upon ocean life, and particularly upon whales. His models integrate several key elements that have emerged repeatedly in recent years, as ocean scientists have begun to draw on powerful computers and sophisticated mapping technologies to integrate an acoustic dimension into population ecology and conservation science.[77] These elements include: the sense of acoustic space as a marker of community and horizon of consciousness; the concept of "masking" and its sensitivity to temporal, spatial, and environmental parameters as well as more basic sound metrics; and methods to quantitatively/isometrically map the acoustic geography of sounds. Truax was an early developer of location-specific, ground-truthed fieldwork methods capable of describing how a wide swath of factors, from a sound's directionality, to the play of winds and the shape of a landscape, to the various metrics of a sound (for example, frequency and intensity) affect the way environmental sounds propagate or are masked even over the course of a day.[78] From such work, Truax generated a series of isometric maps that demarcated and described how acoustic spaces and communities overlay given land-scapes – creating a practical form in which his ideas could literally be "mapped" into science and policy. Examples of this kind of specific, quantifiable modelling and description have proliferated in recent years, and are increasingly being taken up by environmentalists, indigenous groups, and regulators.

In 2009, drawing on a number of key concepts such as acoustic habitat, acoustic scene, acoustic space, and acoustic ecology, Christopher W. Clark et al. developed a sophisticated model of "dynamic spatio-spectral-temporal acoustic habitat," which they then applied "to develop analytical representations by which to study the masking effects of noise on acoustic communication."[79] They used this model to study the degree to which "acoustic bleaching" blocked out the calls of vocalizing fin, right, and hump-back whales in a marine sanctuary as two ships passed through. As one example of their results, only two ships passing near two right whales resulted in an 84 percent reduction of their communication space for well over half a day. Given average volumes of ship traffic of six vessels per day, Clark et al. concluded that right whale communi-cation space was reduced to 16 percent of pre-industrial habitat norms for a majority of the time.[80] Taken with other scientific studies, this evidence strongly suggests that ototoxic effects (including whales colliding with ships because, with their damaged hear-ing they do not sense ships in their path in time) are responsible for the continued decline of the endangered North Atlantic right whale.[81]

In public presentations of his animations and models, Clark has described how ocean background noise has gone up by three orders of magnitude in the lifetimes of many whale species, creating a chronic acoustic fog or smog, punctured by loud noise events which act as an "acoustic blindfold."[82] Yvan Simard's 2008 work applying acoustic modelling in the Saguenay–St Lawrence Marine Park indicates that ship traffic of 6,000 ships a year in the St Lawrence Seaway and up to five ships an hour in the summer months has resulted in severe masking of the calls of blue and other baleen whales at distances of only 30 km, effectively restricting the feeding whales to extremely localized "acoustic cages." Tyack similarly found that call audibility in fin whales has shifted from 7,000 km before industrialization to as little as 32 km in heavily trafficked ocean environments.[83]

Such results have been especially sobering for aboriginal communities attempting to understand how increased seismic surveys, oil and gas exploration and drilling, and ice breaker and other ship traffic will impact marine mammals in a rapidly thawing Arctic.[84] Increasingly, indigenous communities are collaborating with whale researchers to concretely map how specific communities – aquatic and land – may be impacted by Arctic development. For example, Inuit from Pond Inlet/Mittimatalik have lent their support to a narwhal research project in the bays of Eclipse Sound, rich narwhal feeding grounds where icebreakers and barges may be routed to service the St Mary's mine slated for Baffin Island.[85]

What is so hopeful about new acoustic mapping tools is that they are both particular – able to model, for example, how shipping propeller noise falls exactly in the frequencies of deep ocean channel propagation used by mysticetes – and able to accommodate multiple sound sources in order to demonstrate cumulative impacts. As Clark et al. describe: "Cumulative impact has been a long-standing, seemingly intractable issue in the debate over noise effects on marine mammals. Here we have presented a standardized metric to quantitatively estimate how much each sound source contributes to the communication-masking index. Stated from an ecological perspective, we now have a measure for estimating the cost to communication, measured and expressed over ecologically meaningful spatial and temporal scales, for an individual or a population as a result of a particular sound source."[86] Such models of ocean acoustic ecology are increasingly important in establishing the legal basis for limiting industrial ocean noise.

At an international level, acoustic inputs into the ocean are a form of "energy." As Lindy Weilgart explains: "The 1982 United Nations Convention on the Law of the Sea includes the word 'energy' to define 'pollution of the marine environment,' as in 'the introduction by man, directly or indirectly, of substances or energy into the marine environment ... which results or is likely to result in such deleterious effects as harm to living resources and marine life' (article 1.1.4)."[87] Within a North American context, the harm being demonstrated by ocean industrial noise fits within the statutory definitions of Level A and Level B harassment of marine mammals, and therefore subject to the U.S. Marine Mammal Protection Act.[88] The United States has acted to convene an interagency task force on anthropogenic noise in the marine environment, producing a 2009 strategic plan that sets out a roadmap and targets for ten federal agencies, including major players such as the Department of Defense and the State Department, to research and reduce ocean industrial noise. Arctic ocean initiatives were given highest priority as action items. In this atmosphere of increasing openness and willingness to implement practical solutions, in the summer of 2009, the non-profit Okeanos Foundation convened an international, multi-disciplinary group of geophysical scientists, seismologists, biologists, and regulators to review the technological innovations and policy supports that could be put in place to create alternatives and/or modifications to the use of seismic airguns and airgun array configurations.[89] Given proper economic and regulatory incentives, many of the proposed alternatives were feasible either immediately or in a short term of less than five years.

In Canada, a groundbreaking December 2010 ruling on the Species at Risk Act (SARA), based in part on recent scientific evidence of cetacean disturbance from ocean noise, established that quality of the acoustic environment was a dimension of the "critical habitat" of endangered killer whales, and steps had to be taken to limit ocean noise pollution.[90] This ruling has implications for Canada's Arctic, because the bowhead, grey, humpback, fin, and North Pacific right whale species are also subject to various "at risk" designations under SARA.[91]

To conceive of whale habitat as contiguous across vast acoustic spaces (rather than confined to seasonal migratory routes, which encompass many of these spaces in a more temporally limited way) poses new challenges for marine conservation. Fewer than one percent of the world's oceans have protected area status, with conservation groups like the World Wildlife Fund aiming to reach 10 percent.[92] Recent advances in terrestrial landscape ecology suggest that in order to sustain full diversity of species across a landscape, at least 50 percent of the range of large predators (mammals at the top of the food chain) must be set aside from industrial uses.[93] As marine conservation science grapples with the question of how terrestrial ecology concepts of habitat fragmentation, wilderness corridors, and ecosystem continuity apply in ocean environments, evidence concerning the acoustic ranges of whales – large mammals and therefore top predator/indicator species – suggests that preserving marine ecosystem integrity may require far more stringent protection of vast areas of the world's oceans, at least in an acoustic register.

Conclusion

The coming years will be critical in determining the quality of the Arctic marine environment, acoustic and otherwise. As the five Arctic Ocean states settle their sea-floor claims and set up regulatory regimes, as multinational companies move to access the oil, gas, and mineral riches rendered accessible by melting ice, and as northern shipping routes become increasingly viable, there may be little time for the cries of whales to reach us. From an acoustic perspective, it is clear that increasing ocean industrial activity poses a defining threat to Arctic whale survival. The consequences of acoustic pollution – ranging from ototoxic effects to cetacean behavioural changes in feeding and mating patterns – are sobering. These must be addressed not just in terms of cetacean death and population abundance, but also in terms of very real questions of cultural survival and animal suffering.

When whale acoustic ecology is taken into account, troubling ethical issues emerge. Industrial activity is both crippling the senses of individual animals and stressing the social fabric that connects them, inhibiting the communicative behaviours that are so much a part of whales' hunting and reproductive activities. Neither whales nor indigenous communities dependent on whaling have been well served by this industrialization. The sonic life of whales provides a strong case for reconsidering human ethical commitments to and relationships with seascapes and the life they contain. It may seem like a long journey from the cry of a whale to a radical restructuring of ocean governance that effectively addresses ocean industrial noise. But the groundswell of support that ended commercial whaling in the 1980s began with a popular crescendo of whale song almost a decade earlier. It may be that the long-term survival of Arctic whales again depends on a sea change in public opinion – one that begins with learning to listen.

NOTES

1  This chapter presents preliminary conclusions drawn from initial research for a larger project; it explores the interests and conceptual frameworks that shape approaches to a complex conflict. Its assertions should not be understood as definitive statements of the positions, views, and politics of any particular actor, but rather as an attempt to understand and bridge differing perspectives – perspectives that are themselves changing as the regulatory environment evolves. This chapter presents a preliminary formulation, intended as a starting point for consultation and further primary and secondary research, especially with indigenous communities and indigenous governments. As ACUNS (the Association of Canadian Universities for Northern Studies) and numerous organizations involved in aboriginal governance and co-management of lands and resources all make clear, researchers have a responsibility to work with northern communities on issues of mutual concern. Any errors and misinterpretations of viewpoints are mine, and I will endeavour to correct them as the project gets further underway. The author wishes to thank Ed Hudson, PhD (atmospheric and marine chemistry, analytical chemistry) for his careful review of the paper.

2  Taylor, "Shell Cancels."

3  Earthjustice, "Shell Oil's Arctic Offshore Drilling Plan."

4  Earthjustice, "Planned Operations."

5  In the words of UBC adjunct professor and whale researcher Dr Barrett-Lennard, "noise as a form of chronic environmental degradation is a relatively new notion, but

it is my opinion that seismic exploration and the use of sonar are two of the greatest threats to cetaceans at present, and all the indications are that they are going to get worse." See Pamboris, "Sonar and Seismic Exploration."

6   Whitehead, "How might we study culture?"

7   Noise travels roughly five times faster in water than in air, depending on salinity. See Rothenberg, *Thousand Mile Song*, 190.

8   Weilgart, "Impacts," 1092.

9   Cox et al., "Understanding the impacts of anthropogenic sound on beaked whales"; Weilgart, "Impacts"; and Rothenberg, *Thousand Mile Song*, 206–8.

10  Rothenberg, *Thousand Mile Song*, 206–7.

11  Weilgart, "Impacts," 1092.

12  Tyack, "Implications for Marine Mammals," 549–88. The frequencies discussed in my example refer to shipping noise in communicational frequencies; echolocation uses very high frequencies, such as those used in seismic survey/mapping tools and in naval sonar for communications. See Moore, "Whither the North Atlantic Right Whale?"

13  Using echolocation, toothed whales can detect prey sized less than 1 metre at ranges of tens to hundreds of metres. See Tyack, "Implications." While high-frequency ranges used in echolocation are of particular relevance to odontocetes, mysticetes are believed to use very low frequencies to communicate over thousands of kilometres, using the ocean's deep sound channels.

14  Paine, *World of the Arctic Whales*, 25.

15  Weilgart, "Impacts," 1110.

16  It is a common trait of mammals that reproduction rates are higher when animals are healthier. Female fin whales, for example, may reproduce every year when food is plentiful, and only every three years in times of famine. See Lazarus, *Troubled Waters*, 139.

17  Roman, *Whale*, 41.

18  The Alaska Native Claims Settlement Act (ANCSA), passed in 1971, did not protect aboriginal subsistence hunting – these rights were extinguished. Various later legislative solutions, such as passage of Title viii of the Alaska National Interest Lands Conservation Act in 1980, and the recognition of Alaskan subsistence whaling within the Marine Mammal Protection Act of 1972, have attempted to remedy this shortfall, albeit with mixed success.

19  The rationale of the ban was to prevent hunting by sport-hunters during the "off-season" when ducks nested and hatched their young. Unfortunately, in practice the only access Inupiat had to hunting ducks – a key food source – was during this disallowed time frame when the ducks migrated over Barrow en route to their nesting grounds. See Burwell, "Hunger Knows No Law" and Edwardson, *History of the Inupiat 1968*.

20  Hess, *Gift of the Whale*, 8.

21  Ibid.; Brower, *Whales, They Give Themselves*, 7–8; and Alaska Eskimo Whaling Commission.

22  Inuit Circumpolar Council (ICC), *Circumpolar Inuit Declaration*.

23  Kalland and Sejersen offer perhaps the most detailed explanation of the problems with some of these polarities. For example, conservationists and indigenous whalers both have an interest in preserving whale habitat. Equally important is that "subsistence" hunting takes placed in a mixed economy dependent on both non-monetary and monetary economic activity. Particularly as the impacts of climate change require expensive adaptation such as higher fuel costs to reach animals whose migrations have shifted, subsistence hunting cannot be considered without recognizing its place within a larger mixed economy. Divisions between "commercial" and "subsistence," are not as clear-cut in real life as they are in IWC documents. Kalland and Sejersen, *Marine Mammals and Northern Cultures*, 57–90.

24  Lazarus, *Troubled Waters*, 125.

25  Weilgart discusses in detail the problem with making such estimates, based as they are on small sample sizes, data from only a few of dozens of species, and often extrapolations from captive animals who live in the extremely different acoustic environment of a small tank. Weilgart, *Impacts of Anthropogenic Ocean Noise* 1094–5.

26  See "speech." *Encyclopædia Britannica Online* Academic Edition. http://o-search. eb.com.mercury.concordia.ca:80/eb/article-68982.

27  Roman, *Whale*, 157. The amount of light that reaches any particular ocean depth is variable and depends upon a number of atmospheric and oceanic conditions.

28  Sound travels more rapidly in water than air in all circumstances. In addition, however, because of the characteristics of an ocean's water column, low-frequency calls of whales emitted at certain depths can retain a clear or high sound quality for very, very long distances. These calls travel by being reflected within cold, deep water, which is separated by thermoclines (waters with an abrupt transition or temperature gradient) from warmer waters. The calls travel long distances, reflecting within one band of water, in a process somewhat analogous to how signals bend along a fibre-optic cable. See Payne, *Among Whales*, 359–402.

29  "Whale." *Encyclopædia Britannica Online Academic Edition*. http://o-search.eb.com. mercury.concordia.ca:80/eb/article-9076726.

30  That is, 160–168 db; see Lazarus, *Troubled Waters*, 126.

31  Rothenberg, *Thousand Mile Song*, 202–5.

32  Truax, *Acoustic Communication*, 66.

33  In terms of mating calls and reproductive cycles, humpback whales have been studied most extensively. See Tyack, "Implications for Marine Mammals," and Rothenberg, *Thousand Mile Song*.

34  Truax, *Acoustic Communication*, 84.

35  Ibid., 125.

36  World Soundscape Project, quoted in Truax, *Acoustic Communication*, 87.

37  Truax, *Acoustic Communication*, 84.

38  Ibid., 94.

39 Ibid., 93–108.

40 Ibid., 124. The problem of noise obviously predates industrialization: as scholars such as Emily Cockayne have shown, noise problems in urban areas could as easily originate with the cries of animals and humans as with mechanical sounds. However, using acoustic mapping and other techniques, Truax convincingly demonstrates that the power and reach of amplified sounds reconfigure soundscapes in specific ways that differ from the types of noise issues on which Cockayne concentrates.

41 Bijsterveld, "Booming Business."

42 Payne, *Among Whales*, 359–402.

43 Stocker, *Now Hear This*, 7.

44 Weilgart, "Impacts," 1106–9.

45 Truax, *Acoustic Communication*, 110.

46 For instance, see Cockayne, "Noisy."

47 Sterne, *Audible Past*, 92.

48 Rice, *Seeing the World*, 16.

49 Weilgart, "Impacts," 1103.

50 Whitehead, "How might we study culture?" 128.

51 Weilgart, "Impacts," 1102.

52 Rice, *Seeing the World*, 20.

53 Clark et al.'s models of acoustic ecology also begin to conceptualize how different beings or species inhabit multiple overlapping but distinct acoustic spaces: "At any one time an individual animal has multiple acoustic spaces, some dominated by factors operating within the biological, evolutionary domain (e.g. receiver characteristics including hearing abilities as well as source level, directivity, and frequency band of a calling conspecific) and some dominated by physical factors operating outside of an evolutionary domain (e.g. water depth, sound velocity profile, substrate composition, backscatter), and some of which are co-dependent and co-varying." Clark et al., "Acoustic Masking," 204.

54 Dreams and visions are an accepted form of traditional knowledge in much of the North American arctic, and often figure in traditional storytelling. These same traditional stories also often have marine mammals and other animals as characters.

55 Brower, *Whales, They Give Themselves*, 156.

56 Ibid.

57 Ibid., 158–60.

58 For example, see Bodenhorn, "Fall Whaling in Barrow"; Hess, *Gift of the Whale*; and Kalland and Sejerson, *Marine Mammals and Northern Cultures*.

59 Oviok, quoted in Bodenhorn, "Fall Whaling in Barrow," 280–1.

60 Noongwook et al., "Traditional Knowledge," 52.

61 Kalland and Sejerson, 147.

62 Ibid., 146–50.

63 Such prescriptions are common across the arctic – for example, David S. Lee and

George W. Wenzel describe various ways in which Inuit go to considerable effort to hunt narwhal in low-noise environments. See Lee and Wenzel, "Narwhal hunting."

64  See Noongwook et al., "Traditional Knowledge."

65  U.S. Bureau of Land Management, "Northeast National Petroleum Reserve," 3–138.

66  Ibid., 3–109.

67  Roman, *Whale*, 160.

68  Rothenberg, *Thousand Mile Song*, 19.

69  It could alternatively be argued that bird songs are equally complex and that whale calls do not prove that cetaceans have a special intelligence; what is important here is that a complex of cultural and political factors caused whale songs to be articulated with a set of beliefs about whales as intelligent and sentient beings.

70  Roman, *Whale*, 91.

71  Rothenberg, *Thousand Mile Song*, 18.

72  Labelle, "Seeking Ursound," 204.

73  Dolar, *Voice and Nothing More*, 39–42.

74  Calarco discusses voice in a Western philosophical tradition as passage from animality to humanity. Calarco, *Zoologies*, 81–2.

75  Dolar, *Voice and Nothing More*, 42–56.

76  Only whales and human beings have this particular array of cells, responsible for empathy, intuition, and sudden gut reactions, in the frontopolar cortex and anterior cingulate cortex of their brains. See Rothenberg, *Thousand Mile Song*, 160.

77  See, for example, Clark et al., "Acoustic Masking."

78  One particularly interesting case study examined the soundscape of the fishing village of Lesconil, where, depending on the weather conditions and prevailing winds (the "solar wind" cycle), townspeople could generally hear the fishing boats offshore in the afternoons and evenings, but not the morning. Truax, *Acoustic Communication*, 85–6.

79  Clark et al. "Acoustic Masking," 203.

80  Ibid., 219.

81  The North Atlantic Right Whale is a case in point – the small remaining population is heavily affected by commercial shipping traffic and "acoustic smog," and its numbers have never rebounded. Whale mortality is caused primarily by collisions with ships and entrapment in fishing nets – both possibly related to hearing damage. See Moore, "Whither the North Atlantic Right Whale?"

82  Grossman, "Noise Reduces Ocean Habitat."

83  Tyack, "Implications for Marine Mammals," 551–2.

84  For a listing of some of the specific studies of ototoxic effects on arctic marine mammals from these particular industrial activities in the Arctic, see Weilgart, "Impacts," 1101 and bibliography.

85  Marcoux, "Social Behavior."

86  Clark, et al., "Acoustic Masking," 218.

87  Weilgart, "Impacts," 1092.

88  Dolman et al., *Oceans of Noise*, 66 discusses the relevant Marine Mammal Protection Act provisions in more detail.

89  Okeanos Foundation, *Report of the Workshop on Alternative Technologies*.

90  Fournier, "B.C.'s Killer Whales."

91  In February 2012 this ruling was upheld in the Canadian Federal Court of Appeal. However, in spring of 2012 significant changes were made to the Species at Risk Act and other environmental legislation (for example, the existing Canadian Environmental Assessment was abolished/replaced) via an omnibus budget bill, c-38. Details on these changes and their impacts are unavailable at press time. However, as the Canadian government has chosen to dismantle the entire ocean contaminants program of the Department of Fisheries and Oceans, the data necessary to administer a broader definition of critical habitat, as per the ruling, will be increasingly difficult to come by, making the ruling more difficult to enforce, even if the provisions it refers to remain in the Act.

92  See "Our Solutions."

93  Mittelstaedt, "What Amount of Nature."

# Frozen Refractions: Text and Image Projections on Ice (2010)

*Sarah T. Renshaw*

*Sarah T. Renshaw*

DESCRIPTION/ARTIST'S TEXT

Suspended in the air an image is formed in light – water holds it in place, frozen. On one side photographs are projected onto and through the ice tablet. On the other side is text from *Matter and Memory* by Henri Bergson. Images capture something in time. Projecting photographs onto ice gives them a transience that photography generally denies. The melting ice is a metaphor for memory. The images are viewed through the ice and are distorted in the material. Time affects the image as the ice thins and transforms back into a liquid state.

Cross-pollination occurs when sensory impressions of the past intermingle with sensory perceptions of the present. In the initial response to an immediate perception, the mind is instinctively drawn to similar past experiences that in some way relate to what is presently being experienced. Perception (immediate sensory response) brings us into matter, while memory (recollection of past sensory experiences) draws us towards mind.

The past inscribes itself into matter in much the same way it inscribes itself upon the mental process of recollection. The passage of time impresses upon matter, leaving a trace of history. The history recorded in matter by stains, cracks, gouges, and various other markings, is not as clearly written as a history recorded in text, but this material history provides a different kind of reading – one that is perceived directly by the senses. The interpretation of any recorded history will eventually erode with the distortion of perspectives created by the passage of time.

Plates 12–13

Selected images from: *Frozen Refractions: Text and Image Projections on Ice* (2010), artwork by Sarah T. Renshaw (melting canvas of ice, suspended on wire outdoors on a winter evening, projected images and text).

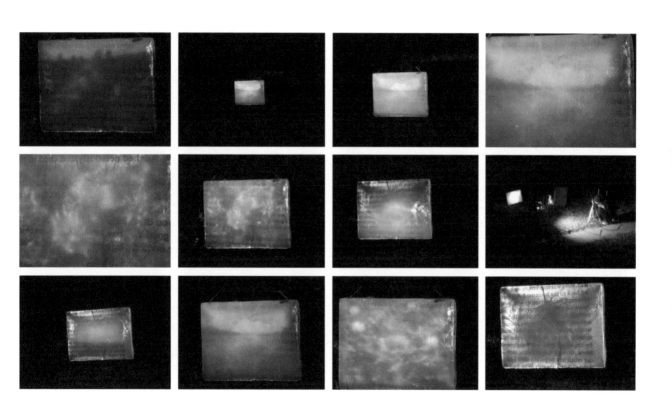

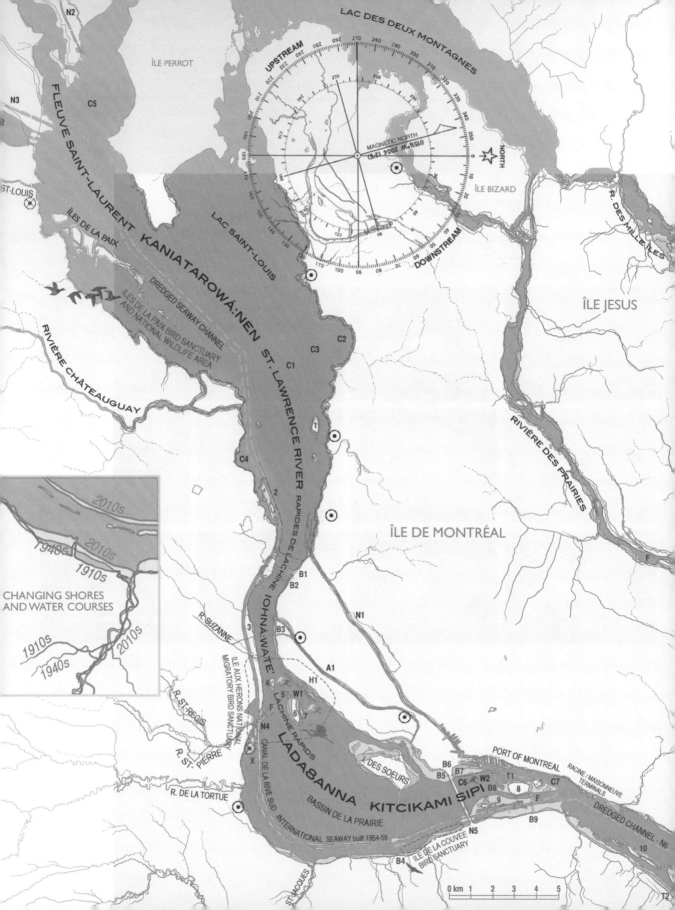

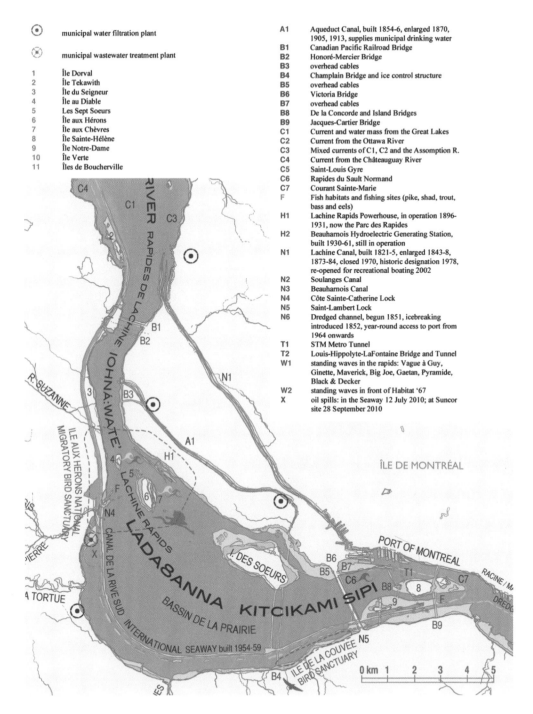

⊙ municipal water filtration plant

⊗ municipal wastewater treatment plant

1   Île Dorval
2   Île Tekawith
3   Île du Seigneur
4   Île au Diable
5   Les Sept Soeurs
6   Île aux Hérons
7   Île aux Chèvres
8   Île Sainte-Hélène
9   Île Notre-Dame
10  Île Verte
11  Îles de Boucherville

A1  Aqueduct Canal, built 1854-6, enlarged 1870, 1905, 1913, supplies municipal drinking water
B1  Canadian Pacific Railroad Bridge
B2  Honoré-Mercier Bridge
B3  overhead cables
B4  Champlain Bridge and ice control structure
B5  overhead cables
B6  Victoria Bridge
B7  overhead cables
B8  De la Concorde and Island Bridges
B9  Jacques-Cartier Bridge
C1  Current and water mass from the Great Lakes
C2  Current from the Ottawa River
C3  Mixed currents of C1, C2 and the Assomption R.
C4  Current from the Châteauguay River
C5  Saint-Louis Gyre
C6  Rapides du Sault Normand
C7  Courant Sainte-Marie
F   Fish habitats and fishing sites (pike, shad, trout, bass and eels)
H1  Lachine Rapids Powerhouse, in operation 1896-1931, now the Parc des Rapides
H2  Beauharnois Hydroelectric Generating Station, built 1930-61, still in operation
N1  Lachine Canal, built 1821-5, enlarged 1843-8, 1873-84, closed 1970, historic designation 1978, re-opened for recreational boating 2002
N2  Soulanges Canal
N3  Beauharnois Canal
N4  Côte Sainte-Catherine Lock
N5  Saint-Lambert Lock
N6  Dredged channel, begun 1851, icebreaking introduced 1852, year-round access to port from 1964 onwards
T1  STM Metro Tunnel
T2  Louis-Hippolyte-LaFontaine Bridge and Tunnel
W1  standing waves in the rapids: Vague à Guy, Ginette, Maverick, Big Joe, Gaetan, Pyramide, Black & Decker
W2  standing waves in front of Habitat '67
X   oil spills: in the Seaway 12 July 2010; at Suncor site 28 September 2010

Plate 14

Evolving qualitative basemap of the rapids compiled by Cecilia Chen from diverse sources (see the bibliography for full details). Among other water-focused gestures, note that the compass rose also indicates upstream and downstream, that overlapping lines show how the shores have changed, and that different colours distinguish water masses from different currents from the St Lawrence, the Châteauguay, and the Ottawa rivers.

Taste the $ource (while supplies last)
2006–present

*Emily Rose Michaud*

DESCRIPTION/ARTIST'S TEXT

A freshwater mermaid offers a taste of her treasured collection of rivers and lakes from various regions of Quebec. Some water samples are out of stock, some taste like blueberry roots and rocks – a rare experience as the commodification of water accelerates and sources of clean water become harder to find. These performances address water at first from an emotional and gustatory place, and then allow the audience to form their own response to the broader social and political issues found within.

Plates 15–17
Images from *Taste the $ource (while supplies last)* 2006–present. A series of performances by Emily Rose Michaud (water, various labelled jars and bottles, mermaid costume, table, signs).

Plate 16

Plate 17

# Jellyfish Science, Jellyfish Aesthetics:
# Posthuman Reconfigurations of the Sensible

*Stacy Alaimo*

> They're slimy, oozy and flimsy. Misconceptions abound. They lead lives of
> mystery, even to scientists who devote years studying their secretive habits.
> Jellyfish and other gelatinous animals like comb jellies, pteropods and
> salps are actually among the most beautiful creatures of the sea.
> (The Jellies Zone)[1]

> . . . is it right
> to call them creatures,
> these elaborate sacks
>
> of nothing?
> (Mark Doty, "Difference")

> The collective is always trembling because it has left outside all that
> it needed to take into account to define itself as a common world.
> (Bruno Latour, *The Politics of Nature*)

Jellyfish and other gelatinous creatures[2] float beyond human comprehension in a zone
where science and aesthetics flow together in baffling ways. As Steven Haddock of the
Monterey Bay Aquarium Research Institute notes, the end of the nineteenth century
experienced a "golden age" of research on jellyfish and other gelatinous zooplankton.
Illustrations by Ernst Haeckel and others were "inspired as much by the beauty of the
organisms as by functional scientific interpretation."[3] Haddock predicts that the start
of the twenty-first century will also become a golden age of research on what he terms,
simply, "gelata." Scientific advances in molecular tools as well as in collection techniques such as the use of deep-sea submersibles and video enable better study of these
creatures. Global climate change and massive overfishing impel research on how gelata
affect and are affected by marine environments. In addition, Haddock argues, basic

research on cnidarians has provided fluorescent proteins and photo-proteins that are now "indispensible molecular and biomedical tools."[4]

Even as there are several reasons for scientists to be interested in gelata, the scientific representation of these creatures is extraordinarily aesthetic. Moreover, against the still-prevalent casting of jellyfish as monsters and beachgoers' experience of their sting, highly aestheticized representations of jellyfish in video and still photography are proliferating in popular culture. These captivating images make me wonder what it means to bring these elusive creatures – many only recently discovered in the deep seas – into view. Also, what are the ramifications, for environmentalism and for critical animal studies, of posing living creatures as "art"? Unlike the early twentieth-century "Teddy Bear taxidermy" that Donna Haraway critiqued, in which specimens were stuffed to serve as "prophylactics" against "decadence,"[5] the extraordinarily beautiful photos and videos of jellies seem the very image of decadence – flimsy, insubstantial, excessive, spectacularly varied, breathtakingly beautiful. If, as Jacques Rancière argues, "politics is an intervention into the visible,"[6] is it possible that the current "bloom" of jellyfish images opens up space for gelata and other non-mammalian sea creatures to provoke posthuman modes of environmental concern? Do these watery creatures, barely distinguishable from their surroundings, suggest the need for a more aquatic environmentalism to emerge, not only from a global mapping of toxic flows and the ravages of industrial extractions but also from some scarcely possible engagement with the heretofore unknown and still barely known if not potentially unknowable forms of life that inhabit the depths?

Animal studies scholarship tends to emphasize animal-human relations, encounters, and similarities. Tom Tyler and Manuela Rossini entitle their new collection *Animal Encounters*. Most notably, Donna Haraway's *Companion Species Manifesto* insists upon the co-constitution and co-evolution of humans and dogs. Furthermore, from Charles Darwin's vivid tales of animal antics and abilities in *The Descent of Man* to the recent work of Marc Bekoff, who documents the emotional lives of animals, those who attempt to include animals within ethical consideration have stressed the similarities between various animals and humans. Jellyfish and other gelatinous creatures whose bodies are 95 percent water, however, float at the far reaches of our ability to construct sturdy interspecies connections, thus posing both conceptual and ethical challenges. As Neil Shubin puts it in *Your Inner Fish*, "How can we try to see ourselves in creatures that have no nerve cord at all?"[7]

Even as we may question the compulsion to see ourselves in every creature, the animals dubbed mere "organized waters"[8] stretch the definition of life itself, as they seem to lack both substance and recognizable organs or features. Although much cultural theory has for the last several decades valued fluidity as a mode of ethical and political possibility, the extreme fluidity and fragility of jellyfish render them almost invisible, almost unrecognizable – at risk, in the human imagination, of being lost at sea. Indeed, siphonophores and jellyfish have been notoriously difficult for scientists to collect. Laurence Madin notes that it has been nearly impossible for scientists to distinguish separate animals within the "shapeless see-through gelatinous blobs" or the "unattractive jello-like mass" brought up in nets and trawls.[9] Another collector concurs: research trawling "reduces most siphonophores to a nondescript goo."[10]

Interestingly, as scientists have struggled to capture, collect, distinguish, and categorize these fluid forms of life, others have transported them from biology to art, rendering them distinct aesthetic objects. Even though people who experience jellyfish in the ocean often have difficulty distinguishing these soft and often translucent creatures from the water itself, photographic representations of jellyfish portray them as glittering "jewels," perfectly set against the sharply contrasting background of black water. Photographic collections, including *Jellies: Living Art*, *Amazing Jellies: Jewels of the Sea*, and the spectacular volume *The Deep: The Extraordinary Creatures of the Abyss*,[11] depict these creatures as stunningly beautiful and profoundly strange. In contrast to the environmental critiques of how standard nature photography objectifies and overly aestheticizes, resulting in the pejorative term "ecoporn,"[12] I would like to argue that these aesthetic presentations of fluid forms of life can be understood as manifestations of care, wonder, and concern. Thinking with these watery and elusive creatures – tracing the currents flowing through science, art, and environmental politics – may reveal an ethics implicit in the desire to distinguish them from the vast oceanic depths. By putting the jellies forward as distinct creatures, these representations may, in Rancière's terms, reconfigure the "partage du sensible," that is, reconfigure the division and distribution of the sensible, making gelata perceptible. Although Rancière's theory is deeply humanist, the current proliferation of stunning photos of jellies, many of which have only been recently discovered, suggests his notion of politics, which "consists in interrupting the distribution of the sensible by supplementing it with those who have no part in the perceptual coordinates of the community, thereby modifying the very aesthetico-political field of possibility."[13] The flimsy, fluid creatures seem unlikely forces within any aesthetico-political field. Gelata, however, may be more potent, both aesthetically and biologically, than they would seem. Even as ocean ecosystems are in crisis and a massive global extinction is underway, jellyfish are thriving. Some scientists claim that in certain areas jellyfish are taking a "joyride"; as "cockroaches of the sea," they are overpopulating the now-numerous marine dead zones, taking us back to a Paleozoic future of "rudimentary flagellate and jellyfish-dominated" ocean ecosystems.[14] Aesthetic attachments overlap and conflict with concern for ecosystem health and biodiversity, as many visual representations of jellies provoke pleasure and wonder that cannot be directly channeled into the ethics, politics, or practices of species protection.

Plate 18
"Discomedusae." Colour engraving by Ernst Heinrich Haeckel.

## Science, Aesthetics, and Fluid Captures

Gelatinous creatures are unlikely candidates for aesthetic attention. Marine scientists may bring up ctenophores in a net, but "only as the formless mystery snot that plankton biologists have always chucked over the side after picking out the hardy copepods."[15] Nevertheless, artists and scientists have long been drawn to jellyfish. Biologist and artist Ernst Haeckel's *Art Forms in Nature* (1904) includes several colourful plates featuring jellies. The "DISCOMEDUSAE: Desmonema Annasethe Haeckel," which he named in honour of his wife Anna Seth, becomes gynopomorphically transformed by Haeckel: "Its tentacles hung like blonde hair ornaments of a princess."[16] His luscious, ornate drawings, recognizable as Art Nouveau, could not be farther from twenty-first-century minimalist photos of jellies. Most of Haeckel's illustrations paint the gelata as solid and substantial; the Antomedusae and Peromedusae resemble *objets d'art*; the decorative forms arranged in a perfectly balanced, symmetrical manner.[17] His illustrations of the Leptomedusae, however, with its delicate blue-grey shading against a white background, suggests their translucence.[18]

The elegant black and white prints included in Elizabeth C. and Alexander Agassiz's *Seaside Studies in Natural History* (1865) intimate how difficult it is for humans to perceive and represent these creatures. Elizabeth C. Agassiz calls the jellies graceful, pretty, elegant, and exquisite. The illustrations, white etchings against a black background, are direct, yet striking. The sharp contrast of black and white seems to render the jellies distinct from their watery world; yet, by drawing only the outline of the creatures, Alexander Agassiz suggests they are nearly indistinguishable from the sea. Elizabeth Agassiz writes:

> The Oceania is so delicate and insubstantial, that with the naked eye one perceives it only by the more prominent outlines of its structure. We may see the outline of the disk, but not the disk itself, we may trace the four faint thread-like lines produced by the radiating tubes traversing the disk from the summit to the margin; and we may perceive, with far more distinctness, the four ovaries attached to these tubes near their base; we may see also the circular tube uniting the radiating tubes, and the tentacles hanging from it, and we can detect the edge of the filmy veil that fringes the margin of the disk. But the substance connecting all these organs is not to be distinguished from the element in which it floats, and the whole structure looks like a slight web of threads in the water, without our being able to discern by what means they are held together.[19]

In Agassiz's description, the jellies hover at the limits of human visual perception, as their insubstantial substance is at times "not to be distinguished from the element in which it floats." The delicacy of the creatures not only sparks wonderment but seems to set the terms for the encounter, as indicated by the repetition of what we may – or

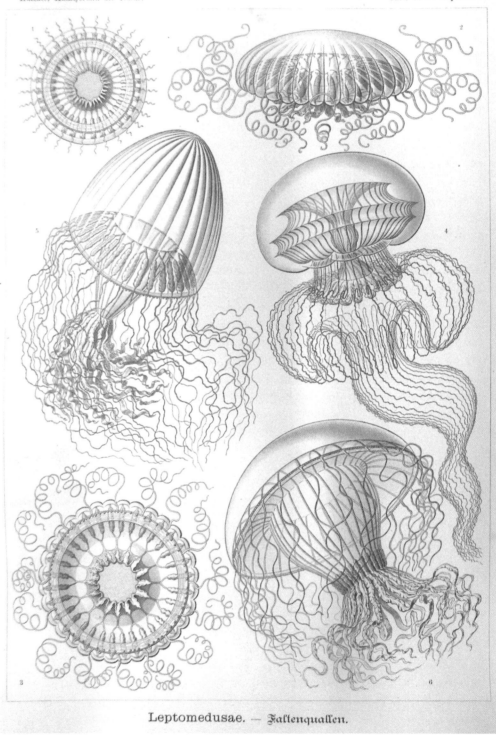

Leptomedusae. — Faltenquallen.

Plate 19
"Leptomedusae." Engraving by Ernst Heinrich Haeckel.

may not – "see," "trace," "perceive," or "detect." Thus, the fluid bodies exert a surprising influence over the human observer. Moreover, they silently subvert the determination of substance, impelling the naturalist to devise metaphors that she herself questions. Explaining the collection of phosphorescent jellyfish at night, she writes, "Our dirty, torn old net is suddenly turned to a web of gold, and as we lift it from the water heavy rills of molten metal seem to flow down its sides and collect in a glowing mass at the bottom."[20] But a few lines later she admits, "it would seem that the expression, 'rills of molten metal' could hardly apply to anything so impalpable as Jellyfish, but although so delicate in structure, their gelatinous disks give them a weight and substance."[21] Agassiz finds herself caught in a paradox whereby phosphorescence lends a perplexing mass to these otherwise transparent creatures, confusing the categories of solidity and liquidity, as light becomes heft.

The photographs of jellies appearing in William Beebe's 1926 *The Arcturus Adventure* and the 1934 *Half Mile Down* are sadly prosaic compared to the art of Haeckel or Alexander Agassiz. Beebe is best known as the explorer, naturalist, and aspiring scientist who descended in his bathysphere half a mile into the Caribbean in 1934. Historian Gary Kroll, calling Beebe the "ad man of natural history,"[22] documents how Beebe struggled to balance funding-generating publicity with serious scientific aspirations. Beebe begins *A Half Mile Down*, by stating: "We should all be happier if we were less completely obsessed by problems and somewhat more accessible to the esthetic and emotional appeal of our materials, and it is doubtful whether, in the end, the growth of biological science would be appreciably retarded."[23] Despite the wretched photos, Beebe's prose attempts to convey the aesthetic appeal of the creatures he has seen. "My inarticulateness and over-enthusiastic utterances may well be excused on the grounds of sheer astonishment at the unexpected richness of display."[24] The captions attempt to arouse an aesthetic appreciation for creatures whose photographs look more like blurry x-rays than a naturalist's illustrations. The caption for Figure 47 reads: "One of the most beautiful of the deep-sea jellyfish is Periphyllum. When brought up out of the eternal darkness it is rich turquoise and maroon."[25] But the photograph itself is a dull black-and-white image of a cone-shaped blob with awkward, spindly legs. Although Beebe includes narratives of discovery, fascination, and aesthetic appreciation of many sea creatures in *The Arcturus Adventure*, the photo of the unappealing, dull grey jellyfish in an onboard tank belies the caption that claims the Porpita is "One of the Most Beautiful of the Floating Jellyfish."[26] Despite the technical challenges, one particular photo of a "Four Inch Quad Jelly-Fish, Tamoya Haplonema, with Twelve Live Fish which were Living Inside It," artfully presents the jelly at a diagonal, its tentacles trailing behind, suggesting propulsion, with the twelve little fishes swimming below in a charming manner. The blurry softness of the image and the fluid shapes of the jelly evoke a tenderness.[27] Indeed, Beebe himself notes that even though we can "coldly analyze and apprehend" the sight of fish pouring out of the jelly, "we must stop to give an incredulous, unscientific gasp of wonder."[28]

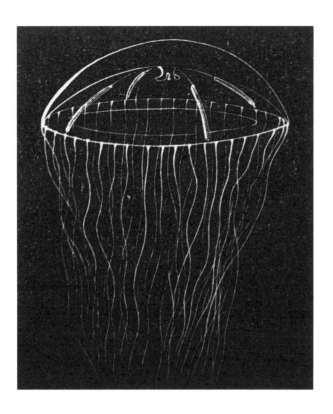

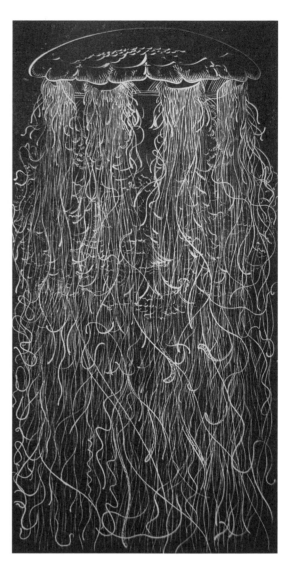

Figure 9.1
"Adult Oceania, natural size [when it averages
from an inch and a half to two inches in diameter]."
Drawing by A. Agassiz.

Figure 9.2
"Cynea arctica; greatly reduced in size."
Drawing by A. Agassiz.

Photography, especially underwater photography, has changed a great deal since Beebe's time, enabling biologists and photographers to take colour photos of jellies in situ and to display them on the Internet where the glowing screen conveys the translucence and even the phosphorescence of gelata. Scientists no longer need words to tell us that the jellies are beautiful creatures. Haddock's Figure 1, for example, portrays ten brightly coloured, glowing creatures – neon purple, blue, pink, and orange – with strikingly different shapes and structures.[29] Visual technologies have by now outpaced marine biology. As Sylvia Earle and other marine biologists remind us, at the start of the

Figure 9.3
"Four-inch Quad Jelly-fish, Tamoya haplonema, with Twelve Live Fish which were Living Inside It." Photograph by Floyd Crosby.

Figure 9.4
"Porpita, One of the Most Beautiful of the Floating Jelly-Fish." Photograph by Ernest Schoedsack.

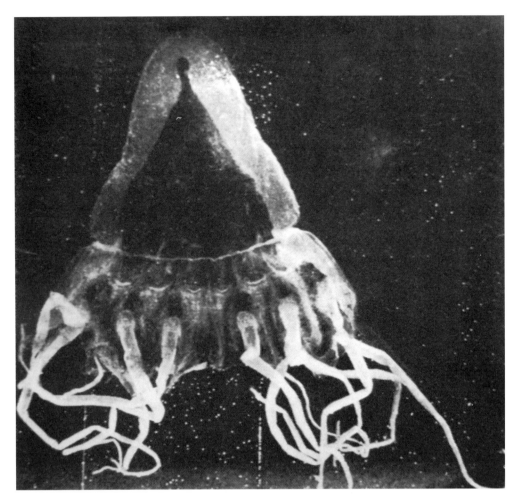

Figure 9.5
"One of the most beautiful of the deep-sea jellyfish is Periphyllum. When brought up out of the eternal darkness it is rich turquoise and maroon." Photograph by John Tee-Van.

twenty-first century, we still know surprisingly little about what inhabits the oceans, especially the deep seas. The similes posing the sea as outer space, which Beebe frequently invoked in the early twentieth century are still in use, although marine biologists now insist we know more about outer space than we do about our own planet's watery environments.

A surge in ocean research may change this state of affairs. The World Register of Marine Species and the Census of Marine Life, a ten-year project, culminating in 2010, are "cooperating to achieve their common goal of inventorying all described marine species by the end of 2010."[30] The business-like term "inventory" minimizes the colossal scope of these projects. Earle notes that the estimates for how many kinds of "plants, animals, microbes and other forms of life" exist in the sea "range from a million to a hundred million," making "the goal of the Census of Marine Life – taking stock of the diversity of life in the sea – one of the most ambitious undertakings in the history of humankind."[31] Despite the overwhelming number of species existing in the sea, the mode of representation that currently predominates is not that of charts of similar species crowded together, or representations of many different species that inhabit the same sort of marine habitat, but rather a portrait-like photo of one single specimen of one species, usually rendered in a hyper-real, strikingly aesthetic mode. Against the vast oceanic realms of the unknown, each species is framed with a certain amount of care.

The World Register of Marine Species (WORMS) aims to "provide an authoritative and comprehensive list of names of marine organisms, including information on synonymy."[32] The register's goal was "to capture all of the estimated 230,000 marine species by 2010, in synchrony with the completion of the Census of Marine Life programme, still 53,016 to go."[33] The photo album for Scyphozoa is an odd combination: rather ugly scientific photos of brownish or greyish jellyfish specimens lying dead in trays with dissecting tools poking them are mixed with bland photos of jellyfish in water or on the sand, and with artistic renditions, primarily on postage stamps. "Art" and "science" visually clash in this hodgepodge of representations. The vibrant photo of the oorkwal (*Aurelia aurita*), taken by Hans Hillewaert, stands as an exception to the rest of the rather clinical, serious photos. The oorkwal, a cobalt blue disk with white markings, glows against the black background. The album for Hydrozoa contains a similar mix of clinical-looking illustrations, plates from Joseph Van Beden (1844), postage stamps, and some spectacular photographs. Since the aim here is taxonomy, perhaps we are intended to look past the aesthetic hodgepodge of photographs, straightforward illustrations, historic plates, stamps, and contemporary high-definition photos – or to look through, as the visual representations are tools for the taxonomic goals. And yet, some of the photos are breathtakingly beautiful. Peter Schuchert's portrait of the Turritopsis rubra medusa, for instance, shows a neon-bright blue creature against a black background, allowing us to see through the medusa to its stunningly orange insides. We may wonder what the orange substance is – organs? food? – but we are not told. The perfectly symmetrical bell is set off by the wild tentacles, impossibly thin, with curly ends, and its position within the frame suggests a human portrait, even though the absence of face diverts our search for the visage toward a posthuman recognition.

Although the glowing, hyper-real spectacle of this and other similar photos of gelata seem at cross-purposes with the rational taxonomic project, their aesthetic power underwrites support for the scientific projects that enable them. Metanarratives of discovery buoy contemporary ocean science. What is discovered can be immediately promoted as valuable for its beauty or strangeness, whereas other sorts of values require more research. As Steven H.D. Haddock argues, "the beauty and mystery of these organisms has sparked broad interest, and the importance of gelata is appreciated now perhaps more than ever before."[34] The U.S. National Oceanic and Atmospheric Administration website, the "Ocean Explorer," features colorful photos of cnidaria, most of them close-ups, except for an "unknown species of jellyfish" whose grey body blends into the background of the lava field.[35] Another "unidentified jellyfish," is presented with no information about its size or about whether the green and white tentacles that appear to be glowing are actually doing so or whether the camera's flash has distorted the image. We are left with a psychedelic image devoid of context or framing – more aesthetic than scientific, yet seducing us into the arc of discovery.

The website for the Census of Marine Life includes a section on "Census in the Arts": "Census discoveries have proven to be an inspiration to artists around the world. The artwork here is a testimony to the excitement generated and the creativity it inspires when the natural and artistic worlds come together."[36] The page includes links to films and documentaries, exhibits, photographs, and sculpture. It may not be clear when scientific photographs become "art," but Kevin Raskoff's work is singled out as simultaneously that of art and science, as he is both a biologist studying the deep water medusae and an (art) photographer. It is his spectacular photo of a deep red Crossota norvegica jelly that graces the cover of the *World Ocean Census* book. BBC's Earth News features his photographs in "Strange Jellies of the Icy Depths."[37]

The Census of Marine Life website also endorses the work of French filmmaker Claire Nouvian, who "worked alongside Census scientists studying the continental margins to capture some amazing photographs for her exhibition 'The Deep.' The exhibit succeeds in relaying a great amount of information about life in the ocean depths, while capturing audiences' imaginations with its powerful and striking imagery."[38] Nouvian's preface to the massive book based on that exhibit, *The Deep: The Extraordinary Creatures of the Abyss*, tells how in 2001, after watching "a stunningly beautiful film" at the Monterey Bay Aquarium, her life "changed direction," as she became fascinated by creatures that she thought could not possibly be real. [39]

> I was dazzled . . . speechless . . . astounded . . .
> As crazy as it might seem, I had fallen in love at first sight . . . It was as though a
> veil had been lifted, revealing unexpected points of view, vaster and more
> promising . . . I imagined this colossal volume of water, cloaked in permanent
> darkness, and I pictured the fantastic creatures that swam there, far from our gazes,
> the surrealist results of an ever inventive Nature.[40]

Nouvian's enthusiasm, bordering on rapture, results in a work of equivalent intensity. *The Deep: The Extraordinary Creatures of the Abyss* is a stunning volume, combining essays by scientists with unrivalled photographs of the creatures. The images in the chapter "Gelatinous but Voracious Predators" portray a surprising diversity of shapes and types of gelata. The essays are often passionate about the creatures they describe, but it is the large, richly coloured, artfully composed photographs that transport their viewers to the place where Nouvian found herself "dazzled ... speechless ... astounded." One reviewer notes simply, "The images astonish."[41]

To be astounded or astonished is to be unmoored, cut loose from an established order of things, to find oneself floating somewhere as yet unmapped, where unexpected, unrecognizable forms of life seem to demand some sort of recognition and response. If, as Rancière puts it, "[T]he dream of a suitable political work of art is in fact the dream of disrupting the relationship between the visible, the sayable, and the thinkable without having to use the terms of a message as a vehicle," then Nouvian's photographs stage the "spectacle" that "does not fit within the sensible framework defined by a network of meanings."[42] These images of bizarre yet visually enticing creatures do not point toward an environmentalist response, say, the way that the polar bear floating on a shrinking iceberg, a bird covered in Gulf Coast oil, or even a chimp on an Endangered Species Chocolate bar do. The sense of dislocation that Nouvian's photos elicit may, according to Rancière, be useful. He argues that "political art cannot work in the simple form of a meaningful spectacle that would lead to an 'awareness' of the state of the world."[43] Instead, he suggests, political art produces a "double effect: the readability of a political signification and a sensible perceptual shock caused, conversely, by the uncanny, by that which resists signification."[44] Although Rancière's theory is not itself posthumanist,[45] we may wish to extend his vision in such a way as to consider the aqueous uncanny nature of the jellyfish portraits, which hover beyond sensible frameworks, such as those that would distinguish between nature, art, and science.

Jellyfish, pulsing beyond the "visible, the sayable, and the thinkable," disrupt and confuse categories with their quiet, understated, inexplicably minimalist mode of being. Judith Connor and Nora Dean, both with professional ties to the Monterey Bay Research Aquarium, declare, in their preface to *Jellies: Living Art*: "We used robotic vehicles to probe the ocean depths. We glimpsed a satellite's view of our blue planet. We studied worms and whales, seaweeds, and snails. But it was the jellies, the gelatinous ocean animals, that showed us living art in motion."[46] The science and technology of exploration and imaging give way here to the aesthetic qualities of jellies themselves, who perform as "living art." This lovely book gathers together photographs of living jellies, jellyfish paintings and sculptures, and first-person narrations of becoming captivated by the gelata. While the chapters devoted to "shape and size" and "color and pattern" render the jellies static art objects, the chapter "Dancing Water – Rhythm and Motion" compares the tempos and modes of locomotion of different jellyfish (a topic better reserved for a DVD perhaps). In a few instances, the sculptures are indistinguishable from the photos of actual jellyfish, and one living jellyfish is explicitly described as art: "the vivid colors of this Atolla take on an appearance of a glass sculpture."[47] The confusion between creatures and artworks frames the flimsy gelata as valuable treasures that are worthy of consideration; the aesthetic response provokes a sense of awe and the impulse to protect.

Nonetheless, the striking photographs of gelata and other sea creatures do, of course, invite the rather predictable, though still vital, critique of their commodification. The images provide instant aesthetic gratification to those whose feelings of connection, even *danger of aesthecisation and commodification*

*Status of jellies*

though genuine, veil the consumer relationship solidified as the coffee-table book. By transforming the jellies from their perplexing liquidity to a more reassuring solidity, the jellyfish no longer provoke the same ontological confusion and panic; the dry, stable photos no longer lure us into pelagic posthumanisms. Worse, the transcendence of the aesthetics removes these particular creatures from the now highly contested, highly fraught environmental political sphere where animals usually appear as threatened and endangered.

Both the aesthetic framing and the accompanying narratives of scientific discovery – as well as the ordinary person's encounter with photographs or aquarium exhibits – remove the jellies from their own ocean environments. This aesthetic segregation from politics and environment is worrisome, given the current surge in ocean conservation movements and the increasingly destructive industries of extraction and fishing. As Rancière explains, there are some versions of aesthetics that promise "a non-polemical consensual framing of the natural world."[48] The aesthetic capture of these creatures, then, implicitly promotes a consensus in which we unite in an appreciation of gelatinous beauty, free from fractious environmental concerns. Unlike a million other creatures, jellies neither ask to be delivered from the fate of extinction nor call us to change North American patterns of consumption, as they are not standard fare for most peoples in the West. Perhaps focusing our attention to these seemingly simple, peaceful creatures serves as an anodyne for the vast landscapes of environmental anxiety, as they become just another New Age packaging of nature for human stress relief.

The DVD *Jellies: The Art of Nature* would suggest as much; it offers up two hours of relaxing images of jellyfish, with no narration, allowing viewer to choose classical, "ambient," or "chill out" music. One reviewer at Amazon.com notes that s/he finds the DVD "mesmerizing": "it adds to the ambiance of any space and not only serves as a stunning background, but also as a source of escapism and retreat."[49] By painful contrast, the large Greenpeace book *Planet Ocean: Photo Stories from the 'Defending Our Ocean' Voyage* includes a photo of a white plastic bag floating among jellyfish, with a caption that explains that this bag may be "easily mistaken for jellyfish." The diaphanous beauty of the plastic bag, an allure that is metonymic with that of the jellyfish themselves, becomes treacherous as the bag may entangle or choke "animals such as turtles, albatross and sea lions that fatally misjudge its shimmering appeal."[50] This photo clearly implicates its viewer, offering up an aesthetically pleasing image of the ocean, only to shift to the perceptions of other species who may suffer the consequences of ingesting the plastic-mistaken-for-jellyfish. More broadly, it warns of the pernicious human modes of perception and consumption, as it subordinates human aesthetic pleasure to the more consequential perceptions of other creatures who are corporeally connected with refuse-ridden seas.

## A Gelatinous Posthumanism?

Notwithstanding the fact that aestheticized images may circulate free from networks of environmental concern, there are particular sorts of engagements with gelatinous creatures that seek to dissolve terra firma presumptions. Humans, as terrestrial creatures whose somewhat watery bodies are distinct from airy atmospheres, expect objects and creatures to be recognizably bounded and assuredly stable. Jellyfish – being watery – exist at the edge of the "visible, the sayable, and the thinkable," barely distinct from the seas that surround them, existing as flowing, pulsing, gelatinous, and just barely organized bodies. Jellies somehow live *as* the very element that surrounds them. (How does this make sense? How do *they* make sense?) Jellies, more than any other creature, would seem to embody Georges Bataille's view that animals live "like water in water," in a state of immanence that humans cannot experience. Tom Tyler critiques Bataille's formulation, arguing that his anthropocentrism "functions as a kind of self-fulfilling prediction" that forecloses "what it is possible for animals to experience, what it is possible for animality to be."[51] The fact that gelatinous creatures are extraordinarily different from homo sapiens could, predictably, be used to widen the abyss between the categories of human and animal. William J. Broad, for example, describes the Apolemia, a large siphonophore that he glimpses during his descent into the Monterey Canyon as "a remarkable adaptation to a place that had no boundaries, no turbulence, and no firm surfaces."[52] He describes another jellyfish in more disturbing terms: "The thing was formidable. Throbbing with slow pulsations, contracting and expanding its leathery bell as it moved through the water, dangling its giant tentacles, the creature looked ugly enough and powerful enough and strange enough to be an extraterrestrial from the Planet of the Jellies."[53] The fear-mongering portrayal underscores the potential for gelata to dissolve categorical assumptions. "Their transparency was so absolute that they almost seemed to defy existence, their body parts trembling on the verge of disappearance."[54]

But philosophical, literary, artistic, and scientific endeavours to understand what it would mean to be, to live as, to perceive as, water in water may also open up posthumanist horizons of possibility that are not structured as anthropocentric or dualistic. While Western humanist subjects have long imagined themselves as distinct from their environments,[55] as subjects acting on passive objects or resources surrounding them, the jellies exhibit another way of being in which the living creature is immersed within and inseparable from its watery world. Jakob von Uexküll, arguing that environment – time and space – differs for different living beings, discusses the deep sea medusa as an example of a creature who experiences a "simple environment." The "eight bell-shaped organs" of the medusa impel a constant "rhythmical up-and-down motion," causing Uexküll to conclude: "In the medusa's environment, the same bell always tolls, and this controls the rhythm of life."[56] His descriptions of the medusa's perceptions counter the "belief in the existence of one and only one world" – the world that humans presuppose.[57]

Uexküll's theory, which insists upon multiple worlds, surrounds the jellies with something that could be considered a posthumanist understanding, a capacious admission that a multitude of other creatures dwell as part of worlds that humans cannot readily or completely access or grasp. Three-quarters of a century later Terry Tempest Williams wonders what it would be like to be a jellyfish. Jellyfish, who have no eyes, nose, or tongue, do have touch receptors on their tentacles and mouths and some have light-sensitive organs. Tempest Williams, in her essay in *Jellies: Living Art*, writes: "Perhaps this is what moves me most about jellies – their sensory intelligence perceived through the clarity of their bodies, the great hunger that is sent outward through the feathery reach of their tentacles. Imagine the information sought and returned."[58] As watery creatures who experience their environs in ways that are utterly alien to humans, jellies stretch our ability to even recognize them as living beings. If the attempt to imagine what it is like to be a bat[59] is fraught with difficulties, how much more impossible is it to imagine being a jelly? Nonetheless, Tempest Williams asks, "What might we come to understand by imagining the world from a fluid point of view?" as she attempts to inhabit their ultimately inaccessible "alien sensibility."[60] Her poetic rendition of the jellies pulsates with single-word sentences: "Of the sea. Open sea. Transparent. Translucent. Transcendent. Bell and tentacles. Nothing hidden. A gelatinous body of nerves. Pulsating. Throbbing. Drifting."[61] Paradoxically, it is the very fact that "nothing is hidden" that makes the jellies so mysterious, so difficult to comprehend, so unnerving. Ron Broglio, in *Surface Encounters*, argues, "If we could think without an inside and outside, if we could be blunt and idiot enough to think without an abyss between humans and animals, we would arrive at another sort of site and productivity – another sort of thinking."[62] Gelatinous creatures, whose transparency allows us to literally *see through them* so that there is no "inside," and jellies, in particular, with their bell-shaped bodies that pull the "outside" waters within, float as extraordinary manifestations of the humanist caricature of the non-human that Broglio analyzes – the belief that animals lack "the substantiality found in the 'depth' of human interiority."[63] Existing in the depths yet seemingly without their own "depth" of secreted interiority, gelata, ever so gently, question the humanist desire for solid demarcations. With their apparent yet unfathomable "lack" of an inside, jellies may entice us into posthumanist states of wonder that extend through manifold modes of being.[64]

Tempest Williams, upon encountering the "shrine" of jellies in the Monterey Bay Aquarium, questions the value of human "gray matter": "Perhaps it is not enough to simply think our way through the world. More important, how do we sense it, absorb it? We have much to learn from these water-based creatures who so fully perceive the world around them in elegance and beauty."[65] The marvellous jellies, so immune to our interest, so utterly different from our primate and mammalian kin, challenge humans to imagine more fluid ontologies and more immanent and immediate modes of knowledge – literal absorption, as Tempest Williams suggests. It would be overreaching, certainly, to argue that encountering these visual images of gelatinous animals unravels the human, but these liquid life forms may well erode a humanist claim to sovereign knowledges, perspectives, or modes of being. Tempest Williams invites us to depart from our assumed proper place. "Can we allow ourselves to be transported by the ciliated plates of comb jellies, their shimmering iridescence that flashes red, yellow, and blue?"[66]

The representational transport of the jellies themselves – from their watery worlds to computer screens, films, and coffee table books – may well give us pause. They are so blatantly exposed to terrestrial eyes, so blithely conveyed from the depths. Is it invasive for us, as terrestrial creatures, to gaze at them? Cary Wolfe, writing about the work of artist Sue Coe, critiques the reinstallation of a sovereign humanist subject – "a subject from whom *nothing, in principle is hidden*." By contrast, he argues that "what must be witnessed is not just what we can see but also what we cannot see – indeed, that we cannot see."[67] While I generally agree that a critical posthumanism entails the critique of human sovereignty and a recognition of human epistemological limits, the photos of gelata in which nothing is hidden may provoke the paradoxical reaction that even when another creature is apparent – even transparent – we cannot ultimately "see" or comprehend that creature. Posthumanist humility may be provoked by wonder as much as by more deconstructive representational strategies. Moreover, within the vast waters of the seas, seeing something rather than nothing may itself be an ethical moment, not because everything is then available to the sovereign subject but because these aesthetic photo-captures of gelata may be a careful, restrained form of recognition.

In fact, photographers need to approach these subjects with special care, as their near transparency means that ordinary lighting techniques will not work: "Standard front lighting will only pass directly through the animal and not reflect sufficient light back to the camera and film to form a distinct image."[68] Within the context of global capitalism, which calculates value of the ocean in the economic terms of "goods and services"[69] and the consumerist discourse that translates ocean life into "seafood," aesthetic encounters may at least gesture toward a recognition that marine animals exist in and for themselves – even if they are unseen and unknown by terrestrial primates.

While cultural theory has long critiqued the image-spectator relation as a matter of consumption, there is, in fact, a crucial difference for the creatures who are literally, as opposed to figuratively, consumed. Moreover, while natural history and wildlife collections exhibit a disturbingly smooth transition from gun to camera, the camera need not harm the creatures it only metaphorically "captures." On the contrary, the desire for a photograph may actually require humans to practise care lest their subjects be destroyed. Contemporary divers photographing jellies, for example, must attend to their own breathing and movements: "The delicate tissue of jellies can be easily damaged or destroyed by careless movement of water or release of air from your regulator."[70]

Despite the concurrent objectification and commodification of the gelata as artistic images for humans, these framings may nonetheless be a way to encircle them with care and concern. Turning a blind eye only gives the sea over to commercial fishing and mining, which haul up catch and "bycatch" indiscriminately, in literal captures that do not respect creature boundaries or aquatic lives. Indeed, ocean conservation movements and organizations disseminate images of ocean creatures in order to battle the invisible plunder of the seas. The Marine Photobank, for example, an organization whose subtitle is "Advancing Ocean Conservation Through Imagery," provides free images of sea creatures, as well as photos of fishing methods, bycatch, pollution, oil spills, and other things that threaten ocean ecologies, because, as their website states, "Out of sight = out of mind."[71]

## Jacques Rancière and Bruno Latour at Sea

Jacques Rancière states, "Political demonstration makes visible that which had no reason to be seen; it places one world in another."[72] Political demonstration is obviously a profoundly humanist performance that makes no sense for the scientific/aesthetic endeavour of representing jellies and other sea creatures.[73] Indeed, it is important to consider that Rancière upholds a conceptual divide between humans and nonhuman animals, as Oliver Davis notes, by preserving "the clear-cut opposition between human speech and animal noises" that he inherits from Aristotle's theory of the origin of politics.[74] Yet, as struggles for ocean conservation gain momentum, the striking images of gelata open up spaces for their recognition – as creatures, as beings, as life forms, if not as political subjects themselves. These images may reconfigure the landscape (or seascape) of what may be perceived and included in consideration. Yves Citton, writing on Rancière, explains that the "reconfiguration of the *partage du sensible*, appears, within Rancière's system, as the founding moment of political subjectivation: whether I stand in front of a work of art or am involved in a social movement, the possibility of politics rests on such a moment when I am led to reconfigure the *partage du sensible* I have inherited from the majoritarian norm (along with its blind spots, its denial of rights, and its hierarchy of privileges.)"[75] Citton puts forth "art" and "social movements" as equivalent sites for the reconfiguration of the sensible. Such a formulation is particularly appropriate for the current moment in which the surge of images of ocean creatures may provoke a transformation in the parcelling out of the world, as anthropocentric and terrestrial hierarchies, blind spots, and denials may no longer be sensible. As Davis explains, in Rancière's work, to be "a political subject is to be heard and seen, and politics is the process of reconfiguring the ways in which subjects are heard and seen."[76] If there is any group most likely to remain unseen and unheard it would, undoubtedly, be that of non-human creatures. That is why, as unorthodox as it may be, it is tempting to think through the potential for Rancière's theory to be transformed by posthumanism. Rancière himself argues that political action "consists in showing as political what was viewed as 'social,' 'economic,' or 'domestic'"[77] – but we could add "scientific" to this list. We could also transport his theory to places – such as the deep seas and the open seas – that are not even remotely political, in that they have never been the habitat of the human. (This is not to say, however, that the oceans have not been the site of more invisible, less public, economic battles over resource extraction.) Rancière argues that "political action … consists in blurring the boundaries": "Politics is a way of re-partitioning the political from the non-political. This is why it generally occurs 'out of place,' in a place which was not supposed to be political."[78]

No doubt scientific projects such as the Census of Marine Life must maintain the stance of scientific objectivity; they are not at liberty to be blatantly political. But the scrambling of scientific discovery and aesthetic awe is more than a veiled strategy to gain political support. The visual images of astonishing gelata and other newly discovered ocean creatures convey an impression of the interconnected networks of science, aesthetics, and politics; the momentous revelation of worlds within worlds; and a vibrant, urgent call to repartition global space in such a way that even the pelagic expanses become political zones of concern. When Nouvian explains what she hoped to accomplish in her stunning collection of photographs, *The Deep: Extraordinary Creatures of the Abyss*, she describes her intentions in terms that are not unlike the reconfiguration of the sensible. "I dreamed of a book that would bring together all the most beautiful images captured in that deep-sea frontier, inaccessible to the majority of us; a book that would give voice to those who held the precious information about this singular environment, a book that would be accessible to all. In short, I dreamed of a book that would bring the deep to light!"[79] Nouvian brings previously unknown creatures to view, jumbling the modern categories of art and science as she ushers forth the creatures of the deep for consideration. When she asks, "Why doesn't somebody stop the world, for a minute, or maybe just a *second,* to announce that these creatures exist down here, at the very bosom of our planet,"[80] her imaginary staging of an earth-shattering announcement suggests that these "marvels" demand a dramatic reconfiguration of the boundaries of what matters.

Floating at the far reaches of human imagination and scientific discovery, the gelata reconfigure the sensible – *both* what we can perceive and what can make sense to us. If politics is "an aesthetic affair," because it is a "polemical form of reframing common sense,"[81] representations of jellies argue for the recognition of creatures at the far reaches of what an animal may be, thus suggesting currents that flow toward a bluer political sphere, a more pelagic posthumanism. The language that often accompanies photos of gelata, describing the creatures as strange, otherwordly, alien, weird, monstrous, or ethereal, establishes these animals as life forms that do not fit within the current configuration of the *sensible*. While Rancière's philosophy enables us to see these photographs as political, Bruno Latour's *Politics of Nature* enables us to imagine a political collective that includes the non-human: "Democracy can only be conceived if it can freely traverse the now-dismantled border between science and politics, in order to add a series of new voices to the discussion, voices that have been inaudible up to now, although their clamor pretended to override all debate: *the voices of nonhumans.*"[82] Drawing upon Rancière and Latour simultaneously – even as they may clash, in many respects – allows us to account for the aesthetic[83] and to open up space for non-human creatures and the scientists who represent them, a space that Rancière forecloses. As we hover in the midst of a veritable explosion of research in the deep sea, which has brought many gelata to light in both scientific and popular culture, it is striking to consider the roles that Latour charts for scientists and "moralists" in his collective. Scientists will contribute by possessing "instruments allowing the detection of invisible entities" and "moralists" will contribute by possessing "scruples that make it necessary to go looking for invisible entities and appellants."[84] The moralists, Latour explains, insist that "we can never call it quits": "With them, the collective is always trembling because it has left outside all that it needed to take into account to define itself as a common world."[85]

Aesthetic representations of some of these heretofore invisible entities may be indispensable for the collective that Latour imagines, as it is these arresting images that may reconfigure the conditions of possibility for the entry of the non-human. Indeed, the book of photographs presented by the Census of Marine Life and National Geographic is entitled, *Citizens of the Sea: Wondrous Creatures from the Census of Marine Life*. Nancy Knowlton introduces this volume of photos and essays by admitting that even after ten years of work, "most ocean organisms remain nameless and their numbers unknown."[86] And yet, she argues that these creatures be treated as citizens with a voice: "The sea today is in trouble. Its citizens have no voice and no vote in any national or international body, but they are suffering and need to be heard."[87] As weird and as anthropocentric as it may be to imagine salps and other pelagic denizens as citizens, such figurations may, possibly, contest the sense that the sea should remain global capitalism's treasure chest for legal plunder. As these unthought lives suddenly appear in highly mediated, highly aestheticized forms, they populate and lay claim to the vast waters.

## Ecology, Environmentalism, and Jellyfish Futures

As Finis Dunaway and others have noted, environmentalism in the United States has been largely propelled by aesthetic conservationism,[88] which depends upon visual representations of nature such as the photographs in Sierra Club calendars and coffee-table books. There is no direct path from gelatinous aesthetics to a blue-green environmental politics, however. As we have seen, most portrayals of jellyfish abstract them from their environment, as they pose one creature against a black background. This portrait-like style encourages a sense of encounter with a distinctive creature but it discourages an understanding of the animal's habitat. As aesthetic and taxonomic purposes converge in this style, the sea itself disappears, rendered transparent rather than substantial. The lack of scientific knowledge about gelata, their habitats, and their ecological relations may contribute to the minimalist, taxonomical "portraits": "Despite the prevalence of photographic images of gelata and their enthusiastic reception by some scientists, artists, and other fans, there are relatively few scientific experts on jellyfish due to "meagre funding in this area."[89] Even basic information about most species, including what they eat and what their polyp stage looks like, is unknown.[90] Their "strange biology," according to Daniel Pauly, has hampered their integration "into the mainstream of marine biology and fisheries research."[91] The role of jellies within their ecosystems remains unknown: "few marine ecosystem models currently include jellyfish, and those that do rarely capture their complex life history and ecology."[92] Moreover, the habitat of many jellies – the pelagic zone (the open seas) – is itself difficult for terrestrials to fathom, as it extends not only horizontally, in vast dimensions, but also vertically, in layers differentially characterized by water pressure and light. Jellies, which live without rigid boundaries, are metonyms of the vast, unthinkable, pelagic expanses.

Although the jellyfish photos represent them as marvels and treasures, they are actually not rare, or fragile, or endangered. The predominant scientific view has been that environmental degradation and climate change have actually resulted in increases, not decreases, of jellyfish populations. Stories such as "Attack of the Blobs," published in *Nature: News and Comments*, report that "an invasion of stinging moon jellyfish, some of which reached the size of bicycle wheels," recently greeted surfers in Florida; and the "gargantuan Nomura's jellyfish" "plagues" Japanese waters, "hampering fishing crews and even causing one boat to capsize."[93] The viewer floats in a puzzling place. Elizabeth Gowell's small book entitled *Amazing Jellies: Jewels of the Sea* introduces jellyfish as among the most "beautiful and unusual animals on earth," treating us to a feast of diminutive but captivating photos. *Amazing Jellies* concludes with the all-too-familiar interpellating moment – a chapter entitled "What You Can Do to Help" – which, oddly, enlists us, not to save these creatures from extinction, but, instead, to help make the ocean healthier to prevent the "population explosions in jellies."[94] While E.O. Wilson, in *The Future of Life*, depicts each species as a "masterpiece" in order to persuade us that we must protect biodiversity and curb the current mass extinction,[95] Gowell similarly depicts the gelata as "jewels" – but as jewels that are in no need of safeguarding. Similarly, in *The World Ocean Census*, a striking photo of an Aequororea macrodactyla is accompanied by the following caption, in which the comparison to the maligned cockroach clashes with the invocation of the aesthetic: "Will the ocean of the future be dominated by jellyfish – known as the cockroaches of the sea because of their ability to thrive under adverse conditions? Shown here is a beautiful example of this adaptable species."[96] Aesthetic pleasure and environmental panic clash in the National Science Foundation's multimedia work "Jellyfish Gone Wild," which warns: "when jellyfish populations run wild, they may jam hundreds and perhaps even thousands of square miles with their pulsating, gelatinous bodies," harming "fisheries, fish farms, seabed mining operations, desalination plants and ships" and even swimmers.[97] The colourful, mesmerizing, drifting series of jellyfish images that accompany the text, however, upstage the warnings. The fear of a clear planet is also provoked by *Discover* magazine's question, "Do Jellyfish Rule the World?"[98] as well as by the ominous news that "'Immortal' Jellyfish Swarm World's Oceans": "A potentially 'immortal' jellyfish species that can age backward – the Benjamin Button of the deep – is silently invading the world's oceans, swarm by swarm."[99]

Such reports of overabundance[100] of gelata disrupt a straightforward relation between the reconfiguration of the sensible and a particular environmental campaign. Notwithstanding the fact that the photographs embody a simple taxonomy of distinct creatures, the broader, more confusing questions about the role of jellyfish within ocean ecologies that are increasingly affected by overfishing, trawling, mining, oil drilling and other extractive industries, climate change, and acidification shifts our attention from "matters of fact" to matters of concern of political ecology. As Latour puts it: "it shifts from certainty about the production of risk-free objects (with their clear separation between things and people) to *uncertainty* about the relations whose unintended consequences threaten to disrupt all orderings, all plans, all impacts."[101] Despite the often-nostalgic narratives of discovery that accompany twenty-first century encounters with dazzling, mysterious gelata, these stories and images must ultimately circulate within the swirling naturecultures of risk, uncertainty, and radical interconnection inhabited by creatures of both land and sea. As these shimmering, pulsing, aqueous creatures provoke aesthetic responses, those responses may become entangled in complicated networks of concern that link human practices and politics with the lives of creatures we can barely begin to imagine, making space for more pelagic posthumanisms.

NOTES

1  From "Photographing Gelatinous Zooplankton," The Jellies Zone. http://jellieszone.com/

2  What most people would commonly consider "jellyfish" are actually animals in two different phyla, Ctenophora and Cnidaria. There are many more types of gelatinous creatures than there are true jellyfish; these animals exist within at least eight phyla. I will use the term "gelata," following Steven Haddock's use: "Here the term gelata is offered as a collective noun to describe the polyphyletic assemblage of medusae, siphonophores, ctenophores, radiolarians, urochordates, molluscs, and worms that eke out a planktonic existence. It is meant to have no taxonomic implication, but rather to evoke these diverse groups of non-crustacean macroplankton that are too fragile to sample with conventional oceanographic methods." Haddock, "A Golden Age of Gelata," 549.

3  Haddock, "A Golden Age of Gelata," 551.

4  Ibid., 555.

5  Haraway, *Primate Visions*, 55.

6  Rancière, *Dissensus*, 37.

7  Shubin, *Your Inner Fish*, 113.

8 Madin, "Gelatinous but Voracious Predators," 103.

9 Ibid.

10 "Siphonophores," n.p.

11 Connor and Deans, *Jellies: Living Art*; Gowell, *Amazing Jellies: Jewels of the Sea*; and Nouvian, *The Deep*.

12 For an excellent history, analysis, and discussion of "ecoporn" see Bart Welling, "Ecoporn."

13 Rockhill, "Translator's Introduction," 3.

14 Richardson, et al, "The Jellyfish Joyride," 318.

15 Kunzig, *Mapping the Deep*, 184.

16 Weissman, "Ernst Haeckel," n.p.

17 Haeckel, *Art Forms*, Tafel 38 and 46.

18 Ibid., Tafel 36.

19 Agassiz, *Seaside Studies*, 53.

20 Ibid., 88.

21 Ibid.

22 Kroll, *America's Ocean Wilderness*, 69.

23 Beebe, *Half Mile Down*, xv–xvi.

24 Ibid., 171.

25 Ibid., Figure 47.

26 Beebe, *The Arcturus Adventure*, Figure 34.

27 Beebe, *Beneath Tropic Seas*, 87.

28 Ibid., 86.

29 Haddock, "A Golden Age of Gelata," Figure 1.

30 WORMS. World Registry of Marine Species, n.p.

31 Earle, "Forward," 12.

32 WORMS. World Registry of Marine Species, n.p.

33 Ibid.

34 Haddock, "A Golden Age of Gelata," 554.

35 NOAA. National Oceanic and Atmospheric Administration (United States), "Ocean Explorer," n.p.

36 Census of Marine Life, n.p.

37 Walker, "Strange Jellies of the Icy Depths," n.p.

38 Census of Marine Life, n.p.

39 Nouvian, *The Deep*, 11.

40 Ibid., 12.

41 Glover, "Worms who Eat Whales," 11.

42 Rancière, *Politics*, 63.

43 Ibid.

44 Ibid.

45 I am not alone in thinking that Rancière's theory could be extended beyond the

parameters of the human. Jane Bennett writes that Rancière has said in public that (in her words) "nonhumans do not qualify as participants in a demos." Despite his statement, however, Bennett contends that "even against his will, so to speak, Rancière's model contains inklings of and opportunities for a more (vital) materialist theory of democracy." One of these opportunities arises, Bennett explains, "when Rancière chooses to define what counts as political by what effect is generated: a political act not only disrupts, it disrupts in such a way as to change radically what people can 'see': it repartitions the sensible; it overthrows the regime of the perceptible. Here again the political gate is opened enough for nonhumans (dead rats, bottle caps, gadgets, fire, berries, metal) to slip through." Bennett, *Vibrant Matter*, 106–7. I think it is important, however, to distinguish non-human creatures from objects, even as it is becoming a thornier theoretical enterprise to do so. My work in new materialism has explored how all sorts of substances, objects, and systems manifest material agencies, but as someone committed to the well-being of nonhuman animals I would distinguish – ethically, politically, and ontologically – living creatures from humanly made objects, despite the undeniable boundary-blurring between living and nonliving, the evolved and the manufactured, the artifacts of "nature" and "culture." The overlaps and divergences between new materialisms, feminist materialisms, posthumanisms, animal studies, the non-human turn, object oriented ontologies, and vitalisms, demand careful debate and consideration.

46  Connor and Dean, *Jellies*, 8.

47  Ibid., 54.

48  Rancière, *Dissensus*, 119.

49  Lesser Knowns, Review, n.p.

50  Holden, *Planet Ocean*, 109.

51  Tyler, "Like Water in Water," 278.

52  Broad, *The Universe Below*, 237.

53  Ibid., 232.

54  Ibid., 239.

55  In *Bodily Natures: Science, Environment, and the Material Self* (2010), I propose the concept of "trans-corporeality" to counter the assumption that the human is separate from the material flows and agencies of the wider world.

56  von Uexküll, *A Foray into the Worlds of Animals and Humans*, 54, 74.

57  Ibid., 54.

58  Tempest Williams, "Foreword," 10.

59  See Nagel, "What Is it Like to Be a Bat?"

60  Tempest Williams, "Foreword," 10, 13.

61  Ibid., 9.

62  Broglio, *Surface Encounters*, 124.

63  Ibid., xvi. Contemplating the jellies reveals some surprising resonances between Broglio and Rancière. Broglio argues that "material surfaces offer a means of thinking

about humans an animals outside the hegemony of the privileged interiority of the human subject." And Rancière describes his method as thinking in "terms of horizontal distributions," rather than searching "for the hidden beneath the apparent," since that establishes "a position of mastery." Broglio, *Surface Encounters*, 85. Rancière, *The Politics of Aesthetics*, 49.

64 For more on oceanic posthumanisms see my essay "Violet-Black: Ecologies of the Abyssal Zone," which explores how prismatic ecologies may lure us into less anthropocentric, less terrestrial modes of knowledge, politics, and ethics (n.p).

65 Tempest Williams, "Foreword," 10.

66 Ibid., 13.

67 Wolfe, *What Is Posthumanism*, 167.

68 "Photographing," n.p.

69 World Ocean Council, n.p. The World Ocean Council's number is between six and twenty-one trillion U.S. dollars.

70 "Photographing," n.p.

71 Marine Photobank, n.p.

72 Rancière, *Dissensus*, 38.

73 See note 43, above.

74 Davis, *Jacques Rancière*, 92.

75 Citton, "Political Agency," 123.

76 Davis, 91.

77 Rancière, "The Thinking of Dissensus: Politics and Aesthetics," 4.

78 Ibid.

79 Nouvian, *Jacques Rancière*, 12.

80 Ibid, 11.

81 Rancière, "Afterword," 277.

82 Latour, *Politics of Nature*, 69.

83 There is not enough space here to sort through the significant differences between the theories of Latour and Rancière. But I should briefly note that I see Rancière's notion of the reconfiguration of the sensible as a productive counterpoint to the way in which Latour's proposal for a collective of humans and nonhumans in *The Politics of Nature* gives short shrift to aesthetic, artistic, and literary forces. The groups that make "contributions" to the "houses" in Latour's collective include scientists, politicians, economists, and moralists. This is not to say that Latour's entire body of work ignores art (or artifacts). His recent book, *On the Modern Cult of the Factish Gods*, for example, addresses artistic, religious, and scientific images.

84 Ibid., 162.

85 Latour, *Politics of Nature*, 158.

86 Knowlton, *Citizens of the Sea*, 9.

87 Ibid., 9.

88 Dunaway, *Natural Visions*.

89  Richardson et al., "Jellyfish Joyride," 320.

90  Ibid.

91  Pauly et al., "Jellyfish in Ecosystems," 82.

92  Richardson et al., "Jellyfish Joyride," 320.

93  Schrope, "Marine Ecology: Attack of the Blobs," n.p.

94  Gowell, *Amazing Jellies*, 42.

95  Wilson, *The Future of Life.*

96  Crist et al., *World Ocean Census*, 233.

97  "Jellyfish Gone Wild," n.p.

98  Mallon, "Do Jellyfish Rule the World?" 42–7.

99  Than, "'Immortal' Jellyfish Swarm Worlds Oceans," n.p.

100  Robert H. Condon et al., in "Questioning the Rise of Gelatinous Zooplankton in the World's Oceans," challenge the idea that "the global ocean ecosystems are thought to be heading toward being dominated by 'nuisance' jellyfish," noting that many reports are unreliable, sensationalistic, based on too little data and/or hampered by inadequate historical memory. They conclude: "A clear need exists to assess historical, current, and future trends in medusa, ctenophore, and salp abundance across the world's oceans, as well as their roles in ecosystems, and the societal and ecosystemic consequences of their proliferation. Consequently, we are creating a global database of gelatinous zooplankton records (the Jellyfish Database Initiative [jedi]), compiled from as many records as possible, contributed by ourselves; by researchers worldwide; and from online databases of zooplankton records such as the Ocean Biogeographic Information System (*www.iobis.org*; see Grassle 2000), scientific literature, and historical records (e.g., nineteenth- and early twentieth-century expedition reports)."

101  Latour, *Politics of Nature*, 25.

## Alsek Lake

*Melanie Siebert*


59° 11′ 06″ N
138° 10′ 38″ W

I wake ancient in the night, ice-kicked, hunkered down
under the thunder-flask, glaciers calving bergs,
drop-boiling three miles away. Rough-tongued,
relentless, the waves trundle in, bucking
the ear's long-handled boom. Bowl of a lake
scummed with ten thousand years of ice. The chest
caves open, glacial ages roll over,
become drinkable. Drink this:
each breath a fist, each fist a hobo,
useless and forgettable.
Listen under,
              way under the thick-slabbed bawl –
the ear picks up tiny-tiny
wasp-winged
      spit-sizzle,
ice shatter,
         chipping
hits of unpolluted
    air.


                  – Tatshenshini / Alsek River

# River-Adaptiveness in a Globalized World[1]

*Andrew Biro*

## Introduction

At the workshop where initial drafts of many of the essays in this book were presented, participants began by introducing themselves, situating their home in relation to local bodies of water; in my case, it was the Annapolis Valley, between the Cornwallis and Gaspereau rivers, near the shores of the Bay of Fundy. The participants had not been instructed to self-identify in this way, but for an event called "Thinking with Water" it seemed a logical, almost natural, thing to do. Like many other workshop participants, though, I had travelled many hundreds of kilometres, to a different watershed, to attend the workshop. As an academic – indeed as a member of a professional class in the global north in the early twenty-first century – travelling a great distance for a conference of a few days' duration also seemed a perfectly normal thing to do. Indeed, academics are likely even more itinerant than most; not only do they regularly attend national or international conferences (virtually a job requirement) but they also in many cases have uprooted themselves to attend graduate school, and then again to take up a job. If thinking with water – a deeper attentiveness to the flows that surround us – began and ended with reference to a *home watershed* as these terms are traditionally understood, then academics might be among the least well-positioned to cultivate such a thinking.

In this chapter, though, I make the case that even if thinking with water might *begin* by identifying one's home with reference to a nearby river or lake, it does not *end* there. Thinking with water means attending not only to hydrological (or even biophysical) flows but also to the historical specificity of the thinking. This means, first, that for late-modern professional subjects (the likely readers of this book), among others, the usefulness of thinking with water depends on the capacity of that thinking to be articulated with contemporary processes of globalization: the compression of space and time associated with late or post-modernity.[2] How do we think with water when, even though we are always to some extent grounded in particular places, we are highly mobile beings, implicated in and to some extent constituted by globalized and deterritorialized networks? At the same time, thinking with water today must not only maintain a sense of the real materiality of watery flows but also attend to the ways in which the structures imposed by thinking on those flows – "basins," "watersheds," "aquifers," "oceans," and so on – are abstractions, grounded in particular cultural understandings.

With these questions in mind, I begin by examining the ways in which hydrological flows have transformed and been transformed by the long sweep of human socio-cultural evolution, tracing and exploring the limits of the "hydraulic society" thesis that Donald Worster draws from the work of Karl Wittfogel, and Worster's prescriptive call to become "river-adaptive" peoples, more attuned to (natural) hydrological flows, rhythms, and limits.[3] Worster presents a powerful indictment of contemporary civilization – that increased power over nature has meant an increase in societal inequality and domination – but he may encourage a tendency to read the notion of "river-adaptiveness" in static and overly naturalized rather than historical terms.[4] Using a more fully historicist account of human biological evolution, I propose that the ecologically appropriate scale of human communities should not be seen in fixed terms (hydrological or physiological). Drawing on the work of Benedict Anderson, among others, I use the example of national identity to demonstrate ways in which the rescaling of community sets in motion political dynamics that shape human evolution, and can thus be seen as "natural," even as they can be revealed as "socially constructed." Rather than champion a particular fixed scale, we can perhaps look at human communities in more multi-scalar and unsettled terms – just as a fixed notion of "watersheds" needs to be questioned if we are to capture the spatial and temporal complexities of real watery flows. Changing our perspective might allow (or force) us to reckon more seriously with the features of late modernity that can serve as resources for, and ought to be preserved in, a transition to a more sustainable society.

I end by looking at a particular contemporary political identity (settler, anglo-Canadianness) to explore ways in which larger-than-local, technologically mediated attachments can both prevent and enable thinking with water. A prosaic example of this abstract paradox was in fact what provoked my flow of thoughts about the possibilities for thinking with water today. On the one hand, the Canadian nation is built on extensive hydrological manipulation;[5] the compression of time and space that makes a coherent national identity across much of the northern half of the North American continent possible relies on the domination of nature. On the other hand, the articulation of nature and nation in Canada is not so completely one-sided. Indeed, one of the striking features of Canadian nationalism is the way that water is inserted into political debates: not merely as a natural obstacle to be overcome or an inert resource to be harnessed, but also as a form of natural heritage under threat, symbolic of the possibility of a more commodious and sustainable mode of living. The prospect of bulk water exports was a major flashpoint in the free trade debates of the 1980s and 1990s. More recently, the most prominent nationalist citizens' organization – the Council of Canadians – has not only campaigned extensively on water issues in Canada but has also been heavily invested in struggles over water privatization and commodification at the global level.

## Donald Worster and the Social Production of Scarcity

In his classic study *Rivers of Empire*, Donald Worster demonstrates that the development of human civilization itself is tied to the perception of water scarcity and the drive to extract and control greater amounts of water for human use. Following Karl Wittfogel's "hydraulic society" thesis,[6] Worster argues that the development of an increasingly complex social division of labour, and hence a greater degree of social stratification, was driven by a desire to increase agricultural productivity through increasingly sophisticated irrigation technologies.

Originally, under what Worster calls the "local subsistence mode," societies controlled water flows using technologies that were simple enough for any of the society's members to understand and operate.[7] Because a division of labour based on specialized knowledge was not required, these societies were characterized by relatively flat social hierarchies. But in many places, this mode of social organization eventually gave way to a structure whereby greater agricultural surpluses allowed some to focus on designing and managing irrigation infrastructure, with the specialization of labour and professionalization of irrigation management in turn yielding even greater agricultural surpluses. Thus, the development of power over hydraulic flows (and over nature more generally) was tied up with the development of increasingly concentrated social power: the visible flow of civilizational development was toward increasing human mastery of the natural environment, but its undercurrent was a growth in social hierarchy and domination.

In Wittfogel's original incarnation of this thinking, however, the tracking of societal power over nature with an emergent bureaucratic state's power over that society's members was a phenomenon found particularly under certain historical and (especially) geographic conditions. Wittfogel goes so far as to assert that the term "hydraulic society" is "interchangeable" with "Oriental" and "Asiatic" society.[8] Writing a third of a century later, Worster sees the problem with Wittfogel's orientalizing stereotype not so much as a mis-characterization of non-Western societies as a failure to see the development of Western societies in the same terms. "Hydraulic society," with its increasing power over nature tied to increased social domination, is found not just elsewhere and in other times, but also here and now.

For Worster, Wittfogel's mistake was to focus too narrowly on the development of state power. Worster looks at power more broadly, in *political-economic* terms: in spite of the formal political equality that comes with liberal democratic institutions, advanced capitalist societies are nevertheless marked by high levels of socioeconomic inequality. Popular consent to strikingly unequal distributions of wealth is achieved by insulating the economic sphere from overt political control: the processes and outcomes of the "free market" are generally (except at the margins) not subject to political negotiation or democratic rule. It is by seeing power as something that operates beyond the development of a bureaucratic state that Worster manages to demolish the boundaries – both geographical and historical – by which Wittfogel had sought to insulate contemporary Western capitalist society from the restricted logic of hydraulic society: the correlation between scaled-up hydraulic control and social domination. As Worster puts it, "the link between water control and social power might occur in places other than the archaic cradles of civilization [and] the past hundred years have seen more irrigation development than all of previous history."[9]

Worster's book offers a political anthropology of the American West, "a principal seat in the world-circling American Empire,"[10] and thus draws a connection between the contemporary moment's unprecedented level of control over nature generally – and hydraulic flows more specifically[11] – and today's unprecedented degree of political-economic inequality. Written just as the statist regimes of Eastern Europe were collapsing, Worster's insights are arguably even more important now, a couple of decades after the end of the Cold War, as capitalism is at least more widely, and arguably more deeply, entrenched as the dominant mode of social organization. If Wittfogel's hydraulic society thesis is really only about the dangers of increased *state* power associated with irrigation technologies, then it is of historical interest. But if, as Worster argues, social domination can proceed in ways other than the expansion of the bureaucratic state, then the hydraulic society thesis can be applied today, and the technologies of capitalist globalization (including irrigation technologies associated with industrial-scale farming for global markets) can be seen in a different light. In other words, Worster allows us to see, in particularly sharp relief, that even while neo-liberal globalization has been marked in many ways by an apparent *retreat* of state power, it has simultaneously been characterized by an *intensification and diffusion* of social domination (power exerted by non-state actors), along with more intensive and extensive interventions into natural processes.

Central to the historical dynamic that Worster describes is the double-barrelled insight that, first, it is the experience of *scarcity* – a phenomenon that is strongly culturally mediated, if not in fact culturally produced – that drives the quest to achieve a greater mastery over the natural world. The modern discipline of economics – arguably the hegemonic way of understanding the social world – takes scarcity as its bedrock presupposition.[12] However, if this presupposition of scarcity is a reflection of cultural prejudices, rather than a trans-historical fact of human life, this surely has important consequences, as we shall see shortly.

In addition to the cultural mediation of the experience of scarcity, the second key feature of Worster's analysis is that the result of increased mastery over nature is not so much relief from scarcity but increased social domination. Paradoxical as it may seem, the pursuit of security through increased technological mastery over nature has in important ways also exacerbated *insecurity*. More people may be better protected from the forces of nature (waterworks providing insurance against periodic droughts, for example). But these same people may simultaneously be rendered more vulnerable to social forces that remain largely beyond their control. With increased societal control over hydrological flows, access to water is unequally distributed throughout society, controlled first through the bureaucratic state and then by the capitalist market, with claims to unequal access – "political" or "economic" – always ultimately backed by force. The technologies that allow for the mastery of nature are thus experienced as themselves impersonal forces of "second nature."[13] As Worster puts it: "Aridity has been a crucial, though not a rigidly deterministic experience for people to deal with. Whenever they attempted to overcome that condition, they gave a new shape to the environment, creating artificial rivers with dams, aqueducts, and the like. But it was not simply a one-way process of humans re-creating nature. *Society, even in its so-called triumphs, inescapably came to bear the mark of the desert* and of its own effort to overcome the environmental exigencies there."[14]

Thus, it seems that the more our *collective* social enterprise has been successfully oriented to the "conquest of scarcity," the more our *individual* lives have come to be governed by impersonal social forces, whose effects turn out to be similar to those natural forces and constraints that we collectively sought to escape. Famines, it turns out, can be as devastating and difficult to control, whether they are caused by drought or by the fluctuations of global markets.[15] If the attempt to conquer scarcity through technological development inescapably reproduces "the mark of the desert" as second nature replaces first nature, then "progress," "development," and even "civilization," as these terms are traditionally understood – increasing social complexity to facilitate a greater range of individual life-choices – turn out in many ways to be a mug's game.

Thus, Worster argues that small-scale, locally-managed water systems are more sustainable – socially, as well as ecologically – than the large-scale systems characteristic of high modernity. Nor is this emphasis on a reversion to smaller-scale systems to escape the dialectic of scarcity unique to Worster: a similar logic drives Vandana Shiva's *Water Wars*, wherein Shiva provides examples of indigenous South Asian cultures that are able to meet hydrological needs in arid conditions by maintaining decentralized irrigation systems along with conservationist technologies and cultures.[16] Like Worster, Shiva emphasizes that the domination of nature associated with modernity *produces* scarcity as much as responds to it. As Shiva asserts in opening the book's penultimate chapter, which is titled "Converting Scarcity into Abundance," "scarcity and abundance are not nature given – they are products of water cultures." Particular "water cultures" (including the dominant culture of Western modernity) can "create scarcity even under conditions of abundance." On the other hand, other water cultures "can create abundance out of scarcity."[17]

Shiva's view, that scarcity and abundance are culturally determined, may be particularly powerful if it is connected to Worster's view that they are not experienced monolithically within cultures, and especially not within complex, stratified social formations. Again, this is a powerful rejoinder to the boosters of technological innovation, focusing as this argument does on the uneven distribution of benefits, and new and unevenly distributed costs of technological development, including such deliverers of water abundance as new irrigation technologies, the construction of large-scale dams and pipelines, methods of accessing hitherto untapped groundwater supplies, desalination technology, and so on.

At the same time, we should be careful not to simply invert the view that technological innovation will create abundance out of natural scarcity. Such an inversion would argue that technological innovation and increased social complexity *necessarily* leads to social domination, and that escaping the constraints of first nature necessarily plunges us into the even tighter constraints of second nature. The alternative to either of these two poles is to affirm critical theory's implicit promise that a greater degree of autonomy for human beings is possible – that we can, not absolutely, but to a greater extent than is currently the case – be liberated from constraints on the free development of our lives, whether these are imposed by "nature" or by "society."[18] Human societies and cultures can produce conditions of abundance (or at least "sufficiency").[19] And while Worster's argument that greater control over the non-human environment has tracked with increased social domination is a historically compelling account, it should not be taken as ontologically invariable: there is at least the possibility of breaking this historical pattern and establishing greater "degrees of freedom" with respect to our (socionatural) environment.

The claim that we should "convert scarcity into abundance," in Shiva's words, may seem strange, particularly to the extent that, at least in the global north, environmental problems (and not only environmental problems) have been driven by a dynamic of overconsumption that displays a reckless disregard for limits. But converting scarcity into abundance is necessary to the extent that the contemporary environmental movement has been politically hamstrung by its focus on "limits" and its consequent failure to offer a positive conception of the good life more satisfying than "we should make do with less."[20] Of course, in an era of rampant consumerism and highly commodified political discourse, "consume less" is a tough sell, so there may be good tactical reasons for not arguing from the premise of scarcity. But more deeply, making a political virtue out of restraint brings with it some worrisome political baggage, especially if (again, following Worster, among others) we understand "scarcity," and hence the need for restraint, as emerging in the first place from a *social* logic of hierarchization and domination. Working our way around this problem – developing a respect for limits while understanding that "limits" are always deployed for political purposes – crucially requires developing an understanding that even, or perhaps *especially*, with respect to something as metabolically fundamental as water consumption, the satisfaction of human needs cannot be divorced from the dynamic evolution of *natural and social* processes by which those needs are satisfied.

Worster begins with the idea of scalar limits (as the term "*local* subsistence mode" suggests), to critique the view that technological means of overcoming limits are required for, or even consonant with, human flourishing.[21] *Rivers of Empire* concludes with a call that is not quite a return to an idealized past, but more an attempt to glean imaginative lessons from an understanding of alternative forms of social organization. "To use a river without violating its intrinsic qualities will require much of us. It will require our learning to think like a river, our trying to become a river-adaptive people. In the past, groups as diverse as the Papago Indians and the Chinese Taoists seem to have met that requirement successfully, and there is much that we can learn from them. If we could cultivate a consciousness like theirs, the effects would be immense."[22] Worster's argument that we ought to become more "river-adaptive" is not couched in the language of abundance, and in fact he is somewhat more sanguine about using the discourse of limits. For example, his *Nature's Economy* concludes that sustainability requires an acceptance of limits: "enduring communities ... have accepted many kinds of limits on themselves and [members of those communities have] enforced them on one another."[23] And, he suggests, a limit on socio-spatial scale in particular can help to ensure two results: first, that people are aware of the consequences of their actions and choices, reducing the opportunities for what Thomas Princen has called the phenomenon of "distancing" that is produced when borders enable some kinds of flows but restrict others;[24] second, and related, that down-scaling, insofar as it reduces social complexity (and reduces the complexity of technologies that mediate relations between people), reduces opportunities for entrenched social domination.

Significantly, the argument that social domination, as well as unsustainability, is correlated with increased social complexity and scale recognizes that a societal or collective commitment to equity and deeply democratic forms of governance requires a level of social solidarity that is best, or perhaps only, maintained in "human-scaled" communities. Beyond a certain point, interactions are necessarily mediated, and, as noted above, the development of mediating technologies is correlated with the evolution, widening, and deepening of entrenched social hierarchies. But does this mean that there is a "natural limit" on the size of human communities?

It is important to note that Princen, in his discussion of distancing, acknowledges that the term "local ... has yet to be assigned an ecologically and socially useful definition in the literatures that use the term."[25] Thus, while it may be tempting to connect the idea of a natural limit on community size with biophysical landscape features, we must also recall that such "natural" features as watersheds are not simply pre-given facts but are also deeply reliant on conceptual (and hence cultural) abstractions.

The point of such a critique of watershed (or bioregional) identification is not a purely intellectual exercise in deconstruction. Rather, it is connected to a *political* imperative, noted at the outset of this chapter, to attend to the historical specificity in which thinking takes place. If thinking with water is to be meaningfully connected with finding more sustainable modes of living, understood as a political project to be undertaken in the current moment, then it must be connected with the ways of thinking and ways of living of late-modern subjects. If human (and, for that matter, non-human) flourishing is only possible in communities of no more than a few hundred people, sustaining themselves (almost) entirely from within the geographic bounds of a particular watershed, then such a vision – however correct from the standpoint of human physiological evolution – is likely to be dismissed as utopian in the context of a majority-urban species of nearly seven billion individuals, already connected and constituted by extensive and intensive global networks and flows.

## Scale, "Human Nature," and Autonomy

Rather than rely on physiologically fixed notions of optimum community size that are at odds with contemporary globalized, urban life, a more promising route may be to emphasize the inherent flexibility of human sociability and neural development. Our starting point can be that while the specific nature of social relations varies tremendously, sociality itself is an invariant feature of human life. This claim is confirmed by findings in evolutionary biology that discern humans' relative lack of genetic "hardwiring" – our "flexibility," or "detachment" – complemented by an extraordinarily highly developed, but also structurally necessary, capacity for social action.[26] In contrast to other primates living in arboreal environments, "hominid survival on the savannah, it is generally agreed, required unprecedented levels of social cooperativity. Human sociocultural life forms are distinguished in their ability to colonize diverse habitats. In order to do so individuals must be deeply susceptible to each other in the flexible co-construction of the sociocultural whole."[27] In other words, our deep interdependence on and with others is what allows human beings to live in very different kinds of ecosystems (arid to humid, coastal to alpine, tropical to arctic, and so on); and vice versa: our lack of a singular pre-given ecological niche makes us deeply dependent on others.

Thus, to the passage from Lenny Moss and Vida Pavesich just cited, we should emphasize immediately that it is not just a "sociocultural" whole that is constructed, but a socio-*ecological* whole. Human beings – like all other species – not only *adapt* to a pre-given environment, but also *transform* that environment. Modern human beings in particular have made themselves relatively unique, however, in the scale of environmental transformations, including of course massive hydrological engineering projects that have turned arid environments into lush ones, and vice versa – as well as massive anthropogenically driven rates of species extinction, and climatic warming associated with anthropogenic greenhouse gas emissions.[28] But, as Moss and Pavesich note, this is still a quantitative, rather than qualitative, difference between humans and other species. Flexibility or detachment from a single rigidly deterministic, naturally given way of living, through cognitive development (and social complexity) is not unique to humans, even if humans do it to a greater degree than other species: "The achievement of a constructed niche, be it a nest, a tunnel, a hive, or a culture, requires a strong measure of 'detached' internal flexibility and a capacity for developmental skill acquisition."[29]

The crucial point here is that social co-operation and *inter*dependence are the necessary flip side to the enhanced mental capacity that gives us the ability to reflect on, and sometimes deny, instinctual urges – human freedom or *in*dependence. Increased detachment is a survival "gambit," as our species' freedom from environmental determination makes us vulnerable. We compensate for this vulnerability by taking an active role in determining our environment.[30] In other words, lack of autonomy does not come from dependence on others *per se*. Rather, dependence on others (both human and other-than-human) is a necessary predicate for a recognizably human existence. Autonomy or freedom, then, can be best understood as a function of our capacity to (collectively) manipulate our environment in satisfying ways, and of the individual capacity to be actively and consciously engaged in the project of co-constructing a socio-ecological whole.[31]

The ability to assert one's individual claims in this regard depends (at least partly) on the extent to which we really mutually are "deeply susceptible to each other."[32] Thus, to the extent that our relations with the others on whom we depend are mediated – literally *depersonalized* – whether through impersonal markets or bureaucratic structures, our mutual susceptibility may be rendered invisible. The cues we depend on to affirm our membership in the social collectivity are both thinned out (the familiar modern sociological problem of *anomie*) and increasingly mediated through objects rather than through direct human contact (reification).[33] A farmer whose water allocation depends on a series of objects (dams, pipes, meters) and institutions (water allocation rights, markets) is less obviously dependent on other people than one whose water allocation depends on the direct communal construction and maintenance of irrigation infrastructure.[34] For the purposes of increasing autonomy in the current context, then, it may not be so much a question of the presence or absence of mediation *per se*, but rather of the distinction between mediation and reification, or in other words whether relations of interdependence are rendered visible or not. The notion of human beings as both highly social (interdependent) and culturally flexible (detached) suggests that mediation in and of itself may be an inevitable aspect of human existence. After all, even language functions as a mediating system (or technology), constituting representations of reality to some extent distinct from the represented world, and allowing for the constitution of relationships across space (with the invention of written language and portable media) and especially over time (both oral and written language used to forge connections between generations that inhabit different points in time). As linguistic beings, even human communities constituted entirely by face-to-face interactions do not live an existence free of mediation.[35]

One of the consequences of the powerful human capacity for complex social co-operation is the very notion of historical development itself, including the capacity for human communities to engage in collective work that spans multiple generations and the capacity to see the present as produced by, and thus different from, the past. But again – precisely because of the biological "flexibility" that facilitates (and necessitates) social action – we have to insist that there is no essentialized humanity that floats above the transformative work of history: we have transformed not only the environment that we inhabit, but also the human beings that inhabit that environment. As Worster poses the question: "How, in the remaking of nature, do we remake ourselves?"[36]

If humanity itself is remade through the process of environmental transformation, then there can be no trans-historical answer to the question: what is a "human-scaled" community? Rather, to return to the issues raised at the beginning of this chapter, the question must be posed as: what is a "human-scaled" community, *today*? Or, to put it in more watery terms: what does it mean "to become a river-adaptive people," *today*?[37] A simple return to the "local subsistence mode" is ruled out by the transformative flow of human history, as it has profoundly reshaped human nature. In this light, we might seek to cultivate a "watershed mind" that does not reify watersheds as a permanently fixable spatial scale, but rather understands "watershed" to be a profoundly unsettled, hybridized concept, with watersheds existing in nested and overlapping scales, ranging from the interiority of individual bodies to the planetary hydrological cycle.[38]

To pose the question more precisely, what does "human-scaled" mean in the context of an environment rich in information, communication, and transportation technologies that are already highly sophisticated, and are increasing exponentially the power not only to collapse space and time but also to provide a depth of experience such that contact across space and time *feels* less mediated (from telegraph to telephone to video conference)? What Moss and Pavesich identify as human flexibility and detachment applies not only to our species' need for social co-operation but also to our capacity to develop technological media (tools) to deliver compensatory mechanisms for social relations in an environment of scaled-up human communities. We feel the lack of intimate connection that comes with increased social scale, and we develop tools to (try to) fill that lack. In a programmatic essay (also cited by Moss and Pavesich), Max Horkheimer emphasizes the dialectical relation between technological and biological evolution: "the proposition that tools are prolongations of human organs can be inverted to state that the organs are also prolongations of the tools."[39] Rather than seeing technological mediation as necessarily ratcheting up the obfuscation of our mutual susceptibility, such a view perhaps opens the possibility that tools could be used to remember, as well as to forget, the ways in which we are connected to, and dependent on, one another.[40] Simply to valorize the local as the appropriate governance scale ignores the ways in which the technological mediation of human relations not only affords greater possibilities for social domination but also simultaneously constitutes new communities as it opens up previously inaccessible scalar levels.

## River-Adaptiveness and Imagined Communities

One prominent example of the analysis of this technologically facilitated re-scaling of community is Benedict Anderson's *Imagined Communities*, which identifies the genesis of modern nationalism with the development of print-capitalism.[41] Even though national identities frequently claim to be rooted in ancient history, as Anderson shows, it is in fact relatively recent technological innovation that has spurred the creation of national communities and identities, where newly forged social bonds across vast distances are "imagined," to be sure (people have personal interactions with only a tiny fraction of their co-nationals), but still powerfully real in their effects. Indeed, nationalism can be seen as having both positive and negative outcomes: anti-colonial liberation struggles (Anderson locates the origin of modern nationalism in Latin America) and the multi-dimensional extension of citizenship rights, on the one hand; the unprecedented slaughter of the First World War, on the other. But from either side, we can hardly avoid the conclusion that a scaling-up of community finds some compensatory mechanisms to deal with the increasingly mediated character of political interaction ("the co-construction of the sociocultural whole," in Moss and Pavesich's terms). In other words, in spite of their highly mediated ("imagined") nature, these social bonds, as twentieth-century history in particular has shown, turn out to be remarkably resilient and salient for mobilizing activity.

For Anderson, the "imagined community" that is precipitated out of the mass consumption of newspapers and national literatures is constituted by both positive acts – the creation and circulation of new narratives about the nation – and negative ones – the culling of historical and geographical facts that is required to make those narratives cohere. As Ernest Renan put it in a lecture given in 1882, "Yet the essence of a nation is that all individuals have many things in common; and also that they have forgotten many things."[42] For Renan, the "forgotten things" may be the historical facts without which differences between co-nationals can be elided, or those that would besmirch rather than stir national pride.

With the advent of a generalized sense of ecological crisis – unknown certainly to Renan in the 1880s, and even perhaps to Anderson a century later – what seems more important now to see as "forgotten" are the ways in which the acts of imagination that constitute human communities are acts grounded in, dependent on, and working with the more-than-human world, and not free-floating metaphysical fiats, the work of pure minds detached from the material realm. Certainly, the zeitgeist of increased environmental awareness implies a greater mindfulness of the ways in which human communities depend on and live with the non-human world. But this mindfulness is not to be conceived simply as a sober, rational assessment of a particular community's "natural capital" or the "carrying capacity" of a certain inhabited territory. Rather, the community's environment is – both figuratively (imaginatively) and literally – actively produced by the community, not least through the community's active engagement with its hydrological environment. Given the necessity for human beings of *constructing* a niche, becoming a "river-adaptive people" cannot be understood as the constitution of a culture that simply transmits natural guidelines or limits. This is particularly the case because waters in general, and rivers in particular, are inherently dynamic and everchanging. As Heraclitus long ago understood, we can never step into the same river twice. How can we adapt to rivers, if rivers are constantly changing? While humans' evolutionary "gambit" requires the intense construction of ecological niches, the very fluidity of watery environments makes them more resistant to manipulations that seek fixity.[43] The process of adaptation thus necessarily involves both a respect for the otherness and autonomy of the waters themselves, including the different timescales of watery flows – from the daily rhythms of tides to the geological work of erosion – *and* their anthropogenic transformations, both physically (storing or directing water to where we want it to go) and imaginatively (representing water as a thing, or things, that, once quantified, can then be defined as "scarce" or "abundant"). Becoming "river-adaptive," in other words, works both ways: people adapt to the river, but also (try to) adapt the river – itself necessarily dynamic and ever-changing – to their purposes.

In this chapter's final section, I offer a more detailed reading of the ways in which water – its management and respect for its otherness – has been bound up with (settler, Anglo-) Canadian national identity.[44] Here, one imagined community is constituted (in part) by imaginatively connecting national identity with a particular hydrological understanding – a contradictory process of adaptation that is also a process of re-scaling (constituting a political community across a broad spatial scale) and, at least to a small extent, a reshaping of human nature.[45] Canadian nationalism is a kind of "thinking with water," although, as I will suggest, it is a kind of thought that is contradictory and as often unthinking (forgetting) as it is thinking (remembering).

Imagining Water Scarcity and Abundance: A Canadian Example

Ask Canadians about Canada's share of the world's fresh water, and they are likely to tell you that it is enormous, perhaps greater than that of any other country in the world.[46] A 2005 Polis Project report on sustainable water management confirms that the belief that Canadian water supplies are abundant is "firmly entrenched" in Canadians' minds.[47] A draft 2007 federal government report states it perhaps most succinctly: "national forecasting of water availability has never been done, because traditionally our use of the resource was *thought to be unlimited*."[48] It should be asserted at the outset that, at least in some ways, this vision of water abundance is a result of Canada's integration into the project of technological modernity. Water "abundance" in many parts of Canada has been made possible by extensive and intensive projects of hydrological manipulation[49] which, because they are mainly in "hinterlands" that are out of sight, remain for many Canadians largely out of mind.[50]

Of course, there are instances when awareness of a regional water shortage does surface, perhaps most notably in Northern Alberta, where the water-intensive extraction of oil from the tar sands has dramatically stressed water supplies. But the response to a great extent is a faith in technological solutions – greater water diversions, more water-efficient extraction technologies, the development of water markets – confirming the dynamic described by Worster's "hydraulic society." In this sense, Canadian techniques of managing water scarcity (or producing water abundance) are entirely consistent with Worster's archetypical modern hydraulic society, the American West, which Worster describes as "a culture and society built on, absolutely dependent on, a sharply alienating, intensely managerial relationship with nature."[51]

This ideological consonance reflects the development of an increasingly continental-scaled economy, whose centre of power lies more and more in the American West (a shift facilitated not least by massive publicly funded water infrastructure projects in the Southwestern United States).[52] The production of a continental economy, largely coincident with the rise of neo-liberalism as a mode of governance, has doubly obscured social relations of interdependence, first by increasing geographic distances, and second by intensifying the role of market forces – acting as a "second nature" – in determining social outcomes. The result has been a perceived loss of community autonomy, frequently articulated as a process of cultural homogenization. This is seen in Canada as the erosion of a distinctive Canadian identity, although it is not a uniquely Canadian phenomenon. As Northrop Frye put it in an address given in 1990 just a few months before he died: "In Canada we say, or have said, that we are being Americanized; but America itself has become Americanized in the same way, and the original contrasts in, say, Philadelphia, St. Louis, and Atlanta have long since been largely obliterated."[53] If the production of culture – a community's distinctive way of life, or, one might say, the fashioning of a particular community's niche – were conceived in a more democratic manner, then the blurring of contrasts between urban centres within a continental society might find its compensation in the (democratic) production of a distinctive way of life for an emergent community constituted at the continental scale. Again, geographic distances or scale *per se* matter only to the extent to which upscaling facilitates "distancing" (in Princen's sense, above) or ecologically unequal exchange.[54] Particular modes of governance (like neo-liberalism) remove or foreclose the capacity for human communities (at whatever scale) to govern their lives autonomously, by using the human capacity for environmental manipulation to produce a "second nature" and reproduce conditions of heteronomy.

But it is just in this sense that Canadian national identity can be seen in a more positive, or at least ambivalent, light. For even though Canadian national identity has been predicated on the technological domination of nature, including massive manipulation of hydrological systems, it has also acted as a brake on neo-liberal continental integration, and not least when continental integration has been seen as a threat to "our" water. This can be traced back at least to the proposals for a North American Water and Power Alliance (NAWAPA) in the early 1960s (a massive engineering project to divert water from British Columbia and Alaska to the American Southwest), to the New Democratic Party's "Waffle" movement in the 1970s (one of whose slogans was "Don't let Nixon drink Canada dry!"), through the free-trade debates of the 1980s and 1990s, to recent dramatic fiction,[55] and right up to contemporary campaigns by the Council of Canadians (a nationalist citizens' organization that features water sovereignty as a key issue, and whose chairperson, Maude Barlow, was appointed the U.N. Secretary-General's first Senior Adviser on Water Issues, in 2008–09).

Canadian "hydraulic society" is thus Janus-faced. Like archetypal modern hydraulic societies, it entails a "managerial" understanding of water – "managerial" both in the sense that watery flows are reduced to objects to be administered, and also in the sense that this task is left to experts, who perform it largely shielded from democratic accountability and hidden from public view. Not least, such "Canadian" projects of hydrological management entail intensified relations of domination between the Canadian state and First Nations communities, and also stark inequalities even within and across Anglo-Canadian communities, as demonstrated in cases of water contamination in Walkerton, Ontario, North Battleford, Saskatchewan, and others.[56] But at the same time, insofar as Canadian identity has been constructed in opposition to American identity and the continental ambitions of American political-economic power, "our" (Canadian) water serves as a touchstone for *resistance to* the archetypal hydraulic society to the south. Plentiful Canadian water supplies in a "natural" setting constitute a key element of the distinctive national conception of the good life – a summer retreat to a lakeside cottage, a hike to a cool mountain stream, skating on a frozen waterway in winter, kayaking down whitewater rapids, and so on. And these images are more often than not grounded in a nostalgic yearning for "authentic" natural environments, rather than a sanitized environment symbolic of techno-managerial progress.[57]

Running beneath the surface of Canadian hydraulic society are thus currents that flow in the opposite direction: the desire to adapt ourselves to rivers rather than adapting rivers to us. In his landmark work, *The Fur Trade in Canada: An Introduction to Canadian Economic History*, political economist Harold Innis argued that the contours of the Canadian nation were structured around hydrological systems. Canada was founded as a staples-exporting country. Making the trade of economic "staples" possible were networks of lakes and rivers, and it was these economic flows, built on (that is, adapted to) hydrological flows, that in a way really constituted the Canadian body politic. Innis's view, that political identity followed from a more or less "organic" inhabitation of natural flows, can be contrasted with Northrop Frye's retrospective view that, prior to about 1960, English Canada "seemed unable to communicate except by railways and bridges"[58] (and, we might add, canals and dams),[59] and that Canadian nationalists sought "to make a nation out of the stops on the Intercolonial and Canadian Pacific lines."[60]

Similarly, the self-conscious production of a distinctive Canadian culture, as in the distinctively Canadian landscape painting of the Group of Seven, was historically grounded in an understanding that the experience of "nature" and the water-/landscape here was very different from the European experience. Thus, a distinctively Canadian culture or way of life was required, one that involved self-consciously adapting to the unique environmental conditions, rather than trying to impose European culture on North American nature.[61]

This theme is also taken up on Environment Canada's webpage on "Water & the Canadian Identity,"[62] which concludes with the claim that "water sustains our Canadian spirit. It forms a link between citizens from every region across the land." Moreover, the social role of artists is to articulate "our understanding of water and land and our relationship with them, [as artists express] things that most of us feel, but few are able to communicate." Even more, Canadian artists (or producers of Canadian culture) facilitate a way of thinking with water: "They are supplying us with the images and information we need to assess our current actions ... Canadians are demanding protection of their natural heritage, and this may slow the rate at which our water resources are degraded."[63]

Slowing the rate of degradation is admittedly a thin sliver of hope, notwithstanding the "Water & the Canadian Identity" essay's final line that such a "trickle" of movement "toward tolerance and stewardship" may turn into a flood of river-adaptive thinking and living. And, if it is to be taken seriously, then the conditions under which such thinking and living can emerge and flourish, and the connections between those conditions and the present, need to be critically examined and not just wished for. In this sense, the professionalization of cultural production might be seen as part of the problem, even as cultural producers continue to articulate important truths.

Becoming a river-adaptive community on national, continental, or even global scales requires us to see rivers (or watersheds) as moments in multi-scalar flows. Thinking with water may begin there, but it cannot simply end at the river's edge or the boundaries of the river's watershed. Multi-scalar hydrological thinking, then, is the correlate of a thinking about sociocultural evolution that can *disarticulate* (the capacity for) environmental manipulation from social stratification and socio-ecological domination. It is neither simply stepping backward to smaller scales of social organization or levels of social complexity nor blindly rising to greater heights of environmental manipulation.

The valorization of earlier, simpler, more river-adaptive modes of living is most useful if it is seen not as directly targeted political goal, but rather as a memento of what has been lost in the production of the present. In 1965 (the year after NAWAPA was proposed), as Canada moved increasingly under the shadow of American influence and into technological modernity, George Grant concluded his *Lament for a Nation* by saying that "the question as to whether it is good that Canada should disappear must be left unsettled."[64] For Grant, the choice was between liberal continental integration and the atomistic culture that its individualized freedoms entailed, and the preservation of a distinctively Canadian tradition. Today, the question of a distinctive Canadian identity continues to be posed, even though neither a return to Tory English-Canadian traditionalism nor an ever-expanding economic liberalism appears to be sustainable. What persists is not the particular content of Canadian national identity, but the underlying desire for communal autonomy that is both facilitated and undermined by technological development.

Technological innovation (the mastery of nature) has fostered social stratification, as socio-ecological governance has jumped scales from local to regional to national to global, even as it has constituted us as the late-modern subjects that we are. In remaking nature, we have remade ourselves as embedded in myriad national and global networks, but still as beings whose survival depends on the capacity to work with others in constructing the environment that we inhabit. As any number of contemporary ecological crises show, such a project is far more likely to be successful if it is undertaken self-consciously, and not as the accidental accretion of uncoordinated individual decisions. Our survival and flourishing thus depends on excavating the possibilities for "human-scaled" (transparent, democratic, sustainable) relations that do not necessarily or only involve a radical geographical downsizing of human social arrangements. Becoming a "river-adaptive people" may not, in the end, require a downscaling of social arrangements as a way to create a circumscribed culture of abundance, but rather the constitution of a socio-ecological community, at any scale, that is a self-conscious project of liberation, not grounded in forgetting. Our task remains the one that Benjamin identified nearly a century ago: "not the mastery of nature but of the relation between nature and man."[65]

NOTES

1 Helpful feedback on earlier versions of this chapter was gratefully received at the "Thinking with Water" workshop, the 22nd annual Reddin Symposium in Bowling Green, Ohio, and the 2010 meeting of the Western Political Science Association. This research was undertaken, in part, thanks to funding from the Canada Research Chairs Program.

2 Harvey, *Condition of Postmodernity*.

3 Worster, *Rivers of Empire*.

4 Ibid., 331. In his concluding discussion of river-adaptiveness, Worster refers to John Wesley Powell's proposal to reorganize the political geography of the American West along watershed lines. Ibid., 332–3 and 138–43.

5 Lasserre, "Drawers of Water."

6 Wittfogel, *Oriental Despotism*.

7 Worster, *Rivers of Empire*, 30–6.

8 Wittfogel, *Oriental Despotism*, 8.

9 Worster, *Rivers of Empire*, 30.

10 Ibid., 15.

11 The World Commission on Dams estimated forty-five thousand large dams worldwide by the year 2000, about 90 percent of which had been constructed in the second half of the twentieth century. WCD, *Dams and Development*, 8. See also the chapter by Haiven in this volume.

12 This is most obviously true of mainstream economics, which separated from the broader field of political economy in the late nineteenth century (a disciplinary reflection of the separation of the political and economic realms under capitalism). But it is also true of heterodox economics traditions, including much of Marxist and ecological

economics. For further discussion see Panayotakis, *Remaking Scarcity*. For an attempt to develop an understanding of economics that starts with a presupposition of surplus rather than scarcity, see Bataille, *Accursed Share*.

13  Although the term is rarely (if ever) used explicitly, Worster's analysis is clearly grounded in a theory of reification – a process by which things are invested with social power (for instance, "commodity fetishism" in Marx's analysis, or "the economy" as a force *to which* human beings are subject, rather than an ensemble of human relations), and human beings become instrumentalized or treated as things. For further discussion of reification, see also the chapter by MacLeod in this volume.

14  Worster, *Rivers of Empire*, 22; emphasis added.

15  Davis, *Late Victorian Holocausts*.

16  Similar claims in favour of downscaling have a fairly long pedigree in environmental thinking more generally, including E.F. Schumacher's iconic *Small is Beautiful* (1973), as well as Marshall Sahlins's description of Paleolithic hunter-gatherers as members of the "original affluent society" (1972) and the anthropological tradition from which Sahlins's work emerges (Claude Lévi-Strauss, Georges Bataille, Marcel Mauss).

17  Shiva, *Water Wars*, 119.

18  For variation of this argument that focuses on the Frankfurt School's "dialectic of enlightenment," see Leiss, "Modern Science."

19  Princen, *Logic of Sufficiency*.

20  For an engagement with this problematic, see the essays collected in Maniates and Meyer, *Environmental Politics of Sacrifice*.

21  Worster, *Rivers of Empire*, 30–6, emphasis added.

22  Ibid., 331.

23  Worster, *Nature's Economy*, 431.

24  Princen, "Distancing."

25  Ibid., 342n5.

26  Moss and Pavesich, "Science, Normativity, and Skill," 155–61.

27  Ibid., 158.

28  McKibben (2010) goes so far as to suggest that anthropogenic environmental manipulation has resulted in the creation of a fundamentally "new planet."

29  Moss and Pavesich, "Science, Normativity, and Skill," 158.

30  Ibid.

31  If the term "satisfying" here connotes too much of a utilitarian or instrumentalist tone, one can think of Marx's notion of the human capacity to "produce according to the laws of beauty."

32  Moss and Pavesich, "Science, Normativity, and Skill," 158. "We share at root the vulnerabilities and susceptibilities of highly detached beings, and from this more anthropologically deep-seated perspective we become only more aware of the misery and immiseration caused by inequitable 'distribution,' not just of material goods as such, or symbolically-mediated acts of recognition as such, but rather of the conditions of

possibility for achieving levels of compensation we will provisionally refer to as 'skill-ful autonomy.'" Ibid., 160.

33 Social status and relations, for example, come to be communicated through a "sign-system" structured around consumption. Baudrillard's (1981) understanding of the "system of consumption" as a linguistic structure that communicates class difference is one aspect of this.

34 For a discussion of the role of reification in water politics, see Loftus, "Reification."

35 See also Biro, *Denaturalizing Ecological Politics*.

36 Worster, *Rivers of Empire*, 30.

37 Ibid., 331.

38 "Watershed mind" is used here in a way that is informed by and borrows from, but is not necessarily identical to, its use in Christian and Wong (this volume). On some of the more pragmatic difficulties of governing at a watershed scale, which highlight the unsettled nature of the watershed concept, see Blomquist and Schlager, "Political Pitfalls," and Sneddon et al., "Contested Waters."

39 Horkheimer, "Traditional and Critical Theory," 201.

40 Citing Richard Terdiman, MacLeod (this volume) describes the process of reification – which I have described as the increasing mediation of social relations by things – as "a memory disturbance."

41 More recently, Peter Cannavo has somewhat similarly argued for "regional" or met-ropolitan-scale governance, citing Iris Young's definition of a region as "the span of a[n] [automotive] day trip ... the range of [non-satellite-based] television and radio transmission" (*Working Landscape*, 235). Andrew Dobson, by contrast, argues that contemporary technologies and practices of globalization demand that a reconceptu-alization of ecological citizenship be scaled up to the global level. *Citizenship and the Environment*.

42 Renan, "What Is a Nation," n.p.

43 Here too, however, the terms are relative rather than absolute. Terrestrial environments – even the most arid – are also constantly transforming as a result of biotic (human and non-human) and abiotic "interventions." These changes also occur at a variety of timescales: "geological" changes take place not only over eons but also in mere moments – tectonic shifts, eruptions, and landslides. All environments are "liquid" in this sense. Berger "Rapid Geological Change"; see also Bennett *Vibrant Matter*.

44 The analysis of Canadian national identity in this paper is focused largely, if not exclusively, on settler English-Canadian nationalism. French-Canadian and First Nations' understandings of the connections between water and national identity are a different set of stories, not told here.

45 For somewhat similar readings of the constitution of national identity through the reshaping of the waterscape, see Swyngedouw, "Modernity" and Worster, *Rivers of Empire*.

46 There are of course many different (and contested) ways to assert national water

abundance. Canada's borders contain about 20 percent of global freshwater by volume. Much of that, however, is "fossil" (or "non-renewable") water. Annual runoff is about 6–7 percent of global totals, which is consonant with the Canadian "share" of global landmass (that is, the land on which precipitation can fall), but far above the Canadian proportion of global population.

47  Brandes et al., *At a Watershed*, ii.

48  "A Federal Perspective," 8, emphasis added.

49  Lasserre, "Drawers of Water."

50  Lasserre notes that the volume of inter-basin water diversions in Canada is greater than in the United States, although most large Canadian diversions are for the production of hydroelectric power rather than urban or agricultural uses. Many of the largest Canadian diversions are in northern Quebec and Labrador. "Drawers of Water," 143–9.

51  Worster, *Rivers of Empire*, 5.

52  Davis, "The Political Economy of Late-Imperial America," 12–13. See also Ross, *Bird on Fire*.

53  Frye, "The Cultural Development of Canada," 669.

54  For one example of an argument that the current global political-economic system is grounded in such a process of uneven ecological exchange, see Rice, "Ecological Unequal Exchange."

55  Burstyn, *Water, Inc.* Burstyn's eco-thriller involves a plot to export water from Quebec to the United States. A similar plot device drives *H2o*, a big-budget CBC miniseries (first aired in 2004), notable also for being the first fully bilingual CBC television production.

56  In the wake of a few high-profile water contamination cases (including the two just mentioned), a survey found over 1,700 Canadian communities under boil-water advisories. Eggertson, "Investigative Report."

57  Thanks to Janine MacLeod for raising this point. Of course, even "wilderness experiences" are often deeply dependent on environmental manipulation (see, programmatically, Cronon, "The Trouble with Wilderness").

58  Frye, "The Cultural Development of Canada," 668.

59  See Lasserre, "Drawers of Water."

60  Frye, "The Cultural Development of Canada," 666.

61  See Biro, "Half-Empty or Half-Full?" and Manning, "I Am Canadian."

62  It is notable that Environment Canada even *has* a webpage devoted to water and the Canadian identity, let alone one with an essay that runs to nearly 7,000 words.

63  Environment Canada, "Water & the Canadian Identity."

64  Grant, "Lament for a Nation," 96.

65  Benjamin, *Reflections*, 93.

# Conceptual Relations: Water, Ideologies, and Theoretical Subversions

*Veronica Strang*

## Disconnecting Water

One of the most striking effects of modernity has been the emergence in Western thought of an extraordinary hubris: a conceptual bifurcation between culture and nature, and the idea that "civilization" has separated humankind from inclusion in and interdependence with ecological processes. This conceptual relation is often gendered, positioning culture with (active) masculinity and nature with (passive) femininity. At times it has also been heavily racialized, aligning notions of culture with primarily Western, more cosmopolitan ways of life, and conflating notions of (unspoiled/unformed) nature and (innocent/primitive) indigeneity.[1]

MALLE

    The sources of this dualism are multiple, entangled in a distant past when shifts into agriculture and irrigation allowed some societies to expand, to override ecological limitations, "subdue" nature, and embark upon escalating programs of environmental engineering.[2] Today, human supremacy is widely taken for granted: contemporary industrialized societies have normalized increasingly intensive self-generative and managerial activities, "gardening the world"[3] in highly directive ways, and believing that when nature revolts this is a mere slippage in patriarchal control. However, under intensifying pressure, nature is revolting more extremely, forcing us all to pay attention both to the lack of reciprocal care in human-environmental relationships and to the reality that global ecosystems cannot absorb misuse indefinitely.

    The dualistic thinking that separates culture from nature has been much critiqued in anthropology.[4] Benefiting from multiple exchanges of knowledge with non-Western, small-scale societies, the discipline has articulated alternate, more integrated conceptual models of human-environmental engagement in which humankind is situated within rather than as a superior "ruler of" the material environment.[5] Recent decades have brought a shift away from the theoretical fixities of structuralism, via feminist critiques and postmodernism, to more dynamic ways of understanding human being and human relations with other species and things. The notion of ecocultural dialectics coheres with this thinking, as do earlier philosophical notions of dialectical relations.[6] Further appreciation of the relational nature of human-environmental engagement has come from progress in understanding the intimacies of cognitive, phenomenological, and sensory engagement with the world.[7]

Thinking with water – making imaginative use of its material characteristics to formulate ideas about flow, permeation, movement, and change – has encouraged this greater theoretical fluidity, highlighting the reality that human-environmental engagements are composed of shifting and mutually constitutive processes, rather than the more static and fixed relations suggested by notions of culture or civilization, which depend heavily on images of "structure," artefacts, and built urbanity.[8]

A more connective view, building on Vladimir Vernadsky's ideas about the flows between all biota, situates humankind within an all-encompassing "hypersea" of spatio-temporal relations.[9] This view draws attention to the reality that human agency intersects with that of many other actors and "actants."[10] There is an ongoing negotiation with the activities and behaviours of non-human species and things; with the circulations of hydrological and ecological processes; with the currents of histories and changing imagery; and above all, with the inexorable flow of time.

In stressing the interdependence of all species and ecological processes, relational approaches strive for a less anthropocentric vision. As Mielle Chandler and Astrida Neimanis observe, an understanding of the "hypersea" challenges the notion of humans as actors in relation to a passive nature and, with a more modest ethic of self-erasure, presents them as fellow subjects within and part of an all encompassing gestational "milieu."[11] A similar point is made in Anna Tsing's work on "friction," which presents a connective world in which species, things, processes, and ideas work upon and shape each other.[12]

In contrast, a bifurcated concept of culture and nature retains a positivist view of human agency in relation to an objectified "other." In these terms, culture is defined in terms of human abilities to act directively and to control natural processes: in other words, an ability to override the agentive forces of non-human actors and actants. Most critically, I would like to suggest, it comprises an endeavour to resist the flow of time. I will return to this point, but let us first consider some examples of different ways of relating to and thinking with water. One is small-scale and "holistic," having no conceptual separation between nature and culture (and no traditional terminology for such ideas) and the second is large-scale and emphatically dualistic in its framing of human-environmental relations. The contrast is useful in illustrating how different ways of "thinking with water" enable people to inhabit different worlds, even when they share the same material environment. But although these examples may exemplify very different positions vis-à-vis water and nature, they are not binary opposites. Both describe the application of considerable human agency; both contain hybridities and elements of each other. Where they differ most radically is in the extent to which they consider human agency to be morally superior to that of other species and things, and in the degree to which human dominance is manifested and asserted in material terms. I have also included a third example, which considers groups who, though socially enmeshed in a dualistic and directive mode of environmental interaction, seek to promote more relational practices.

## Coming From the Rainbow

My first example draws on long-term ethnographic research in far-north Queensland, in the catchment area of the Mitchell River in Cape York.[13] The community of Kowanyama is located in an ex–mission reserve area near the Mitchell estuary, which flows into the Gulf of Carpentaria. The area was colonized by European graziers in the early 1900s; local language groups were then subject to the "protection" of the church and – from the mid-1960s onward – the more distant governance of the state. Situated in an area that was until recently remote from urban centres, they have maintained an equivocal relationship with the state and the wider population, achieving some degree of self-governance, and making use of a long history of political, social, and economic marginalization to retain their own lifeways; for example, continuing to hunt and gather, and to maintain practical and ritual management of their clan estates. They have determinedly retained their own beliefs and knowledges and, despite adopting increasingly hybrid[14] ideas and practices, still present a worldview that is radically different from that of the wider settler society in Australia.[15]

Aboriginal people in Cape York, as in other parts of Australia, lived as hunter-gatherers for many millennia prior to the European colonization of this area. Their society was composed of several hundred language groups scattered across the continent, thinly in the central desert regions, more densely in coastal regions and the resource-rich areas of the tropical north.

In traditional Aboriginal cosmology, which Indigenous Australians describe as "the Law," the world was formed in a "long ago" era – more commonly known as the Dreamtime or, in Cape York, as the Story Time. In this particular story of genesis, non-human species played a central role in transforming the world and creating humankind. Ancestral beings, in the form of animals, birds, and other aspects of the environment, emerged from within a flat, featureless landscape and journeyed across it, creating all of its topography, geology, and ecology, and populating it with flora and fauna as they travelled. Having made the world, they "sat down," sinking back into the land and becoming the totemic ancestors for the Aboriginal clans into which Indigenous language groups were divided.

Creating concentrated wellsprings of power at sacred sites – and more generally permeating the land – the ancestral beings defined the range of clan estates and each clan's inalienable and collective ownership of them. In this way they organized people spatially in relation to resources and to each other, enabling low-key and thus highly sustainable systems of resource use and economic and social exchange. Water was central to this organization: the majority of ancestral tracks or "story lines" followed water courses

Child with yabbie (crayfish) trap at Maggie's Well, a sacred site near Kowanyama.

and paused for important events at key water places. Clans were therefore distributed along waterways and defined themselves by water: people were upstream or downstream; fresh or saltwater. Waterways were only minimally manipulated: small and generally only temporary fish traps and weirs were built, but they had little or no effect on hydrological processes. Groups moved seasonally, shifting onto high ridges in the Wet and travelling further afield to meet other groups and to make use of other resources in the Dry. Thus, they moved with water and other ecological flows through time and space.

Aboriginal relationships with places were (and remain) deeply affective and protective, while being simultaneously pragmatic and opportunistic. The continued sentient presence of ancestral beings in the land casts the material world and all its species and processes as active and equal partners in a reciprocal human-environmental relationship that may be said to epitomize one of the world's most enduring examples of relational ethics. Such a modest, non-directive positioning of humanity alongside other species was matched (as typified by many hunter-gatherer groups) by "flat" socio-political

relational
ethics

arrangements in which gerontocratic leadership ensured egalitarian access to wealth and power in the form of collective ownership of clan estates and of sacred and restricted knowledge.[16] This commitment to equity was made possible, in part, by the small scale of Aboriginal communities and commensurately low pressures for expansion or intensification in land and resource use.[17]

Water in Australian Aboriginal cosmology is presented as a form of creative potential that clearly expresses the notions of "gestationality" and "futurity."[18] It plays a central role in conceptualizing human-environmental relationships over time. All things – ancestral beings, their human descendants, and other species – emerge from the Rainbow Serpent. As the elders in Cape York say, "we all come from the Rainbow."[19] The elders' vision presents human being as part of the whole stream of life generated by water and the hydrological cycle.[20] Thus, "the Law" can be seen as an intensely localized hydrotheology in which spirit is embodied in the material substance of water (as with the cosmological ideas expressed by Rita Wong and Dorothy Christian in this volume). The rising of ancestral beings from the earth, their ability to manifest everything in the visible dimension of the world, and their return to an invisible spiritual domain within the land is simultaneously a story about the cyclical movement of water through the environment; its essentiality to all ecological and human processes of generation and reproduction; and its capacity to contain past, present, and future. Thus, it also encapsulates temporal change, being a wellspring of memory[21] and "uniquely capable of symbolizing multi-generational time."[22]

Aboriginal thinking with water is further illustrated through ideas about individual spiritual and social genesis. According to the Law, water in the land provides pools of ancestral force from which spirit children "jump up" to provide the vital spark of life to the foetus in a woman's womb. Individuals rise to "become visible," like their totemic ancestors, from water sources held within the land. The emergence of their spirit from a "home" in clan land, assures their identity as a member of the clan, defines their rights to land and resources, and provides the basis for close and affective ties to place.[23] People are keenly aware that they are composed of water and spirit, which is temporarily made corporeal through combination with the material substances they consume from their clan estates, which "grow them up." Human lives are believed to echo the hydrological/ancestral cycle, the objective being to relive ancestral lives, drawing upon environmental resources, and reciprocally nurturing these for future generations. As people age, they draw closer to the ancestral beings. When they die, their spirit has to be sung ritually back to their home place, so that they can be reunited with their totemic "mate" and so re-enter the pool of ancestral forces and the regenerative power of the Rainbow.

Aboriginal Law therefore provides a sense of the fluid and processual nature of all domains of human and non-human activity, underlining the reality that these are continuously connecting and mingling. In this small-scale, localized, and beautifully precise cosmology, it is not difficult to see how water, and metaphors of water, move freely across ecological, social, imaginative, and corporeal domains, bringing them together in a flow of human and environmental changes over time and space. It is equally clear that water and notions of flow are ways of conceptualizing time in cyclical terms, describing how collective human and non-human actions circulate into and out of the material world and, on an individual scale, portraying the nascence, progress, dissolution, and regeneration of individual lives.

*water, flows and cyclical time*

## Emu Lagoon

The intimacy of this cyclical relationship with land and water can be illustrated through a brief visit to a lagoon near the confluence of the Alice and Mitchell rivers, which is an important sacred site in the traditional "country"[24] of the Kunjen-speaking people. Having been appropriated by European graziers in the early 1900s, this area was given back to the state (in an effort to avoid rent and taxes) in the latter part of the century, and became the Mitchell-Alice River National Park. Emu Lagoon is a large permanent water source in the flat open-forest country that characterizes much of the Cape York Peninsula. According to the Kunjen elders, its name comes from a major ancestral story about a fight between Emu and Brolga in which at one point Brolga, having burned Emu's wings off, carries her into the sky and drops her, leaving "for all time" an emu-shaped creek feeding into the lagoon.

The waterhole is thus perceived as the product of ancestral actions, and the spiritual home of many members of the local Emu clan. As a significant sacred site, it is also the focus for important ceremonies – for example, "increase rituals" designed to encourage the ancestral beings to provide food and necessities. The lagoon was a rich resource of fish, spear rods, timber for boomerangs, bush foods and medicines, and reliable water throughout the dry season. It has several ancient campsites and a long history of use. It remains a focus for ritual and social engagement for the traditional owners, and they also take care of it not just by conducting ceremonies but also by "cleaning" the landscape with fire and, more recently, by taking over the management of the national park. Newcomers to the area have to be "baptized" so that the ancestral beings will recognize and not harm them, and the totemic forces held in the water continue to generate human spiritual being. As part of the wider canon of ancestral stories that compose "the Law," the Emu and Brolga story contributes to this blueprint for Aboriginal life, defining who belongs where and has rights to resources, and situating each individual in a network of kin relations and responsibilities.

The lagoon therefore manifests a relational ethic that connects human and non-human realms. Socially, it provides people with a collective identity and social belonging that carries with it powerful obligations toward others. As Nic Peterson and John Taylor observe, in Indigenous Australia "a child is born into a web of connectedness" in which core values of sharing and equality pertain.[25] Les Hiatt also points to a central ethic of "generosity" in Aboriginal society.[26] Equally vital to hunter-gatherers is the vast lexicon of local ecological knowledge and close, long-term relationships with places, all of which is mnemonically held in the land and its stories. These interrelationships are mediated by the land and waterscape; thus, the waters of Emu Lagoon connect the Kunjen people to their material environment and to each other. According to ancestral Law, the lagoon cannot be compromised by being drained, dammed, overfished, or polluted: any usage must be sustainable, to provide "for future generations."

In a contemporary political arena, the Kunjen people have struggled to reclaim ownership and control of Emu Lagoon. In Aboriginal terms, this ownership has never been in question, but it took European Australians two hundred years to acknowledge formally (in 1993) that legal title to land and resources had existed prior to the European invasion.[27] Native title claims have been rumbling slowly through the courts ever since. In 2009 the people in Kowanyama finally regained ownership of the former mission reserve area under the Native Title Act.[28] In the same year, the Kunjen people also succeeded in formalizing an agreement with the state to take over the management of the Mitchell-Alice National Park, now renamed *Errk Oykangand*. In English this means the "home of the Oykangand/Kunjen-speaking people," but it also refers to an important term, *Errk Elampungk*, which describes the "home place" in the ancestral domain from which a person's spirit emerges, and to which it must eventually be returned.

Despite massive disruptions in the last century, Aboriginal people in Kowanyama have maintained the core tenets of a way of being in the world which is based on equitable partnership with a sentient land and waterscape in which non-human beings engage – and indeed merge – with human beings, and time is cyclical in its form.  Although the environment is humanized and "acculturated" in imaginative and practical terms, these tenets of equality have traditionally resulted in non-directive, ecologically collaborative economic practices which, despite some undeniable impacts on other species, have proved to be highly sustainable. Thus, while adopting new social and environmental practices, and recognizing the necessity of involvement in what Pearson calls "the real economy,"[29] Aboriginal people have other goals: to maintain their own places and their own "life projects" independently of the state and the market. They hope to reproduce their own cultural beliefs and values – to "hold the Law." But to hold their own Law, they must also strive to hold water.

Hydrological Diversions

A tidal wave of very different ideas and practices flowed into Australia with European colonization. These ideas and practices share with indigenous law some fundamental commonality in the ways that people make conceptual use of the fluid characteristics of water, but this commonality is obscured by major shifts in scale to more abstract notions of flow, and by the channelling of ideas into separate conceptual domains. Along with other writers, I have previously pointed to the way that the hydrological cycle provides a vision of time and flow in larger societies,[30] most particularly in conceptualizing the movements of spiritual being through material and non-material dimensions. Vestiges of a long history of hydrotheology remain visible in Biblical imagery and, at a secular level, rivers provide a common metaphor for the passage of time. Water imagery is used ubiquitously to describe the currencies of wealth and resources, social circulations, population movements, and the spatio-temporal circulations of information and ideas.[31] "Scientific" concepts of flow illuminate ideas about hydro-ecological processes.

But these ideas are abstract and displaced colonial imports, reflecting a focus on a larger scale of engagement. This degree of abstraction differs crucially from the firmly located ways of life still experienced in many Australian indigenous communities. Despite the demands of colonial assimilation into larger social schemes and more ephemeral networks, Aboriginal people have maintained a "place-based" way of life in which ideas and identity are intricately woven into, and so supported by, an intense focus on the immediate material environment.

For larger, more geographically and socially mobile societies, the various dimensions of life – and the connections between them – are not so firmly emplaced. Andrew Biro (this volume) is optimistic about the potential to imagine multifarious interconnections on a large scale, but it is a big task to "think globally" and imagine whole nations and their transnational connections and interrelationships with each other, with other species, and with multiple geographic and ecological contexts.

At one level, of course, all Australians inhabit immediate physical environments and localized cultural landscapes encoded with meaning in which it is easier to discern some of the cross-flows between different domains. In a river catchment, for example, it is possible to connect hydrological flows, the abstraction and use of water in various forms of production, and the effects of these activities on local ecosystems. There is an awareness of how the human communities in the area reproduce themselves and engage with the material environment and its other inhabitants over time, not just through economic activity and consumption but also through social and political processes, and through imaginative, emotional, and sensory engagements with places. But while such immediate material location serves to provide some foundation, a societal focus on the broader picture and the mobility of the settler population makes the achievement of deeply rooted local identities less attainable.[32]

Without a secure anchor in place, the hypersea is very large – maybe too large – to think with. It might be sensed within individual consciousness, pulsing through the heart, or swirling in the deep currents of the psyche, and it might be imagined with Vernadskian holism in abstract organic terms;[33] but for the most part, in dealing with its complexities, industrialized societies have come to think of – and not *with* – water in more channelled and specialized ways. Thus, human life becomes divided into distinct domains: social life, economic activity, and so forth; and non-human life is seen in terms of biology and ecology. Forgetting that these are mere heuristic devices, societies have further reified and parsed these domains, so that they now seem conceptu-

*[margin handwritten note: Thinking of water "divided life in modernity"]*

ally disconnected from each other. Economic flows and the movement of money and resources in global terms are generally separated from ideas about social or ecological flows, and – increasingly – this separation has encouraged ideological positions (by which I mean the promotion of particular values) in which commercial activities are heavily prioritized.

Further damming one flow from another is the separation of culture from nature which, with the gendering and racializing of these dualistic concepts, appears to encourage a differential evaluation of the relative importance of each. This may provide a clue to the emergence of ideologies that valorize human/male agency above all other forms. Critically, a dualistic view suggests that human activities are not part of the non-human material world we inhabit, but are somehow, through a magical sleight of hand, independent of it. We know, of course, that this is not true: we know that we live in physical places, consume material resources, interact with other species, and are subject to other agentive processes and events. We know that we place anthropogenic strains on all these things, often with disastrous outcomes. So what is the purpose of this conceptual separation?

## Time and Resistance

I want to suggest that one of the key reasons for separating culture from nature is to provide an illusion of fixity and permanence: of something that enables resistance to the currents of time that, in earlier Western metaphors, carried departing souls downriver into a final sea of dissolution.[34] This notion of culture is concerned with active creativity: an ability to "make things" – to make concrete material objects, to make events happen, to make a mark. As well as being seen to mark and claim place and territory, it can be seen as a way to capture and hold time, or – by leaving a legacy – to transcend it. If nature and the hypersea represent a flow of water and time, then culture signifies the impounding dam: an attempt to stem the flow of both water and time and to direct these into manifestations of human agency.[35] This concept of culture may tend, fundamentally, toward a human-centred (and male-centred) ideology of control in which the world is surveyed as an array of resources and materials for constructing artifacts that fix human agency in time – rather than consisting of flows in which humans participate.

There are wide cultural variations in the extent to which different societies conceptualize Nature as Self or Other.[36] This observation accords with a Durkheimian view, which posits that societies categorize and imagine the world in accord with their own social arrangements.[37] Thus, Philippe Descola and Gisli Palsson note that patriarchal, hierarchical societies tend to designate non-human species as a feminized "other" – that is, as Nature – while those whose social organization can be described as "communal" are more likely to reject such a clear distinction.[38] Comparative anthropological and historical perspectives have shown that cosmological principles shift in concert with important changes in social and economic practices. Therefore, conceptual dualism may be conterminous with the development of more directive modes of environmental engagement: for example, irrigated agriculture,[39] industrialization, resource extraction, some Western scientific practices, and even urbanization.[40]

While scientific deconstruction of the material world enabled some recognition of shared human and non-human materiality,[41] it also laid the foundations for more secular cosmological ideas. As Peter van Wyck notes,[42] a "rational" materialistic view presents a different notion of mortality, leading not to the hopeful cycle of dissolution and regeneration implicit in hydrotheology but to a more brutal loss of animation, a complete cessation of being. This echoes Max Horkheimer and Theodor Adorno's observation[43] that modernity brought disenchantment and a loss of animism. The undermining of firm beliefs in spiritual renewal, or a sense of spiritual involvement in the environment (whether in the form of ancestral beings or as a generalized omnipresence) sparked what they describe as a fear-driven battle for domination. Possibly, this fear also strengthened desires to "dam time" through the construction of artifacts.

These seismic cosmological shifts created multiple changes in ideas and social practices, and contained two key trends: a massive intensification in material efforts to direct and "fix" the environment; and a related competitive drive to "fix" ownership of it through the enclosure and privatization of land and water. What were once socially and ecologically embedded economic activities have become increasingly fragmented, leading to what Karl Polanyi called "disembedding": the process by which "capitalist economic institutions achieved their own, autonomous logic vis-à-vis other dimensions of modern society."[44] Disembedding takes both material and imaginative forms: in material terms, the abstraction of resources from the physical environment represents a literal dislocation. Water, abstracted from nature for industrial or domestic purposes, is taken through various stages of treatment and delivery and is thus transformed into a product of industrialized culture.[45]

As Monica Minnegal and Peter Dwyer point out,[46] such disembedding and acculturation can also be virtual: for example, the distribution of fishing quotas or of water allocations relies upon entirely imaginary notions of how many fish, or how much water, can be disbursed in a "virtual market." In Australia, water allocations, traditionally held in conjunction with land ownership, can now be traded away from the land, leaving dry blocks. Water trading relies on "virtual" water: volumetric abstractions theoretically available for trade and speculation in an equally intangible market. This has enabled powerful elites to "impound" water, regardless of its physical location and to alienate it from a conceptual hydrocommons. In this way, water is reframed as a "cultural" resource and channelled into a speculative water market detached from local ecosystems and communities.

This dynamic movement is greatly enabled by the material qualities of water.[47] Its fluidity enables notions of ownership and control that are not constrained by conventional property rights. Virtual or physical abstraction from the common pool enables more exclusive forms of ownership and agency. As water has been reframed as a "resource," there have been increasing efforts, by powerful elites, to discard ideas about it as a common good, to commoditize and privatize it, and thus to draw it into their particular spheres of control. These spheres are themselves perceptually and physically disembedded – and thus disconnected – from social and ecological systems: the world that is being made "productive" is not a shared, communal world, but an enclosed and isolated space. With a dualistic concept of nature and culture and a compartmentalized and abstract view of economic activities, efforts to "fix" time and appropriate space can therefore be made at the expense of other species and indeed other humans.

*Property rights and water*

## Dams and Directions

A journey down the Brisbane River illustrates the cosmological shifts discussed above, offering a spatio-temporal journey through increasingly directive engagements with water. The Europeans who settled along Australia's rivers brought with them a vision of the material world shaped by processes of industrialization in which dualistic concepts of culture and nature influenced their initial experiences of this new continent – a seemingly hostile and unforgiving place in which nature dealt with humankind in adversarial terms. Importing economic practices developed in more temperate zones, early settlers found themselves engaging with a more variable climate that offered radical shifts from drought to flood; a range of unsympathetic insects, reptiles, and plants; and dusty, readily eroded, and often infertile soils. Unlike the indigenous population, they were disinclined to go with the flow, preferring to become "Aussie battlers" determined to tame recalcitrant (female) Nature and bend it to their cultural will. The introduction of irrigation technology was central to this adversarial contest, enabling settlers to override ecological pressures and direct water into their own activities – even though, two hundred years later, the widespread ecological damage across the continent suggests that there have been no winners in this contest.

*Western settler perspective → adversarial nature, battling, taming*

In south Queensland, cattle graziers were among the first European settlers to shift inland. They cleared the upper reaches of the Brisbane River, violently displacing local indigenous groups. Running cattle in the thin forests of the Jimna Ranges, they drilled water bores and diverted water from creeks, in order to maintain stock. Thus, they turned water into beef. Holding both land and water, the "squattocracy" was for a long time central to Australian settler society, and very much in charge of its governance. Today, though sidelined by new industries and a more urbanized population, the graziers continue to hold the land and to have both political and economic influence.

Further downstream major dams were constructed, creating the Wivenhoe and Somerset reservoirs. These huge structures provide flood control and domestic water supplies to the spreading urban sprawl of Brisbane and its satellite towns, and capture water

Wivenhoe Dam.

supplies for the arable farmers in the central catchment area, whose activities are heavily reliant on irrigation.

With supplies from these reservoirs, or abstracted from local aquifers and creeks, the farmers turn water into melons, pineapples, carrots, garlic, and so on. There is also a dairy industry in the central valley which requires substantial irrigation to create pastures and fodder, to maintain intensive herd populations, and to turn water into milk, cream, cheese, and butter. Like the graziers, the longstanding rural community of farmers in south Queensland comprise an important part of the state's social and political history, and make a significant contribution to its economy.

Another powerful economic and political role is played by the industries in the lower catchment area. Extractive industries take not only water but also sand and gravel from the river. Closer to the city, factories refine and package agricultural outputs, and redirect water to produce things like fertilizer, paper, paint, chemicals, and timber products. In the city itself, the port (which was Brisbane's original *raison d'être*) disburses these goods, linking Queensland to a wider international economy. The city council also makes use of the dammed water, turning charges for domestic and commercial water supplies into a "cash flow" that supports health care, education, social services, infrastructure, and a range of other goods and services.

Water is thus directed into a range of products and services: each group draws it physically and imaginatively into their spheres of influence, most often in accord with what Max Haiven calls "the austere logic of economic imperatives."[48] Just as the river is turned into beef, crops, and dairy products, industrial water users transform it into a range of material goods, and the council uses it to support a fast-growing urban community. Over the last several decades, as economic priorities have taken centre stage and globalized economic forces have been brought to bear, each of these productive activities has come under increasing pressure to grow and intensify. Cattle farmers have increased the number of stock per hectare. The use of water for irrigation has doubled in every decade since the 1960s. Industrial water users have done their best to expand their activities as rapidly as possible and, in recent years, with a population drift northward in Australia, Brisbane has absorbed fifteen thousand new domestic water users a week.

But south Queensland is pretty dry, and this rapid intensification has led to major ecological impacts in the form of degraded soils, damaged and polluted aquatic systems, and a loss of biological diversity. Sociocultural well-being has been similarly affected, with primary producers crumbling under competitive pressures and a widening rural-urban divide. There are rising conflicts over access to water, and the population is being forced to confront a reality in which – even with desalination plants, recycling pipelines, and other new technologies – there are limits to how much local ecosystems can be coerced. This process of intensification – and its effects – is materialized in a water body which, in every respect, is a long way away from Emu Lagoon.


## Cubbie Station

In southern Queensland, close to the New South Wales border, lies Cubbie Station. With the construction of vast dams running for 28 kilometres alongside the Culgoa River, Cubbie became internationally notorious as the largest privately owned irrigation property in the southern hemisphere. It was created by amalgamating a dozen properties and acquiring fifty water licences, permitting the impoundment of 460,000 megalitres[49] of water a year for an annual payment to the state of just AUD 3,700.[50] This is roughly the amount of water it would take to fill Sydney Harbour, and equivalent to all of the irrigation entitlements downstream of the station. In a "good" (that is, wet) year, the station may irrigate up to 200 square kilometres of cotton, one of the thirstiest of all crops. The station also produces wheat and – from both of these crops and from water trading – has the potential, it is said, to produce an income of AUD 50 million a year.

Cubbie Station is the product of a competitive economic system that now includes water trading, allowing farmers to sell their water allocations in a privatized market. The station captures about a quarter of the water that would otherwise flow into the Darling River and thus on into the Murray-Darling Basin, one of the most over-allocated, ecologically degraded catchment areas in the world. The costs of Cubbie's impoundments are externalized not only to the aquatic ecosystems and non-human species downstream, but also to the farmers and other water users who depend upon the river's flow. Thus, although Cubbie's story is often presented heroically, as enterprise winning over a harsh land, Phil Dickie and Susan Brown also describe a series of favours from government and a dogged fight by the station owners to frustrate any regulation, squash the objections of other water users, and block any effective opposition to their activities.[51]

To some extent, they are merely acting in accord with the larger structural arrangements and practices of dominant ideologies. The majority of large stations and farms in Australia are held under long-term leasehold arrangements that require leaseholders to engage in economically productive activities. Water allocations are issued with similar requirements. Thus, Cubbie's CEO, John Grabbe, maintained: "None of us want to destroy the environment ... If the river is being destroyed, it is being destroyed because we are doing what we were told to do. We were given entitlements to do things and we are doing nothing but developing those entitlements – clause one is that we have to do certain works and clause two is that we have to beneficially use the water."[52] In a 2004 interview with Paul Lockyer on the ABC, he went on to say, "I'm extremely proud of what we've done ... extremely proud."[53] As the company maintained on its website, "The Cubbie Group Irrigation Project is an economic and ecological model for sustainable development in inland Australia."[54]

But New South Wales (NSW) National Parks and Wildlife Service river ecologist Dr Richard Kingsford warned that Cubbie is contributing to "a major long-term ecological collapse" of a world heritage–listed wetland just south of the station, across the NSW border.[55] And farmers downstream of Cubbie's dams had the following comments: "Cubbie's got a diversion channel ... It's three times the width of the river ... And what doesn't go into the diversion channel gets backed up by their weir, so, you know, they got the bulk of it ... We are the first property south of the border and ... we still can't get any water. So, you know, you have to feel terribly sorry for everybody below us."[56]

By competing successfully to impound water resources, Cubbie Station has thus contributed to the failure of smaller, more vulnerable farms downstream. Many are already under pressure, as water trading and competition for limited water resources also drives irrigation costs up. Few farmers can contemplate the kind of infrastructural investment made by Cubbie Station and, in any case, there is only so much water to be impounded. At the top of the river system, Cubbie was built to take advantage of both this scarcity and the potential for speculative trade. However, this proved to be somewhat risky: in the lengthy drought that followed its establishment, the station acquired debts of AUD 320 million and in October 2009 it went into administration. Long-awaited rains provided a reprieve in 2010; then there was a lengthy wrangle about whether the Cubbie Group would be sold, and to whom, with various (unsuccessful) government efforts to buy back some of its water allocations. Despite intense public (and some federal) opposition, in October 2012 the station was sold to a Chinese-led consortium, in which 80 percent of the shares were held by the Shandong RuYi Group.[57]

As will be clear from this example, the competitive advantage provided to those willing and able to engineer the environment radically, and the creation of a mercilessly commercial water market, has had considerable effect in Australia. The accumulation of water licences by wealthy elites, in a pattern of appropriation repeated all over the country, has accelerated the dissolution of rural farming communities already crumbling under the pressure of deregulation and the cheap importation of foreign foods. It has greatly increased the gap between rich and poor, with concomitant social and political effects. Many farmers are angry and disaffected; suicide rates and other signs of stress in rural communities have gone up; and, increasingly, there is talk of violent protests and active resistance to the state and to the imposition of market forces.

*[margin annotation: social + ecological consequence]*

In reality, water users are caught in a competitive spiral: small farmers must either sell out to major agricultural corporations or further industrialize and intensify their activities. For cattle farmers, more animals per hectare and more irrigation and fertilization for fodder equals more erosion and pollution. To pay for more costly water, arable farmers must switch to "high value" crops like cotton or even rice, which require heavier irrigation, have major impacts on delicate soil systems, and add to the soil salination that is now a widespread problem in Australia.[58] Further development in urban areas is leading to an increasingly volatile competition for water.

The microcosm of Cubbie Station and the wider issues related to water in Queensland reflect patterns that are being repeated on regional, national, and international scales all around the world. There are limited freshwater resources, and certainly not enough to support unlimited growth and expansion of populations and commercial activity. Nevertheless, in broad terms, the Australian government has maintained a commitment to neo-liberal ideologies in which growth is good and economic rationalism rules. The justification for creating a "water market" is that competition is "healthy" and forces "efficiencies." In these terms, by diverting water flows into its own interests, Cubbie Station is a winner whenever there is water, and the externalization of its costs is just part of the competition. The losers are people, other species, and environments from which water – and thus health and wealth – are being lost. As Rory Treweeke, a grazier downstream put it: "It's a gross transfer of wealth from the floodplain down here to the irrigators upstream."[59] It is also a gross transfer of well-being from non-human to human species. The notion of water as a hydrocommons is thus overridden

Irrigation in south-east Queensland.

by a vision of "water resources" as exclusive private assets, acquired in a competition in which might is right.

This picture of inequity reminds us that water both represents and constitutes power. As Karl Wittfogel made clear fifty years ago,[60] people's ability to own and control water is fundamental to their political enfranchisement and their inclusion in collective decision-making; in other words, the control of water reflects the extent to which individuals and groups have social and political agency. As illustrated by Aboriginal Law, egalitarian political arrangements depend on the collective and inalienable ownership of land and water. Water privatization in Australia underlines widening social, economic, and political disparity, empowering ever-smaller numbers of people, reducing the role and authority of democratically elected institutions, and disenfranchising the majority from real participation in processes of governance.

Along Queensland's rivers, commercial water users are either swimming successfully or drowning in the mainstream, with a commitment to productivism that demands constant growth and intensification of their activities. Yet, even within more successful groups, there are undercurrents of doubt about the wisdom of this direction. And such doubts are more keenly felt among other water users. The emerging crisis over water

Irrigation channel.

has brought to the surface real differences in ideological values, between those dedicated to (or pressured to conform to) *über*-economic rationalism and the control of nature, and those concerned to uphold a wider set of priorities and to acknowledge a more relational ethic.

## Contraflows

Alternative priorities are encouraged by recreational activities, and this is demonstrated along the Brisbane River. Its catchment area contains a major tourist industry that is an increasingly important contributor to the state economy. While this industry constitutes a further economic use of the river (albeit one that generally has less radical environmental impacts than those created by industrial agriculture), it also leads to some different engagements with the environment, and thus to more relational ways of thinking with water. Through recreational activities, people "commune with Nature" and aquatic

Canoeing on the Brisbane River.

*re creation*

environments in ways that are "re-creational" and "re-generative." They participate in *leisure –* pleasant sensory interactions with places, and immerse themselves both literally and *water –* imaginatively in water. Whether in the flickering leaf-green of the river, or in the rhyth- *sensory* mic swash and backwash of the sea, immersion is a powerful experience. Offering free- *engagement* dom from physical and mental gravity, the amniotic embrace of water enables flows between mind and heart, between human and non-human water bodies, and between self and other.

Environmental anthropologists have long observed that sensory and aesthetic engagements with the material environment enable affective connection with places and evoke a sense of belonging and protective concern.[61] Greater recreational use of the land- and waterscape has encouraged support for a lively conservation movement in Queensland. This movement has strongly (and, for the time being, successfully) opposed proposals to build new dams in the area, in the belief that it is more important for the river to "produce" biodiversity and maintain local communities. It has raised awareness about anthropogenic impacts on other species, and argued that human societies have a collective responsibility in this regard. Conservation groups have, with increasing volume, articulated a critique of industrial farming practices and their environmental impacts, protesting against pollution and the intensive use of fertilizers and pesticides. They have drawn attention to the effects of overfishing in river estuaries and offshore, and pointed to the environmental degradation caused by mining and other local industries. More broadly, they have supported Australia's moves to become a signatory to the Kyoto Accord, and its various efforts to address the issue of climate change.

In recent years, as irrigation has further intensified, conservationists have become particularly concerned about the overabstraction of water from aquatic ecosystems and the externalization of costs to other species. The ecological disintegration of the Murray-Darling Basin has been a salutary lesson, garnering considerable political support for a change in direction. In October 2010 the Murray-Darling Basin Authority (MDBA), which was appointed to initiate change, published a management plan that proposed cutting allocation permits in the basin by nearly one-third, in order to return between three and four thousand gigalitres (four million megalitres) to the waterways.[62] This proposal was received enthusiastically by conservation groups such as Environment Victoria: "For the first time, serious proposals are being put forward to return significant amounts of water to the rivers of the Basin to achieve two things – a big improvement in ecological health AND a sustainable future for agricultural communities across the basin. It envisages real action to rescue our rivers and we've warmly welcomed it."[63]

However, following intense debates between conservationists, right-wing groups and irrigators, and major criticisms of the plan's potential social and economic effects on rural farming communities, a revised document was released in November 2011.[64] It proposed rather more modest cuts to water allocations and excluded from the MDBA's river-modelling processes the extraction of more groundwater (though this does feed into river systems). Even this new proposal didn't satisfy the Victorian Farmers Federation: "The Murray-Darling Basin Authority has developed a plan that, if left unchallenged, will destroy communities, industries, businesses, farms, and families across rural Victoria. A government-imposed 'drought' will inflict permanent damage on Basin communities."[65]

Still, as long as they are neither socially nor economically costly, ideologies of conservation continue to receive increasing support at a local level, particularly in urban areas. Brisbane City now contains over thirty-five catchment management groups in which people engage collectively with the river and its numerous tributaries. They "garden" their environs enthusiastically, clearing debris and weeds from local streams and planting riparian areas with native flora, to create more habitable and ecologically robust waterways. These management groups express concerns about the alienation from Nature often experienced in large-scale and socially mobile urban contexts, and aspire to create neighbourhoods and places to which people can "belong." Their focus on local streams and creeks expresses an implicit understanding of the connectivity of water in defining localities and providing a common substance of identity for humans and other species. However, their focus is more on rebuilding a sense of social connection and belonging, and their primary aim is to establish distinctive local communities.

Catchment group endeavours are therefore generally framed in politically anodyne terms, most often expressing ideas about "community" or "ecological health and well-being." But there is an important subtext to their activities – a concern with participating directly in managerial processes and maintaining common ownership of water and of public space. It is these grassroots groups that are often the most resistant to the enclosure of water. In this regard, they share common ground with more overtly political social justice and environmental activist groups, who are openly critical of the efforts of particular elites to impound resources, exclude others, and externalize the costs of their activities.

For the most part, recreational, conservationist, and community groups in Queensland work within a conventional societal view of nature as "other." The term "nature" (and its implicit separateness) is normalized in their everyday discourses, and their representations about "taking care of the natural world" or "protecting ecosystems" implies a position of benign stewardship rather than co-identification.[66] However, in these groups' endeavours to recreate themselves, ecosystems, and communities there is an important underlying theme of reconnection and reintegration, and some acknowledgment of the need to establish more egalitarian relationships with other species. Although these ideas are rarely articulated to the extent of challenging the deeply entrenched conceptual dualism of nature/culture, there is clearly some potential for them to lead in this direction.

Recreational groups use water to bring about personal revitalization and affective connections with places. Conservationists hope to direct water into "producing" biodiversity, as do local catchment groups, although their emphasis is more on reproducing communities and socially cohesive neighbourhoods. To this extent, such groups share with primary producers a desire to control water for particular purposes, reflecting an assumed ability to "garden the world" successfully, and to manifest their particular beliefs and values. But a key difference between them and commercial water users is in the extent to which their efforts are directed toward a common good rather than toward individual gain at the expense of the commons. Their "contraflowing" ways of thinking with water are much less holistic than those of indigenous Australians, and there is not, except in the deepest green groups, a self-erasing sense of equality in relation to non-human beings. But some commonality is nevertheless present in these non-profit groups' striving for an ethic of "sharing," and in their willingness to recognize and valorize long-term human-environmental interdependencies. This desire to re-establish a more relational ethic between human groups, and/or between human and non-human species, therefore challenges dualistic notions of culture and nature and the ideologies that such polarized thinking promotes. Though conceptual partition continues to dam the mainstream, separating it from the hypersea, alternative ideas flow around, seep through, and threaten the foundations.

Water itself plays a role in inspiring contraflowing ideas, regularly asserting the ephemerality of human agency. No amount of desperation or desire can break a drought or halt a flood, and attempts to "hold" water illustrate a central tension between "cultural" efforts to dam the flow and water's fundamental elusiveness and fluidity. This brings us back to the idea that cultural creativity represents attempts to manifest human agency in the face of temporal pressures. Individuals and communities beaver away to build their dams, only to be overcome, eventually, by the currents of time. We might conclude, therefore, that the conceptual dam of culture expresses both creative joy *and* fear.

*[handwritten margin note: conceptual dam of culture.]*

## Conclusion

There is an obvious resonance between a separation of culture from nature and the literal and metaphorical abstraction of water from its social and ecological location. This parallel suggests an important correlation between dualistic and boundaried notions of human-environmental relationships and exploitative productivism. What I want to point to here is a recursive connection between conceptual models and ideology, whereby ways of understanding the world encourage or discourage particular values and practices.

On the one hand, cosmological understandings in which humankind is held *within* "nature" appear to support a relational ethic whose aim is to sustain collective social and ecological well-being. In these terms, water is necessarily a common good. With a more disconnected view, which deems humanity or "culture" to be somehow *separate from* the material world, it is possible to act more competitively, treating nature in adversarial terms, and asserting the primacy of human agency. With this view comes the privatization of resources and their use, and the externalization of costs to other people, species, and ecosystems.

Along the rivers of the world, groups are increasingly competing for water. They are also involved in a critical competition about whose concepts, ideologies, and values prevail. A conceptual reconciliation between culture and nature would require a sea change in ideological direction. Though such a reorientation would undoubtedly be embraced by some groups, it is likely to be deeply unwelcome to elites currently empowered by their ownership and control of water and by their perception of nature as "other."

In public discourses and mainstream practices, as illustrated by events in the Murray-Darling Basin, a boundaried, primarily economic view of water resources continues to dominate policy and decision-making, while more fluid and inclusive perspectives are consistently marginalized. In the academy, this conceptual dualism is manifested in structural terms: the "hard" (masculine) sciences are clearly separated from the "soft" (feminine) social sciences, and the flow of funding to those comfortable with an instrumental techno-managerial view of water is a torrent compared to the trickle diverted to social and cultural issues. This reality both affirms dualistic visions of culture and nature, and discourages the alternative perspectives that envision connective flows between human beings and the hypersea.

In thinking with water, the theoretical debate is thus also a political one, in which more fluid theories are regularly dammed. The implication is that social scientists must also be social activists, committed to resisting intellectual impoundment and breaking through the boundaries in public debates on water issues. We must continue to lay charges at the base of the dam.

NOTES

1   There is an extensive canon of anthropological literature on this issue(e.g., Descola and Palsson, *Nature and Society*; Escobar, *After Nature*; Langton, *The "Wild", the Market and the Native*; MacCormack and Strathern, *Nature, Culture and Gender*; Strang, *Uncommon Ground*). Aboriginal communities in Australia, New Zealand and elsewhere continue to be critical of essentializing visions of Indigeneity, but are also keen, in the political arena, to stress their traditionally relational engagements with the environment and their particular expertise as its custodians. The complexities of simultaneously repudiating essentialism and making an identity-based case for such expertise are considerable. There have also been changes in ideas about who has "culture": in some parts of the world (for example, New Zealand and Australia) there is a growing tendency to conflate notions of "tradition" and "culture," and to see indigenous people as maintaining authentic cultural practices that have been lost by larger, more cosmopolitan societies.

2   There has been considerable debate about how a dualistic vision of nature and culture

emerged and became dominant. A Cartesian vision of consciousness and its alienating potential to objectify is affirmed by Roy Ellen, who points to a cognitive imperative for an inductive understanding of nature as a realm outside human being. As Wittfogel's work observes, though, power over Nature may also provide political and social power over human subjects. Descartes, *Philosophical Works*. Ellen and Fukui, *Redefining Nature*. Wittfogel, *Oriental Despotism*.

3  The term "gardening the world" refers to a specific concept of human agency: "'gardening the world' can be seen as a process through which individuals and groups assert ownership or control of resources and extend their agency across time and space, ensuring their social and cultural reproduction." Strang, *Gardening*, 35.

4  For example, Descola and Palsson, *Nature and Society*; Ingold, *The Perception of the Environment*; and Milton, *Environmentalism and Cultural Theory*.

5  There is no space here for a disquisition about the complex history of ethnographers' relations with indigenous groups. But, whatever the real or presumed disparities in power relations between researchers and host communities, anthropology has always entailed an exchange of worldviews and knowledges. Today, thankfully, ethnographic research is conducted in an explicitly collaborative and egalitarian way, and in accord with strict ethical guidelines. A fuller acknowledgment of the active role of host communities in research permits a clearer understanding of the discipline as a mutually/multi-culturally produced artifact. Caplan, *Ethics*; Strang, "Happy Coincidence."

6  Hegel explores the dialectical process through which humans engage with their environments. The concept of "ecocultural dialectics" was introduced in the call for proposals for the Thinking with Water project "to renegotiate the material-semiotic border" between terms (such as "nature" and "culture") that are often opposed in a Western critical tradition. Hegel, *The Phenomenology of Spirit*. Chen, MacLeod, and Neimanis, "Call for Proposals."

7  For example, Damasio, *The Feeling of What Happens*; Howes, *Empire of the Senses*; and Ingold, *The Perception of the Environment*.

8  Although Ingold eschews notions of "culture," preferring to consider humans as organisms, there are resonances here of his work on "Building, Dwelling, Living" (1995), which draws in turn on Heidegger's "Building, Dwelling, Thinking" (1977).

9  McMenamin and McMenamin, *Hypersea*. Based on ideas about the biosphere first put forward by Vladimir Vernadsky in the early 1900s (and further elaborated by James Lovelock and Lynn Margulis), the "hypersea" is composed of all land biota, including humans, which depend on and are thus interconnected by water. This notion might also be said to have longer historical roots, in early Greek debates about the "nature" of the earth and its waters, and in Johannes Kepler's ideas about the earth as a living being, composed of sentient, interactive particles. Kepler, *Harmony*.

10 The term "actant" is often used to describe the agentive properties and behaviours of things and purportedly non-sentient species. I feel it is useful in acknowledging a

difference between these and "actors" with reflexive consciousness, though whether this line can really be drawn between human and non-human is another matter. Haraway, *When Species Meet*; Latour, *Reassembling the Social*.

11 Chandler and Neimanis, in this volume, reference but diverge from the thinking of Gilles Deleuze.

12 Tsing, *Friction*.

13 Since first going to Cape York in 1982, I have conducted extensive ethnographic research with the three Aboriginal language groups – the Kokobera, Kunjen, and Yir Yoront people – in Kowanyama. I have also conducted research along several rivers in southern Queensland, again working with different groups of water users.

14 Altman, "Indigenous Interests and Water Property Rights."

15 I am keenly aware of the pitfalls in presenting radical cultural differences, and of common assumptions that such representations must be both romantic and reductive. See Ellen, "What Black Elk Left Unsaid"; Krech, *The Ecological Indian*. There are various political reasons for representing greater homogeneity among human societies, and sometimes people simply find it difficult to imagine inhabiting the world in ways that are genuinely alternative to mainstream experiences. But indigenous communities in Australia, particularly those that remain geographically distant from urban centres, have gone to great lengths to protect and maintain their own beliefs and values, despite multiple pressures to "assimilate." In this sense they have maintained what Scott, in *The Art of Not Being Governed*, calls "zomia": a social and geographic space that successfully eludes externally imposed governance. After several decades of collaborative research with groups in Far North Queensland (and exhortations by their elders to help "teach whitefellers about Aboriginal custom"), I would argue that there remain quantum differences in Aboriginal Australian views of the world, their relationships with their environment, and their values. Their unique cultural perspectives ought to be acknowledged rather than subsumed by anxieties about the recreation of reductive binary differences or romanticism.

16 There was clearly some differentiation in gender roles, and there has been some tendency to assume that it translates into gender inequality; but in Aboriginal Law, although women and men have their own "business," all become elders and so acquire gerontocratic power; all own common property; and in an animistic cosmos, the ancestral beings, and the all-important Rainbow Serpents are both female and male (and often an androgynous combination of the two) without any apparent difference in status.

17 See Biro, this volume.

18 See Chandler and Neimanis; and Speigel, this volume.

19 Lefty Yam, interview, quoted in Strang, "Life Down Under."

20 Strang, "Life Down Under."

21 Bachelard, *Water and Dreams*.

22 MacLeod, this volume, page 49.

23 See Morphy and Morphy, "Tasting the Waters."

24 The term "country" is used to define the areas traditionally owned by specific language groups or clans.

25 Peterson and Taylor, "The Modernising of the Indigenous Domestic Moral Economy," 109.

26 Hiatt, "Traditional Attitudes to Land Resources."

27 In what became known as "the Mabo case" in 1992, the High Court ruled that, despite denial of this reality during the period since colonial settlement, Aboriginal people had had a system in which people held legal title to land. This ruling resulted in the Native Title Act of 1993, which allowed groups to submit claims for certain kinds of land, including Crown land, such as national parks.

28 The Anglican mission reserve area established in 1903 was handed from the church to the state in 1964 (following a devastating hurricane) and designated as Aboriginal land under a Deed of Grant in Trust in 1987. This area was deemed, in 2009, to meet the requirements of the act and thus returned to its traditional owners.

29 Pearson, *Our Right to Take Responsibility*, 8.

30 Blatter and Ingram, *Reflections on Water*; Lakoff and Johnson, *Metaphors We Live By*; and Strang, *The Meaning of Water*.

31 See, for instance, the discussion of water and metaphor in MacLeod, this volume, and the introduction to this volume.

32 Of course in recent decades indigenous Australians have also become more geographically mobile. An intense cultural emphasis on maintaining place-based identity has counterbalanced this to some degree, but there are inevitable effects.

33 Regarding Vladimir Vernadsky's holism, see also endnotes 9 and 41 in this chapter.

34 This vision may be said to link, metaphorically, with Jung's notion of the "great sea" of a shared human unconscious, which, in its turn, suggests a connective cognitive "hypersea." Jung, *Archetypes*.

35 See Haiven, this volume.

36 Strang, "Knowing Me."

37 I refer here to Durkheim's well-known assertion that human societies make their religious cosmologies in their own image. Durkheim, *Elementary Forms*.

38 Descola and Palsson, *Nature and Society*.

39 My current research (in progress) suggests that along with irrigated agriculture came a related emergence of religious beliefs in which increasingly monotheistic (male) humanized figures superseded (previously predominant) multiple and variously gendered, non-human spiritual beings.

40 Industrialization relocated the majority of people into largely human-made urban surroundings. While urbanization may not preclude connective human-environmental relationships, research on urban consumption patterns suggests that physical and

perceptual detachment from material production and related ecological processes is a powerful factor in enabling a critical disassociation from their realities – and needs. For example, research on water and other resource use indicates that the more invisible processes of production and related ecological issues become, the more likely people are to be resistant to pleas for conservation and profligate in their patterns of consumption. Conversely, where production and ecological processes, as well as the effects of consumption, are visible and immediate, and particularly when people are directly involved in these, they tend to make greater efforts to be conservative. See Shove, *Comfort*; Strang, *Meaning of Water*.

41 For example, enabling an appreciation of the organic composition of all species, which underpinned Vernadsky's holistic views of the biosphere and later iterations of this perspective by Lovelock and Margulis. Lovelock, *Gaia*. Margulis and Sagan, *Dazzle Gradually*.

42 Van Wyck, email to author. August 21, 2010.

43 Horkheimer and Adorno, *Dialectic of Enlightenment*.

44 Hornborg, "Money and the Semiotics of Ecosystem Dissolution," 149; Polanyi, *The Great Transformation*.

45 Illich, $H_2O$ *and the Waters of Forgetfulness*; Strang, *The Meaning of Water*.

46 Minnegal and Dwyer, *Appropriating Fish*.

47 See Strang, "Fluid Forms."

48 Haiven, this volume, page 216.

49 One megalitre is 1,000,000 litres.

50 Dickie and Brown, *The Rise and Rise of Cubbie Station*.

51 Ibid., 1.

52 Grabbe, quoted in Dickie and Brown, *Rise*, 6.

53 Grabbe, Interview. Australian Broadcasting Corporation, "Bitter Water Feud."

54 Cubbie Group.

55 Kingsford, quoted in Dickie and Brown, *Rise*, 7. Narran Lakes is a world heritage–listed wetland hosting migratory birds from Siberia and Western China. It is also one of the last major breeding grounds for the straw-necked ibis, known as "the farmers' friends" because of their appetite for plague locusts.

56 Pop Peterson and Peter Peterson, quoted in Australian Broadcasting Corporation, "Bitter Water Feud."

57 There is a requirement in Australia for the Federal Treasurer and the Cabinet to approve sales of over aud 231 million to foreign investors.

58 Irrigation in Australia has doubled every decade since the 1960s. Land-clearance and irrigation brings salt to the surface of the soil, creating vast areas of land in which nothing – not even native vegetation – will grow successfully. csiro calculates that approximately 2.5 million hectares are affected, and that a further 15 million hectares of currently productive agricultural land could follow.

59  Treweeke, quoted in Australian Broadcasting Corporation, "Bitter Water Feud."

60  Wittfogel (1981 [1957]) argued that control of water was a precondition for the establishment of despotic regimes. More broadly, it can be seen as fundamental to political dominance as expressed, for example, in the colonial appropriation of key water sources, and more recently in the appropriation of water through enclosure and privatization by particular elites.

61  See Milton, *Loving Nature*; Reason, "Reflections on Wilderness"; and Strang, *Gardening the World*.

62  The report observed that more than twice this amount (up to 7600 gl) was needed to ensure the long-term ecological sustainability of the basin, but conceded that such an aim was not socially or economically viable. Certainly the uproar over its much more modest proposal suggests that the earlier proposal would have been politically impossible. Murray-Darling Basin Authority, *Basin Plan 2010*.

63  Environment Victoria.

64  Murray-Darling Basin Authority, *Basin Plan 2011*.

65  Victorian Farmers Federation, "Submission."

66  I am drawing here on discourse analysis of interviews with a wide range of informants in Queensland, carried out in various research projects, 1992–2007.

# Erratics

*Adam Dickinson*

Here, the water is several hounds
clapping on the rocks around us.
Dogs in place of lapping waves –
such substitutions often go unnoticed,
unconsidered where they are found.
Like the tower of a church
that becomes a chain of lakes
as its windows exchange in the sun,
one seldom sees the ascension,
the division that has come.
The sky that turns to a field of mares
and then to the flesh of a trout,
assumes its weight above us
as if by right, or consequence.
I have kept my eye to the surface
and to the lie of sand just beneath,
but still I cannot say when the movement took place
when exactly the water grew round
and folded upon the beach
as wind in a dress,
then into the feet of a hound.

# The Dammed of the Earth: Reading the Mega-Dam for the Political Unconscious of Globalization

*Max Haiven*[1]

I typed these words on a windy day in Hamilton, Ontario, an industrial city, once powered only by Niagara Falls, today by a grid that harnesses power from hundreds of rivers across the Province of Ontario, connected to dams at James Bay, Quebec (protested by the Cree and the Inuit),[2] at Churchill Falls in Labrador (under claim from the Innu of Sheshatshiu and Natuashish),[3] at Wuskwatim, Manitoba (where the Nisichawayasihk Cree blocked construction),[4] at The Oldman River in Alberta (protested by the Peigan Lonefighters),[5] and at the Gardner Dam near Saskatoon on the South Saskatchewan River (where I was taken most years of grade school to bear witness to the wonders of modern engineering, the serenity and scientific value of man-made lakes, and the basic principles of power).

As a settler on these lands, my existence is a materialization of flows harnessed by dams on stolen rivers. My ancestors flowed in from Europe and, like so many today, met the dam of the border, pooled, got lucky, and proceeded to lend their lives to the dynamo of Canadian capitalist modernity. I reproduce this body with domestic foodstuffs grown on dam-irrigated lands and with imported food traded on unequal footing for the dam-powered products of Canadian industry. The early Canadian establishment chose the beaver as the icon of this colonial-settler state, a creature whose instinct to dam is so strong it literally changed the topography of the land; a creature whose pelt, oiled by glands deep in its body, made for fine hats and boots in Europe. Wars were fought for this skin; multiple attempted genocides were powered by the fur trade. Whole civilizations drowned in the floodplain of imperial commerce. Pelts sold in the same currency and flowed in the same financial current as spices and slaves, opium, and rubber.

The power that courses through my damming device, my computer and its word-processor, the means by which I arrest my flow of thinking and the associated currents of knowing and acting of which I am a small part, is a haunted power. Its circuitry is produced in Chinese factories where the world's largest dams, including the Three Gorges Dam on the Yangtze, displaced millions of peasants and townspeople to empower massive industrial growth in the production of export-oriented consumer goods.[6] The lowest estimates of the quantity of purified water consumed in the production of a personal computer is about 1,500 litres, about twice what an adult should drink in a year.[7] Presently, the power that courses through the keyboard stems in part from dams here in Canada.

The university, the intimate master (my under-employer) under which I write this paper, is a dam of knowing.[8] Its disciplinary turbines spin out articles and books, "research," and "excellence" by harnessing the power of inquiry, curiosity, and the organic, day-to-day production of knowledge. Of dams and universities we must ask: to what powers do these concretizations of authority answer? Whose magnanimity or acumen, seduction or coercion brought together the epic flows of human cooperation to make such mega-projects possible? Whom do mega-dams and universities em-power; whom do they dis-place? Whom do they enlighten and whom do they drown? Dams force us to attend to the interconnectivity of power, the way sources of energy are converted into one another: from hydrokinetic to direct-current to alternating-current to thermodynamic; or between cultural, economic, historical, and material forms of power.

○

Damming rivers and streams has been a vital part of countless human societies. Damming practices have been and continue to be a crucial and sustainable part of many Indigenous and non-Western engagements with nature, and small run-of-the-river dams have been built and mobilized by communities to make relatively sustainable interventions into their habitat to control flooding, provide irrigation, or generate modest flows of electricity. But dams have taken on a different significance and scale in the last century of Western capitalism and its attendant histories of colonialism, racism, patriarchy, and other forms of oppression and exploitation.

While the industrial revolution may have been driven largely by energy derived from coal, it is critical to recall that, even in the age of the steam engine, industrial economies and their colonial orders were facilitated by waterways, canals, and locks, all of which demanded new technologies for attenuating rivers and creating artificial hydrostructures and hydrographies. The rise of urbanization was in its turn facilitated by "advances" in water management and the damming of rivers to mitigate flooding and provide irrigation for intensive, industrialized agriculture. Public waterworks not only brought running water to the growing urban working-class populations of Europe and North America but they also gave firefighters access to water, thereby offering significant insurance relief to factories and landlords, and facilitating larger industrial investments.[9] A critical aspect of steam power is, of course, water. Dams and other forms of water-redirection were necessary to fill the water towers that fed the infernal boilers of sweatshops, locomotives, and other parts of the modern industrial apparatus. Much is made of the importance of water to a maritime mercantilist economy; but the industrial revolution floated on water and was an era of massive improvements in the civil engineering and management of waterways that also birthed modern dam-building in the nineteenth century.

The dam's fullest moment in the history of capitalism was concurrent with the widespread adaptation of electricity and the birth of hydroelectric power (among the first and still most effective and widespread means of generating electricity). By the turn of the twentieth century, dam-building had become a near obsession for Western powers. Today, some forty-five thousand dams provide about 16 percent of the world's electricity, 69 percent of global energy from so-called "renewable" resources.[10] But beyond this, the hydroelectric dam has become an icon of a century of electrification consonant with imperialist themes of modern progress and enlightenment, national uplift, and the triumph of man over nature.[11] By the Great Depression, projects like the Hoover Dam in the United States were key sites in the renegotiation of nature and nation; dams were presented as evidence of industry, providence, and ingenuity.[12] In them, massive public investment and privatized proficiency came together not merely as make-work infrastructure projects but as massive and shared symbols that represented the modern conquest of fate and the weaving of a national imaginary around the myth that the causes and consequences of life were no longer subject to nature's whims but could be directed by the will of a people. Nor was this mythology absent from non-capitalist societies: the Soviet Union and China also highlighted their dam construction as evidence of the benevolence of the state and the ability of communist regimes to best mobilize the flows of human energy toward the common good.[13]

Today, in a global age, dams continue to animate the imagination. China's purportedly insatiable appetite for reckless industrialization and urbanization has made that country's recent mega-dam–building spree a topic of global concern. But this concern is shaped less by deep ecological and humanitarian worries than by the cut and thrust of geopolitics: in the imaginary of the West, as xenophobic and colonial tropes are clothed in environmentalist robes, China's mega-dams have come to symbolize the monolithic economic and cultural juggernaut of a coming "Chinese century." While there is much to concern us about the enthusiasm of so-called emerging economies for ecologically disastrous mega-projects, without a focus on the way global capitalism drives these processes (and is, in part, driven by Western capital), these concerns easily slide into pernicious nationalisms or ignorant globalisms.

Dams are built to generate, harness, and shift the circulation of *power*. Not merely do they convert kinetic-aquatic power into electrical energy but they also fundamentally reshape the flows of social and economic power. In their planning and their construction, dams both draw on and reproduce social power relations. They depend on and serve to generate certain types of social, cultural, political, and economic relationships, and particular historical and local configurations.[14] The building of a mega-dam is an almost sublime intervention into what John Holloway calls the "social flow of doing"; that is, into the way social cooperation is constantly in the process of organizing itself.[15] Through their ability to harness, produce, materialize, and symbolize power, dams are a *concretization* of power relations. As such, they empower some and disempower others. While they are very real material manifestations of political, economic, and social power, dams are fundamentally *cultural* edifices: not only do they organize waters but they organize meanings and relationships.

I use the term "mega-dams" to refer to dams typical of large-scale hydroelectric projects, as distinct from ancient damming projects or smaller-scale modern dams.[16] Beyond their importance as nationalist icons or modernist fetishes, mega-dams are megalithic nodes in networks of cultural power. They are both the product and the producers of cultures of modernity. Mega-dams are, for instance, manifestations of a highly complex convergence of modern, capitalist, and patriarchal institutional cultures whose components include: the training of civil and electrical engineers; the institutional cultures of state bureaucracies that both approve and finance mega-dams and carry out (more and less genuine) environmental and social impact assessments; the legal and bureaucratic cultures necessary to facilitate the control of land and resources; the private and international finance that must first see the mega-dam as a worthy investment and then organize the capital required to bankroll these massive projects. At the same time, these institutional cultures mobilize narratives of epistemic superiority that allow them to ignore or dismiss the concerns of the people who will be displaced or dispossessed by mega-dams, thus giving them a sense that the cultures of soon-to-be-flooded areas are worthless in comparison to a dream of nationalist, technocratic progress, "the greater good,"[17] or the austere logic of economic imperatives. Mega-dams concretize these cultural politics, mobilizing a vast array of material and labour resources.[18]

But as much as mega-dams are manifestations of cultures, they also *transform* cultures; they do a profound work *on* culture. Perhaps most important is their contribution to electrification, without which we would not have electric lights, microprocessors, advanced robotics, contemporary pharmaceuticals and medicine, the advanced refinement of chemicals – let alone radio, television, and other mass media, or the world of cheap consumer plastics we enjoy today and which have dramatically reshaped lived and material culture around the world. But the arrival of dams in an area also fundamentally transforms local cultures. Boyce Richardson, for instance, notes the dire challenges posed to the Cree traditions in Northern Quebec in the wake of the James Bay hydroelectric project.[19] Similarly, Sanjeev Khagram documents the ways in which peasant, Indigenous, and rural cultures around the world are radically transformed by their proximity to the sites of dam construction and by the dramatic ecological changes that follow in the wake of these dams' construction.[20] As might be expected, some of these changes tend toward the spread of consumer capitalism, possessive individualism, social drift, and Westernized/colonial forms of modernization. Above all, though, dams fundamentally transform the cultural relationship of people to the forces we have come to call nature and, in particular, our relation to water. By providing consistent irrigation, easy and seemingly consequence-free electricity, and security against flooding, mega-dams reorganize our relationship to one of the Earth's (and our bodies') most elemental substances, and they do so on a global scale.

Mega-dams represent sites where cultural energies and histories pool; they are turbines of subdued and churning meaning-making. This is in part because dams are such massive interventions in "causality," in the way we imagine that the world fits together, the way we imagine cause and effect (and the causes of causes, and the effects of effects). By causality, here, I do not mean the great cosmic ordering of reality, but rather the dense, necessary web of collective fictions that we weave to explain why and how things occur, and especially to explain our own individual and collective agency to ourselves.[21] Within the history of Western modernity, our sense of causality has generally narrowed to a highly technocratic explanatory framework that ecofeminist Vandana Shiva likens to a "monoculture of the mind."[22] This framework fundamentally excludes a consideration of more-than-human agency (or, more properly, the way any notion of human "agency" is always already implicated beyond the human) and tends toward a sequential and linear logic. Within this framework, humans are seen as "cultural" and agentful, in contrast to "nature," considered passive and reactionary.[23] Dams are a product of this cultural logic of causality in the sense that they manifest a technocratic and reductionist worldview. But they also (re)produce and reinstantiate that worldview and help install the form of global capitalism under which we live. A massive array of global forces must convene to manifest in a mega-dam; and, in turn, the mega-dam becomes a generator and reorganizer of global material and power relations.

As a result, despite their relative remoteness from densely populated areas, mega-dams are particularly revealing of cultural politics and power relations. While dams appear in relatively few cultural works, I suggest that they "haunt" the cultural imagination and cultural production in the present moment. At a time of globalization characterized by the increasing liquidity of social, political, and economic relations, a time when a language of "flows" speaks of the complex and frenetic interplay of cultural, financial, social, religious, and ecological forces,[24] the hydroelectric mega-dam is a spectral presence – a critical historical factor in the constitution of our present condition as well as a vital nexus of contemporary relations of power and struggle.[25] Throughout the nineteenth century, Western colonial administrations touted dam construction as an example of their paternalistic benevolence and intellectual and technological superiority (hence their right to rule).[26] By improving water supplies and preventing floods, administrators sought to demonstrate the supremacy of Western science, industry, and management of labour and society. Even today, Canada's "signature project" for a reconstructed Afghanistan is the rehabilitation of a large dam in Khandahar that, it is promised, will improve the health of urban populations and facilitate the agricultural transition from opium poppies to more acceptable forms of export-oriented cash-crops.[27]

Following decolonization, the mega-dam became a critical icon of post-colonial nation-building, the royal road to an autonomous modernity that promised electrical power for civil infrastructure and industrial use, better irrigation and access to intensive agricultural practices, and more stable water transportation and water supplies.[28] But dams were also to provide massive collective projects thought capable of unifying diverse and factionalized post-colonial polities. Jawaharlal Nehru, India's first prime minister, famously called major hydroelectric dams "the temples of modern India," demonstrating his faith in the power of the dam to transform Indian society and generate new forms of collective economic agency.[29] Gamal Abdel Nasser, the iconic president of Egypt, was to make that country's decisive break with the imperialist powers by opting to finance the Aswan dam of the Nile without Western backing. This nationalist decision was an act of independence that led directly to the 1956 Suez crisis, to new cultures of Western internationalist imperialism, though the construction of the dam still led to the displacement of some fifty thousand Nubian villagers.[30] Indeed, as Vijay Prashad notes, the Suez crisis was a critical turning point in neocolonial strategy, spurring Imperialist powers to develop new techniques of harnessing and reorienting the "third-world" and its threats of economic independence, cartelization, and Soviet affinity – a new politics of coercive international debt and compulsory dependency enforced (primarily) by the "disinterested" hand of the market.[31] Mega-dams soon became signature projects for "structural adjustment" and a fetish of the World Bank and its associated "economic hit-men," who promised third-world nations around the world that hydroelectricity was the key to modernization and economic uplift, at the same time compelling or coercing these nations to borrow billions of dollars from Western creditors to spend, ironically, on Western materials and expertise for their construction.[32] The latter half of the twentieth century may have been publicly characterized by the shadow of "The Bomb"; however, mega-dams must be held responsible for the massive liquidation or dislocation of whole civilizations, from the Amazon to Northern Quebec, from India to Indonesia. Dams have both concretized and facilitated the flows of power that course into our present moment. In this sense, hydroelectric mega-dams haunt the current global economy as almost no other single manifestation of global forces.

Indeed, the money invested in mega-dams has been a crucial outlet for the over-accumulated capital of the Global North and, more recently, for the petro-dollars and sovereign wealth of oil-rich nation-states. Debt for mega-dam construction represents a relatively stable investment because it is backed not only by the promise of the indebted dam-building nation-state in question but also by transnational lending institutions with access to state treasuries in the "developed" world.[33] In an age when speculative investments penetrate economies and societies around the world, and when these financial flows are continually being deconstructed and reconstructed by sublimely complex digitized risk vehicles,[34] the financial ghost of the mega-dam lurks in almost every major financial institution, bank, mutual fund, pension program, and investment portfolio, including the endowments and investments of universities. We cannot escape its shadow. The mega-dam is the icon, manifestation, and generator of complex and intertwined forms of global violence: ecological, social, economic, and epistemic.

A major source of dam failure is sedimentation: the gradual build-up of infinitesimal silt and grit from the rivers that are blocked, redirected, or harnessed. Gradually, the particulate gums up the turbines and accumulates in the riverbed and flood plain, rendering the dam less effective and often unusable, if not at risk of breach. In the same way, dams build up a sedimentation of meanings, cultural resonances, and ideological dissonances. As such, dams are singular sites that help us to read the cultural politics of their day and, what is more important, to bear witness to the ways cultural politics flow into and out of material power relations. For this reason, I suggest that we "read" the dam as a "cultural text," a liminal site hovering at the cusp of the cultural and the material that manifests hopes, dreams, desires, nightmares, perils, and possibilities.

Key to water as a critical heuristic and material/cultural problem is its unimaginable *causality*. There is something fundamentally sublime about how water "works," something beyond the human imagination, beyond even the metaphorical powers of science. While there have been major advances in the scientific study of water systems and hydrodynamics over the past hundred and fifty years, especially where they have been aided by computer-modelling technology, the full cyclical nature of water systems remains elusive because there are simply *too many factors* to consider. This is the case, for instance, in predicting the possible ecological impacts of large dams.[35] Water defies our ability to fully chart how one thing affects another, or the way the chain of causal events leads to a predictable conclusion – it exceeds our capacity for narrative. The irony is that water is always already all around us, always already in us, but we do not (and perhaps cannot) understand fully how it works.

On the one hand, this situation speaks to the terrible hubris materialized in the mega-dam – the tragic and devastating arrogance of humans in presuming to command the flow of so elemental and unpredictable a force as water, and the broader arrogance of a society that believes it can master causality through the subjugation of nature. But it also implies that dams are a cultural problem, a loaded and ambiguous signifier or icon of the imagination. Dams are both metaphors and materializations of deep cultural patterns and contradictions. For this reason, I want to identify the dam as an archetype of the "political unconscious" of neoliberal capitalist globalization which recurs again and again as the symbolic and physical manifestations of the mega-dam both haunt the hopes, fears, desires, and revulsions of this global moment.

The association of dams with the unconscious was pioneered by Sigmund Freud in his development of a theory of sublimation, which alludes to the way primal sexual drives are channelled into socially acceptable behaviour, and the way subjects of analysis come to develop themselves through this work of redirection. For Freud, the cultivation of "civilized" subjectivity was akin to the erection of mental "dams" to hold back or harness unconscious energies.[36] He was particularly concerned with the constitutive forms of psychological anxiety born of a constant fear of the "return of the repressed" in potential explosion or collapse of the mental dam and the consequent bursting forth of unmediated primal drives. Later psychoanalytic thinkers like Jacques Lacan and Slavoj Žižek were to suggest that the ongoing work of worrying about the "return of the repressed" was critical to the constitution of the subject, and that our psychic life is a constant, frantic effort to convince ourselves that we are more than merely the drives we have sought so hard to sublimate, an effort that leads us to draw on a pool of social meanings and significations and common imaginaries to fortify our ego.[37] For Freud and others, pent-up anxiety over the repressed is the source of the urge towards self-abnegation, the "death drive" that fills us with fantasies of self-harm, suicide, and disappearance as a final escape from the war in our minds between what we take to be "natural" drives and the "cultural" work of sublimation.

In his influential book *The Political Unconscious*, Frederic Jameson seeks to wed these Freudian metaphors with an understanding of the conditions of cultural production under capitalism.[38] For Jameson, the capitalist system is an accumulation of the repressions and sublimations of the contradictions, crises, and unanswered injustices inherent in a complex system of exploitation. The history of economic violence and other forms of violence necessary to create the capitalist order, as well as the perverse threat of total revolution (the possibility that things could be radically different), is always repressed and sublimated within capitalism's political unconscious. The system is haunted both by the ghosts of the violences that brought us to this moment and the ghostly presences of what-might-have-been and what-could-be. For Jameson, cultural texts can offer theoreticians the opportunity to "psychoanalyze" the underlying material conditions of a cultural moment because they not only speak to the particular themes and preoccupations of their creators' intent but also emerge, circulate, and gain currency in a particular historical moment. In other words, cultural production both symptomatizes the political unconscious at the moment of its emergence (or the moment of its reception and decoding) and helps contribute to or reproduce this moment (although the exact form, politics, and potential of this reproduction are far from certain).

It is important to note, as Jameson makes clear in later work, that the ideological work of cultural texts is to provide a "causal map" of social reality: both the forms and the content of fiction, film, and other mediations offer their user a sense of the way things work and the causes and consequences of social life and action. But for Jameson, social life and the systems of power that structure it are "sublime" – too massive in scope and complexity for the imagination to fathom. This is especially the case in an age of globalization when those former containers of the causal imagination (for instance, the nation, ethnicity, or religion) have been fundamentally ruptured and provincialized.[39] Thus, all texts (but especially fictional ones) are ideological in the sense that, by necessity, they all offer a coherent sense of a causality that masks and reduces the complexity and scope of life. Without this deceptive "ideological" coherence, such narratives would seem implausible or disjunctive. In order to make sense to their audiences, all texts draw on the reservoir of the "political unconscious" and succeed to the extent that they are able to speak to shared archetypes, tropes, and dominant notions of social causality.[40]

It is in this sense that I read the mega-dam as a cultural text and as a quintessential liminal site in the political unconscious. In the language of psychoanalytic theory, "liminal" sites are thresholds[41] between the conscious and unconscious mind. Liminal figures are those that offer a unique moment to witness the play of signification and sublimation, an eerie border between worlds. Because mega-dams are such dense sites of intention and consequence, and because their career over the past century has been so influential and violent on the global stage, their ascendancy stands out as a poetic and potent moment in the political unconscious. The mega-dam is perhaps the signature icon of Western modernity's drive to conquer causality and to convince the "natural" world to conform to the dictates of "progress."

○

In what follows, I chart the presence of the mega-dam in several filmic "blockbusters" over a period of roughly seventy years, to uncover some of their cultural meanings. I am interested in the ways these films play off, express, and, in many ways, anticipate deeply seated anxieties in the political unconscious – a role that blockbuster films enact particularly well by virtue of their location within the political economy of culture (they are extremely expensive productions that must be surefire hits to buoy the finances of major studios). But I also suspect that the more recent blockbusters are popular in part because they incorporate and seduce us with an invitation to a vague critical reading, usually in the form of a juvenile and contradictory environmentalism, an "untransformative catharsis" for the sublimated violence of the dam that haunts our existence. In general, while early cinematic representations of mega-dams are filled with triumphant optimism, more recent appearances betray deep anxieties about the world that has created mega-dams and that has been shaped in their shadow.

The first major cinematic appearances of mega-dams were newsreels featuring the construction of the century's iconic dams in the United States and the Soviet Union in the 1920s and '30s.[42] What is notable about these early newsreels is that the majesty of the dam and the miracle of the moving picture are made to complement each other. Not only do such films glorify the mega-dam as an almost sublime mobilization of labour and ingenuity, but mega-dams, in their massive scale and scope, glorify the emerging medium of film. The transitions between wide, establishing shots, close-ups of workers laying cement, and even aerial shots of dammed river gorges lionize the cinema as the new sensory organ of the mega-dam–empowered polis. Indeed, film proclaims itself the medium for capturing the full magnitude of the mega-dam's intervention in causality: we are offered not only a visual panorama of titanic, concrete edifices but a full explanation of the forces at work in their design and construction (interiors of laboratories, close-ups of cement mixers) and what the dams will produce or make possible (crude animations mapping the flow of electricity to cities and water to fields, images of electrified homes and factories, of bustling cities). Their filmic portraits illustrate the process by which mega-dams became fused with the promise of a bountiful modernity, constant progress, and a taming of waters – and, therefore, of causality.

Both the medium of film and the mega-dam were iconic of an age where superpowers competed to fulfill the promises of modernity. Indeed, films and dams are both products and producers of mass publics, sites of phenomenal investment, and the coming together of particular constellations of economic and cultural power. Susan Buck-Morss has expanded on Benedict Anderson's notion of "imagined communities" to map the emergence, during this time, of mass political imaginaries and utopian visions of collective possibility in both the United States and the Soviet Union.[43] She documents the ways in which the emerging medium of film and the construction of major public works became critical sites of struggle over how mass publics might imagine themselves and their future. In her reading, collective imaginaries are characterized as flow-like – always shifting, changing, and evolving. Films and major infrastructure projects operate as dams in these flows, attenuating, harnessing, redirecting, and channelling the power of mass public imaginaries in particular ways. I further suggest that they are concretizations of the imagination that, in turn, shape the imagination – acute sites of the intersection of the cultural and the material. It is for this reason that we can read dams as cultural texts. They help conscript us into a shared imaginary or collective fiction through which we explain causality and agency to ourselves.

By the postwar period, however, early cinematic valorizations of the dam were slowly to give way to a more ambivalent and anxious signification. The 1955 British film *The Dam Busters* celebrates the real-world scientists and pilots who developed innovative "bouncing bombs" and flew them deep into Nazi territory during the Second World War to destroy mega-dams and thus disrupt German industry and agriculture. Despite being one of the most popular films of its day,[44] this film is marked by masculinized sobriety, and its jingoism is moderated (although in some ways consummated) by a melancholic note: the force of human ingenuity and courage must be applied to building and delivering bombs to destroy dams. Here, the breach of the dam represents the violent liberation of modernity from the shackles of German fascism, pictured as an unnatural dam both on the European landscape and on history, a blockage that could be cleared only by the combination of tireless British ingenuity and stiff-upper-lipped aerial heroism. And while the mass national imaginary of British valour here is far from ambivalent, the location of the dam is. The closing moments of the film follow the pilots as they land after a successful sortie and retire to their quarters. While the narration calmly and authoritatively notes the triumphant place of the dambusters in history, the eye is drawn to the evidence of the high human cost of these missions: haunting photographs of downed pilots, empty cots, and vacant seats in the mess hall. These visual cues quietly register sacrifices to the dam, troubling the more celebratory voice-over and closing the film on a somber note. No longer a symbol of unproblematic progress and modernity, the dam here begins to emerge as a dangerous Promethean gift, accessible to enemy and ally alike.

While such pageantry was possible in 1955, by the time of the production of the first *Superman* film in 1978, matters were considerably more complex. The Oil Crisis of 1973 had stemmed from a problematic act of economic resistance to an emerging neocolonial world order, and represented a substantial threat to the postwar economic supremacy of the United States. Further, it instigated widespread inklings that a culture dependent on oil to maintain its domestic prosperity and its international military hegemony was fundamentally unstable, that its own empowerment relied on the disempowerment of others, and that the ability to generate and acquire its needed energy was altogether uncertain. The "energy crisis," as it came to be known, ushered in a new age of concern for the future. The celebratory vision of the mega-dam as the icon of the national command of causality gave way to a sense that things had slipped beyond control.

*Superman* drew on and contributed to a cultural zeitgeist in the shadow of U.S. president Nixon's revolutionary severing of the hegemonic U.S. dollar from the gold-standard in 1973, a move that entailed entrusting the fate of the nation and the global economy to the fabled power of the free market. In addition, as David Harvey points out, it ushered in an age of economic and financial uncertainty that had its cultural expression in the rise of postmodernism.[45] Inklings of a postmodern skepticism about the metanarratives of industrial modernity and its attendant euphoric national imaginaries creep into the film's epic climax in which Superman, the American icon and champion, fails to prevent one of his enemy Lex Luthor's two terrorist missiles from striking the precarious San Andreas Fault. Tellingly, Luthor's plan is an act of terrifying speculative investment: he anticipates the sinking of California into the Pacific Ocean, leading to a boom in the value of his property investments in the (soon-to-be-coastal) states of Nevada and New Mexico. The unstopped missile causes a massive earthquake and widespread havoc, including the breach of the iconic Hoover Dam (washing away houses and farms) and the death of our hero's beloved Lois Lane. Bereaved beyond reason, this all-American hero from outer space chooses to breach intergalactic rules and test the limits of his powers by (implausibly) flying backward around the world to reverse the flow of time and return to the past to stop the second missile and save the day.

In *Superman*, the dam is a site of anxious and vulnerable disenchantment. The breach of the Hoover Dam, once the site of national hope, aspiration, collectivity, and modernity, betrays a profound fear of being swept away by the flood of events triggered by the psychotic excesses of Luthor's capitalist greed if taken to their grotesque conclusion. Superman's inability to save the dam in time resonates with an interpretation of a superpower experiencing the "return of the repressed," a sense that global violence, which was once kept in check, threatens now to inundate the national imaginary – a sense of belatedness and the speeding up of events beyond rational control. Luthor's act of financial terrorism echoes the sense, already gaining momentum in the late 1970s, that American capital had betrayed American society. Businesses could no longer be trusted to be motivated by civic responsibility.[46] Instead, immaterial speculation was evolving into a period of neo-liberal callousness.[47] Meanwhile, Superman's humanitarian justification for breaking the interstellar taboo against intervening in the flow of time eerily foreshadows and normalizes more recent American imperial adventures that have flaunted international agreements and covenants in the name of "human rights" and a unilaterally defined "greater good."

That Superman ultimately saves the dam and the woman he loves betrays an aspirational nostalgia for a time when things seemed to flow properly and a deep-seated desire for a strong, superhuman force to put the world back to rights. This nostalgia would become a key affective resource for the neo-conservative movements of the 1980s and 1990s, which mobilized the fears of a coming flood of internal and external social "evils" (migration, feminism, greedy unionized workers, and ungodly academics, for example) to reinforce the power of the free market and the repressive and punitive power of the state. That Superman alone is able to take command of causality (turning the clock back to an incisive point where "it all went wrong" and redirecting the flow of events) is less an articulation of hope than a manifestation of a recognition that only some sort of superhuman force can rescue us from our own creations.

The anxiety, ambivalence, and disenchantment associated with dams has persisted through the rise to supremacy of global neo-liberalism and the dawn of a largely disenchanted twenty-first century. Dams today are understood as part of an industrial modernity gone terribly wrong. In more recent films, the mega-dam resonates with anxieties that rarely achieve coherent articulation in mainstream discourse beyond the movie theatre: industrialized warfare, entrenched poverty, the breakdown of society in the solvent of the free-market, and a vague ethos of resigned helplessness in the face of imminent ecological and social collapse. Indeed, the dam has emerged as an archetype of the anxieties of globalization precisely because of the development of a neo-liberal cultural politics that (as critics like Henry Giroux, Zygmunt Bauman, and Jean and John Comaroff note) has engendered a culture of fatalism, disenchantment, and fear.[48] Where the consolidation of media power has severely limited public discourse and where people's lives are more and more dominated by the harsh imperatives of the unfettered free market, political agency is increasingly reduced to spectacle and neo-conservative reaction. In this context, ever-more dramatic representations of dams swing between exposing the repressed violences of globalization on the one hand, and revealing and throwing into relief a sense of political impotence and pointlessness on the other. The films to which we now turn both seize and capitalize upon this contradiction.

In the second of the Lord of the Rings trilogy, *The Two Towers* (2002), among the highest-grossing films of all time,[49] "nature" literally uproots itself in anger to destroy a dam. Motivated by fatalism (the "end of history" in the form of the feared "inevitable" triumph of the evil warlord Sauron), a once nature-loving wizard has betrayed his alliance with the forest and is razing it in order to power a magical forge in which he is bioengineering a hybrid race of super-soldiers for world domination. Through most of the film, "nature" is represented by sentient walking trees ("Ents" or tree-shepherds) who stoically declare their neutrality in the looming war, explaining that "men" will eventually wipe themselves out and that "nature" need only wait. However, upon seeing the rampant destruction of the forest at the hands of the now-evil wizard, "nature" awakens and seeks revenge, tearing apart a dam, which releases a river that floods the wizard's tower and its satanic mill.

We can read here an allegory of humanity's hubris in its perceived mastery over nature, which will eventually overtake us, drowning us in calamity. The film comes at a time when ecological crises of global warming, air and water pollution, drought, and famine seem increasingly uncontrollable and a spirit of confusion and fatalism descends on public discourse.[50] These environmentalist themes are clearly director Peter Jackson's preferred interpretation, but we must wonder why this image would gain such currency at the present moment, when ecological issues otherwise remain woefully underaddressed. Some might see this as a rather hopeful image, insofar as nature's (feminized) passivity and withdrawal give way to insurgent (masculinized) rage. But what is missing here is a sense of a transformative mobilization of agency and possibility. "Nature" here comes alive as a discrete and separate phenomenon to wreak retributive justice on "culture," reinforcing the same untenable dualism that gave rise to our ecocidal system in the first place. The response to the dam here is not so much revolutionary as apocalyptic, echoing Frederick Jameson's suggestion that it has become easier to imagine the end of the world than the end of the present global capitalist order.[51] There is a millennial logic to the closure that the Ents' destruction of the dam brings to *The Two Towers*, something more of the cleansing wrath of God (for which we must merely wait and pray) than an image of revolutionary transformation. What we have here is not an image of resistance but a cathartic and titillating glimpse of the "return of the repressed," a cinematic gesture to a systemic death drive. This climactic destruction of the dam capitalizes on and reinforces deep-seated anxieties and their accompanying political paralysis, rather than offering new perspectives toward a more substantive ecological politics.

A year later, in *X2: X-Men United* (2003), the second in the extremely popular adaptation of the classic X-Men comic books, the dam harnessed and generated similar anxieties. The series imagines that our world is shared by mutants with superhuman powers. The mutants are at war among themselves: between those (antagonists) who believe in mutant superiority and supremacy and those (protagonists) who believe their powers should be used to help humanity. The latter are led by the wise, just, and paternal "Professor X" who, although confined to a wheelchair, wields acute telekinetic, telepathic, and psychic powers and has founded a school to help mutants control their gifts and put them to the service of humanity. In *X2*, the professor is kidnapped by a ruthless mutant-hating military contractor, William Stryker, and secreted into a remote hydroelectric dam where Stryker plans to use the professor's powers, amplified by the dam's massive generating capacity, to launch a global genocidal psychic attack on the world's mutants. But at the eleventh hour, the chauvinistic mutants arrive and reverse this weapon, targeting all non-mutant humans on the planet. The day is saved not through any dramatic acts of heroism but by a breach in the dam caused by a "domestic dispute" between the professor's psychic protégé, Jean Grey, and her husband (at the time under mind-control but, we are given to understand, generally displeased with his wife's sexual feelings for another mutant hero, the inestimable Wolverine). Their powers run amok within the brittle shell of the dam, and the final third of the film is a dramatic race against time as the edifice crumbles and the once-arrested river breaks through. Wolverine discovers the dam is his own "primal scene" where, years before, Stryker had transformed him from a near-feral mutant into an indestructible super-soldier, through genetic and surgical manipulation. Our heroes manage to stop the genocidal plot, rescue the professor, and escape the dam just moments before it breaks, but Grey must pay for her "infidelities" (or non-monagamous desires) and sacrifice her life to hold back the flood while her comrades escape. She, Stryker, and the remnants of the dam and its genocidal machinery, are swept away in the ensuing flood.

Once again, we find the dam as a site of ambivalence, apprehension, degeneration, and catastrophe. In *X2* the spectre of genetic engineering and the fear of military experimentation identify the dam as the site of a gathering darkness, its power being harnessed to the most anti-human causes with potentially genocidal implications. The ultimate breach of the dam resonates with concern over the impotence of modernist institutions of containment such as the cohesive nation-state, the patriarchal nuclear family, the psychological labour of sublimation, and the postwar compact of state, capital, and labour. The mega-dam here becomes quite literally a site that harnesses and amplifies psychic desires and antagonisms; it is the political unconscious concretized, which risks being overcome by that which it increasingly fails to repress, literally emanating the death drive as it amplifies the primal powers of the professor (that paragon of control and civility) toward irrational genocidal ends.

We might read the collapse of the dam in *X2* as a critical commentary on the evils of industrial modernity, capitalism, and globalization. But it is once again important to recognize that the destruction of the dam in this film is framed only as a catastrophe, albeit ultimately a cleansing one. While Stryker and the dam are washed away, the antagonism between mutants and humanity remains. While the film may provide a catharsis for a political unconscious haunted by the dam and offer a release for the pent-up psychic energies bound up with this liminal edifice, these images are far from transformative. The film thrives on something like a cultural death drive that expresses itself through our desire to see the dam collapse. While we fear the breach of the mega-dam at the core of the economic, cultural, and social ontology of the present global moment, we also desire, perversely, to see this final scene, this unspeakable catastrophe, replayed and replayed.

In the 2007 blockbuster *Transformers* we revisit the Hoover Dam. This time the massive power plant is portrayed as a secret government military facility that both masks the presence of a giant evil extraterrestrial robot and maintains its frozen stasis. The dam does not break (though it does crack) but the film's denouement reveals that the U.S. government built the dam solely to hide this alien danger that they exploited both for its advanced technology and for its potential for gaining military supremacy. Inevitably, the robotic menace escapes to wreak havoc on Californian cities. Here, the Hoover Dam, once a site of state benevolence, national aspiration, and a Keynesian care of the population, reveals that it harbours a potentially massively destructive alien presence, with a potential for a reckless abuse of national trust that strikes deep into any sense of national cohesion: the merciless alien is truly at the heart of the national project. As in the other recent blockbusters, there is a sense that technology has overstepped itself, in this case releasing near-indestructible artificial intelligences to destroy America. And, while we might be tempted to laud this criticism of modernist hubris, once again the scenes of destruction echo a general sense of resignation and desperation. The transformers who emerge from the dam are unstoppable by any human agency, and we can do nothing but sit back and enjoy the strangely "just" destruction they mete out to civilization.

What accounts for the commercial and cultural success of the imagery of the collapse of the mega-dam in these blockbuster films? We comprehend that we are trapped within a modern, capitalist worldview of causality of which the mega-dam is both an instance and an engine. We are witness to the ecological and human violence of the mega-dam and this entire system – to the causes and effects of our collective behaviour. But we cannot imagine our way clear of this worldview or system. Hence, we are addicted to images of our own annihilation.

○

Mega-dams have occasionally featured in films and literature with a more critical orientation. Documentaries such as the popular *Up the Yangtze* (2007)[52] have highlighted the human and ecological costs of dam-building and garnered worldwide sympathy for anti-dam movements.[53] Ahrundhati Roy's Booker Prize–winning novel *The God of Small Things* (1997) mobilizes rivers as a key literary trope, foreshadowing the author's own widely publicized anti-dam activism against the Narmada Valley project in India.[54] And popular non-fiction books such as *Confessions of an Economic Hitman*[55] have highlighted the way the World Bank and other transnational financial institutions promoted dam construction as a means of recolonizing the postcolonial through a politics of foreign ownership and control, debt and, in many cases, "regime change."[56]

But I want to conclude by considering Canadian/Cherokee author Thomas King's now-classic *Green Grass, Running Water*. The narrative of this novel, based on a composite of indigenous experiences and hydroelectric construction in Canada, takes place in the actual shadow of a mega-dam.[57] King's fictional Blackfoot community in Southern Alberta has lost the political battle against the "Great Baleen" dam, whose construction has fundamentally disrupted local ecology and further circumscribed traditional Blackfoot lifeways. Yet before the dam can be opened (leading to the flooding of a large area), Eli, a retired literature professor, returns to his childhood home on the reserve and refuses to leave his mother's cottage in the dam's prospective floodplain, gaining an injunction to block the opening of the floodgates. While the dam functions as a literary device to announce a fundamental impasse or tension that shapes the novel, it also highlights indigenous experiences of the imposition and false promise of hydroelectric development in Canada and the imposition of colonial-settler "development" more generally. Further, the dam represents a historical blockage and comes to represent the hubris of Western capitalist modernity. As numerous commentators on the novel have observed, King mobilizes tropes and signs of liquidity, fluidity, and water as a playful counterpoint to the rigidity of colonial-settler culture as well to the formal strictures of the novel form: water lubricates, erodes, and bursts through the liminality of written and oral storytelling, linear and cyclical temporalities, and Euclidian and metaphysical space.[58] Indeed, the very "causality" of the story – the ability of the narrative to proceed in the expected canonical Western arc of conflict, climax, and resolution (as is so faithfully repeated by the Hollywood blockbuster) – is constantly interrupted by the refrain "First, there was only water." With this refrain, the narrator attempts to tell a creation story to the metafictional trickster figure Coyote but is stymied (diverted) each time by the course of events and Coyote's antics.

At the climax of the novel, the dam is (inadvertently?) broken by the actions of Coyote, leading to Eli's death in the resulting flood. Indeed, the destruction of the dam is represented as the culmination of the contradictions, confusions, injustices, and ironies of indigenous-settler relations that animate the novel. Specifically, the cars of three of the key characters are magically transported into the river and crash into the dam, causing a fatal breach. But unlike the previously examined Hollywood narratives, the collapse of the dam is far from cataclysmic. While Eli dies and while the collapse of the dam results in temporary ecological havoc, King highlights the intertwined resilience of the human and non-human community. The destruction of the dam is featured neither as an apocalyptic fantasy of totally cleansing destruction nor as a "return" to a pre-colonial time. Instead, just as the metaphors of water tease and chide any desire for clear causality (and erode the hubris of controlling water emblematized in the mega-dam), so too King's narrative offers no clear or simple closure but opens instead to multiple possibilities. The Blackfoot community and the individual characters are, we understand, stronger and more united by the end of the novel. The Blackfoot Sundance gathering, which is threatened in various ways throughout the novel, continues and thrives. And the novel concludes on a note of playful optimism with the mercurial Coyote unchastened by his actions and the narrator continuing his efforts to tell the story of creation whose opening refrain is always "First, there was only water."[59]

Unlike the cataclysmic parables of the Hollywood mega-dam narratives, King's conclusion does not offer us easy answers. Rather, it asks us to imagine the before and the after of the mega-dam with a sort of revolutionary patience – revolutionary at least within a society addicted to simplified maps of causality. His playful evasion of clear distinctions between heroes and villains, between written and oral culture, between "natural" and "human" forms of agency, or indigenous and settler culture – in short, the subversive fluidity of his intervention – highlights an alternative approach to the mega-dam.[60] King seeks to tease open the knotted roots of a culture that fetishizes mastery and control of causality. While far from writing a neo-primitivist rejection of all technology or a postmodern rejection of all literary form, King teases out the knots of a Western worldview that spawned both the dam and the novel. Rather than offering an alternative, post-apocalyptic vision, however, he seeks to remind us of the power of relationships and possibility, a power emblematized in the run of a river or the sublime interconnectivity of a watershed.

While numerous narratives and cultural productions celebrate the collapse of mega-dams or criticize mega-dams for a great many admirable reasons, King's novel is perhaps unique in its perception of the way the dam concretizes global power relations and its sensitivity to the roots of the relations deep in the dense intersection of spirituality, community, epistemology, and economics. In this sense, King intimates a vision of life beyond the dam, and beyond the dam of the present, a vision that is neither atavistic nor apocalyptic nor techno-utopian, but which hints at a healthier approach to causality. King's work, mischievous in both form and content, subtly offers a foil to the mega-dam and all that the mega-dam imposes, represents, and insists upon. He makes a playfully light yet genuine and mature gesture toward a revolutionary *patience* and *compassion* for our selves as watery bodies[61] that can never be fully aware of or control all our causes and consequences.

NOTES

1 My sincere thanks go to the editors of this volume for their extensive assistance with this chapter, as well as to all the other "Thinking with Water" participants for their inspirations and insights. Previous imaginings of this chapter have benefited from the feedback of William Coleman, Imre Szeman, A.L. McCready, and audiences at the Université de Montréal and the Canadian Association for Commonwealth Literature and Language Studies.

2 Richardson, *Strangers Devour the Land*.

3 Samson, *A Way of Life That Does Not Exist*, 102–6.

4 "Native protesters blockade Manitoba dam project"; Kulchyski, *È-nakàskàkowaàhk (A Step Back)*; Yan, "Canada's Hydro Partnerships No Panacea for First Nations."

5 Glenn, *Once Upon an Oldman*.

6 Qing, Thibodeau, and Williams, *The River Dragon Has Come!*; Chetham, *Before the Deluge*.

7 Grossman, *High Tech Trash*, 73–5.

8 For a cogent collection of analyses of the current state of higher education, see The Edu-Factory Collective, *Towards a Global Autonomous University*.

9 Grossman, *Watershed*; Nelles, *The Politics of Development*, 215–55.

10  Lucky, "Global Hydropower"; *Renewables 2011*, 73.

11  Froschauer, *White Gold*; Nelles, *The Politics of Development*, 215–55.

12  Stevens, *Hoover Dam*.

13  Josephson, *Industrialized Nature*, 1–5.

14  Strang, *The Meaning of Water*, 113–28.

15  Holloway, *Change the World Without Taking Power*, 27.

16  The distinction is far from exact or scientific, although the literature in development studies almost always makes one. On the devastating social and ecological ramifications of these, see Dorcey et al., *Large Dams*; Froschauer, *White Gold*; Goldsmith and Hildyard, *The Social and Environmental Effects of Large Dams*; Grossman, *Watershed*; Josephson, *Industrialized Nature*; Khagram, *Dams and Development*; Leslie, *Deep Water*; McCully, *Silenced Rivers*; Pearce, *The Dammed*; Qing, Thibodeau, and Williams, *The River Dragon Has Come!*; Scudder, *The Future of Large Dams*.

17  Roy, "The Greater Common Good."

18  On "industries" as both products and producers of "culture," see Mato, "All Industries Are Cultural."

19  Richardson, *Strangers Devour the Land*; Carlson, *Home Is the Hunter*.

20  Khagram, *Dams and Development*; Goldsmith and Hildyard, *The Social and Environmental Effects of Large Dams*; Leslie, *Deep Water*.

21  Graeber, *Towards an Anthropological Theory of Value*, 49–90.

22  Shiva, *Monocultures of the Mind*, 9–17.

23  On modes of knowledge and experience beyond/against this colonizing worldview, see Christian and Wong, this volume; also Coulthard, "Place Against Empire"; and Alaimo, *Undomesticated Ground*.

24  Appadurai, *Modernity at Large*, 27–47; also MacLeod, this volume.

25  On this notion of spectrality, see Derrida, *Specters of Marx*, 10.

26  See "The Assuan Dam" from the *Times* (1912) for a vivid example of the rhetoric of imperial benevolence and European ingenuity.

27  Potter, "Security standoff stalls Canadian dam project in Kandahar"; Government of Canada, "Signature project: Dahla Dam and Irrigation System."

28  On the cultural politics and political economy of dams, see Benjamin, *Invested Interests*, 107.

29  Scudder, *The Future of Large Dams*, 5.

30  Fahim, *Dams, People and Development*, 43.

31  Prashad, *The Darker Nations*.

32  Khagram, *Dams and Development*; Perkins, *Confessions of an Economic Hitman*.

33  Worm, Dros, and van Gelder, *Policies and Practices in Financing Large Dams*; Perkins, *Confessions of an Economic Hitman*; McCully, *Silenced Rivers*.

34  LiPuma and Lee, *Financial Derivatives*, especially 141–60; on "flows" and capital, see MacLeod this volume.

35  See, for instance, Dorcey and Others, *Large Dams*; World Commission on Dams, *Dams and Development: A New Framework*.

36  Freud, *Three Essays on the Theory of Sexuality*, 43, 54.

37  Lacan, "The Mirror Stage"; Žižek and Daly, *Conversations*, 65–72.

38  Jameson, *The Political Unconscious*; see also Dowling, *Jameson, Althusser, Marx*.

39  Jameson, "Postmodernism"; Jameson, "Notes on Globalization."

40  Jameson, for instance, is primarily concerned with the way the novel's narrative form is consonant with a pattern of expectations germane to capitalist modernity.

41  The Latin root word *liminus* literally means "threshold."

42  Josephson, *Industrialized Nature*, 15–40.

43  Buck-Morss, *Dreamworld and Catastrophe*. On a related note regarding the importance of control over water to the imagining of the nation, see Biro, this volume.

44  Ramsden, *The Dam Busters*.

45  Harvey, *The Condition of Postmodernity*.

46  Billington and Jackson, *Big Dams of the New Deal Era*.

47  Harvey, *A Brief History of Neoliberalism*.

48  Bauman, *Liquid Fear*; Giroux, *Against the Terror of Neoliberalism*; Comaroff and Comaroff, *Millennial Capitalism*.

49  In November 2010, this film was the twelfth-highest grossing film worldwide. See "All Time Box Office: Worldwide Grosses."

50  See, for instance, Žižek, *Living in the End Times*.

51  Jameson, *Archaeologies of the Future*, 199.

52  *Up the Yangtze*, directed by Yung Chang. See also Chetham, *Before the Deluge*; Qing, Thibodeau and Williams, *The River Dragon has Come!*

53  See, for instance, the International Rivers website.

54  Roy, "The Greater Common Good"; *The God of Small Things*.

55  Perkins, *Confessions of an Economic Hitman*.

56  See also Grossman, *Watershed*; Khagram, *Dams and Development*; Pearce, *The Dammed*.

57  King, *Green Grass, Running Water*.

58  Bailey, "The Arbitrary Nature of the Story"; Cox, "All this Water Imagery"; Fee and Flick "Coyote Pedagogy"; Lousley, "Hosanna Da, Our Home on Natives' Land."

59  Fee and Flick, "Coyote Pedagogy"; Goldman, "Mapping and Dreaming."

60  Ibid.

61  Neimanis and Chandler, this volume.

# Untapping Watershed Mind

## Dorothy Christian

*To begin, I need to acknowledge and give thanks to the spirits and the people of these lands: (Montreal, where the Thinking with Water workshop occurred in June 2010), the Gan-ya-ge-haga of the Haudenosaunee Confederacy – the People of the Flint who you may know as the Mohawks, and who I know as the Keepers of the Eastern door. All too often in our stressful, busy lives we forget to exercise the fundamental protocols of our co-existence. In my culture, it is "good manners" to acknowledge whose land you are on. And part of that is to introduce yourself, so people can know who you are and where you come from.*

Part of respecting different systems of knowledge involves valuing oral cultures as much as written discourses; for that reason, and because it is important to keep situating the places from which we speak, I have decided to share what I presented at the "Thinking with Water" workshop in Montreal in a revised and transcribed form in this anthology, with a number of the local references intact. I invite readers to consider what is gained, lost, or shifted in the movement between oral and written approaches.

*I carry three tribal names from the land, one from my Secwepemc (Shuswap) community, one from the Syilx (Okanagan) people, my Grandmother's people and one from the Anishnawbe peoples who adopted me into one of their clans when I lived in their territories. My colonial name is Dorothy Christian; I am the eldest of ten. I have one daughter. I bring greetings from my Splatsin community to the Gan-ya-ge-haga and to all of you who have come to dialogue about Water, a very critical part of who we are as human beings and which I have heard Elders refer to as the "life blood" of Mother Earth.*

*My aw(o) kwe (meaning Sister/Friend in my Secwepemc dialect), Rita Wong, and I would like to acknowledge that we have travelled from the traditional unceded Coast Salish territories of the Squamish, Musqueam, and the Tsleil-Wau-tuth, the lands where we live, work, and, in my case, study as guests, as visitors. I am part of an Indigenous diaspora; many of us have moved from our traditional territories in order to survive. I*

# Untapping Watershed Mind

*Rita Wong*

Rain teaches me to be humble. Its gentle persistence gives life to the unceded Coast Sal-ish land known as Vancouver, where the Musqueam, Tsleil Watuth, and Squamish have made their home for thousands of years. Thanks to the grace of rain and the generos-ity of these Indigenous peoples, whom I would like to acknowledge, I live in Vancou-ver, which the Chinese used to call Saltwater City (in contrast to New Westminster, Freshwater City), part of the *Stal'əw* watershed that flows out toward the Pacific Ocean.

Rain, falling steadily over millions of years, gradually gathered, pooled, and swelled into the bountiful watersheds that now provide my drinking water: Capilano, Seymour, and Coquitlam reservoirs. Rain, falling steadily over millions of years, created what the Musqueam call *Stal'əw*,[1] what English speakers call the Fraser River. As my co-author Dorothy Christian shows in the way she introduces herself, names matter, as they can honour a lineage and a history, or obscure it through colonial amnesia. Though my drinking water doesn't come from the *Stal'əw*, the *Stal'əw* is crucial to the formation of the land that I currently live on, through millennia of silt deposits from the Rocky Mountains, travelling over 1,300 km to shape the rich delta on which local farmers grew tons of produce, before industry pushed out much of the agriculture that flourished along what is now called Marine Drive.

> *saltiness grows over eons     plankton provide half our oxygen*
> *what we cannot see     matters as kin*

*Stal'əw* is a twelve-million-year-old[2] elder, an immense force that drains a third of Abo-riginal Columbia as it moves ceaselessly from its headwaters in the Rockies down, down, down to the ocean. It is a rare creature for its size: an undammed river, though some of its tributaries have been dammed, with great devastation to Indigenous peoples' homelands.[3]

As a resident of Vancouver, I need to acknowledge the TseKehNay people because the electricity that we use everyday results from the W.A.C. Bennett Dam completed in 1967 on the Peace River, which flooded the traditional territories of the TseKehNay (consis-ting of the Tsay Keh Dene, Takla Lake, and Kwadacha First Nations), devastating their *also speak as an Indigenous filmmaker and scholar. The observations that I share below are from multiple locations: they may begin in Montreal, but they move from the river delta of Stal'əw (also known as the mouth of the Fraser River or Vancouver), through to the Nile, the Mississippi, and the Shuswap rivers, and I meditate on the sacred waterways and watersheds where my people continue to live today.*

What might a watershed moment look like? It would, I think, require us to be conscious, to be mindful of our actions, our thoughts – how we live our daily lives. It would require us to take up the challenge of responding to the crisis posed by mega-projects like the Tar Sands, which are devastating the Athabasca River and the Arctic Ocean watershed. For me, it requires being painfully aware of the contradictions within my Western consumerist lifestyle and my Indigenous ways of knowing, seeing, doing, and acting. It takes a conscious and conscientious effort to continually bring my Indigeneity forward and not allow myself to be "paved over" by the ever-constant colonizing forces in my world. It is within this complex framework that I stand up to speak with water, because many humans are not listening to her voice carefully enough. A useful strategy toward a watershed moment may be for all of us to reframe our identities in relation to water, recognizing how the water that constitutes us is always "simultaneously real, like nature, narrated, like discourse, and collective, like society."[1]

This reframing of identity involves facing colonial divides and dismantling them, slowly rebuilding and acknowledging the Indigenous histories and perspectives of water that precede us everywhere on this continent and indeed the world.

*It is not comfortable being the only Indigenous person in the room when I know there are many Indigenous people who know much more about water than I do and who should be part of this conversation. I would like to explain why I put myself in this place of discomfort. Over twenty years ago, at the so-called 1990 Oka Crisis, I worked behind the scenes with two of the Iroquois Confederacy negotiators (Mike Myers, Seneca, and Bob Antone, Oneida) in the communications arena to elevate international consciousness about the land rights that the Mohawk and many other Indigenous peoples were defending. In 1995, for the last twelve days of the Gustafsen Lake stand-off, I worked with Jeannette Armstrong, Marlowe Sam (Okanagan), and the Shuswap Liaison Committee in the communications of that land rights dispute. Since my involvement in those two modern-day Indian wars, I have examined Indigenous-settler relationships in this country to search for ways and means to a peaceful coexistence on these lands.*

*These two situations were very visible because the people had picked up arms to illustrate how serious the land question is to Indigenous peoples. There have been many unreported situations of the people standing up to prevent the extraction of the natural resources that are directly tied to environmental degradation on our lands. It is in this context that I put myself into many intercultural environments where I am the only Indigenous person in the room.*

communities, those of people who once lived on the 1,773 square kilometres of flooded land, and communities like the Athabasca Chipewyan First Nation whose ability to hunt and gather was severely harmed by the dam's redirection of water, which dried up the delta they relied on for food and medicines. TseKehNay families did not know that their homes would be destroyed, and people suddenly found their homes burnt down by the government.[4] I cannot change this violent past, but what I can change is how I respond to this historical inheritance. One of colonization's common tactics is to divide and conquer different groups in the takeover and privatization of land, water, and resources; those of us who want to walk a peaceful path have a responsibility to build relationships and alliances that recognize interdependency and love for the watershed commons on which we live, even "at this late hour, under these imperfect conditions," as Larissa Lai has phrased it.[5] While this may be a daunting challenge, it is a worthy one, and we are fortunate to have many teachings to assist us: be they from the rain; Indigenous knowledge keepers; sometimes submerged aspects of various cultural traditions; the planet itself as its changes are translated by observers and scientists; and creatures large and small – what Dorothy Christian calls the seen and unseen – if we are open to a wide path of learning and peace.

The dam started operating in the late 1960s and has provided British Columbia, and in particular the Lower Mainland and the City of Vancouver, with electricity ever since. The TseKehNay have documented their history and their recent protection of Amazay Lake from Northgate Minerals Corporation's proposal to use it as a toxic tailings pond for their mining operations, in their film *Amazay,* which testifies to their resilience and dedication to water. Their story is something I didn't learn in school, but it should be taught there. It takes time, but I am steadily making efforts to remedy my ignorance about the watershed where I live and its many inspiring keepers.

For over a decade, I lived in a place made by the accumulated rain, *Stal'əw,* and powered by hydroelectric dams; yet, I remained for the most part unaware of my dependence on the river. Out of sight (unless I was driving to the airport), out of mind. If I ate salmon, it was in a restaurant, from a supermarket, or if I was lucky, from the boat of a fisherman near Granville Island. Never had I seen someone catch a salmon from the river that is famous for its salmon runs. Only this year have I actually seen salmon swimming in a stream, through the Mount Currie Reserve. Such disconnection from the river is not unusual for a city person. But thanks to Dorothy Christian and Denise Nadeau's invitation in 2007 to protect our sacred waters,[6] I've undertaken a journey to reconnect to the watershed in creative, practical, spiritual, and philosophical ways. Having met Dorothy at a gathering in 2002 organized by Lee Maracle, "Imagining Asian and Native Women: Deconstructing from Contact to Modern Times," I feel fortunate and honoured to rethink and relearn water in sisterhood with her in an unfolding process, many years later, to embark on a journey of enacting *LaxHösinsxw* (described in her section) in humble, respectful proximity with her.

In the past, I've moved constantly over various micro watersheds, unaware of the

*My personal resolve is that our current environmental reality is so urgent that I grit my teeth and grin and bear it for the most part, so as to bring an Indigenous perspective to the discourse. In my interface with settler peoples, I have developed allies within both the white settler and the Chinese settler populations to do collaborative work. My work with Rita Wong on the Downstream Project is one of those collaborations. In this work, I acknowledge the complexities, contradictions, and paradoxes that I experience as an Indigenous woman living in an urban centre in the twenty-first century who has purposefully worked toward reclaiming and revitalizing my Indigenous knowledge base for the past twenty-five years.*

It is from this point of view that I speak of the "cultural interface"[2] and some of the Indigenous concepts that directly affect the ways human beings intersect with the water systems of our physical environment. Doreen Jensen, an important Gitxsan Elder and scholar who has passed on to the spirit world, gives a critical insight into one of the concepts from her culture, which may assist in how we meet each other in a shared space. She writes that the word *LaxHösinsxw* "is a very important word in the Gitxsan language. It means honoring and respecting others, place, and space. In this city, at this site and at this time in history, it is a word we might learn from. The place and space in which ... Vancouver ... stands, physically and metaphorically, is a contested one. Here, where a city has been incompletely exchanged for the forest and newcomers have incompletely replaced the aboriginal inhabitants, LaxHösinsxw may be key to the creative process and to our future."[3]

In considering the "honoring and respecting" that Jensen points to, it may serve us to think of this interaction as working toward what Torres Strait Islander Martin Nakata calls the "cultural interface."[4] Nakata dismantles very tired colonial binaries and liberates Indigenous peoples from the role of victim to assume agency in their own system of knowledge. This meeting place is a domain where Indigenous knowledge and Western knowledge meet on an equal footing, where each system of knowledge is valid, a place to explore the notion of a peaceful co-existence, within academic discourse and our physical environments.

Though our efforts to build such respectful relationships are very important, structurally, we are not yet in that place of equality. Often, I find myself observing how institutional contexts work to encourage, discourage, objectify, ignore, or marginalize Indigenous voices on water issues. If the gap between good intentions and effective practices is to be closed – whether at other events, or this one – conscious efforts need to be made to cultivate a cultural interface that is respectful and welcoming to more Indigenous peoples, early in the planning of events, anthologies, and conversations. This inclusion could involve formally acknowledging whose traditional lands we are on, or inviting a range of Indigenous participants so as to broaden and deepen intercultural conversations.

subtle shift in topography whereby the water underground flows south to the Fraser, or north to False Creek, or even further north to the Capilano River. Water knows gravity intimately, sensitively, and moves accordingly.

Looking at Vancouver as a nested series of watersheds, I begin to learn about dispersal and accumulation as I try to perceive time and space through the lens of water. For instance, the Coquitlam River is a tributary of the Fraser River, which flows into the Georgia Strait, whereas the Capilano and Seymour rivers flow into Burrard Inlet. All of it flows, eventually, into the Salish Sea and, then, the Pacific Ocean. It's a question of whether one takes the ocean, the river, or the smaller streams and tributaries as the main point of reference by which to define the drainage area of the watershed.

Valuing water intrinsically, not as a commodity, not for its use value or its exchange value, but as agent in and of itself both plural and singular, I've had to suspend the property framework imposed by what the writer SKY Lee has called imperial delirium.[7] Vancouver is in the throes of real estate speculation and intensive finance capitalism, and land prices have steadily and rapidly increased over the years. One of the desired attributes for which people will pay lots of money is a view of expansive saltwater. As Lance Berowitz describes in his book, *Dream City*, Vancouverites favour waterfront property.[8] Ironically, in the rush to build expensive waterfront developments, in the rush to look out over the Burrard Inlet and False Creek, most of the city's occupants have overlooked and devalued the fresh water within. Instead of protecting and valuing over fifty salmon streams that historically ran through the area now known as Vancouver, the city gradually paved over most of them, culverting the wild streams, and burying them under concrete. As Dorothy Christian notes, a parallel can be drawn here with how original, Indigenous spiritual practices were paved over by the Christianizing process of colonization, practices which are now in the process of revitalizing or being "unpaved" as people return to honouring the whole of Creation, including watersheds.

At the scale of the local, I've embarked upon the task of learning about the many streams that used to flow freely in Vancouver. Less than two hundred years ago, before the onslaught of pavement and sawmills, Vancouver was a rich, abundant place, with streams slowly fed by rain, wet earth, and the natural dams we call cedars and Douglas firs. Today, only the Musqueam Creek near the Musqueam reserve still survives as a wild salmon stream, with the odd salmon struggling to return each year.

Amazing accomplishments in the midst of an urban space are due to the efforts of volunteer groups like the Musqueam Ecosystem Conservation Society (MECS) who've heroically and steadily worked to protect and replenish the stream habitat.[9] They've organized monthly stream clean-ups, and they offer public walks as well. On one of these walks, Will Sparrow taught us about how leaving fallen trees near the stream helps to keep the water cool for the salmon.[10] The city's parks staff had been removing such natural "debris" and thus inadvertently starving the creek; Sparrow persuaded them to leave the logs alone – substantially saving staff labour costs, and also feeding the creek

The cultural interface is a place to embed underlying principles of reform in the relationships we build with one another. From an Indigenous perspective, everything within Creation is sacred and interrelated. Human beings have a relationship with the seen and unseen worlds, with the entirety of the physical environment that includes the trees, the four-legged animals, the birds, the fish, the insects, and, above all, our waterways, which include our streams, our rivers, our lakes, our oceans, and our watersheds. A phrase that Indigenous peoples use that encompasses this interrelatedness is "All My Relations." Within this context, we ask you to conceive of water as the embodiment of spirit.

Many Indigenous thinkers perceive the self as composed of four capacities: the intellectual/mind, the physical/body, the emotional/heart, and the spirit.[5] Of these four parts of self, it may be spirit that is most elusive or challenging for many non-Indigenous peoples to approach. It is important to delve into the spiritual because it has been a site of oppression, one that needs much unpacking and rethinking. From my Indigenous way of seeing, we humans are a very small part of the rest of Creation, which we believe is infused with spirit. In the way that water gently and unstoppably finds its path everywhere around the world, so does spirit.

*[handwritten margin note: Western indi-vidualism/ indigenous responsibility/ environmentally embedded worldviews]*

When I look out to the world, I am at the centre as an individual, with three concentric circles surrounding me that represent my family, my community, and my Nation; therefore, included and embedded within my worldview is a responsibility to be respectful of the consciousness of the collective. The ways in which Indigenous peoples see, think, act, do and listen stand in stark contrast to dominant strains of Western thought that imagine the individual as primary, as being more important than community, notwithstanding Western intellectual efforts to challenge this thought structure, which works in the service of a capitalist imaginary.

From an Indigenous perspective, how we "see, think, act, do, and listen" is very different from the Western mindset, because we contextualize our physical relationship with a multidimensional point of view and with a multi-layered connection with seen and unseen beings – we relate to the land, the waters, the animals, the plants, and the spiritual realms. All beings are considered sacred, including water.

The Christian-centric perspective, which takes its cue from the first verse in the Christian bible, empowers man in the anthropocentric form of a God who has dominion over all things. I realize this is an overgeneralization; however, theologian Thomas Berry[6] has deliberated on this very question when looking at the state of our environment. With human dominance over watersheds, an extreme imbalance exists today, manifesting in an everyday urban culture that ignores or takes for granted the watersheds that we live in.

As writers, poets, filmmakers, and scholars, we make our homes in watersheds, not just in cities. If I map my life, my work, my communities, and my impact in terms of watersheds, then from my Indigenous perspective I look at "All My Relations," which as logs slowly decay, releasing nutrients, and cooling the water through their shade. What looks "messy" to an urban dweller might look and function like a pleasant retreat to a salmon fry or other water creatures. Meanwhile, volunteers keep removing plastic bottles, tin cans, and invasive species like ivy, laurel, and Himalayan blackberry, in diligent attempts to give Indigenous plants like the salmonberry a chance to survive. So, careful effort in some areas to reduce the impact of human pollution, and conscious non-effort in others to respect the ecology of the creek, provides a balance that gives the creek a better chance at survival.

Another example of how "chaotic" or "natural" ecological processes may be more desirable than "neat" or "tidy" human control can be found at nearby Langara College. On one end of the campus, perched on the edge of a parking lot, exists a small, reclaimed wetland,[11] a body of water that is home to a diverse range of Indigenous plants and birds. Guided through the wetland by Kelly Sveinson, I learned that the campus site used to be occupied by forests, ponds, streams, and swamps, of which the small wetland is a tiny reminder.[12] On the other end of the campus is the new energy-efficient library, which has a large rectangle of water outside it – monocultural and quite inhospitable to most nonhuman forms of life. The controlled water takes up more prominent campus space and arises from a well-intentioned desire for "green" buildings, but I find it rather sterile in contrast to the lively, aerating flow through the wetland, as water is jostled by ducks or trickles through green sedges.

The tension between pre-existing hydrological flows and currently imposed controls has often come to mind as I've taken various "lost stream" walks offered by the False Creek Watershed Society, organized by Celia Brauer.[13] On these walks, I cannot help but listen for water, and look for dips and cracks in the ground that might signal stubborn streams underneath. Thanks to the volunteer efforts of local historians like Terry Slack, Bruce Macdonald, and Dan Fass, I know of at least two supermarkets built on top of where streams used to run; where one could have fished for plentiful salmon for free a hundred years ago, today one has to purchase the salmon at the IGA or Famous Foods. In the alley behind one of Vancouver's hippie restaurant establishments, the Naam, only a small depression in the cement now indicates the stream underneath. Where people would have seen Brewery Creek a century ago, today we find a shiny Starbucks at the corner of Main and 14th.

Though the signs of human occupation are everywhere, we would do well to keep in mind what Squamish storyteller Wes Nahanee says: "water can never be stopped."[14] Whether it flows slowly, almost imperceptibly, beneath our feet, or rapidly in the big storms that tore down huge trees in Stanley Park, water moves inexorably through and around us. Most of the streams that used to exist are no longer visible to the eye because they have been buried under concrete, diverted or piped into sewers. But we can still hear them.

On the corner where I live, almost every day I hear the creek beneath the manhole include the waterways with which I co-exist. In this way, I can better understand and relate to the local connections and global flows of the place where I am situated.

On the Coast Salish territories where I live, the water in the Capilano, Seymour, and Coquitlam watersheds gets chlorinated and piped into our homes; moves through our bodies, hydrating and replenishing us, before being released into toilets; and is briefly and inadequately treated at the local sewage plants. Then, the water is released into the Georgia Strait, the Fraser River, the Burrard Inlet, and eventually the Pacific Ocean, to possibly evaporate up into the clouds in an infinitely dynamic hydrological cycle.

As a director of cameras for film and video, I have tried to imagine my camera eye following the path of water, from the point of view of water. Humans are connected to those aspects of water that we can see (clouds, precipitation, rivers, ponds, and lakes) and to those we may not see in our daily lives (underground aquifers, distant wetlands, sewage, glaciers, changing ocean currents, and the blood inside us). When we allow our imagination to flow with the water, from its many perspectives we get a small glimpse into how profound a connector water is for all of us. It is a connecting force that defines some physical boundaries and some would say, *defies* all boundaries. We begin to see how each of us is related through water; even that which falls from the sky is a gift from the cloud people.

You and I are part of that flow. Human beings are roughly two-thirds water, and the Earth's surface is roughly two-thirds water. We are part of the hydrological cycle, not separate from it. Some of the water that is in our bodies may have previously circulated in woolly mammoths millions of years ago, or swelled up in a plump, juicy salmonberry, or jostled around with fish in lakes and rivers, or been processed by our local sewage treatment plant. Water connects us to places, people, and creatures we have not seen, life that is far away from us, and life that came long before us.

If I look out at the world through the lens of water, I might notice "how close in salinity I am to ocean water,"[7] or, as Basia Irland puts it, how "each of us is a walking ocean, sloshing down the hallway with damp saline innards held together by a paper-thin epidermis."[8] I might start to think of myself as a porous body of water. I might see myself as part of the hydrological cycle, this planet's crucial circulatory system, my moist breath returning water vapour to the environment, the way trees do through transpiration. I might also notice how one person's bottled water means another person's dried-up aquifer when rapid, mass extraction is allowed to happen.

How many people take the time to intentionally build a relationship with our waterways as Rita Wong has done? How different would our world be, if we took the time to interrelate with our water systems in a mindful way? Water is what keeps us alive. What does it mean to bury this life force under concrete and to control its flow in pipes? When we start to trace its complex paths, how do we change our perceptions of water?

A very literal tracking of water may be what it takes to bring an understanding of how each of us is connected to one another, that a larger flow of energy – what some of us call Spirit, and what some of us do not name, notice, or acknowledge – links us both to covers, calling to me, gurgling its longing to return to sunlight and to reconnect with birds, fish, plants, and people. Because it's hard to ignore its insistent song, I helped organized a neighbourhood conversation on the topic of daylighting streams at the Native Education College a few blocks from what we tentatively call St George Creek (because it runs along what is now St George Street – and we've also thought about calling it Tenas Chuck, the Chinook term for "little water" or creek). At the suggestion of a city councillor who attended the event, that conversation became a neighbourhood group, and three months later, to our surprise, we had organized our first St George Creek Street Party.[15]

> *where the hydrant bursts*
> *water shoots exuberant into sky*
> *hear here*

> *coincidence, haunting, or the stubborn stream's refusal to be confined?*

> *one of fifty-plus former salmon streams on the old map*
> *what's lost may not be the streams but the people*
> *when they try to control the stream's knowledge*

> *re-pair tributary with daylight*
> *twin riparian zone with home*

What might be called the "St George Watershed" at this point is primarily a series of underground pipes that follow the grid, a very manufactured affair to be sure, but one also complemented by rainwater that overflows at times, exceeding the capacity of man-made systems. I rely on this urban watershed, whose piped rhythms follow people's preferred washing and cooking times. But it's the watery flow beyond the pipes, fed by clouds and rain, that intrigues me with its potential for infinite resilience, its generative production.

I've learned from other daylighting efforts that it's a very slow, difficult, and expensive process to try to unpave a street and restore a creek.[16] But even so, there are resident-driven efforts to return some of the streams to daylight, and, due to them, we can now see parts of Still Creek, the Renfrew Ravine, the Sanctuary in Hastings Park, and historical markers along Brewery Creek in Vancouver. It's important to restore, however partially or imperfectly, that broken connection to the water underneath even in the heart of the urban grid, because it shifts perception and awareness of place, and one's relationship to place. The streams call us to wake up and return to earth, return to water. And even if some daylighting efforts do not succeed, they still invite us to contemplate the underground life of unseen water, and how the unseen relates to the seen.[17]

On one of the stream walks, Chief Bill Williams of the Squamish Nation said that his one another and to the Earth to which we belong. Wonder and respect for this larger flow, this watery network, can be cultivated through poetry, through oral and visual storytelling, and through education. Most Indigenous peoples have stories of the waterways that bless their physical existence.

The storytellers from my Splatsin community, which is on the banks of the Shuswap River in the interior of British Columbia, have many stories about what that river means to us and particularly what it means to one of our food sources, the salmon. The Shuswap River watershed that I come from flows into the Thompson and Fraser river basins that affect our families, our communities, our Indigenous and non-Indigenous neighbours, and our Nation.

*I have a very personal relationship with the streams and other waterways of my land. I do not usually share this kind of information with people outside my culture because it is considered to be "insider" knowledge, earned through shared experiences and the sustained building of relationships. However, in this cultural interface, I have come to see it is necessary to explain some of our spiritual practices that are based in our Indigenous knowledge with concrete examples. For instance, when I returned to my territories, I sought guidance from the Elders. One Elder woman recommended that I re-introduce myself to the land and she instructed me to go to the streams and rivers "to talk and listen to them – to pray with them." Under her tutelage, I followed a strict program of instruction for one year. At the beginning of every season, for four days in a row, at the first light of day, I sat beside the waterways to meditate and pray. I re-introduced myself to the stream, the trees, and the rocks. With humility, I asked for cleansing, guidance, and strength.*

In 2005, when I had the privilege of visiting the Mississippi and Nile rivers, I felt in the very cells of my body, in a very visceral way, that I had to take personal action about the state of my sister, the waters of the Earth. In June 2005, I witnessed the Mississippi River in the bright sunlight of Minnesota. The source of this mighty river is Lake Itasca. My Anishnawbe friend and her Seneca husband were checking on the wild rice, a major food source for the people of that region that depends on water for its abundance. I wondered, "What challenges does the Mississippi overcome before reaching the Gulf of Mexico?"

Later that summer, in August 2005, I visited what I thought was the headwaters of the Nile River, basking in the moonlight of Uganda. When I came home, I researched the Nile River and found a complex system of rivers that come together to form the longest river in the world. I learned there is a White Nile and a Blue Nile, which merge near Khartoum, Sudan, to form what we in the West know as the Nile. It flows through Sudan and Egypt as it makes its way to the Mediterranean Sea. I discovered that the source of the Nile is actually the Luvironza River in Burundi, a tributary of the Kagera people paid attention to the direction that the water flowed, in order to describe their traditional territories.[18] That is, they were guided by the watersheds that they lived in. This is a radically different way of navigating land and space than imposing a concrete grid and price tag upon what was here.[19] It arises from a long-term view that listens to and works with the water's energy, its dynamics.

Prior to the urban infrastructure of water and sewer pipes, people had lived very well for millennia in what we now call Vancouver. In her short story "Goodbye Snauq," Lee Maracle observes that food was so plentiful near the shores of Snauq Staulk (False Creek is a misnomer that takes pride instead of shame in colonial errors)[20] that the Coast Salish called that area their garden or supermarket.[21] Working closely with what nature provided, they gathered oysters, clams, fish, wild cabbage, mushrooms, berries, camas, and much more. Most of this natural wealth became polluted and destroyed by newcomers; but today, Vancouver sees a rising popularity in urban food cultivation, ranging from community gardens to guerrilla gardens to programs like the Good Food Box Program started by the Vancouver Native Health Society and coordinated by artist/ethnobotanist Cease Wyss. With this, we also see more attention to how water flows. For instance, in the past, rainwater was usually diverted straight down into the sewer pipes when it would have been better to direct the water into the ground to nourish plants and gardens. This is changing slowly.

Among these small, hopeful signs around Snauq Staulk, a mass of contradictions and contestations abound. Such contradictions are the legacy of colonization, as my co-author Dorothy Christian points out. Today, it is not only a commercial space (including the billboards that the Squamish have placed on Burrard St Bridge),[22] or a residential space (high-rise condo heaven), or a recreational space (witness the dragon-boaters practising assiduously in teams), but a place whose identity is undergoing transformation.

Maracle writes in her story that "we are built for transformation," and that our challenge is to find freedom in the context we inherit. Although flashy capital demands our attention, it may be a very old and sacred relationship to water that we need to freely and wildly reclaim in this moment. We can't return to the past, but both Indigenous and non-Indigenous (or displaced, migrated) people can integrate a deeper respect for Indigenous ways of knowing into our current lives, working toward what Kuan-Hsing Chen has called a critical syncretism in a very different context, in his study of decolonization and de-imperialization in Asia.[23]

*"It was only when we learned the term acid rain*
*and saw the fish floating belly-up in lakes*
*hundreds of kilometers away*
*that we knew the death*
*had not vanished into thin air*
*as eagerly announced,*

River, which forms the border both between Rwanda and Tanzania and between Uganda and Tanzania, and then flows into Lake Victoria, from which the White Nile emerges in Uganda, which is where I connected with the Nile River. I wished I had a year or two to trace the flow of that river. I wondered what stories have come from the peoples who live along all those rivers. The vastness and beauty of these far-away rivers also reinforced my sense of connection to the waters that I grew up with. My community lives next to the Shuswap River, and we have many stories of our relationship with that river. The energies of the Nile and the Mississippi touched me in ways I cannot articulate. I was not immediately clear on what I should do, but the sense of water's connectedness lingered in me, eventually unfolding into personal actions.

*Another very intimate spiritual process in which I engage is in a community ceremonial context, which again is very private. Some Indigenous peoples may say I am breaking cultural protocols to even include this brief explanation, in this non-Indigenous environment. However, I choose to share a scant amount of information to assert the importance of an Indigenous approach to the Earth and all the seen and unseen beings, including water.*

*In 2007, I sent tobacco, a sacred medicine plant which assists in spiritual communications with other humans and non-humans (with a woman Sun Dancer) to the sacred Sundance Tree to ask whether or not I was ready to extend myself to this very sacred ceremony. I was given my answer, and I made a pledge to start a four-year cycle to Sundance in 2008. I will not go into the details of what this ceremony means, but I will explain that it requires a deep commitment to Indigenous ways of knowing the Earth and all of Creation. For four years, I sacrificed of my physical being by going without food and water for four days. During those four days, I danced and I prayed with a community of people for many things, including water. I prayed that the water of the Earth would continue to provide sustenance to humanity and I prayed for its protection.*

*Due to an illness, I was unable to sundance the summer of 2011; however, I completed my vow in August 2012. It is very difficult to share this kind of information with a non-Indigenous world that usually either does not give credence to the Indigenous ways of knowing or veers to the opposite extreme where individuals become so enamoured with Indigenous spiritual ways that they appropriate what little knowledge they glean for personal gain. While it is difficult to discuss cultural appropriation in this forum, it is necessary to acknowledge that this highly volatile issue makes it necessary for Indigenous people to be cautious and to protect our cultural knowledge from the exploitation that occurs when opportunistic, self-appointed "experts" assume the privilege of conducting Indigenous ceremonies.[9] There is a difficult balance to be struck between being vulnerable and generous with one's knowledge, and protecting against abuse and exploitation; I tread cautiously in maintaining this balance.*

For many Indigenous people, their original spiritual practices have been paved over by

*knew it would take a new kind of thinking*
*that was actually old*
*ancient*"[24]

The dominant colonial systems we've inherited run on a somewhat predictable logic: capitalist, hierarchical, predatory, exploitive. But underneath them, quietly persisting, are the watersheds and the underground streams, reminding us that another world is possible, and will indeed continue with or without us. The streams might be piped now, but unless they are painstakingly maintained, the pipes will leak and eventually burst. Before the water was piped, it was wild. What would it take for us to reconnect to that wildness? Urbanized, alienated, and ecologically illiterate, we cannot return to wilderness so easily, and may not want to, but perhaps we might explore what it means to go feral, to find some hybrid state that respects what has not been piped, controlled, regulated – what flows as the earth, the rain, and the ocean have a power and vitality that replenishes us.

Moving in that feral direction, I borrow the term "watershed mind" from Peter Warshall,[25] a former editor of the *Whole Earth Review*, who sees watersheds as necessary sites from which to support a cultural shift that values and substantially reconnects to water. When I walk through the city streets now, I think in terms of watersheds – which way is the water flowing underneath the ground? Why? How much is piped and controlled and chlorinated; how much left to wander freely? Where was the water last year; and where will it be in five years, in five centuries? How are the seen and unseen related through watershed dynamics?

I also find myself turning to a member of the Earth Ministry as I explore the possibility of untapping watershed mind. Considering the critical role that primary aquifers under the West Bank play in struggles between Israel and Palestine, Doug Thorpe notes how, in the Bible, "living water" signifies "fresh water that hasn't been controlled by human means – thus water that comes from God – but the phrase also conjures up some quality that transcends this literal definition."[26] Go back into history and you will find the idea that water is a sacred gift from the heavens (god, nature, or mother earth), and that people are grateful for this water. Thorpe compares us to the Roman empire, which was also able to pipe and divert water through huge feats of engineering. He suggests that the Romans "secularized the water. It no longer came from heaven; it came from Rome."[27] But empires and governments do not make water; they only redistribute what already exists in the living world.[28] When we can turn the tap on and off at will, it's easy to forget the vast rhythms and cycles of which we are part, and then slide into taking water for granted as a utilitarian resource, losing a mindful sense of connection to and reverence for the water that keeps us alive – what Thorpe calls "a mystique of rain."[29]

Thorpe starts his paper by quoting a Salish elder: "If you take the Christian Bible and put it out in the wind and the rain, soon the paper on which the words are printed will be gone. Our Bible is the wind and rain."[30] It was not until I made trips out to the

the Christianizing process of colonization, much as the streams in many urban centres have been paved over. However, like the streams, there are many of us who continue, quietly and persistently, trying to reclaim, revitalize, and return to our original ways of honouring the whole of Creation, including our water systems. All over Turtle Island, or North America, every summer there are Sun Dance circles praying for humanity and the Earth and all that it provides, including the abundance of our water systems. In our way, we are *giving back* to the Earth and the other beings who bless us with life.

In many Indigenous cultures, we have a concept of *giving back*. We try not to take without giving something back. What do we give back in return to our watersheds, our streams, our rivers, our oceans? What might be worthy gifts to offer sister water for all that she gives us? How do we remember our relationship with the natural world, what came before us, and who and what will come after us?

In the reclaiming of my own Indigenous spiritual practices, I acknowledge the sacredness of water as the "life blood of Mother Earth," as a gift from the sky and as a reminder of larger rhythms and cycles of which human beings are part. I connect to the water with an understanding that humans are only one kind of living being in a world that consists of millions of kinds of living beings: bears, salmon, deer, frogs, horsetails, berries, and moss all have as much of a relationship to water as I do. That is, I bring what Ardith Walkem calls a kin-centric perspective to my relationship with water. She writes: "When indigenous peoples say that the waters, lands, and resources are related to them, these are not merely words but, rather, deeply felt and acted upon beliefs … A kin-centric notion of ecology 'is an awareness that life in any environment is viable only when humans view the life surrounding them as kin' … and it calls upon humans to honour these relationships."[10]

With colonization, the story of Indigenous communities and water is also a story of people repeatedly displaced and devastated by dams, in different configurations, again and again around the world – their kinship to waters and lands disrupted. One inspiring example of resistance and resilience is documented in the film *Upstream Battle* (2008), which tells the story of the Karuk, Yurok, and Hoopa tribes that have dedicatedly struggled to remove dams and return salmon habitat along the Klamath River, and are in the midst of a successful effort to achieve this huge feat. They work for their relatives the salmon people by integrating a wide spectrum of imaginative tactics that range from actively lobbying Warren Buffet, to building alliances with historical enemies like the white fishermen, to practising traditional spiritual rituals and dances.

Though many of us are land-centric, it bears repeating and remembering that the planet's surface is roughly two-thirds water, just like our human bodies, and that this place that humans call "Earth" would more accurately be named Ocean. Writers like Alanna Mitchell argue that the ocean is the planet's primary life-support system.[11] If all the creatures on the land were to disappear tomorrow, the creatures in the water would be fine without us. But if all the creatures in the ocean were to disappear tomorrow, we would perish with them. Half the oxygen we breathe is created by plankton in the ocean.

Seymour, Coquitlam, and Capilano watersheds that I finally understood, in a visceral way, that I drink rain every day. Rain that has collected and pooled into lakes over centuries and millennia. Rain that connects me to oceans and clouds and places I have never seen with my own eyes. With the encouragement of watershed educator Ficus Chan,[31] I've begun to imagine more of the water's path, its complex relationships to hemlock, cedar, birds, frogs, lichen, moss, fungi, and all the delicious edibles that grow in the forest. Water is a gift from the sky that trickles, dissolves into, and invigorates complex ecosystems and human infrastructures before it arrives, chlorinated and resilient, through my tap.

Stream walks and watershed tours have changed how I see and imagine water; no longer is it merely an inert substance, but rather a larger process of ongoing transformation that slowly shapes where and how I live.

"Watershed mind" perceives how we are situated and embodied within micro- and macro-flows, moving at rates that range from the barely perceptible to the sudden extreme. I hear watershed mind in Jeannette Armstrong's poem "Water is Siwlkw," which opened the 2003 World Water Forum. She writes, "knowing that you   are the great River   as is   the abundant land   it brings   to carve / its banks   then spread   its fertile plains and deltas and open its basins / its great estuaries   even to where it finally   joins once again the grandmother ocean's vast and liquid peace."[32] In asserting that people are water, she articulates an Okanagan understanding of interconnectedness.

We are connected through what we receive and what we give back. As Dorothy [Christian] phrases it, "we try not to take without giving something back." This is a worthwhile principle for both Indigenous and non-Indigenous people to consider. At the moment we release many unworthy gifts into the watershed. Wastewater treatment plants do important but inadequate work. Sludge sinks and scum floats in the Annacis Island, Lulu Island, and Langley wastewater treatment plant. Tons upon tons of sludge sink and scum floats in the Lions Gate and Iona Island sewage plants. Once the solids are removed, the water that remains is chlorinated before it's returned to the Fraser, the Burrard Inlet, and eventually to the Pacific. These sewage plants were not designed to deal with medical waste – their engineers did not imagine Prozac, birth control pills, antibiotics, fire retardants, PCBs, and much more, dissolved and floating in their smelly, watery depths.

A worthier gift would be to restore or even improve conditions that enable living water. Such a gift involves understanding the colonial history that led to the increasing toxification, instrumentalization, and objectification of water, and realizing that Indigenous alternatives to it have survived, despite all attempts at obliteration. The logic of colonization involves defining and speaking for the other, pretending to know better, rapidly asserting mastery rather than humbly acknowledging one's limits – becoming a better listener before one slowly decides to act. With that in mind, as an uninvited guest on this watershed, I'm hesitant to speak *for* water in the abstract, and find myself drifting toward what Trinh T. Minh-ha has called "speaking *nearby*."[33]

Both saltwater and freshwater are crucial to our survival. And the cultures that form around saltwater are distinct from those that form around freshwater.

Maybe it is time for humans to grow up, to remember that the water in our bodies has flowed for millennia, to move slowly like a mature species that knows its ecological limits rather than an immature adolescent species that seeks only to instantly gratify itself and rapidly grow, like a cancer all over Mother Earth. The oil, the hydrocarbons, that we rely on in the cities are actually "ancient sunlight," to borrow Thom Hartmann's phrase, the remnants of our ancestors, turned into earth, into fuel.[12] In the shift from a society predicated on hydrocarbons, to one that respects the hydrocommons, Rita [Wong] and I propose that it is possible to shift society radically from a mindset of human domination to one of human coexistence with all other forms of life, who also need clean water. Our survival as a species depends on deeply understanding and propagating such coexistence.

As Mitchell points out, it is "the ocean that contains the switch of life. Not land, nor the atmosphere. The ocean. And that switch can be flipped off,"[13] as it has been during the five previous mass extinctions that have occurred on this planet. Perhaps it is time for global civilization to realize and accept that our collective actions as humans have brought the very real possibility of our extinction as a species. Here, in the midst of what many have suggested is the sixth mass extinction, we are living in "watershed times" where humanity has some critical choices to make. Is it a coincidence that the species that has caused this situation is the one with the responsibility to respond to it? For many Indigenous peoples and cultures, we have what Maori filmmaker Barry Barclay calls "a palpable awareness of [our pending] extinction,"[14] which is why I choose to put myself in the uncomfortable place of the "cultural interface" to bring some understanding of how we "see, think, act, do and listen" in the world, which has direct consequences to the survival of us all.

○

There are many indigenous approaches to respecting water. The practices I've mentioned for myself: Jeannette Armstrong's water poetry, Ardith Walkem's kincentric perspective, and the Karuk, Yurok, and Hoopa's protection of the Klamath River are all part of a larger body of knowledge that is both grounded in specific histories and, what is more important, looks toward a long-term future of coexistence with all beings who rely on water. Contrary to the falsehood of *terra nullius*, Indigenous peoples have been interacting with our environments for millennia, carefully passing on clean water and healthy forests to our future generations. Michael Blackstock, a Gitxsan forester, describes blue ecology as a "water-first approach to planning human interventions in the environment."[15] Interviewing three elders – Mary Thomas from the Secwepemc, Mary Louie from the Syilx, and Millie Mitchell from the Nlaka'pamux, he contrasts their assertion of the spiritual importance of water with Western science's focus on water's chemical and physical properties.[16]

How might I, as a watery being, speak *with* water, as an ally to it, knowing it is both within and without, always in movement? Taking on this watery lens may reorganize our structuring of self-identity, introducing a revelatory breakthrough, rather than a threatening one. The water that is inside me is part of the hydrological cycle around me, as water shapeshifts through me. The distinction between inside and outside, me and the surrounding watershed, becomes phased and rhythmic if we track the subtle dance of water molecules, floating through lively green wetlands and dark linear pipes on their way from you to me.

Speaking nearby still involves positioning oneself, being attentive to building relations with others, human and nonhuman. I am struck, for instance, by how the Musqueam language integrates a careful attentiveness to water in its very structure. While I am not a hən'q'əmin'əm' speaker, I have read that, "the vast majority of Musqueam verbs take their cue from the subject's orientation to the water."[34] In hən'q'əmin'əm', verbs change form depending on your relationship to the direction of river, whether you are upstream or downstream. This orientation embodies a daily relationship to water that is engrained through daily speech acts. How might this attention to water be translated into the structure of English verbs? Or how might Indigenous ways of knowing and articulating leak into English and transform it?[35]

> the city paved over with ~~cement~~ english cracks open,
> stubborn hən'q'əmin'əm' springs up

Piping and damming water has changed the rhythms and patterns of its flow, and I find myself reflecting on the many disrupted and rerouted watery rhythms that make up my everyday life, from irregular menstrual cycles[36] to the surge of the spring freshet down the *Stal'əw* to the cement-bound gurgling beneath the city streets. When I flip the electricity switch on, as I mentioned earlier, I am connected to the violent displacement of the TseKehNay, through the system of hydroelectric dams that have made the city possible. I am also more likely to disregard solar and lunar cycles because I rely on artificial light, and I can thoughtlessly flush without paying attention to seasonal flows of water, which may be higher in winter and spring and lower in the summer. There is so much to learn if we are to reconnect to the nonhuman world that gives us life; even today, I don't know when the full moon and the high tides are unless I consult a Web site. I seek the larger picture, learning from the rain that it will take a long time to evolve. Though the pipes might temporarily confine the water, flow will continue to the ocean, to the sky, to the planet.

> water has a syntax     i am still learning
> a middle voice     pivots where it is porous

A watery lexicon and syntax, a hydro logical approach could cultivate our capacity to scale down to the level of molecules and up to the level of oceans.[37] It could also

There are many creative and public ways to build relationships with the people and with water. Cathy Stubington, for instance, artistic director of Runaway Moon Theatre in Enderby, the small town next to my community, co-wrote a play called *Not the Way I Heard It*[17] with Secwepemc historian Rosalind Williams, who also co-directed the play in May 1999. They produced an amazing interactive theatre performance that incorporates both the settler and the Indigenous perspectives on the history of the lands and waters in the region on which our peoples coexist. This play worked as an amazing community development tool to develop relationships between the people of my community and the surrounding settler peoples who have, at times, had a very difficult history together. Since 1999 Cathy [Stubington] has deepened her relationship to my community, and one of her latest creative works was developed in July 2010;[18] it is a wonderful, large-scale community performance called *Sawllkwa* (the Splatsin word for water), bringing together a cast of people from my community and from the surrounding settler community, to celebrate and learn about water. This was followed by *The World Is Upside Down*, a bilingual (English and Dholuo) show that explores our personal and global relationships with water, arising from Cathy [Stubington]'s visit to a Kenyan village where she met performer Jimmy Ouma. Such creative works fosters a culture of respect and love for the people and for water, through the humour and inventiveness of theatre. Popular theatre, scholarly discussions, community organizing, spiritual gatherings, and creative practices – all these and more are needed to cultivate resilient watershed cultures.

Like Cathy [Stubington] who takes the time to build a deeper relationship with the people of my community and the surrounding waters, I am building a deeper relationship with water. I've imagined my camera eye way up in the sky looking down at the mouth of the Mississippi and the Nile rivers; I pan over to the watersheds of Turtle Island, then the watershed of Vancouver and the Lower Mainland of BC, and then the watershed of my home territories in the interior of BC. I wonder what a camera lens might see when it looks upon the waterways of your specific location. Do you know what it would see? Would your camera lens see the Indigenous peoples with whom you coexist and on whose ancestral lands you live? Yes, it is a challenge layered with complexities to simultaneously think with regionally specific waters while attending to the global relations of water. The waters we live with are part of a complex multi-body organism that envelops the earth and connects us all. Maybe the time has come for a cultural interface where all cultures shift into a paradigm that puts the WATERS of the EARTH at the front and centre of our human needs.

NOTES

1   Latour, *We Have Never Been Modern*, 6, quoted in Linton, *What Is Water?*, 177.

2   Nakata, *Disciplining the Savages*, 195.

3   Jensen, "Metamorphosis."

better attune our senses to the range of languages that traverse the human and nonhuman realms, enabling us to transition between the dialects of the domesticated, the wild, the feral. If I can learn to parse a salmon's journey or a human sentence, then hopefully, I might be able to speak *nearby* river, if I keenly listen to its shapeshifting grammar, its stubborn flow despite human obstacles and impositions. These are the fluid literacies I believe we need to relearn and adapt for the future.

NOTES

1 Victor Guerin, e-mail correspondence with author, 30 July and 6 September 2010. Guerin is a Musqueam community member and language speaker who provided this spelling of the Musqueam pronunciation, which was used in the City of Vancouver's "Wild Salmon Month" Proclamation in September 2010.

2 Bocking, *Mighty River*, 3.

3 For more discussion of the effects and representations of dams, see Haiven, this volume.

4 Daniel Sims, email correspondence with author, April 2011. A graduate student at the University of Alberta, Sims is also a member of the Tsay Keh Dene and is doing important historical research in this area. See also Sims, "Ware's Waldo."

5 Lai, "Radioactive Time," 2.

6 Christian and Nadeau, "Protect Our Sacred Waters."

7 Lee, Keynote speech.

8 Berelowitz, *Dream City*, 25–7.

9 *Musqueam Ecosystem Conservation Society* website.

10 This walk took place on 26 September 2009.

11 *Langara Wetland Project* website.

12 I visited the Langara campus on 7 May 2010.

13 Most of the walks I went on happened in the month of September in 2009, but the walks have been offered for a number of years by the False Creek Watershed Society.

14 I remember hearing him say this at a community mapping workshop organized by the False Creek Watershed Society in April 2010.

15 The first St George Creek Street Party happened on 11 September 2010.

16 On the expensive and inspiring side, see Andrew Revkin's story about Cheonggyecheon in Seoul, "Peeling Back Pavement to reveal Watery Heavens."

17 For more discussion of the unseen or non-visible, see: Neimanis and Chandler in this volume on a watery sociality that flows "beneath" human ethics; Alaimo in this volume on how a posthumanist approach to gelatinous creatures could reconfigure the seen/sensible; and Irene Klaver on reconnecting visible and invisible water structures with water bodies.

18 This walk took place on 26 September 2009.

19 Also see Chen in this volume, "Watering Mapping."

4  Nakata, *Disciplining the Savages*, 195.

5  See Archibald, *Storywork*.

6  Thomas Berry was a Catholic priest who died 1 June 2009. He named himself a "cosmologist," a "geologian" and an "Earth scholar." Berry was identified as part of the "new breed of eco-theologians." See Heffern, "Thomas Berry, Environmentalist Priest," pars. 3–4; Heffern also cites an article in *Newsweek*, 5 June 1989. See also Berry, "Thomas Berry and the Earth Community."

7  Wong, "Watershed," 116.

8  Irland, *Water Library*.

9  For example, in October 2009, "New age guru James Arthur Ray" charged $9000 for a sweatlodge experience where three people died. See Gumbel, "Death Valley." In February 2010, Ray was charged with manslaughter in the three deaths. See *Mail Foreign Service*, "Sweat lodge deaths."

10  Walkem, "The Land Is Dry," 314. Walkem here cites Salmon, "Kincentric Ecology," 1332).

11  Mitchell, *Sea Sick*, 22.

12  Hartmann, *The Last Hours of Ancient Sunlight*.

13  Mitchell, *Sea Sick*, 5.

14  Barclay, "Exploring Fourth Cinema," 17.

15  Blackstock, *Blue Ecology website*.

16  Blackstock, "Water: A First Nations' Spiritual and Ecological Perspective."

17  For more details, see Wellburn, "'Not the way I heard it.'"

18  For further details, see Runaway Moon Theatre.

20 George Henry Richards (1820–1896) thought it was a creek, but found out it was an inlet.

21 Maracle, "Goodbye, Snauq," 201–20.

22 See the *Digital Natives* project.

23 Kuan-Hsing Chen, *Asia as Method*, 99.

24 Ruffo, "Ethic," 53.

25 Warshall, "Watershed Governance," 47.

26 Thorpe, "Living Waters," 2 and 4.

27 Sawicki, *Crossing Galilee*, 24, quoted in Thorpe, "Living Waters," 10.

28 Chandler and Neimanis, this volume, describe the repetition and the infinitely creative reiterations of the hydrological cycle.

29 Thorpe, "Living Waters," 7.

30 Ibid., 1.

31 I went on a number of watershed tours offered by Ficus Chan through Metro Vancouver in 2009.

32 Armstrong, "Water is Siwlkw," 18, also, this volume, 104.

33 Minh-ha, *Framer Framed*, 96.

34 Zandberg, "Reviving a Native Tongue."

35 See, for instance, Roburn in this volume on the importance of primal sound for some Indigenous cultures.

36 It is worth noting that ancient Chinese medicine practitioners called menstrual blood "heavenly water." See Zhao, *Reflections of the Moon on Water*.

37 With regard to scale, also see Biro in this volume.

# Pond

*Don McKay*

Eventually water,
having been possessed by every verb –
been rush been drip been
geyser eddy fountain rapid drunk
evaporated frozen pissed
transpired – will fall
into itself and sit.
                              Pond. Things touch
or splash down and it
takes them in – pollen, heron, leaves, larvae, greater
and lesser scaup – nothing declined,
nothing carried briskly off to form
alluvium somewhere else. Pond gazes
into sky religiously but also gathers in its edge, reflecting cattails, alders,
reed beds and behind them, ranged
like taller children in the grade four photo,
conifers and birch. All of them inverted, carried
deeper into sepia, we might as well say
pondered. For pond is not pool,
whose clarity is edgeless and whose emptiness,
beloved by poets and the moon, permits us
to imagine life without the accident prone
plumbing of its ecosystems. No,
the pause of pond is gravid and its wealth
a naturally occurring soup. It thickens up
with spawn and algae, while,
on its surface, stirred by every
whim of wind, it tranlates air as texture –
mottled, moiré, pleated, shirred or
seersuckered in that momentary ecstasy from which

impressionism, like a bridesmaid, steps. When it rains
it winks, then puckers up all over, then,
moving two more inches into metamorphosis,
shudders into pelt.
                   Suppose Narcissus
were to find a nice brown pond
to gaze in: would the course of self-love
run so smooth with that exquisite face
rendered in bruin undertone,
shaken, and floated in the murk
between the deep sky and the ooze?

# Footbridge at Atwater: A Chorographic Inventory of Effects

*Peter C. van Wyck*[1]

> Away to the westward, the valley of the Ottawa opens out, and the river itself, splitting upon the Island of Montreal, sends its waters upon either side to mingle with the St Lawrence. Lake St Louis is spread out like a sea, and the Lachine Canal gleams like a ribbon of silver, and, upon occasion, one may see the leap and sparkle of the Rapids.
> (*The Montreal Electrical Handbook*, 1904)

> Interestingly, few species of mammal occur in or near the canal.
> (Canadian Environmental Assessment Agency, 1996)

The Lachine Canal is a vestigial corridor that draws a shallow line through the south-western portion of the island of Montreal, linking the Old Port with the town of Lachine, on the shores of Lac St Louis.[2] Constructed in the early nineteenth century, an era of great enthusiasm for canals in North America, the canal's purpose – part commercial, part military, and part hydraulic – was to bypass the otherwise unnavigable rapids on the St Lawrence River, the principal impediment to the smooth flow of (European) trade between Upper and Lower Canada. Between 1825 and its closure in 1970 the Lachine Canal became a trade and industrial terminus through which virtually all rail and water traffic on the St Lawrence corridor passed. The spatial and economic logic of Montreal – between Church and State, industry and urbanization, land ownership and production – came to be organized around this hydro-corridor. Tanning, livestock, lumber, agricultural goods, sugar, flour, cotton, textile and silk, rubber, shoes and boots, tobacco, slaughterhouses, dyes. And then hydroelectricity, iron, steel, foundries, munitions, electric wire and cable, ships, bridges and rail cars, paint and varnish, industrial chemicals, electroplating, coal to gas production, coke, batteries. In the years following its closure – and with much of the industrial infrastructure now in ruins – the Canal gradually reinvented itself as a recreational corridor. In 2002, under the auspices of Parks Canada and the Old Port of Montreal Corporation, the canal and its five refurbished locks were reopened to pleasure boating and designated as the Lachine Canal National Historic Site.

What has captured my imagination in all of this is not only the formal history of this corridor, nor the social and industrial transformations wrought by it. Rather, it is the material and sedimented accumulation of "past" that is very much alive in the present; the very toxic and archival quality of the site of the Lachine Canal calls for a procedure both lyric and chorographic. By *lyric*, I mean the overcoming of a distance through metaphor and imagination, and by *chorographic*, I signal a descriptive mode of proximity, an intensification of reading and writing, feeling and thinking in a particular locale or place. The itinerary of this text proceeds from a federal inventory of thirty-two contaminated sites on the canal (there are today more such sites, but this is where it began). The Atwater Footbridge secures for this work a platform from which, in thirty-two movements or gestures – let's call them variations – one may reflect on the layered social and industrial flows.

I

Rimbaud figured it thus:

> Skies the grey of crystal. A strange design of bridges, some straight, some arched, others descending at oblique angles to the first; and these figures recurring in other lighted circuits of the canal, but all so long and light that the banks, laden with domes, sink and shrink. A few of these bridges are still covered with hovels, others support poles, signals, frail parapets. Minor chords cross each other and disappear; ropes rise from the shore. One can make out a red coat, possibly other costumes and musical instruments. Are these popular tunes, snatches of seigniorial concerts, remnants of public hymns? The water is grey and blue, wide as an arm of the sea. A white ray falling high from in the sky destroys this comedy.[3]

2

To begin with, imagine that you and I were standing together on the footbridge at the Atwater Market. Rimbaud's cinematic prose could seem to us an invitation, perhaps an invocation, of sorts; a whimsical if impressionistic checklist, just for us. Canal, check, obviously. Minor chords, yes, in a sense, yes. Hovels, some remaining. Frail parapets, most certainly. Public hymns, of course. And a sky the grey of crystal. Yes, crystal. Always. But this isn't exactly about us. And you are not really here on this bridge in Montreal with me.

3

This bridge, owned by the federal ministry, Parks Canada, is known as the Atwater Bridge – a footbridge possessed of no inspiration, of no special attributes. It merely cuts a low arc across the canal, joining one side with the other. This is the *Bridge without Qualities*. "And since the possession of qualities assumes a certain pleasure in their reality," writes Musil, "we can see how a man who cannot summon up a sense of reality even in relation to himself may suddenly, one day, come to see himself as a man without qualities."[4]

4

None, really. And certainly nothing of technical, historical, or aesthetic distinction. No pleasurable baroque cantilevers, no clockwork turntables (telling perhaps), no stonework, no appointments as they say (again, tellingly; it has no itinerary). It is vaguely bureaucratic-looking. Incongruous in relation to the lovely deco-inspired Atwater Market. Instrumental, one might say. That is, it does the job – if we understand the calling of the bridge in a certain functional fashion – drawing on the paradigm of possible bridges quite without recourse to anything we might call a gesture of art. It is, after all, only a footbridge, merely a portage for *les couriers de baguette*: travellers, traders, and tourists to and from the market at Atwater.

Nice view from up here, though.

5

Of course we must remember that this is a bridge over the Lachine Canal; though moving as we do, we sometimes forget. Part sewer, part trench, part recreational corridor, part territorial archive, it cuts a topographic swath through the lower part of the island of Montreal, through its deep and sedimented history. A history, one must recall, that stretches back considerably further than that fall afternoon in 1535 when Cartier stumbled ashore.

The canal was opened to traffic in 1825.[5] In the beginning, the alignment from the Old Port of Montreal to Lachine was controlled by a series of seven locks, each one hundred feet long by twenty feet wide, and the canal was excavated to a depth of five feet. The first major enlargement of the canal occurred between 1843 and 1848. During this period the number of locks was reduced to five, and these were re-engineered to more than double their original size, and the canal itself was increased to a depth of nine feet to accommodate deeper draft boats. Another expansion, undertaken between

1875 and 1899, saw the canal deepened again, this time to fourteen feet, and widened to between 150 and 200 feet.

A westward journey with an eastern itinerary for the European imaginary. Lachine, *La Chine* – forever a cycle of possession and dispossession.


6

Between the mid-nineteenth and mid-twentieth centuries, this long line, this route, was the most intensively industrialized region in Canada, a huge economic engine for the region and the nation. A cradle, as it was (and is) ceaselessly called, of economy, of industry, of nation, of anything nascent and valuable.[6] And it would be still, a cradle, that is, if the opening of the St Lawrence Seaway had not set in motion the canal's transformation to anachronism with the first flush of its locks in 1959.


7

By 1965 the eastern end of the canal at the Old Port was closed and filled. In a kind of zero-sum game of urban transformation, the materials used to fill the lower basins of the canal are presumed to have come from the excavations undertaken for the expansion to the subway system in the lead-up to Expo 67.[7] This closure left ship access only from the Lac St Louis (Lachine) end – a strange reversal of its founding (hydro)logic. In less than a decade, Canal traffic had declined from over one thousand boats a year to fewer than a hundred. The turning basin, upstream from lock no. 3 (St Gabriel Lock) was maintained so ships did not have to back out of the canal to Lachine. A Lachine Canal with one opening is not really a canal. A loading dock, a driveway. A *cul de sac*.

The end came in 1969 when the St Lawrence Seaway Authority announced the permanent closure of the canal, rendering the site of nearly a century and a half of continued investment, development, expansion and transformation – from the Old Port of Montreal to the municipality of Lachine – a telling scar, a land-locked artifact and archive.


8

It wasn't a quiet transformation.[8] The remaining industries along the corridor attempted to contest the closure and potential filling of the canal, arguing their continued demand for water (upward of 25 million gallons a day), waste disposal (some 6.4 million gallons a day), and at least partial navigability – minimally, from Lachine eastward to the

LaSalle Coke Company plant. Nonetheless, in 1970 the canal came to an end. The single entrance to a very narrow lake closed – an oxbow, not of riparian but of techno-political origins. Vestigial, obsolete.

By 1982, having been deemed by the government to be sufficiently contaminated to warrant the protection of the public, it was closed to any and all recreational activities. Neighbourhoods that had been socially, economically, and geographically formed by the canal over the course of its history were set adrift: Lachine, LaSalle and Ville St Pierre to the west; Ville Émard, Côte-Saint-Paul, Saint-Henri, La Petite Bourgogne, Pointe-Saint-Charles, Faubourg-des-Récollets, and Griffintown to the east.[9] Towns with no cheer.

9

But here it is. Naked, curious. A murky fact. Topographically and economically useless, it soon became a jurisdiction pariah as well. Transport Canada, the ministry responsible for the canal, negotiated transfer of jurisdiction to Public Works in 1974, and Public Works handed it off to Parks Canada in 1977.[10]

And if we were to ask, "What is the Lachine Canal?" of that most contemporary of oracles, Google, we would learn many things about this urban route.
For instance,
where I get my daily dose of weather, and trees ...
Or,
Once a humming artery of shipping and ...
located in a heavily used urban park where one does not expect ...
            (We are not sure what not to expect.)
And, part of Parks Canada's historic sites
noted today for ...
            (Dot dot dot.)
Located in Montreal, the Lachine Canal stretches 14.5 km from the Old Port to
Lake Saint-Louis
an integral part of Montreal's sea port
a key part of Montreal's past as a shipping and industrial centre
hard to imagine that placid little Lachine Canal used to be interior Canada's sole
artery to the Atlantic...
            (Yes it is.)
ideal for activities that are as cultural and historical as they are sportive and
recreational
            (Having fun?)
It is: due to a clearance of 8 feet under the Canadian National Railway

designed for vessels with a clearance of 8′

open from May 14 through October 14

stirring up as much enthusiasm among Montrealers now as it did two hundred years ago during its construction

(Never mind that the dates don't quite line up.)

business owners on Montreal's Lachine Canal were told to close down Tuesday after the city was forced to dump raw sewage into the Canal to avoid sewer backups during Monday's heavy rainfall ...

(History *is* the site of the now.)[11]

intimately tied to Montreal's economic growth

full of human patterns

the oldest canal in Canada

destined to become a favorite tourist attraction

a green wonderland of leafy elephants

(My personal favourite.)

opened after five years of construction

an important and complex historic site

more severely contaminated

also scenic

finished

completed

full

experiencing an expensive but exciting rebirth as a centre for culture

now a popular tourist area

the oldest industrial area in Quebec

planned for this summer

a picturesque spot popular with Montrealers

finally finished and allows boats to reach the west without having to go through the rapids

presently being refurbished to once again give pleasure boats direct access to the Old Port of Montreal

(Once again?)

a nationally significant cultural and historical resource

good riding so I took my time and made it to downtown just before dark

a storm was coming so we docked at the Atwater market

("The storm is what we call progress.")[12]

Although,

there may not be an opera ...

(Always a risk.)

And so on.

10

Anyway, apart from its rich setting, its apparent indifference thereto, and its utter structural artlessness, it is, like most of the bridges over the length of the Lachine Canal, an abridgement of the work of the canal itself. That is to say, to have a canal – the Lachine, or otherwise – mustn't one also have at the very least the *idea* of a bridge to cross it? The invisibility of our tools – bridges, search engines, and otherwise – testifies to their embeddedness in our thinking and speaking. The blindness of practice – a precondition for practice itself – is a Faustian bargain that grants continued "productivity" at the price of knowledge, awareness.

11

No need to be overly metaphorical here; after all, the bridge is already performing in the service of metaphor; it can hardly do otherwise: *to carry-over, to bear, to transfer*. That said, this is not the bridge as a symbol of fraternity, as a reaching-out and holding-together across the waters – the communicative bridge. This *is* a bridge that we *have* come to and *will* cross over. That metaphorical bridge is freighted with travellers and tropes stretching back into antiquity. Heidegger's bridge, for example, does not simply "connect banks that are already there."[13] The banks, he writes, "emerge as banks only as the bridge crosses the stream."[14] On this account, the bridge is a gathering.[15]

But not all bridges are gatherings, of course, and for Heidegger, not equally so.

> The city bridge leads from the precincts of the castle to the cathedral square; the river bridge near the country town brings wagons and horse teams to the surrounding villages. The old stone bridge's humble brook crossing gives to the harvest wagon its passage from the fields into the village, and carries the lumber cart from the field path to the road. The highway bridge is tied into the network of long-distance traffic, paced as calculated for maximum yield. Always and ever differently the bridge escorts the lingering and hastening ways of men to and from so that they may get to the other banks and in the end, as mortals, to the other side.[16]

The point here is different, and is simply this: the hydrotechnics of the canal – connecting two distant bodies of water by drawing a line deep into the earth – is unthinkable without a parallel technology of the bridge. Together they form a practice or a circuit.

The canal presupposes the bridge, just as the bridge presupposes something for it to purposefully cross over.

12

Indeed, when legislation was first enacted to allow the construction of the Lachine Canal, it specified that where the canal severed a public road – which of course it did at numerous points in its alignment from the town of Lachine to the Old Port of Montreal – within a period of one month a new bridge was to be built.

13

When you think of it, this is a long time to sever a road, and a very short time to build a bridge. Nonetheless. Gathering.

When the canal was twice widened in the middle of the nineteenth century, some fourteen bridges had to be rebuilt – more or less one per kilometre of canal. Some of these constructions were impressive structures indeed, drawing from the leading edge of design and technology, and many were the work of the renowned Canadian engineering firm, the Dominion Bridge Company: the Gauron, the Des Seigneurs, the Charlevoix.[17]

14

From the bridge, the territorial archive is but a conjecture. The water below, as water, reflects the sky above (incidence), not the archive beneath (incidents). But this is only partially about the visible to begin with. The archive of toxicity is only ever legible, and only then aided by multiple literacies and actors – from benthic organisms, macrophytes and mammals, to biochemical transactions and curious academics. Another bridge, then, is required; a conceptual and hermeneutic bridge between the metropolitan archives and the territorial indices – inscriptions, traces, florescences and absences. A reader, then, am I of this dilatory place, sifting and gleaning through the remains. In other words, the movement is not from archive to site – the indexical imaginary[18] – but to see the site *as* archive, dispersed as it is.

While there is something hopeful about the inclusion of toxic sites within the rubric of Canada's National Historic Sites, the history Parks Canada wishes to promote excludes mention of the word toxicity itself. Perhaps, then, the role of the chorographer is in part to return this toxicity to its very archival site – that is, to understand and accept this historical, industrial excess, without disavowal, without erasure. And of course, why stop there? The canal did not exactly appear, *ex nihilo* – it is and was already predicated on prior erasures.

15

Today, the canal is crossed by some twenty-five bridges and structures, a number of rail-ways, and the improbable and crumbling aerial catastrophe of ramps and overpasses, linking together three expressways, in airborne symmetry, conventionally known as the Turcot Interchange. Crossing beneath it are two tunnels, two Metro lines, a clutch of conduits together with hydro, telephone, and gas lines.

16

Through the nineteenth century, right up until the point in 1970 at which boats plied the canal no more, divers were employed periodically to remove objects that might prove hazardous to navigation. Having been designed for shallow-draft, flat-bottomed canal boats, the canal was never very deep. Stones, pieces of wood and metal, dross from construction. Carts, carriages and other castoff debris. Bodies, supposedly. Who knows? But everything had to be located and removed.

17

Here, in the early twenty-first century, crossing the bridge at Atwater in winter, one can enumerate many such objects arrayed on the grey January ice. Remnants of public hymns perhaps. An installation of debris, of signs. A shopping cart maquillage of frozen fresh-water clams. The back of a Petula Clark CD. Greatest hits. One tire. A small, cross-country ski boot. Left, by the looks of it. A blue hat, a red scarf, and a mitten that may have been brown. Many small objects not easily identifiable. (No stray dogs or suckling pigs.) A constellation of empty, and largely domestic, beer bottles. A bowling ball. (Actually that's not true. There was no bowling ball – that was a different bridge, and a different canal, and a very different time.)

18

The scene in the summer months is remarkably different. Commencing with the fanfare of the 2002 official reopening of the Canal, a veritable flotilla of boats has taken to the waters. This had not been part of the original plan proposed by Parks Canada, nor part of the environmental impact statement they undertook. But during the public consul-tation process, it became cast as the key issue for the success of the project. Boating would potentially generate "substantial economic spin-offs in the tourism sector, cre-ating new jobs and contributing to the economic development of the region."[19]

In 1989 Parks Canada requested an environmental assessment of its proposed decontamination project. At the same time the Old Port of Montreal Corporation requested that the portion of the canal under its jurisdiction be subject to the same review. The Government of Quebec and the Federal Government initially agreed to conduct their assessments jointly, but eventually decided to conduct a single assessment that would satisfy both provincial and federal requirements.

By 1998 a plan was proposed for the complete refurbishing of the locks, construction and reconfiguration of bicycle bridges, and the raising of the Charlevoix, Des Seigneurs and Côte-Saint-Paul bridges.[20] The question remained, though, concerning the effect power-boats and the newly functioning locks would have on the fourteen-kilometre layer of contaminated sediments. There was talk of placing protective covers on top of the sediments downstream of the five locks to prevent re-suspension. "Cover-ups," as I heard one French-speaking journalist inadvertently put it. This was never done. And as for the boat traffic, computer modelling suggested that a speed limit of 10 km/h would prevent the re-suspension of sediments.[21]

Several remediation alternatives were imagined and assessed in the Environmental Impact Statement (EIS) submitted by Parks Canada and the Old Port of Montreal Corporation (otherwise known as the proponents): terrestrial containment, where the sediments are dredged and stored, somewhere; *in situ* containment, where the sediments are covered up, so to speak, on the bottom of the canal with a geotextile membrane; encapsulation, where the sediments are dredged from the canal and stored in containment cells built into the canal embankments; *in situ* solidification, where the sediments would be chemically treated and solidified on-site; *ex situ* solidification, where the sediments are first dredged, then solidified and stored elsewhere; and finally, physico-chemical extraction, where the sediments are first dredged, then treated to remove contaminants, then put back into the canal.[22] Costs for the various options varied wildly. Estimates were in the range of six to forty-three million dollars (in 1993 Canadian currency).

The option that was selected by the proponents – based on a curiously weighted technical, economic, and environmental analysis – was to encapsulate the sediments on the banks of the canal in a number of specially constructed containment cells. Estimates of the volume of sediment to be contained varied according to the reporting agency: from 122,000 m² to nearly three times that amount. To picture this, imagine a layer of sediment, from Lachine to the Old Port, somewhere between 26 and 78 cm deep.

The joint panel review of the impact statement did not concur with the project's proponents; the encapsulation proposal was flatly rejected on the grounds that it was effectively a temporary solution, and that it would further compromise the adjacent environment. And furthermore, since Parks Canada had abandoned hope for swimming as a recreational value, removal of contaminated sediments posing no immediate health risk was not economically justified. Although the review panel agreed that decontamination was a good in and of itself, it failed to agree that it was a particular good that "we" could afford.

Their review, scathing at points, criticized the EIS for not having considered the *status quo* as a viable (and in any case, important comparative) option. (The *do nothing*, or null hypothesis option is conventionally included in impact statements.) Their argument was simple: Since Parks Canada had downgraded the proposed recreational use of the canal to include only "secondary-contact" uses (such as rowing, canoeing, and paddle-boating) and excluding "primary-contact" uses like swimming – and, at that point, was not proposing to open the canal to boat traffic – the canal sediments would pose no significant public health risks. And since the bacterial quality of the water was determined by factors other than the sediments, the proposal to encapsulate the sediments in three containment cells was not sufficiently justified. "Regardless of the future uses of the Canal, the joint panel finds it incomprehensible that the proponent is proposing to decontaminate the sediments in the Lachine Canal for the purpose of cleaning up the environment, without first ensuring that it is aware of and controls the main sources of contamination of the local environment."[23]

## 19

But in any case, the bridge today affords a kind of archaeological viewpoint. It is an irreducibly modern bridge, but it looks over something built up from layers and layers of history. It would be useful, for those inclined to think about the canal in this manner, "to examine the stratigraphic context, to identify what seems to be a fire layer, to locate any trace of occupation."[24] Such traces are of course everywhere, though the apparently inexorable process of commoditization of the canal's historical built resources threatens to stage all of this as a *second* disappearance of the canal. The sediments, though – these are the only remaining *in situ* record. The sedimentary archive remains today, as testimony to the disavowal of those in charge, and as the repressed material of the discursive and rhetorical transformations of the canal.[25]

## 20

Imagine, suggests Don McKay, "a trail made of moments rather than minutes, wild bits of time which resist elapsing according to a schedule. Pauses. Each one bell-shaped, into which you step as an applicant for the position of tongue."[26] To imagine this is to arrest one flow in order to see another: a landscape where water is not a supplement. It is to think of the archive as a territorial proposition. It is to understand something of the relations between a route and a place. A route is visitable, but not habitable, to badly paraphrase Barthes.[27] A place is habitable, we might say, and in addition to its occupation and identifications, is constituted by everything in that some*where* that if excluded or erased would diminish it.[28] But a route, a route is a foil – that is, a track (a mark, a line) *and* a concealment … the effacement of the line. As visitable only – although perhaps a succession of habitable places – a route is a problem.

21

If we were standing on the footbridge now, or any time at all, we would be roughly midway along what is prosaically called Basin no. 3 of the Lachine Canal; the language of the lockmaster is always used to describe this place. This was a difficult basin during the clean-up phase of the of the canal's redevelopment. Not that there was much of a cleanup undertaken. The worst was Basin no. 4; there were bikes and mattresses, furniture and picnic tables, and "so many cars that it would have been impossible for a boat to cross it."[29]

22

Apart from the contaminated sediments, and the various and sundry objects that find their way into the murky shallows, the other (or an other) vector of contamination, one that is infrequently cited in official documents, but was crucial during the review of the impact statement, concerns bacteriological contamination. Several times a year, according purely to rainfall intensity, waste water and household sewage in the Côte-Saint-Luc collector overflows, and is diverted through a four-hundred-metre-long, rectangular conduit into the Rockfield Overflow outlet, directly into the Lachine Canal.[30] The frequency of these punctuated events varies; the environmental impact review estimated forty events per year, equivalent to roughly 100,000 kg of sediment discharged annually into the canal, prompting the review panel to note that "based on the metal content of this suspended matter, recontamination of the bottom sediments to level 3 would take only 25 years."[31] Other estimates report smaller loads of less frequency (such as 70,000 kg/yr). No one seems certain. Nor, it seems, is anyone quite sure how many active discharge points there are along the length of the canal.[32] Parks Canada estimated over two hundred drains and intakes exist, some active, some not.[33] So much for decontamination. And swimming. And skating.

23

One must resist the idea that the basins of the canal are somehow interconnected lakes communicating via locks. This could not be further from the truth. The Atwater Bridge overlooks the real secret of the canal: it is a river, a river in slow-motion. A post-industrial river.

24

From Lachine to the Old Port of Montreal the canal drops over five metres. In other words, the water one sees in calm reflection (yours or its) is moving. From the vantage point of our bridge at Atwater, the water falls. Hardly a torrent, but it falls. And it falls at something on the order of 6 cm per second.[34] That's a little over five kilometres a day. Think of it: the water flowing past the Fur Trade Museum in Lachine this morning will pass under the Atwater Bridge tomorrow afternoon, and will flow into the Old Port the day after that. Down to the sea.

25

Yet our inventory here is hardly complete. Beneath the bridge, and beneath the water, it is a river, after all.

26

In the water here, beneath the bridge, in addition to things that might impede navigation, the river with its tributaries supports life. A lot of life, actually. One can find such denizens of the not-so-deep as pelecypods, and oligochaetes. And fish. I've seen them. Chromatic fish, like Emerald Shiners, and Yellow Perch, some sixteen species in all; I have often seen intrepid urban fishers casting their lines.

And there are metals too: zinc, mercury, chromium, cadmium, nickel, lead, phosphorus, and copper. In the sediments below the bridge, copper, chromium, lead, zinc, and particularly mercury, all exceed provincial guidelines. Traces all, to be sure, of the serial history of production along this route. Pulp and paper, iron, rubber, leather, textile, beverages, steel, printing, non-ferrous metals, electrical appliances, petroleum, coal, industrial chemicals, flour, nails, sugar, non-metallic ores, and so on. History here is not just built. It is contained in the stratigraphic record of the canal's sediments. The challenge is to think all of this history in the "now." The real of the sediments, of course, makes this somewhat easier to accomplish. Unlike radiological contamination, matter that seeks to efface itself, these materials simply persist, indifferent to time. Dispersion or containment (that is, spatialization or localization) – these are the modes proper to toxic materials. The passage of time here indexes only to memory and forgetting.

27

If you consult the "Directory of Federal Real Property," managed by the Treasury Board of Canada, you will see that the Lachine Canal is home to a number of such contaminated sites. It is of course not possible to tell with any real precision where these thirty-two individual sites might be, nor the precise extent of the contamination.

Each of the contaminated sites, however, indicates the presence of heavy metals and organic compounds like petroleum hydrocarbons, polychlorinated biphenyls (PCBS), and the wondrously synesthetic polycyclic aromatic hydrocarbons (PAHS).[35] Odd name, that. Quips Rimbaud: "it ends in a riot of perfumes."[36]

## 28

Even from this vantage point atop the Atwater Bridge, the very concept of contamination is ambiguous. What would count, exactly? By "contaminated site" is meant: "a site at which substances occur at concentrations (1) above background levels and pose or are likely to pose an immediate or long term hazard to human health or the environment, or (2) exceeding levels specified in policies and regulations."[37]

## 29

Contamination. Either dangerous, or illegal. Or both. The de-coupling of the toxic and the political-juridical is interesting, and telling. This, one might add, mimics perfectly the structural form of the alibi. Its very ambivalence takes care of everything.[38]

## 30

Contaminated sites; toxicological or juridical, invisible or recreational. A brownfield, as it is sometimes called, is: "a former industrial or commercial site where future use is affected by real or perceived environmental contamination."

Real or perceived. Full fathom five.

## 31

Musil saw things differently:

Dark patches of pedestrian bustle formed into cloudy streams. Where stronger lines of speed transected their loose-woven hurrying, they clotted up – only to trickle on all the faster then and after a few ripples regain their regular pulse-beat. Hundreds of sounds were intertwined into a coil of wiry noise, with single barbs projecting, sharp edges running along it and submerging again, and clear notes splintering off – flying and scattering … the general movement pulsed through the streets. Like all big cities, it consisted of irregularity, change, sliding forward, not keeping in step, collisions of things and affairs, and fathomless points of silence in between, of paved ways and wilderness, of one great rhythmic throb and the perpetual discord and dislocation of all opposing rhythms, and as a whole resembled a seething, bubbling fluid in a vessel consisting of the solid material of buildings, laws, regulations and historical traditions.[39]

Were this a piece of music – a composition of sound, of sounds, with which it is certainly filled, a quodlibet let's say (though perhaps more in the archaic sense of a *topic* than a medley) – we might think of the canal as a very long line, a rhythmic line in extension, and we could also imagine – not a hard thing to do – that this line had a thickness, a depth, say, a harmonic depth. That would be something to think about. It would be a very complicated place, a place that would require a very special mode of engagement. A mode of theory that retro-navigates an idea of place as inseparable from experience, but not in any way reducible to it. In a word, *theoria*.[40]

## 32

And then, we would have something very special indeed, a remarkable line, that we will call a route or a watery foil – with a thickness and extension, or better, an amplitude and a frequency, the *waves* of the route falling down through the canal to the sea; we would have a strange and wonderful polyphony of industry and water, and history and time, and progress and struggle and change. And the lives of men and women, of runners and riders and boats with Bob Seger; of immigrants and owners, lockmasters and ship-builders, and Styrofoam water lilies (unstable objects for sure[41]); and steersman, stonecutters, masons and machines, iron-workers, pipe-fitters, dog-walkers, and those without homes; all of these things would be there, as they *are* there, here, traces of them at least, and of course the contamination – each of the thirty-two sites – about which we know so little,[42] yet each subsists, each perfectly real wherever they are; and then we think of the bridge from which we survey this strange cacophony, and there *we* are: an encounter by chance, by accident.

NOTES

1  I want to thank the organizers of the Thinking with Water Workshop for their thoughtful advice (and patience) in bringing this work from speech to text. I am particularly grateful to Stacy Alaimo and Rita Wong for their probing comments and suggestions.

2  My interest in the Lachine Canal began at the invitation of sound artist and scholar

Andra McCartney, who commissioned a text for an installation at the Lachine Museum. See Peter C. van Wyck, "Footbridge at Atwater."

3  Arthur Rimbaud, *Illuminations and Other Prose Poems*. Des ciels gris de cristal. Un bizarre dessin de ponts, ceux-ci droits, ceux-là bombés, d'autres descendant ou obliquant en angles sur les premiers, et ces figures se renouvelant dans les autres circuits éclairés du canal, mais tous tellement longs et légers que les rives chargées de dômes s'abaissent et s'amoindrissent. Quelques-uns de ces ponts sont encore chargés de masures. D'autres soutiennent des mâts, des signaux, de frêles parapets. Des accords mineurs se croisent, et filent, des cordes montent des berges. On distingue une veste rouge, peut-être d'autres costumes et des instruments de musique. Sont-ce des airs populaires, des bouts de concerts seigneuriaux, des restants d'hymnes publics? L'eau est grise et bleue, large comme un bras de mer. – Un rayon blanc, tombant du haut du ciel, anéantit cette comédie.

4  Musil, *The Man Without Qualities*, 12. See also Finlay, *The Potential of Modern Discourse*.

5  The morphological dimensions of the Lachine corridor and its articulation with the historical built form of Montreal is well documented. See Bliek and Gauthier, "Understanding the Built Form of Industrialization Along the Lachine Canal in Montreal." And for an analysis of brownfield environments as historically significant elements of urban space, see Bliek and Gauthier, "Mobilising Urban Heritage to Counter the Commodification of Brownfield Landscapes."

6  Google search for "'Lachine Canal' Cradle" turns up about 2,740 results.

7  It is, however, only a presumption; the records to support this have not to my knowledge been discovered amid the Byzantine record-keeping practices of Montreal. Parks Canada: "Theoretically, these soils should not be contaminated." Parks Canada, "Project to Reopen the Lachine Canal to Through Navigation," 37.

8  See in particular the plea on behalf of the "Lachine Canal Committee" – an organization representing industries located on the canal – to ensure the continued well-being of the industrial dimensions of the canal corridor in Montreal Engineering Company, Limited, "The Importance and Potential of the Lachine Canal."

9  See Desloges and Gelly, *The Lachine Canal*; Desloges, "Behind the Scene of the Lachine Canal Landscape"; Fitterman, "Lachine Canal"; Gedeon, "History's Floodgate"; Hamilton, "Boat at Your Own Risk on Fetid Former Sewer"; Lalonde, "Old-Timers Recall Glory Days"; Lejtenyi, "Affluence, Boats and Condos"; Parks Canada, "Project to Reopen the Lachine Canal to Through Navigation"; Thompson, "Toxic Sites Worth Billions."

10  Canadian Environmental Assessment Agency, "Lachine Canal Decontamination Project."

11  See Benjamin, "Theses on the Philosophy of History," § xiv.

12  Benjamin's figure of the *Angelus Novus* watching the past as a single catastrophe is

apt in this present context. This text would seem to refigure this angel as watching a history of toxicity. Ibid., § ix.

13  Heidegger, *Poetry, Language, Thought*, 152.

14  Ibid, 152.

15  "But the bridge," he continues, "if it is a true bridge, is never first of all a mere bridge, and then afterward a symbol. And just as little is the bridge in the first place exclusively a symbol, in the sense that it expresses something that strictly speaking does not belong to it ... The bridge is a thing and *only that*." Ibid, 153.

16  Ibid, 152–3.

17  Founded in 1882, the Dominion Bridge Company was involved in the construction of numerous bridges, the most noteworthy of which include: the Jacques Cartier Bridge (1929); Honoré Mercier Bridge (1934); Golden Gate Bridge (1937); Lions Gate Bridge (1938); Champlain Bridge (1962); Port Mann Bridge (1964); Pont de la Concorde (1965); Laviolette Bridge (1967); Pierre Laporte Bridge (1970).

18  I develop this idea of the indexical imaginary at length in my *Highway of the Atom*, 138–42. Essentially, I am trying to understand how it is that one may encounter a place without, in some sense, *already* understanding it.

19  Parks Canada, "Project to Reopen the Lachine Canal to Through Navigation," 2.

20  All structures crossing the canal had to conform to a minimum elevation of 2.4 metres, and at the canal itself, to a minimum draft of 2.14 metres. Ibid., 9–13.

21  The only way to enforce this speed limit is to time the travel of individual boats between locks. Not exactly a foolproof system.

22  Parks Canada, "Environmental Assessment," 16.

23  Canadian Environmental Assessment Agency, "Lachine Canal Decontamination Project," 66. A more recent assessment: "The Lachine sediments have been shown to contain large quantities of contaminants in which the inorganic contamination was dominant. Heavy metals (Zn, Pb, Cr, Cu, Ni and Cd) and other toxic metals (As and Hg) were found to surpass in all instances various governmental criteria, especially those relating to a medium management level. Hence the Lachine sediments have become carriers and a potential source of heavy metals, and may affect the water column and groundwater quality." Galvez-Cloutier and Dubé, "An Evaluation of Fresh Water Sediments Contamination, Part ii," 299. And further: "With respect to heavy metals, the Lachine contamination followed a specific sequence… : Zn > Pb > Cu > Cr > Ni > Cd > As > Hg." Galvez-Cloutier and Dubé, "An Evaluation of Fresh Water Sediments Contamination, Part i," 277.

24  See Ethnoscop. "Site de L'ancienne Usine Stelco, Canal de Lachine," cited in Parks Canada, "Environmental Assessment," 11.

25  These sorts of transformations are increasingly staged on sites of former industrial and particularly, military production. I think here of Shiloh Krupar's work on the Rocky Flats plutonium factory. See Krupar, "Alien Still Life."

26  McKay, *Vis à Vis*, 31.

27  See Barthes, *Camera Lucida*, 38.

28  This formulation is, I think, quite similar to the way Jonathan Bordo put it to me in conversation sometime in the summer of 2009.

29  Gedeon, "History's Floodgate," 40.

30  See Emond, "Following Riviere St Pierre Under Lachine."

31  Canadian Environmental Assessment Agency, "Lachine Canal Decontamination Project," 48.

32  See Ibid., 54.

33  Parks Canada, "Project to Reopen the Lachine Canal to Through Navigation," 69.

34  Ibid., 32.

35  "Generally, the sediments all along the canal present average concentrations of chromium, copper, mercury, lead and zinc that are higher than level 3." Ibid., 38. In the language of the environmental assessment, these contaminants are in concentrations at or beyond level C (for soils), and Level 3 (for sediments) of the Politique québécoise de rehabilitation des terrains contaminés. Both designations signify an adverse effect threshold in which immediate action is called for. In the case of sediments, Level 3 indicates that 90 percent of benthic organisms are affected, and that any and all dredged materials must be sequestered or treated. See Environment Canada and Québec Department of the Environment, "Critères Intérimaires"; Quebec Department of the Environment, "Politique de Réhabilitation."

36  Rimbaud, *Illuminations and Other Prose Poems*, 41.

37  Treasury Board of Canada, "Federal Contaminated Sites Inventory."

38  On this sense of the structural form of the alibi – the alibi as a primarily spatial function – see Roland Barthes' "Myth Today," in *Mythologies*.

39  Musil, *The Man Without Qualities*, 3–4.

40  Walter, "Placeways."

41  See Daigneault, *Artefact 2001*.

42  Commissioner of the Environment and Sustainable Development, "2002 October Report."

# Mapping Waters: Thinking with Watery Places

*Cecilia Chen*

I live near the rapids called *Iohná:wate'* in the archipelago of *Tiohtià:ke*. Put another way, the Lachine Rapids in the Montreal archipelago influence and shape the place where I live.[1] The rapids are both watery event and place. Never still, these waters are a turbulent stretch of river that resists easy navigation and mapping. The river, *Kania-tarowá:nen*, or the St Lawrence, flows between the rocky Precambrian Shield to the north and the Appalachian Plateau to the south and finds an intense diversity of life at *Tiohtià:ke*, where the Ottawa River offers its sediment-rich waters to the archipelago. Distinct from other watery events both upstream and downstream, the rapids occur, in the first place, because the wide volume of *Lac Saint-Louis* is squeezed into a narrow passage between stubborn shores, even as a suddenly shallow rocky riverbed pushes the river currents into noisy turbulence. These waters, then, fall thirteen metres to the *Bassin de La Prairie* and the Port of Montreal. Although from the shores we see the rapids only for a stretch of about four kilometres, the force and the complex currents of these fast-flowing waters are felt far beyond their visible extents both upriver and downstream.

This chapter has emerged through my attempts to think with these multiply named rapids[2] – to think with watery place. In so briefly describing them, I have already begun to frame these fast and tangled waters, their places, and their meanings. It is in trying to articulate these particular waters and their human and more-than-human communities that I have come to explore a series of assumptions, theories, and practices that influence and limit how we usually map and understand situated waters. To engage the critical and generative potential of mapping with water, I ask: How do the ways in which we think and map with water predetermine, limit, or enable the way we then construct our relations to place, to others, to environments, to shores, and to communities? I hope to uncover how we may better think, represent, and make places in relation with diverse waters and with our more-than-human others. Finally, I suggest that the mapping process most appropriate to the watery places in which so many of us dwell is a process that is multivocal, responsive, and heuristic.

Mapping involves a set of actions that gather, present, and articulate imagined understandings of place. To change these understandings – the perceived and practised relations of dwelling with many others in evolving ecosystems of matter and meaning – we may need to examine and alter the practices with which we articulate place. In this regard, it may be radically informative to move mapping processes toward a critical and generative inclusion of the communities convened by waters. We may begin by learning how to think *with* water and with our watery places. Consider, for instance, how the *Iohná:wate'* rapids have repeatedly brought various peoples together in exchange and conflict over time. The Iroquois, St Lawrence Iroquoian, Algonquin, and Huron-Wendat nations likely met in, on, and near these river waters.[3] Certainly, in North America, the waterways navigable by nimble canoe were often the site of early contacts between Indigenous peoples and foreigners, who arrived with strange languages and technologies, new bacteria, and goods. These encounters catalyzed new sets of relations, encompassing trade, disease, war, and subsequent settlement patterns among both Indigenous peoples and newcomers. Among the technologies employed to support often violent colonial relations were the imported European cartographic practices that imposed an instrumental understanding of waters, lands, and peoples. Unfortunately, similar inventory-like mappings continue to be used in our time to appropriate and to narrowly constitute landed territories and watery resources. What we understand about the communications of different waters is necessarily limited by our use of languages and concepts –the apparatuses with which we, in effect, constitute knowledge. As has been diversely argued in this volume as a whole, we need to move away from narrow representations of water as a seemingly tractable resource toward an understanding that waters are situated, lively, and shared.

## Watery Place

Waters take place. The movements of water in our daily lives link us to places and to each other. Whereas, for many, "place" is strongly associated with landed territories, thinking place in terms of water may dissolve certain land-based preconceptions. Unlike thinking with land, thinking with water asks that we deterritorialize *how* we understand where we live and that we consider ongoing relations with others – whether these relations join us to other locations, other beings, or other events and spacetimes. Understanding waters in place helps us to engage with waters and places as mutually transforming and transformative phenomena. It is neither that waters contain places nor that places contain waters: the specificity of situated waters articulated with places, with space and time, with dynamic bodies, materials and semantic contexts can enable a more thoughtful discussion of watery relations. These relations may include communities of disease and environmental toxicity as well as the many everyday watery places that we make together. Thinking with watery places asks us to recognize places as always permeable and permeated with water – as shaped by water quality, scarcity, or abundance. Further, it requires that we consider a lively relationality and an ethics of environmental community.

However, place is a sometimes messy process. For geographer Doreen Massey, place is open, simultaneous, "internally multiple," and therefore incoherent and inconsistent. This "throwntogetherness of place demands negotiation ... [Places] implicate us, perforce, in the lives of human others, and in our relations with nonhumans they ask how we shall respond to our temporary meeting-up with these particular rocks and stones and trees."[4] To this last, I would add "water." Moving waters and the changing shores articulated with land, humans, and other life forms make up many of the incoherent common places where we live. Therefore, just as the constant flow of river waters defines and constitutes *Tiohtià:ke*, or the archipelago of Montreal where I live, so also, places are made and re-made with each narrative, cartographic, and toponymic iteration. In this way, places – such as the hydrocommons of a watershed or an underground aquifer – are always shared, local, and topical.[5] By seeking to understand the full complexity of situated waters, we must also consider the relations and often-unexpected communities convened by unruly waters. Unlike the abstract and dislocated idea of resource, the waters that join us in relation are articulated with space and time.

Places emerge out of the articulations of our embodied and socially entangled experiences with nonhuman phenomena and contexts; they shape and are shaped by the conversations we weave with space, time, and matter. How, then, might we adequately articulate places with their wealth of (muddy, humid, frozen, fully-immersed, and foggy) watery relations? Even as we recognize how place is a layered confluence of multiple processes (material and discursive, sensorial and habitual) we also need to attend to what is emphasized, disputed, or entirely left out of our representations of place.[6] And, to share these thoughts we need to represent them legibly in some way: each human practice of "knowing" simultaneously articulates and delimits what may be intelligible. To better understand how we claim to "know" the inclusive relations of watery place – particularly through mapping practices – I explore the ways in which many relations of water may exceed conventional limits of intelligibility and how thinking with water may enable novel perceptions of spacetime, place, and community.

*More Than Resource*

The conceptual place of waters has been parsed in particular ways in globalized commodity cultures and adheres closely, if not only, to resource-related discourses. There is a wide range of nuance in how water is articulated as resource – whether as natural, sovereign, a common good, or even a human right.[7] Thinking of water as a resource is a way of thinking *about* (and not *with*) water. Yet, any critical examination of water needs to consider the common political-economic discourse wherein water is reduced to being a useful support for agriculture, industry, commerce, power-generation, and the well-being of people and cities – a substance that is (equitably or inequitably) organized to serve human cultures. As resource, water is discursively contained and conceptually ordered, even as it is physically extracted, treated, and piped to where we live. This limited and limiting approach to water has become a part of humanity's relation to itself, to nature, to the world, and to its internal and external others.[8] However, even in societies that have most benefited from the asymmetries of resource extraction industries and global capitalism (such as the one from which I write), many debate whether water can indeed be traded as if it were solely an abstract commodity. And the idea of resource inevitably raises (or buries) the idea of its opposite – that which is judged un-useful, excessive, or unintelligible.

Water is much more than a resource. It is a socio-natural *force* – an active agent of overflow, creation, and destruction. The movements, transformations, and relations of water seasonally overflow neat categorizations and normative discourses. As a responsive and promiscuous solvent, water is rarely pure and is always picking up, carrying along, dropping off, and bonding with other elements. In this sense, it materially communicates where it has been, what has occurred elsewhere, and even what is possible. And whereas useful waters easily find articulation within human practices, "useless" waters (waters that exceed anthropocentric ideas of service) are less intelligible, as agents of troublesome, unpredictable, and transformational energies – energies that are integral to risky processes of becoming, including but certainly not limited to death.[9]

Referring to a poetic process of becoming-in-the-world, Elizabeth Grosz writes of "a nature that is always the supercession and transformation of limits and thus beyond the passivity of the reserve or the resource, nature as becoming or evolution."[10] For Grosz, the transformative energies of excess and superabundance are a powerful dynamic of a "nature as becoming" – a nature that exceeds narrow and constrained discourses of "natural" resource.[11] Her philosophical approach, when applied to current water discourses, helps us to think beyond their normative bounds. Human expectations are inevitably transformed, as the dynamics and physics of water influence the relations of life, death, and becoming. Although these ineffable aspects of water may never be fully mappable, acknowledging water's transformational powers is humbling in regard to what we may or may not articulate about watery place in a way that can move us towards better mapping practices.

*Intelligibility and Babble*

As they exceed political, semantic, and material containments, waters challenge us to understand situations and relations beyond previously established human logics. Greater awareness of the habitual assumptions that limit the ways in which we listen to (and think about or with) water could aid in opening up critical human discourses towards larger environmental communications. Indeed, attending to the way in which waters exceed intelligibility may be key to transforming our understanding of where and how we live. For intelligibility is political,[12] and mutual intelligibility is a mark of a respectful relationship between interlocutors in acknowledged conversation. When one set of interlocutors (for instance humans intent on unfettered industrial activities) refuses to listen to the communications of another (for instance dying fish populations), the rejected communications are relegated to non-sense, constituting a denial of the intelligibility of the other. Once the voices of others are relegated to non-sensical noise or even to mere static, then a response is no longer required. I make the assumption here that humans are part of an ongoing conversation with other living entities – although it is currently a lopsided conversation in which the communications of the more-than-human and other phenomena are often willfully ignored.

Prior to and after its socializations, water is often treated as unintelligible, excessive, and formless. In this way, phenomena (aqueous and otherwise) that disturb human ideals of normative order are frequently excluded from social articulation. Denied intelligibility, these phenomena are also often denied visibility[13] – except as the distorted and monstrous. The power and risk of disordered chaos lurk at the margins of social order like medieval sea-monsters swimming at the unmapped edges of the known (or knowable) world. When the perceived order of social norms is achieved through a selective editing of an otherwise messy world of infinite and therefore dangerous potential, the act of denying the intelligibility of certain phenomena helps to maintain the status quo – it is from disorder that new social and conceptual patterns emerge.[14] As Grosz suggests with her "nature as becoming," it is from the amorphous realm of disturbing potential that risky, transformative, and generative powers may emerge. As has long been related in myth and story, a transformational and generative anarchy is carried within the vague and less comprehensible spacetimes of water.[15]

Unsurprisingly, the common parameters of intelligible political discourse in Canada are usually limited to human perspectives and heavily favour forms of evidence rooted in scientific and legal traditions continuing from Enlightenment Europe and its colonial legacies. For this reason, certain kinds of testimony, especially documents such as contracts, diagrams, photographs, and maps, are privileged as legitimate evidence. Certainly, the assumed authority of maps is one of the reasons that I am so interested in examining how we practise the mapping of waters. Other kinds of witness or non-hegemonic forms of knowledge are perhaps less easily recognized.[16] And communications from inarticulate non-citizens such as animals, plants, water, and rock are often rejected as noisy babble – except where the more-than-human are represented by human "experts."[17] Even when inarticulate non-citizens find sincere representation, there are limits to what can be articulated and what might be knowable.[18] Yet, it is only when we move beyond normative articulations of water that we encounter its volatile semantic and material potential. For this reason, we may need to listen more carefully to our noisy surrounds – for the babble of water – its excess "noise" – may in fact be a communication that fruitfully expands the limits of intelligibility, the bounds of shared conversations and the parameters of how we map.

## Mapping Watery Places

Mapping is a human practice – a conceptual apparatus and an approach to articulating watery place. Apparatuses, as varied as languages, boats, cameras, sketch-books, bodies, and identities, focus a set of social and technical assumptions, conventions, and relations that we bring to a situation. As such, mapping both emerges from and feeds back into larger meaning-making practices. Each mapping describes an implicit or explicit set of relationships among landscapes, waterways, populations of the human and more than human, and other lively agents.

Specifically, I am seeking an approach to mapping that is appropriate to articulating the heterogeneous relations of shared watery places – our hydrocommons. Whereas capitalist desires to stake out territories and to locate and extract resources may wish to present the world as singularly passive and claimable, "watershed mind" and other similar approaches described in this volume[19] recognize the ways in which the active materialities of the world push back. We are in constant, if often unacknowledged, conversation with what Alphonso Lingis calls "the murmur of the world,"[20] – or what I think of as the babble of water. Whether we participate as map-makers or map-readers, the way we recognize or deny these conversations with human and more-than-human others will result in significantly different kinds of maps. Our very sense of orientation, and consequently our perceived locations in the world, may emerge through the socio-technical process of mapping. Indeed, mapping is one way to actively articulate what matters in the world. However we choose to map, we selectively frame a range of possible understandings and subsequent actions. As a strategically powerful way to construct, communicate, and represent the places where we (and many others) live, mapping practices need to be constantly and critically re-evaluated. We may more thoughtfully articulate how we know watery place by better understanding the conceptual and socio-technical processes of mapping.

### Apparatuses of Knowing

Map-making engages a set of practices that gather knowledge and representations of place – through hydrographies, cartographies, topographies, chorographies[21] or other graphings. Mapping is a practice and apparatus of knowing that shares aspects with both scientific measurement and descriptive narration. Karen Barad observes that: "There is an important sense in which practices of knowing cannot fully be claimed as human practices, not simply because we use nonhuman elements in our practices but because knowing is a matter of part of the world making itself intelligible to another part. Practices of knowing and being are not isolable; they are mutually implicated. We don't obtain knowledge by standing outside the world; we know because we are *of* the world."[22] For Barad, the conventional Western division of knowing into epistemological, ontological, and ethical approaches results from a metaphysics that separates humans from nonhumans and matter from discourse. She calls for a greater "appreciation of the intertwining of ethics, knowing, and being […] because the becoming of the world is a deeply ethical matter."[23] Thus, how we know watery place, and how we know ourselves as watery bodies, is not separable from the material and discursive apparatuses that we use to articulate this knowledge.

There is no "knowing" without a conceptual and material commitment to an apparatus of knowing. In a seminal example drawn from the history of quantum physics, Barad (a physicist as well as a cultural theorist) describes how the choice of measuring apparatus predetermines how a light photon is perceived to move. We can measure how light photons move like a wave or we can measure how they move like particles – however, we cannot measure (or know) both phenomena simultaneously.[24] Indeed, Barad recounts how the apparatuses designed and built to *measure* the light photon in fact *constitute* phenomena. Each apparatus enables a particular relationship and configuration of space-time-matter – and therefore enacts a way of knowing that we then distinguish as either "wave" or "particle."

Whether we understand water as a molecular matrix, as a supple liquid, as part of our bodies, or as a place we call home depends upon our approach to knowing. Humans enact relations with water daily: individually as we drink (from a well, a tap, or a bottle) and wash (with plumbing or in a pond); and collectively as we practice agriculture, with our thirsty cities, through shipping, fishing, the pulp and paper industry (among the many industries that involve large quantities of water), and through oil extraction. Implicit in each habitual relation is a way of knowing water.

Here, I propose that an oil rig in the Gulf of Mexico may be understood as an apparatus of knowing. The oil rig commits us to knowing the ocean solely as a place from which to extract oil; it is a complex device in the larger apparatus of global capitalism that constitutes the world as instrumentalized resource. Under normal operating conditions, the oil rig is a useful, controlled place in the ocean, "challenged-forth" by global resource-extraction industries that materialize an impoverished framing of the world.[25] At least circumstantially, a constructed platform floating mid-ocean would seem to be a very watery place. However, the deep-water oil rig is an apparatus designed to endure and to bypass the ocean entirely with drills, pumps and pipes to access reservoirs below the seabed. As such, the deep-water oil rig is an anthropocentric instrument that allows only a severely reduced understanding of the ocean around it.

The maps and hydrogeological surveys that precede the capital-intensive placement of any oil rig likely support this same narrow knowledge of the ocean. As a practice that selectively conveys location and relations – and although it is only one among a multiplicity of practices with which we claim to know water – mapping is a commonly employed and widely understood apparatus of knowing. As already noted above, mapping practices are thus entangled in determining what "matters." How we choose to practise mapping is therefore critical.

Unlike narrative or acoustic media that unfurl sequentially in time, maps offer a visual simultaneity of information keyed to a selectively framed spatial expanse. Almost all maps begin with a graphic interface. And this initial interface offers the map-reader many simultaneous choices. Reading a conventional roadmap with intent, an individual will focus on one route over another. Navigating an online map, such as *Waterlife*,[26] each reader will choose to first focus on different aspects or segments. Viewing a map, such as Figures 20.1 or 20.2, you may initially find one layer of information more compelling than another. Nonetheless, each map offers a finite and edited data set. Given the diversity of what might possibly be engaged through mapping, we must carefully choose how we deploy this selective apparatus of knowing that can so powerfully articulate what is intelligible – what *matters* – about watery place. Keeping Barad's observations in mind, we know ourselves to be part of any mapping. Therefore, how and what we habitually know is not separable from our thinking apparatuses; the way we map water and place is simultaneously enabled and delimited by what we think we may understand about watery place.

### Water and Heterotopia

Watery places are not always comfortable or even familiar. They can be uncanny – a place of others, or an *other* place – especially, in the sense of Michel Foucault's heterotopia.[27] Indeed, humans cannot actually dwell for any length of time *in* water without some kind of prosthetic mediation (such as scuba gear, diving bells, or submarine vessels). Most commonly, land mammals that we are, humans have devised ways to move *on* water. Boats may be understood as a human response to oceans and rivers – an apparatus with which to know watery place. In the context of European colonialism in the Americas, Foucault proposes that, from the sixteenth century onward, the boat has been the most important instrument of Western economic development; it has also been a deeply charged object of imagination (*la plus grande réserve d'imagination*).[28] He further suggests that the boat is the epitome of heterotopia – a vessel with which to imagine and explore beyond familiar waters. If the figure of the boat is the epitome of heterotopia, then, what is water – *where* is water?

How should we understand the oceans, lakes, and rivers plied by this floating place without place (*un lieu sans lieu*)? Foucault's boat is a place (*un lieu...*) tossing about in a non-place (*... sans lieu*) – the watery *utopia* of the ocean.[29] Any breach of hull midocean would lead to a dissolution of boat-place for the land animals within. And without the boat, the land animals would be lost at sea and without place. Or, would they? For eminently pragmatic reasons, the oceans are the resting place of more than one sailor's body. For many other reasons, an overwhelming number of land animals seek to live and die near oceans and other bodies of water. Indeed, the concept of hypersea[30] suggests that not only did all life emerge from the sea, but that all land biota also carry pockets of the ocean within us. Water buoys and gestates life, but it is also a medium that, as humans, we cannot breathe – therefore, it also offers us places at the thresholds of experience and comprehensibility.[31] So water may be construed as a non-place where one becomes lost, a home to many, *and* a place of rest in the otherness of death.

Place may begin as strange: a restrictive apparatus like the oil rig described above. However, a watery place may *become* uncanny where once it seemed quite homey. With its explosion in April 2010, British Petroleum's (BP) Deep Water Horizon oil rig cat-alyzed a heterotopia of disastrous excess.[32] This event cataclysmically redrew the imag-ination of the Gulf of Mexico as a watery place with new monsters of untracked underwater oil plumes, an ocean bed smothered by dispersant, and sensitive wetland shores altered by petro-chemical compounds. The dwellings of all those living in the range of effects from the spill suffered a radical dislocation without geophysical dis-placement. The transformative effects of environmental contamination have altered the imagination of place and ecosystem, as well as the health and identity of local popula-tions (human and more than human). Haunted by past and future excesses that corre-late to deep-sea drilling, the effects of this spill are most closely observed and profoundly lived all along the shores and shallows of the Gulf of Mexico.

### Gaps, Lines, and Coasts

Many of us live near a threshold between water and land – a transitional zone between terrestrial and aquatic ecosystems. Whether we live on the drier part of the shore, in tidal pools, or in the eddies and shallows of an oceanic or riparian ecosystem, it is in these thick thresholds of overlapping water and land that there is a great density of life. At these intensely inhabited and biodiverse margins – shores, coasts, wetlands, estuaries, floodplains, and river valleys – terrestrial and aqueous communities mingle. These changeable places have been engaged variously as shore, as ecotone, as breach – and even as a kind of heterotopia where we may meet unexpected others. Although coasts are typically mapped as a wavy line blithely dermarcating a seemingly simple border between water and land, this simplification is generally inadequate to the wealth of these complex zones.

The lived thickness of the coast is distinct from the thin abstract coastline drawn on a map. Paul Carter engages the gap between the illusory mimesis of the world presented by a stable, triangulated terrestrial cartography and the "rough and ready" running sur-veys and dead reckoning of coastal maps sketched out mid-current in the 1700s off the coast of Australia.[33] In this regard, Carter notes that: "Whatever the thin ambitions of the cartographer might be, the coast remained fat from the point of view of the coastal surveyor and hydrographer." Even from a landed perspective, the coast is "a region, tract or district … a distinct transitional zone including sandhills, shore and shallow water."[34] For Carter, metonymically contained in the "difficulty of drawing a continu-ous, dimensionless line"[35] – as charged to the skillful map-maker – is a tension between abstractly representing authoritative knowledge, and the actual uneven and recalcitrant phenomena of shores and coasts. He argues that this tension reflects an epistemological paradox in Enlightenment thinking that demands seamless reasoning but nonetheless requires a: "little *saltus* of imagination, the gift of intellectual wit, or what Vico called *ingenium*, to see relationships and grasp their significance."[36] Gaps threaten the conceit of authoritative knowledge. To remedy inconvenient gaps, then, "the instrument of elimination is the continuous line."[37] However, to draw a continuous line requires a steady hand that is likely powered by a willful imagination and projected "significance."

Unless they could be explained, "gaps were an offence against logic: only as sources of legitimate speculation, as sites of unbounded advance, could they be recorded [...] rivers were coastlines by another name; they were gaps where imagination coincided with reasonable expectation."[38] Thus, seeking the Northwest Passage in 1778, James Cook named a gap along the coast of Alaska the Gulf of Good Hope.[39] This was subsequently renamed Cook Inlet upon further examination by George Vancouver in 1794. Cook's desire that the gap resolve itself into the mouth of a navigable trade route between Europe and Asia proved to be wishful projection – provoking Vancouver's bitter lament that this body of water was instead "[a] coastline that folded back on itself like some marine flagellate, yielding no new body of knowledge ... horrible to contemplate."[40] Both of these colonial mapping expeditions produced maps according to "the thin ambitions of the cartographer," noted by Carter. The disappointment of these brittle desires may explain Vancouver's horror. Yet, had they been asked, the Dena'ina, who have long called this gulf or inlet *Tikahtnu* or "big water river," would have been able to tell Cook and Vancouver that this was not the sought-after Northwest passage navigable by British sea-going vessels. The Dena'ina knowledge of this coast – accumulated over generations and built upon through innumerable daily contacts – is infinitely thicker and more nuanced than the slender hopes and thinner lines drawn by Cook and Vancouver. Indeed, oblivious to Vancouver's sour disappointment, the tidal waters of *Tikahtnu*, or Cook Inlet, rise and fall along some of the most densely populated and biodiverse shores of Alaska.

Many practices of making and reading maps in North America are still largely shaped by conventions that date back to the ambitions of colonial cartography.[41] Clearly, the ways we recognize or interpret gaps are important – along a coast, within stuttering narrations, between words and knowing, or in the empty spaces of a map. The ways we understand and interpret watery places – what we cannot know about them as much as what we may think we understand – are critical. If and when mapping practices are able to acknowledge and articulate the varied knowledges of watery place – such as that lived by the Dena'ina on the shores of *Tikahtnu* – then we may better understand waters and coasts as richly storied and lively places.

Practising Mapping with Water

We may need to practise the making and reading of maps with more care. Thinking wholly in human terms, geographer Denis Cosgrove understands mapping as a complex cultural, technical, and semantic practice. He makes an important distinction between the process of mapping and the produced map itself. The "map" is a partial articulation within the larger socio-technical process that constitutes mapping: "Any map may thus be regarded as a hinge around which pivot whole systems of meaning, both prior and subsequent to its technical and mechanical production."[42] A map is a determined cultural production, but it is also an element within material culture. An individual map may be thought of as a distinct entity emerging from and subsequently re-inserted into an ongoing cultural process of mapping and meaning-making.

In related thinking, landscape architect James Corner understands the practice of mapping as a precondition of maps, but not as a process that can fully predetermine the subsequent fate of any individual map. Thus, the process of making a map creates relationships that might not have previously existed: "mapping engenders new and meaningful relationships amongst otherwise disparate parts … something constructed, bodied forth through the act of mapping."[43] Moreover, once the map is published and shared it is impossible to predict how it will be received, circulated, and interpreted. New relations may emerge in the way that a map is read. And while maps might be criticized for attempting to fix a set of normative understandings of place, map-reading is not prescribable.[44] If we take these insights about mapping practices to water, we may better map our relationships to watery place.

*Shores to Ecotones*

Defining coasts as thresholds between land and water is key to current efforts to map watery place. For many land animals, the shore and its shallows may be as far as we usually get in our direct interactions with larger bodies of water. Human relations with watery place are often materially revealed along the shore – from fishing and drilling zones to constructions such as harbours and ports, canals, dams, boardwalks, jetties, and beaches, and even to efforts to protect and restore coastal ecosystems. Thinking with *Tiohtià:ke*, for instance, we may ask how its urbanized shores make evident the assymetric negotiations between and among humans and the more-than-human. As a thick threshold *between* ecosystems, the shore is an important site from which to develop a relational approach to mapping waters. And to better map these liminal places, we must first examine how shores are conventionally represented.

Maps typically abstract the shore to a sometimes kinked but continuous line that serves as a radical reference for those on land and on water. But, as already visited with Paul Carter, the shoreline confidently represented on many maps is a kind of fiction. Shores morph with seasonal or tidal fluctuations, and banks are coerced by water currents, sedimentation, erosion, and vegetable or animal interventions. The shoreline drawn on many maps is a pragmatic abstraction. On nautical charts, such as those prepared by the Canadian Hydrographic Service (CHS), the shoreline and all given water depths are based upon something called Chart Datum or Low Water Datum.[45] This is a conservative way of ensuring that navigators do not over-estimate water depths and founder their vessels. However, in a dry season like the summer of 2012 in the Montreal archipelago, even this low-water datum is not low enough.[46]

The CHS declares that "Nautical Charts Protect Lives, Property and the Marine Environment."[47] These charts are specialized maps that are commercially sold and intended to aid in the navigation of watery places. However, they facilitate only a very limited kind of navigation and are particularly disappointing when it comes to describing watery places, like the *Iohná:wate'* rapids, that have long resisted domesticating human efforts. Chart 1409 names the *Rapides de Lachine* but not *Iohná:wate'*. We are presented with the information necessary for commercial (and some recreational) navigation. After all, the chart is named for the St Lawrence Seaway's "Canal de la Rive Sud" and not for the rapids that catalyzed the building of both the Lachine Canal in the 1800s and the Seaway in the 1950s. As the rapids are un-navigable by contemporary freight vessels, only abstract symbols for white water and its name are scattered through its watery extents (see Figure 20.3). Depth readings given elsewhere are not offered for these tricky waters that flow outside of shipping channels.

Skilled river pilots in canoes and steamships "ran" these rapids in the past;[48] and white water enthusiasts kayak, raft, and surf their tumultuous waters in the present day.[49] Nonetheless, these daring interactions with the intricate highs and lows of the rapids are quite possibly thrilling – but not conventionally useful – and therefore do not appear on Chart 1409. This omission is not surprising, given a history of Canadian surveying and mapping that is tied to colonial appropriations of land and water and to nation-building efforts eager to prove the pragmatic resource wealth of its territories. This kind of mapping tends to reduce water to a resource in the vocabulary of global capitalism and continues to profoundly limit understandings of water. Yet, closer study of Chart 1409 reveals other less obvious kinds of watery place. Two bird sanctuaries and many potable water intakes are marked on this nautical chart. Depending on how we read this map, we may understand that migratory birds and surrounding municipalities also depend upon the same river waters that float commercial shipping activities. A critical commentary on these nautical charts is important. For, although other ways of mapping these rapid waters do exist, few have the systematized expertise, wide distribution, and seemingly weighty authority of these CHS documents.

However, a mapping practice intended to ease the transportation of commercial freight will necessarily differ from a mapping practice that seeks to articulate the place-based relations of watery home. One way that we might begin to articulte the latter is to vary the gestures with which we map shores: conceptually and graphically, the thin continuous line may be mitigated by the deliberate use of gaps, tones, textures, and overlapping lines of varied thickness. The line may also thicken to a threshold by embracing the idea of the ecotone. One team of hydrologists and ecologists, Verry, Doloff, and Manning, define "ecotone" as a "gradient across ecosystems"[50] – a three-dimensional zone of varying shape and thickness where diverse biological communities coexist. Where "eco" is derived from the Greek *oikos*, or dwelling, and "tone" means tension, identifying an ecotone requires that we first recognize the correlation of two or more overlapping systems. Moreover, the vibrant tension of this threshold requires an inclusive approach to mapping that encompasses the conflicts, negotiations, and unpredictable encounters within the tangled overlap – a robust approach that differentiates between layered systems while also recognizing the energies generated by their coexistence. Whereas "ecotone" is a term used more commonly in the physical sciences, it offers, here, a way to understand shores and coasts as lively places where land and water meet; it allows us to consider the particularities of encounter between diverse systems, populations, and even practices – of which some may be more land-based, others largely aqueous, and yet others existing only in the complex mingling of both.

Excerpts from related maps published more than two centuries apart: (left) Samuel de Champlain's 1613 map of "Le grand Sault Saint Louis" as published by Jean Berjon – note that "N" marks where two men drowned in the rapids; (right) a later version of this map from 1884, rendered by Pierre-Louis Morin for a historical atlas of Montreal.

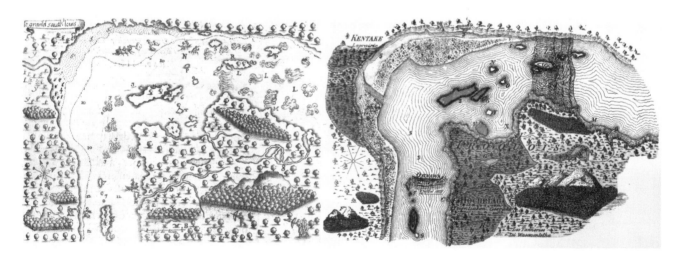

## Open Waters

Watery places, like shores and ecotones, are thick and negotiated thresholds between different ways of life and varied hybrid communities. In any consideration of place, space and time are inseparable movements; the spatial imagination of place is tied to the duration and movements of time. In underlying representations of place (whether mimetically "real" or imagined topia), there are always implicit framings of the present and selected projections into the future and the past. Historical maps and narratives are as malleable, partial, and selective as interpretations of the present and imaginings of the future. Remembering this facilitates a critical approach to understanding how we negotiate and construct place.[51] An edited past may be used to support, justify, and even critique the current situation and its possible futures. Telling or retelling stories of the past, the present, or the future is never a neutral action. Reiteration and re-membering are always selective.

We are reminded that we cannot understand time in a linear way: instead we practise and imagine the past and future only through continuing iterations. Elizabeth Grosz proposes that, where utopia emerges from a projection of the present-past that closes

Excerpts from two watercolour sketch maps of the rapids concerned with the navigable channel: (left) Louis Charland's 1805 plan proposes a new mid-stream structure to facilitate navigation of the channel through the rapids; (right) Thomas C. Keefer's 1850 sketch map, oriented with South at the top, also shows a structure in the water and marks the shipwreck of the *Dawn*.

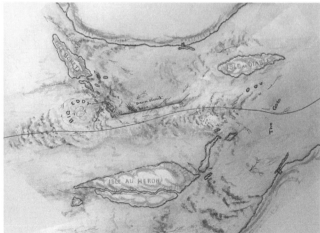

down the future, *atopia* – the idea of an "embodied utopia" – is an opening up of the present to an unpredictable future.[52] In her considerations of time, and specifically the future, as a concept important to architectural, spatial, and environmental imaginations, Grosz rejects deadening and prescriptive utopia and argues instead for atopia. This rejection is consistent with her vision of futures that are open to the processes of becoming, where and when the meanders of matter, time, and space are allowed to carry us into lively and unknown futures; and where the effects of drift, current, wind, water, and the agencies of the more-than-human help to deterritorialize the future.

Atopia offers a generative approach to place; it helps to open up the way we imagine places evolving. Whether consciously or not, imagination and perception are very much a part of the semantic and material construction of places. Places become material – are materialized – through active perception, imagination, and iteration. Places are in process; they are dynamic events unfolding from collective and contested efforts to make intelligible the environments in which we live. However, when approaching watery places as open to unknown futures, we risk getting lost even as we seek previously unimagined relations with place.

Excerpts from two hydrographic charts that indicate the rapids: (left) an excerpt from a 1925 chart published by the Canadian Hydrographic Survey; (right) an excerpt from Canadian Hydrographic Service Nautical Chart 1409, "Voie Maritime du Saint-Laurent: Canal de la Rive Sud" from 2002.

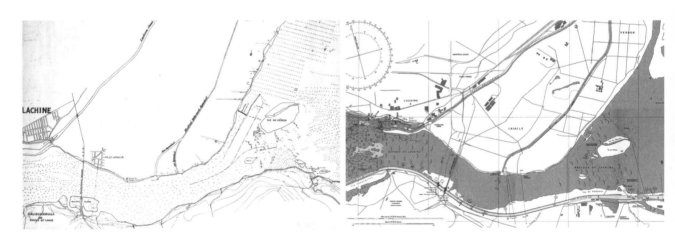

## Getting Lost, Navigation, and Synaesthesia

If lost, the shore may be a good place to go. From this threshold between land and water, distant horizons, other shores, and approaching weather are both visible and audible. Large bodies of water (such as lakes and reservoirs) can affect local weather. A chorus of frogs or a slight whiff of decaying vegetation tells us of a nearby marsh. The taste of humid salt breezes or the roar of breaking waves may signal the ocean. From low tide to high tide, from sere to wet, or from rain to snow, we read the changing presence and quality of water to understand where we are geophysically, temporally, and seasonally. As discussed in the introduction to this volume, the presence of water is often taken for granted, yet its manifestation in our surrounds is radically important to a sense of place.

Similarly, a sense of being in-place is frequently assumed and even subconscious. Feeling in-place may be defined negatively: as *not* thinking about place at all or as *not* feeling out-of-place. Our ability to orient and navigate in an environment – to locate ourselves – involves many senses and multiple ways of knowing. Brian Massumi proposes that "place arises from a dynamic of interference and accord between sense-dimensions" –

Excerpts from two proposed (but unrealized) plans to harness the rapids: (left) an excerpt from a plan drawn by engineer Charles Legge in 1867 for the St Louis Hydraulic Company scheme; (right) a sketch plan by the author derived from Volume 3 of the Feasibility Report produced for the Projet Archipel in April 1986.

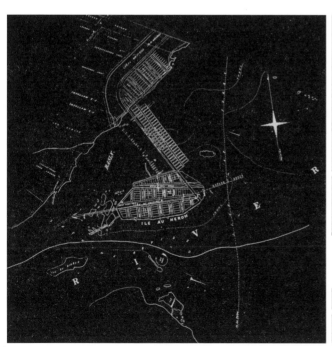
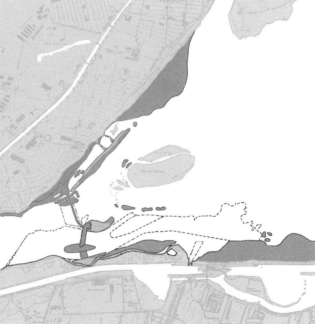

a sense of being placed emerges out of "a *synesthetic* system of cross-referencing" that involves at least two "sense systems."[53] The first navigational sense system he identifies is analytic and strongly tied to visuality and the Euclidean geometries of static space – an "exoreferential visual-cue system." The second system encompasses the proprioceptive and kinaesthetic sense of our surrounds that guides how we more habitually navigate through familiar environments – a set of practices based upon a "self-referential orientation."[54] Our constant, if often unconscious sense of water (or its lack) is likely part of this second more somatic sense system. When these multiple ways of navigating come into conflict, we may become misplaced: "The alarmingly physical sense we feel when we realize we are lost is a bodily registering of the disjunction between the visual and the proprioceptive." The moment we become aware of, or question, the "accord between sense-dimensions" is the moment when we are misplaced – the moment when the unconscious performance of being in-place is interrupted.

These moments of feeling out-of-place are important to renewing our sense of orientation and to discovering other ways to relate to place that escape habitual assumptions.[55] Those who dare to experiment (to seek atopia) run the risk of getting lost – with or without being found later on. Yet, a willingness to get lost is key to finding innovative ways of mapping watery place. Beyond the conceit of the continuous line of enlightenment logic described by Carter, the messy, stuttering maps of experimental practices lend themselves to the inclusion of that which is currently excluded and may, in this way, further expand mapping practices beyond the cartographic traditions that firmly link European colonialisms and contemporary resource extractions.

There are sophisticated ways of mapping that are indigenous to the Americas (and many other parts of the world), which have been strategically obscured and deemed less valid than colonial cartographic practices. To decolonize our mapping habits, not only must we recognize how apparatuses of mapping shape what "matters," but we may also note how non-hegemonic apparatuses have often received less regard. Multi-sensory approaches to navigation, place, and other watery phenomena are not exclusive to experimental practices. Traditional Inuit navigational practices, for instance, are notable for their synaesthetic approaches. "Elaborate navigational concepts, skills, and technologies for *moving through* space along tens of thousands of kilometres of traditional travel routes," include the reading of snow and snow drifts, the deciphering of distant land configurations through their luminous reflections in low-lying clouds, orientation by sun, moon, and stars, and various other mnemonic mapping practices.[56] Although Inuit mappings were sometimes made into objects, they were more often performed: sketched in sand, snow, or air, while being narrated from memory in great descriptive detail. When fixed into portable objects, Inuit maps were not limited to two-dimensional diagrams. East Greenland coastal maps, for instance, were carved from driftwood to become tactile devices that might be deciphered by mittened hands even in bad weather.[57] Their articulations felt like the coastline and were understood in conjunction with a kinaesthetic sense of the coast being travelled. Engaging multi-sensory intelligence, these way-finding devices worked at night, floated if dropped in the water and did not require paddlers to take their eyes off the coast itself.

According to Cosgrove, "All the resources of visualization and graphic communication are combined in mapping; the map is perhaps the most sophisticated form yet devised for recording, generating and transmitting knowledge."[58] Yet, while this may be true in a limited sense, experimental and traditional mapping practices employ more than solely visual and graphic communications. Mapping practices that include sound, oral histories, and performance (such as soundscape studies and storytelling[59]) engage time, space, and our understandings of place more broadly. The toponymic and tactile navigational practices of the Inuit, the songlines of Australian Aborigines, the cognitive maps used by many in the navigation of our daily environments, even the visionary maps of seers, thinkers, and artists, are all practices that work on the assumption of some form of articulable and navigable space-time-matter. Most important for this project, synaesthetic and experimental approaches to mapping often engage mapmaker and mapreader in more ways than just visually – and these more inclusive and multivalent practices may therefore better respond to the unique wealth of each watery place.

### Invoking Watery Places

Articulations of watery place emerge through the synaesthetic practices of orientation and navigation. However, we also invoke places through naming and identifying locations, by narrating, iterating, and claiming situations. In the Inuit topographic knowledge described above, the naming of places enacts important environmental and biophysical details about lands and coasts. Myths, stories, songs, rites, and playful tongue-twisters all incorporate valuable information about places and paths of travel through arctic topographies. Toponymic knowledge is constantly iterated and performed for and with an eager communal audience: "Topography is made intelligible and mapped into memory through its articulation with a store of cultural knowledge, and at the same time the community comes into being through the enculturation of individuals to a local history embedded in places."[60] In placing them-our-selves in a landscape, individuals identify with its places. In this way, calling to and re-calling place performs our locational relations within a larger environment. In actively listening and responding to the mapper-narrator, the community and audience also help to enact a resonantly imagined topography.

As a city dweller, with less than a decade of ties to the urban landscape I inhabit, I nonetheless find myself with friends and colleagues taking pleasure in sharing recent experiences of this or that neighbourhood, this or that street, park, bakery, or local adventure. We may debate the character of a place – or lament or celebrate recent changes. However, each iteration adds to a nuanced understanding of the place discussed. A place, a *topos*, comes into being through a collectively performed process. Each iteration repeats and constructs place, but always with a slightly different space-time-material configuration, always with atoms and molecules arrayed somewhat differently.

Moreover, each narration of place enacts a minor identitary claim: "Well, *my* experience ..." Certainly, my own invocations of place – via mapping or otherwise – emerge from an instinct to locate myself and my home. As a second-generation immigrant and someone who is visibly Asian, my sense of belonging to the northern shores of the Great Lakes and the St Lawrence River is regularly questioned. Speaking about watery place enacts a claim – an insistence that I know these waters in some way even if my family has only been living in this watershed since 1968. In this way, our invocations of place also map the presence and experience of the speaker in relation to a common landscape – shared watery places that also shape our sense of self.

However inconsistently, landscapes are first imagined and narrated – and then planned and built with water, earth, wood, stone, metals, and synthetics – often at the extended site of shores. Through maps, surveys and plans, new articulations of existing places precede these constructions. In this way, the shores of *Tiohtià:ke* were renamed by colonists before and even as they were radically reconfigured to become piers and harbours, aqueducts, canals, dams, bridges, and man-made islands. And the naming and narration of place is key to these strategic representations. For instance, mapping many names for one river immediately evokes the generative tensions of shared waters (see Plate 14). Robustly diverse relations to water may be encouraged by iterating a greater variety of names and stories of watery place. If we can learn to invoke more inclusively the way that places are shaped through generative relations with water and a community of many others, then perhaps we can also enable wiser ways to map and inhabit the world *with* each other.

## Heuristic Process: More Ways to Map Water

I have asked how we might begin to think with water, how the places where we live may be articulated with these fluid relations, and how our understandings of place may emerge newly wet through expanded practices of mapping situated waters. Above, I have only begun to explore how the ways in which we currently map water may both limit and enable how we then construct our relations to place, to others, to shores, communities, and environments. Here, in conclusion, I offer some further thoughts that might move us toward more open apparatuses of knowing, such as a heuristic process of mapping watery places.

A heuristic approach implies an evolving and responsive practice that is open to trial and error, as well as to improvization.[61] While this kind of mapping process may refer to convention as a starting point, it will also encourage a questioning (and possible rejection) of these same conventions. This mapping process favours experimentation and may generate diverse ways of map-making that are open to collective authorship, multiple interpretations, and the potential communications of as-yet-unintelligible noisy excess. Mapping watery place in this way could encourage an idiolocal community of map-makers and map-readers who recognize the intense material negotiations of place engaged by watery phenomena and diverse forms of life.

Without wanting to restrict experimentation, there are a couple of aspects of mapping watery place that are worth emphasizing:

*Individual mapping efforts are part of a larger whole*: Each map is composed of omissions and inclusions; each map is incomplete. Indeed, certain kinds of knowledge are not easily mappable.[62] Each map needs a readership. Highlighting the continuity of authorship and interpretation in mapping practices helps to shrug off the fiction that each map is a discrete and authoritative iteration. A map can be further contextualized, not only by listing who composed and compiled the map, but also by revealing how a mapping effort is funded and organized, how the map-makers relate to their human and more-than-human informants, how difficulties or opportunities enliven and alter both mapping process and resulting map, and how other maps inspire, provoke, critique, or re-interpret a particular effort.

*Mapping watery place is best practised by taking multiple perspectives into account*: Given the complexity and wealth of watery place, the very least evolution in mapping practices would include a deliberate plurality of maps – overlapping but differing iterations and re-iterations of situated waters, a generative ecotone of water mapping. Mapping multiply would certainly include collaborative authorship. It would also heighten awareness of how any watery place is home to a larger more-than-human community. Mapping in this way may include: (1) more than one understanding of water (for example, the differing perpectives of those standing on shore, mayflies, fisherfolk, migratory birds, kayakers, or the crew of a freighter); (2) an awareness of the same watery place or event over time, thus recording slow and fast transformations; (3) a selective layering of information to give depth to watery place (such that a geophysical base is enriched with the representation of ecotones, multiple toponyms and hydronyms, stories of watery place, records of changing shorelines, and seasonal variations); (4) a deliberately synaesthetic use of many senses and various kinds of media, as discussed above; 5) the relation of the produced map to other maps of the same watery place, thus revealing an evolving community of maps.

Certainly, there will never be only one way to map water. Although I suggest particular approaches above, a thoughtful mapping of watery place is in part enacted by its readers. So, even though this volume is, first of all, a book, an inventive reader might also approach this work as a map – a survey of ecocultural theory that thinks with water.

○

Figure 20.1 and Plate 14 begin to map the rapid waters that have inspired this study. I am far from achieving the water-mapping ambitions sketched out above. That said, I draw selectively upon a broad community of other maps to represent this watery place in a way that differs significantly from more conventional maps like the CHS Nautical Chart

1409 (excerpted in Figure 20.3). The river flows (with gravity and text conventions) from the top of the page to its bottom; with its compass rose we understand that upstream and downstream are as important on this map as the cardinal directions. The map deliberately downplays land-based information such as roads, streets, and territorial boundaries. Instead, this *water* map highlights surface waters and their watersheds,[63] as well as water infrastructures, such as canals, bridges, municipal drinking water intakes, and wastewater outlets. It includes multiple names for the river and the rapids;[64] it shows changes to the shorelines over time and distinguishes different water masses and currents, including standing waves named by whitewater aficionados; it marks protected and unprotected places frequented by birds and fish, birdwatchers and fisherfolk. While I have not been able to show seasonal variations in this set of maps, the Montreal Flood Commission, for instance, assembled some wonderful ice and frazil studies of the rapids in the winter of 1886–87. Finally, an earlier on-line version of Plate 14 narrates a series of relations with this watery place.[65]

○

Expanding the current limited discourses of waters beyond constructions of resource and utility is important in this effort. Moreover, for future mappings of water and place to have any weight, they will need to engage wide participation and even wider consideration if they are to shift the way we collectively imagine and make places – a shift, not just beyond resource, but also toward an environmental intelligence and watery sociality that necessarily includes the more-than-human. To be engaged broadly, these mappings need to be recognizable. However, to catalyze changes in our perception of our daily environments, they also need to articulate and include phenomena at the thresholds of intelligibility which may initially seem strange. Water maps that challenge habitual ways of relating to place may inhabit a material and discursive threshold – an ecotone between intelligibility and incomprehensibility and between the known and the not-yet-recognized. Any heuristic mapping process will therefore seek an inclusive, generous, and generative approach that moves toward open futures (atopia and not prescriptive utopia). The relations and understandings drawn from these kinds of mapping practices will necessarily be unpredictable and will escape any map-maker's intentions.

We live and think with water. The places where we live are fully awash with its movements – waters flow in and draw out tangled relations with our many others: from the radical chemistries of life and death to the equally transformative effects of pollutions, toxins, and disease. Thinking with water may lead to new approaches to understanding place and practising mapping. Situating our complex relations with water engages thought in particular and *placed* iterations of space-time-matter. Mapping practices are key among the apparatuses that organize and selectively represent the way we know watery places – and, therefore, the way we imagine and negotiate the past, present, and future relations of watery community rich with entangled forms of life. Mapping *with water* helps us to more critically and generatively articulate the precarious and responsive watery places that we make and inhabit together.

NOTES

1 *Iohná:wate'* and *Tiohtià:ke* are Mohawk (*Kanien'kéha*) place names for the Lachine Rapids and the archipelago of Montreal, respectively. See Appendix, 299.

2 This chapter emerges from my dissertation research.

3 Jack and Wright, "Tiohtiake." *Tiohtià:ke* means "where the people divide" in Mohawk or *Kanien'kéha*, one of the Iroquoian languages. Douglas Jack and Roy Wright suggest that, like the waters of the Ottawa and St Lawrence rivers, peoples both move apart and come together in this archipelago – a complex dance of islands and lakes just east of the Beauharnois Axis.

4 Massey, *For Space*, 141.

5 Haraway, "Monsters," 65. Like Massey, Donna Haraway remarks upon the unruly collective negotiations that nonetheless cohere to become the places that we share. Haraway links *topos* and *tropos* by locating "nature" as both an evolving rhetorical construction and a contested common place. This juxtaposition suggests an agonistic realm where rhetorical representations are inextricably tangled with the way we negotiate shared places and waters.

6 See the work of political ecologists such as Gandy, Kaika, and Swyngedouw.

7 Recognizing access to safe drinking water and adequate sewage as human rights gives important moral weight to efforts that seek to protect the health of humans in relation to local waters. See Knight "The Right to Water"; United Nations General Assembly, ga/10967. However, the discourse of human rights can perpetuate the anthropocentric assumptions that narrowly frame water as resource and commodity. See also Neimanis "Bodies of Water."

8 Heidegger, "The Question Concerning Technology," 14–19.

9 Stoekl, *Bataille's Peak: Energy, Religion, and Postsustainability*.

10 Grosz, *Architecture from the Outside*, 101.

11 Ibid., 162.

12 Warner, *Publics and Counterpublics*, 21–63.

13 In this volume, Ælab's work, *light, sweet, cold, dark, crude* (2006–ongoing), makes visible wastewater and wastewater systems. See also Spiegel, this volume.

14 Douglas, *Purity and Danger*, 94–5.

15 From Noah's Ark to the countless contemporary tales, such as *The Life of Pi* (2001) by Yann Martel, being "at sea" is a common metaphor for being lost and for transformation. The metaphoric powers of water are addressed by MacLeod in this volume.

16 Roburn, "Literacy and the Underdevelopment of Knowledge." See also Christian and Wong, this volume.

17 Attempting to speak for and represent others, whether human or more-than-human,

is rarely without some distortion. For this reason, in the *Politics of Nature*, Bruno Latour has proposed the figure of the stuttering spokesperson in his Parliament of Things. Here, I am the stuttering and problematic speaker. See more questions about "speaking for," "speaking with," or a possible "affinity of incomprehension" in van Wyck's *Primitives in the Wilderness*, 121–6.

18 In "Water and Planetarity," Neimanis discussed the radical unknowability of waters and the importance of humbly acknowledging the limits of what we can know.

19 Christian and Wong, this volume. As we outline in the introduction, each chapter in this book challenges reductive definitions of the aqueous by mapping diverse relations to water.

20 Lingis, *The Community of Those Who Have Nothing in Common*, 69–105.

21 See van Wyck on chorography in this volume.

22 Barad, *Meeting the Universe*, 185.

23 Ibid., 185.

24 Ibid., 97–106.

25 Heidegger, "The Question Concerning Technology"; Grosz, *Architecture*, 100–1.

26 The *Waterlife website* is a filmic and narrative map that offers an alternate way to engage the materials of the documentary film, *Waterlife* (2009), directed by Kevin McMahon.

27 Foucault, "Des Espaces Autres (1967) Hétérotopie," 47–8. Foucault offers an extended definition of heterotopia here. See English translation: "Michel Foucault: Of Other Spaces."

28 Ibid., 49.

29 Ibid.

30 Hypersea is a concept described by the McMenamins and also referenced by Strang and Chandler and Neimanis in this volume,

31 See Chandler and Neimanis, this volume.

32 See the Introduction and Chandler and Neimanis in this volume in regard to this spill.

33 Carter, "Dark with Excess of Bright," 130: "The coastal survey stood to one side of the classic ambition of Enlightenment science to map the world, preserving in the awkwardness of its practices a recognition of the refractory nature of the phenomenal world, an awareness of the approximate and constructed nature of its designs … The geographer's coastline signifies rather the desire of signification, the condition of bringing into circulation the field where power relations will be played out" (130).

34 Ibid., 131.

35 Ibid., 128.

36 Ibid., 128–9.

37 Ibid., 129.

38 Ibid., 127.

39 Ten years later, one interpretation had this gulf named Cook's River. It is interesting to

compare James Cook's 1778 map with Rigobert Bonne's map of 1788 for the differ-ences in toponyms that are not solely due to translation from one language to another.

40 Carter, "Dark with Excess of Bright," 127.

41 See Harley on reading maps of colonial "encounter."

42 Cosgrove, *Mappings*, 9.

43 Corner, "The Agency of Mapping," 229.

44 In an extreme example, Guy Debord's reports: "A friend recently told me that he had just wandered through the Harz region of Germany while blindly following the direc-tions of a map of London." Debord, "Introduction to a Critique of Urban Geogra-phy," paragraph 17.

45 Canadian Hydrographic Service (chs). Nautical Chart 1409. *Canal de la Rive Sud.* This chart is now replaced by Chart 1429. See chs, *Nautical Charts and Services* website.

46 "Record low water levels in Quebec," *Radio Noon Montreal*, 12 July 2012. As a result of drought and low water levels in July 2012, the St Lawrence Seaway was put on "Alert Level": ships were asked to lighten their loads by 10 percent; and naviga-tion through Lac St-Louis was micro-managed so that heavier ships rode a contrived surge of water released from upstream. Low water levels affect everything from muskrat homes to municipal drinking water systems.

47 Canadian Hydrographic Service (chs). Nautical Chart 1409. *Canal de la Rive Sud.* See also chs, "Hydrographic Surveys" webpage, where chs promises to "capture water depths, geographical features, hazards to navigation, man-made and natural features that aid navigation, tides, currents and water levels, and sea bottom characteristics."

48 Many of these skilled river pilots were *Kahnawakero:non* (from Kahnawake). See Phillips, "The Kahnawake Mohawks and the St Lawrence Seaway," 13, 33.

49 See Fortin, "Guide"; Myosis, "St-Laurent, Rapides de Lachine"; and ksf. See also Accès Fleuve / zip Ville-Marie, "Guide de randonnée: Route bleue du Grand Montréal."

50 Verry, Dolloff, and Manning, "Riparian Ecotone," 76–7. They propose that where "Ecosystem has that troublesome characteristic of being applicable at all scales: single cell, Earth, universe and most everything in between ... ecotone is a gradient across ecosystems (for example, the prairie-forest ecotones; the estuary, salt-fresh water ecotone)" (76–7).

51 Said, "Invention, Memory, and Place."

52 Grosz, *Architecture*, 198. See also MacLeod, this volume.

53 Massumi, "Strange Horizon," 182.

54 Ibid., 180.

55 Massey, *For Space*, 109–11; Sadler, *The Situationist City*, 20–1. The Situationists are known for their pursuit of creative disruptions to daily life, exemplified in part by their experimental re-mappings of Paris, such as *The Naked City* (1957) by Debord and Jorn.

56  Whitridge, "Landscapes," 219–26. See also Collignon, "Inuit Place Names."

57  Morgan, "Tactile Maps"; "Reading Maps"; and Greenland Inuit. See also "Eskimo's Map of Driftwood."

58  Cosgrove, *Mappings*, 12.

59  For example: see Lockwood and McCartney on soundscapes of water; see Stein's *Montreal Sound Map*; see the Centre for Oral History and Digital Storytelling for oral history mapping projects; see also *Waterlife website*; and Parr, van der Veen, and van Horssen for online maps that employ image, sound, and sometimes film or animation.

60  Whitridge, "Landscapes," 220–1. Whitridge is citing Nuttall, *Arctic Homeland*.

61  In this, I am inspired by the inventive methodologies described by Gregory Ulmer in *Heuretics* and many of the examples of innovative mapping already cited in this chapter.

62  See Chen, "Ville de Sainte-Catherine," for an attempt to map certain place-based narratives.

63  Currently, information about Canadian groundwaters is far from complete. See National Resources Canada "Groundwater"; Patterson, "Canadian Groundwater"; and "Harper's."

64  See also the Place Names Appendix

65  See Chen, "Mapping Watery Relations," *Alternatives Journal*.

# Appendix of Place Names

| Anishinabe / Algonquin | English | Français | Huron-Wendat | Kanien'kéha (Mohawk) |
|---|---|---|---|---|
| Kitcikami sipi | St Lawrence River | Fleuve Saint-Laurent | Lada8anna | Kaniatarowá:nen |
| Kanawageng / Moniapawitik? | Lachine Rapids | Rapides de Lachine* | | Iohná:wate' |
| Monia Minitikoka? | Montreal Archipelago | Archipel de Montréal | | Tiohtià:ke |

*Pronunciation for Kanien'kéha names:*
Kaniatarowá:nen [ga-nya-da-ro-wáa-nunh] = St Lawrence River
Iohná:wate' [yohh-náa-wa-de7] = Lachine Rapids
Tiohtià:ke [djohh-djàa(7)-geh] = Montreal Archipelago
Kahnawà:ke [gahh-na-wàa(7)-geh] = "on the rapids" (or "by" or "at" the rapids)

*with this key:*
[g] hard as in get or gift;
vowels as in French, NOT slurred (as in English);
[áa] / [àa] held longer, with higher/lower pitch on the next syllable;
[hh] strongly aspirated/puffed, NOT as weak as [h] or silent;
[7] glottal stop/catch in throat, as in English "uh-(7)oh" (oops) (optionally dropped
   after [àa] as in 'Tiohtià:ke' and 'Kahnawà:ke').

Sources for place names: Roy Wright, e-mail correspondence with author regarding *Kanien'kéha* place names (including their pronunciation), 14 October 2010. See also Wright, "Le Plan Vincent"; Douglas Jack, "History Map 10.4"; and Cuoq, *Lexique*. This table is only a partial record of the many names of the waters of *Tiohtià:ke*.

*According to *La commission de toponymie du Québec*, this naming of the rapids seems to emerge from a colonial desire for an unattainable other. Granted a territory beside the rapids in 1667, René-Robert Cavelier de LaSalle soon abandoned the working of his lands to seek a trade route to China. Although subsequent explorations proved more successful, his first venture foundered and, upon an early return, he and his men became mockingly known as "the Chinese," while his lands by the rapids were called *La Chine* – the place they did not reach. The polished-by-use-into-one-word toponym of Lachine has endured.

# Works Referenced

Accès Fleuve / ZIP Ville-Marie. "Guide de randonnée: Route bleue du Grand Montréal: Édition 2012." *Fédération québecoise du canot et du kayak*. http://www.routebleue.com/guide-des-itineacuteraires-agrave-teacuteleacutecharger-gratuitement.html. Accessed 30 July 2012.

Adorno, Theodor and Max Horkheimer. *Dialectic of Enlightenment*. (1944). Edited by Gunzelin Schmid Noerr. Translated by Edmund Jephcott. Stanford: Stanford University Press, 2002.

"A Federal Perspective on Water Quantity Issues: December 2007: Draft." *Council of Canadians*. www.canadians.org/water/documents/FederalWaterQuantity.pdf

Agassiz, Elizabeth, and Alexander Agassiz. *Seaside Studies in Natural History*. Boston: Ticknor and Fields, 1865. Reprint. Michigan Historical Reprint Series. Ann Arbor: University of Michigan Press.

Alaimo, Stacy. *Bodily Natures: Science, Environment, and the Material Self*. Bloomington: Indiana University Press, 2010.

– "The Naked Word: The Trans-Corporeal Ethic of the Protesting Body." *Women & Performance: A Journal of Feminist Theory* 20, no. 1 (2010): 15–36.

– "Trans-corporeal Feminisms and the Ethical Space of Nature." In *Material Feminisms*, edited by Stacy Alaimo and Susan Hekman, 237–64. Bloomington: Indiana University Press, 2008.

– "Violet-Black: Ecologies of the Abyssal Zone." In *Prismatic Ecologies: Ecotheory Beyond Green*, edited by Jeffrey Jerome Cohen. Minneapolis: University of Minnesota Press, forthcoming.

– *Undomesticated Ground : Recasting Nature as Feminist Space*. Ithaca: Cornell University Press, 2000.

Alaimo, Stacy, and Susan Hekman, eds. *Material Feminisms*. Bloomington: Indiana University Press, 2008.

Alaska Eskimo Whaling Commission. alaska-aewc.com.

"All Time Box Office: Worldwide Grosses." *Box Office Mojo* website. http://www.boxoffice-mojo.com/alltime/world/. Accessed 12 November 2010.

Altman, John. "Indigenous Interests and Water Property Rights." *Dialogue* 23 no. 3 (2004): 29–34.

*Amazay: A Film About Water*. JP Laplante, dir. Tse Keh Nay, 2009. Online Film, 57 min. http://www.youtube.com/watch?v=pypoI54tLxg. Accessed 24 July 2012. [Defunct link, http://tsekehnay.net/index.php?/news/article/81/, accessed 8 June 2010].

Anderson, Benedict. *Imagined Communities: Reflections on the Origin and Spread of Nationalism*. London: Verso, 1983.

Apffel-Marglin, Frédérique and Loyda Sanchez. "Developmentalist feminism and neocolonialism in Andean communities." In *Feminist Post-Development Thought: Rethinking Modernity, Postcolonialism and Representation*, edited by Kriemild Saunders, 159–79. London, England: Zed Books, 2002.

Appadurai, Arjun. *Modernity at Large: Cultural Dimensions of Globalization*. Minneapolis: University of Minnesota Press, 1996.

Archibald, Jo-ann. *Storywork: Educating the Heart, Mind, Body and Spirit*. Vancouver: UBC Press, 2008.

"Arctic." *Scripps Whale Acoustics Lab*. http://cetus.ucsd.edu/projects_Arctic.html.

Arctic Council. *Arctic Environmental Protection Strategy*. Rovaniemi: July, 1991. http://arctic-council.org/filearchive/artic_environment.pdf.

– *Arctic Marine Shipping Assessment 2009 Report*. Second printing. April 2009.

– *Nuuk Declaration*. Nuuk: 12 May 2011. http://www.arctic-council.org/index.php/en/about/documents/category/5-declarations.

Arendt, Hannah. "Introduction." In *Illuminations: Essays and Reflections*, edited by Hannah Arendt, 1–55. New York: Schocken Books, 1968.

– *The Human Condition, 2nd Edition*. Chicago: University of Chicago Press, 1998.

Armstrong, Jeannette. "Water is Siwlkw." *Proceedings of the Theme "Water and Cultural Diversity."* Kyoto, Japan: Third World Water Forum. March 16–23, 2003. 17–18.

Åsberg, Cecilia, Redi Koobak, and Ericka Johnson, eds. NORA: *Nordic Journal of Feminist and Gender Research: Post-humanities* 19, no. 4 (2011).

"The Assuan Dam." *The Times* (London), 26 December 1912, p. 11, issue 4002. Accessed online from "The Times Digital Archive."

Australian Broadcasting Corporation. "Bitter Water Feud Grows in Queensland." Television Program Transcript. Reporters Paul Lockyer and Kelly O'Brien, with interviewees John Grabbe, Pop Peterson, Peter Peterson, Rory Treweek, et al. Broadcast 24 February 2004. http://www.abc.net.au/7.30/content/2004/s1052459.htm

Bachelard, Gaston. *Water and Dreams: An Essay on the Imagination of Matter*. 1942. Translated by Edith Farrell. Dallas: Dallas Institute of Humanities and Culture, 1983.

Bailey, Sharon M. "The Arbitrary Nature of the Story: Poking Fun at Oral and Written Authority in Thomas King's *Green Grass, Running Water*." *World Literature Today* 73, no. 1 (1999): 43–52.

Bakker, Karen J., ed. *Eau Canada: The Future of Canada's Water*. Vancouver: UBC Press, 2007.

Ball, Philip. *Life's Matrix: A Biography of Water*. Berkeley: University of California Press, 2001.

Barad, Karen. "Post-humanist Performativity: Toward an Understanding of How Matter Comes to Matter." *Signs* 28, no. 3 (2003): 801–31.

– *Meeting the Universe Halfway: Quantum Physics and the Entanglement of Matter and Meaning*. Durham and London: Duke University Press, 2007.

Barclay, Barry. "Exploring Fourth Cinema." Talk presented at "Re-imagining Indigenous

Cultures: The Pacific Islands," National Endowment for the Humanities, Summer Institute, Honolulu, Hawai'i, July 2003. kainani.hpu.edu/hwood/HawPacFilm/BarclayExploring FourthCinema2003.doc

Barthes, Roland. *Camera Lucida: Reflections on Photography*. Translated by Richard Howard. New York: Hill and Wang, 1981.

– *Mythologies*. London: Paladin, 1973.

Bassey, Nnimmo. "UN report on Nigeria oil spills relies too heavily on data from Shell." *Guardian*, 25 August 2010. http://www.guardian.co.uk/environment/cif-green/2010/aug/25/un-nigeria-oil-spill-shell. Accessed 25 March 2010.

Bataille, Georges. *The Accursed Share, Volume 1*. Translated by Robert Hurley. New York: Zone Books, 1991.

Bate, Jonathan. *The Song of the Earth*. London: Picador, 2000.

Baudrillard, Jean. "The Ecstasy of Communication." In *The Anti-Aesthetic: Essays on Postmodern Culture*, edited by Hal Foster, 126–34. Port Townsend, Washington: Bay Press, 1983.

– *For a Critique of the Political Economy of the Sign*. Translated by Charles Levin. St Louis, Missouri: Telos Press, 1981.

Bauman, Zygmunt. *Liquid Fear*. Cambridge and Malden, Massachusetts: Polity Press, 2006.

Beebe, William. *Beneath Tropic Seas*. New York: G.P. Putnam's Sons, 1928.

– *Half Mile Down*. New York: Duell, Sloan, and Pearce, 1934.

– *The Arcturus Adventure: An Account of the New York Zoological Society's First Oceanographic Expedition*. New York: G.P. Putnam's Sons, 1926.

Benjamin, Bret. *Invested Interests: Capital, Culture and the World Bank*. Minneapolis and London: University of Minnesota Press, 2007.

Benjamin, Walter. *Illuminations: Essays and Reflections*. Edited by Hannah Arendt. Translated by Harry Zohn. New York: Schocken Books, 1968.

– "Theses on the Philosophy of History." In *Illuminations: Essays and Reflections*, 253–64. New York: Schocken Books, 1968.

– *Reflections*. Edited by Peter Demetz. Translated by Edmund Jephcott. New York: Schocken Books, 1978.

Bennett, Jane. *Vibrant Matter: A Political Ecology of Things*. Durham, North Carolina: Duke University Press, 2010.

Berelowitz, Lance. *Dream City*. Vancouver: Douglas & McIntyre, 2005.

Berger, Anthony R. "Rapid Geological Change Challenges Concept of Sustainability." *Geoscience Canada* 34, no. 3–4 (2007): 81–90.

Berland, Jody. "Walkerton: The Memory of Matter." *TOPIA* 14 (2005): 93–108.

– "What is Environmental Cultural Studies?" Symposium on Environmental Cultural Studies. Toronto: York University, 2006. http://www.yorku.ca/jberland/docs/whatis.pdf. Accessed 22 June 2011.

Berry, Margaret. "Thomas Berry and the Earth Community: Thomas Berry Short Biography." http://www.earth-community.org/bio.htm. Accessed 9 October 2010.

Bhopal Gas Peedit Mahila Stationery Karmachari Sangh, Bhopal Gas Peedit Mahila Purush

Sangharsh Morcha, Bhopal Group for Information and Action. "Press Release: Benign Buffet, November 28, 2009." *International Campaign for Justice in Bhopal, Students for Bhopal.* http://www.studentsforbhopal.org/node/292.

Bhopal Medical Appeal, Activists and Yes Men at Dow Live Earth. http://www.youtube.com/watch?v=N5IUaU9BfhY.

Bigwood, Carol. *Earth Muse.* Philadelphia: Temple University Press, 1993.

Bijsterveld, Karin. "A Booming Business: The Search for a Practical Aircraft Noise Index." In *Mechanical Sound: Technology, Culture and Public Problems of Noise in the Twentieth Century.* Cambridge: MIT Press, 2008, 193–232.

Billington, David, and Donald Conrad Jackson. *Big Dams of the New Deal Era: A Confluence of Engineering and Politics.* Norman: University of Oklahoma Press, 2006.

Biro, Andrew. "Half-Empty or Half-Full? Water Politics and the Canadian National Imaginary." In *Eau Canada: The Future of Canada's Water*, ed. Karen Bakker. Vancouver: UBC Press, 2007: 321–33.

– *Denaturalizing Ecological Politics: Alienation from Nature from Rousseau to the Frankfurt School and Beyond.* Toronto: University of Toronto Press, 2005.

Blackstock, Michael. "Water: A First Nations' Spiritual and Ecological Perspective." *BC Journal of Ecosystems and Management* 1, no.1 (2001): 1–14.

– *Blue Ecology.* http://blueecology.com. Accessed 9 October 2010.

Blatter, Joachim, and Helen Ingram, eds. *Reflections on Water: New Approaches to Transboundary Conflicts and Cooperation.* Cambridge, Massachusetts: MIT Press, 2001.

Bliek, Desmond , and Pierre Gauthier. "Mobilising Urban Heritage to Counter the Commodification of Brownfield Landscapes: Lessons from Montréal's Lachine Canal." *Canadian Planning and Policy – Aménagement et politique au Canada* 16, no. 1 Supplement (2007): 1–20.

– "Understanding the Built Form of Industrialization Along the Lachine Canal in Montreal." *Urban History Review* 35, no. 1 (2006): 1–17.

Blomquist, William, and Edella Schlager. "Political Pitfalls of Integrated Watershed Management." *Society and Natural Resources* 18 (2005): 101–17.

Bocking, Richard. *Mighty River: A Portrait of the Fraser.* Vancouver: Douglas & McIntyre, 1997.

Bodenhorn, Barbara. "Fall Whaling in Barrow, Alaska: A Consideration of Strategic Decision Making." In *Indigenous Ways to the Present: Native Whaling in the Western Arctic*, edited by Allen P. McCartney. Edmonton: Canadian Circumpolar Institute Press. 2003.

Bonne, Rigobert. *Carte de la Rivière de Cook, dans la partie N.O. de l'Amérique.* Princeton University Library, 1788. Map. http://libweb5.princeton.edu/visual_materials/maps/websites/pacific/cook3/map-cook-river-1788.jpg.

Boswell, Randy. "Feds plan to probe for oil in proposed conservation area: Move to protect Lancaster Sound conflicts with search for seabed resources." *Vancouver Sun.* Vancouver: 8 April 2010.

– "Inuit claim whale as proof of importance of controversial survey site." *Postmedia News, www.canada.com.* 10 September 2010. http://www.canada.com/travel/Inuit+claim+whale +proof+importance+controversial+survey+site/3377950/story.html.

– "Judge grants temporary injunction against seismic testing." *Postmedia News, www.canada.com.* 10 September 2010. http://www.canada.com/technology/Nunavut+judge+ grants+temporary+injunction+against+seismic+testing/3375321/story.html.

Boundas, Constantin. "What Difference Does Deleuze's Difference Make?" In *Deleuze and Philosophy*, edited by Constantin Boundas, 3–27. Edinburgh: Edinburgh University Press, 2006.

Brady, Jeff. "Shell Pushes Forward to Drill Well in Arctic." *National Public Radio.* 24 December 2010. http://byers.typepad.com/arctic/2010/12/shell-pushes-forward-to-drill-well-in-arctic. html#more.

Braidotti, Rosi. "Becoming-Woman: Or Sexual Difference Revisited." *Theory, Culture and Society* 20, no. 3 (2003): 43–64.

Brandes, Oliver M., Keith Ferguson, Michael M'Gonigle, and Calvin Sandborn. *At a Watershed: Ecological Governance and Sustainable Water Management in Canada.* Victoria, British Columbia: Polis Project on Water Governance, 2005.

Braun, Bruce, and Sarah Whatmore, eds. *Political Matter: Technoscience, Democracy and Public Life.* Minneapolis: University of Minnesota Press, 2010.

Broad, William J. *The Universe Below: Discovering the Secrets of the Deep Sea.* New York: Touchstone, 1997.

Broglio, Ron. *Surface Encounters: Thinking with Animals and Art.* Minneapolis: University of Minnesota Press, 2011.

Brower, Harry, with Karen Brewster, ed. *Whales They Give Themselves: Conversations with Harry Brower, Sr.* Fairbanks, Alaska: University of Alaska Press, 2004.

Buck-Morss, Susan. *Dreamworld and Catastrophe: The Passing of Mass Utopia in East and West.* Cambridge, Massachusetts: MIT Press, 2000.

Buell, Lawrence. *The Future of Environmental Criticism: Environmental Crisis and Literary Imagination.* Malden, Massachusetts: Blackwell, 2005.

Burstyn, Varda. *Water, Inc.* London and New York: Verso, 2005.

Burwell, Mike. "Hunger Knows No Law: Seminal Native Protest and the Barrow Duck-In of 1961." United States Department of the Interior, Minerals Management Service. Paper presented to the 2004 Alaska Historical Society. http://www.uaa.alaska.edu/cafe/upload/ Hunger-Knows-No-Law-AAAMarch2005Last.pdf.

Butler, Judith. *Bodies that Matter.* New York: Routledge, 1993.

Byers, Michael. "It's time to resolve our Arctic differences." *Globe and Mail.* Toronto: 30 April 2010: A15.

Calarco, Matthew. *Zoographies: The Question of the Animal from Heidegger to Derrida.* New York: Columbia University Press, 2008.

Canadian Environmental Assessment Agency. "Lachine Canal Decontamination Project. Report of the Joint Environmental Assessment Panel." Ottawa, 1996.

Canadian Hydrographic Service (CHS). "Hydrographic Surveys." *Nautical Charts and Services.*

Accessed 7 July 2012. http://www.charts.gc.ca/data-gestion/hydrographic/hydrographic-eng.asp.

– *Nautical Charts and Services* website. Accessed 7 July 2012. http://www.charts.gc.ca.

– Nautical Chart 1409. *Canal de la Rive Sud: Voie Maritime du Saint-Laurent / St Lawrence Seaway*. 1:20 000 (45°28'N). Ministry of Fisheries and Oceans Canada, 2002-04-12 (updated 2008-04-18).

Canadian Hydrographic Survey, Department of Marine and Fisheries, Department of Railways and Canals, and Charles McGreevy. Map. "Canada: River St. Lawrence, La Prairie Basin." Compiled from a survey by Chas. McGreevy, C.E., 1911, and from air photos and survey by the Railways and Canals Department, 1925. Published by the Canadian Hydrographic Survey, Department of Marine and Fisheries Canada, 1925. Scale 1 inch: 1000 feet, blueline print, 107 cm x 135.7 cm. Library and Archives Canada, Microfiche number 51986 (2 sections), Call number MIC/312/[1925], Record number 9780.

"Canadian Tar Sands: Impacts to US and Canadian Indigenous Communities." *Indigenous Environmental Network*. http://www.ienearth.org/tarsands.html

Cannavo, Peter. *The Working Landscape: Founding, Preservation, and the Politics of Place*. Cambridge, Massachusetts: MIT Press, 2007.

Caplan, Pat, ed. *The Ethics of Anthropology: Debates and Dilemmas*. New York: Routledge, 2003.

Carlson, Hans M. *Home Is the Hunter: The James Bay Cree and Their Land*. Vancouver: University of British Columbia Press, 2009.

Carr, Nicholas. "Is Google Making Us Stupid?" *Atlantic Monthly* (July/August 2008): 56–63.

Carter, Paul. "Dark with Excess of Bright: Mapping the Coastlines of Knowledge." In *Mappings*, edited by Denis Cosgrove, 125–47. London: Reaktion Books, 1999.

Castricano, Jodey, ed. *Animal Subjects: An Ethical Reader in a Posthuman World*. Waterloo: Wilfrid Laurier University Press, 2008.

*Census of Marine Life website*. http://www.coml.org/. Accessed 1 October 2010.

*Centre for Oral History and Digital Storytelling*. "Our Projects." http://storytelling.concordia.ca/oralhistory/projects/projects.html.

Césaire, Aimé. *Discourse on Colonialism*. (1955). Translated by Joan Pinkham. New York: Monthly Review Press, 2001.

Champlain, Samuel de (1574–1635). Map. "Le grand Sault St. Louis." In Samuel de Champlain, *Les Voyages du sieur de Champlain, Xaintongeois, capitaine ordinaire pour le Roy en la marine, divisez en deux livres [...]*. Paris: Jean Berjon, 1613. 1 map, 11 cm x 16 cm. Bibliothèque et Archives nationales du Québec, numéro catalogue Iris 0002663504, http://services.banq.qc.ca/sdx/cep/document.xsp?id=0002663504.

Chandler, Mielle. "Creation, Sovereignty, Ethics: Private Property and the Infraction of Infinity." PhD diss. Toronto: York University, 2009.

Charland, Louis (1772–1813). Map. "A plan of that part of St. Lewis Falls and Rapids comprehended between the Isle au Diable and Isle Boket drawn by order of the Gentle [...] Commissioners appointed under the authority of an Act intitled: An Act for applying the sum of one thousand pounds, towards the improvement of the inland navigation of this Province," scale 2 arpents: 1 pouce (1: 4 608), 1805, 1 plan, colour, 63 cm x 79 cm, Bibliothèque et Archives nationales du Québec, cote E21, S555, SS1, SSS18, P01 1/2 E.

Chen, Cecilia, Janine MacLeod, and Astrida Neimanis. "Call for Proposals: Thinking With Water – An Anthology of Cultural Theory on Water." *NiCHE Network in Canadian History and Environment*. http://niche-canada.org/node/2500.

Chen, Cecilia. "Mapping Watery Relations at the Lachine Rapids." *Alternatives Journal* 37.1 (2011): 20–1. Also online: http://www.alternativesjournal.ca/articles/mapping-watery-relations-at-the-lachine-rapids.

Chen, Kuan-Hsing. *Asia as Method: Toward Deimperialization*. Durham, North Carolina: Duke University Press, 2010.

Chetham, Deirdre. *Before the Deluge: The Vanishing World of the Yangtze's Three Gorges*. New York and Basingstoke: Palgrave Macmillan, 2002.

Chingari Trust. http://www.chingaritrustbhopal.com/

Christian, Dorothy, and Denise Nadeau. "Protect Our Sacred Waters." *Common Ground*. June 2007. http://commonground.ca/iss/0706191/cg191_waters.shtml. Accessed 8 June 2010.

Citton, Yves. "Political Agency and the Ambivalence of the Sensible." In *Jacques Rancière: History, Politics, Aesthetics*, edited by Gabriel Rockhill and Philip Watts, 120–39. Durham, North Carolina: Duke University Press, 2009.

City of Vancouver. "Wild Salmon Month" Proclamation, September 2010. www.falsecreekwatershed.org/pdfs/salmon_month_proclamation_2010.pdf. Accessed 8 October 2010.

Cixous, Hélène, and Catherine Clément. *The Newly Born Woman*. Minneapolis: University of Minnesota Press, 1986.

Clark, C.W., W.T. Ellison, B.L. Southall, L. Hatch, S.M. Van Parijs, A. Frankel, and D. Ponirakis. "Acoustic masking in marine ecosystems: intuitions, analysis, and implication." *Marine Ecology Progress Series* 395 (2009): 201–22.

Clark, C.W., Moira W. Brown, and Peter Corkeron. "Visual and acoustic surveys for North Atlantic right whales, *Eubalaena glacialis*, in Cape Cod Bay, Massachusetts, 2001–2005: Management Implications." *Marine Mammal Science* 26, no. 4 (2010): 837–54.

Coase, Ronald H. "The Problem of Social Cost." *Journal of Law and Economics* 3 (1960): 1–44.

Cockayne, Emily. "Noisy." In *Hubbub: Filth, Noise and Stench in England*, 106–30. New Haven: Yale University Press, 2007.

Colebrook, C. "On Not Becoming Man." In *Material Feminisms*, edited by Stacy Alaimo and Susan Hekman, 52–84. Bloomington: Indiana University Press, 2008.

Collignon, Béatrice. "Inuit Place Names and Sense of Place." In *Critical Inuit Studies: An Anthology of Contemporary Arctic Ethnography*, edited by Pamela Stern and Lisa Stevenson, 187–205. Lincoln, London: University of Nebraska Press, 2006.

Comaroff, Jean, and John L Comaroff. *Millennial Capitalism and the Culture of Neoliberalism*. Durham, North Carolina, and London: Duke University Press, 2001.

Commission de Toponymie du Québec. "Lachine." *Banque de noms de lieux du Québec*. Last modified 3 March 2011. http://www.toponymie.gouv.qc.ca/ct/ToposWeb/fiche.aspx?no_seq=98645.

– "Rapides de Lachine." *Banque de noms de lieux du Québec*. Last modified 3 March 2011. http://www.toponymie.gouv.qc.ca/ct/ToposWeb/fiche.aspx?no_seq=33166.

Commissioner of the Environment and Sustainable Development. "2002 October Report of the

Commissioner of the Environment and Sustainable Development." *Office of the Auditor General.* http://www.oag-bvg.gc.ca/internet/English/att_c20021002xe01_e_12327.html.

Condon, Robert H. et al. "Questioning the Rise of Gelatinous Zooplankton in the World's Oceans." *BioScience*, February 2012, 62.2: 160–9.

Conley, Verena Andermatt. *Ecopolitics: The Environment in Poststructuralist Thought.* London: Routledge, 1997.

Connor, Judith L., and Nora L. Deans. *Jellies: Living Art.* Foreword by Terry Tempest Williams. Monterey: Monterey Bay Aquarium Foundation, 2002.

Cook, James. Sketch of the Gulf of Good Hope [Cook Inlet]. *Colonial Despatches* website, University of Victoria, 1778. Map. http://bcgenesis.uvic.ca/map.htm?id=mpi_1-81_2_1778.

Coole, Diana, and Samantha Frost, eds. *New Materialisms: Ontology, Agency, and Politics.* Durham, North Carolina: Duke University Press, 2011.

Corner, James. "The Agency of Mapping: Speculation, Critique and Invention." In *Mappings*, edited by Denis Cosgrove, 213–52. London: Reaktion Books, 1999.

Cosens, S.E., and L.P. Dueck. "Icebreaker noise in Lancaster Sound, N.W.T., Canada: Implications for marine mammal behavior." *Marine Mammal Science* 9, no. 3 (1993): 285–300.

Cosgrove, Denis. "Introduction: Mapping Meaning." In *Mappings*, edited by Denis Cosgrove, 1–23. London: Reaktion Books, 1999.

Coulthard, Glen. "Place Against Empire: Understanding Indigenous Anti-Colonialism." *Affinities: A Journal of Radical Theory, Culture, and Action* 4, no. 2 (2010): 79–83. http://journals.sfu.ca/affinities/index.php/affinities/article/view/69/211.

Council of the European Union. *Council Conclusions on Arctic Issues.* Brussels: 8 December 2009.

Cox, James H. "'All This Water Imagery Must Mean Something': Thomas King's Revisions of Narratives of Domination and Conquest in *Green Grass, Running Water*." *American Indian Quarterly* 24, no. 2 (2000): 219–46.

Cox, T.M., T.J. Ragen, A.J. Read, E. Vos, et al. "Understanding the impacts of anthropogenic sound on beaked whales." *Journal of Cetacean Research Management* 7 (2006): 177–87.

Crist, Darlene Trewe, Gail Scowcroft, and James M. Harding, Jr. *World Ocean Census: A Global Survey of Marine Life.* Foreword by Sylvia Earle. Buffalo: Firefly Books, 2009.

Cronon, William. "The Trouble with Wilderness; or, Getting Back to the Wrong Nature." In *Uncommon Ground: Rethinking the Human Place in Nature*, edited by William Cronon, 69–90. New York: W.W. Norton, 1996.

*Cubbie Group.* http://www.cubbie.com.au/

Cuoq, Jean André (prêtre de Saint-Sulpice). *Lexique de la langue Algonquine.* Montreal: J. Chapleau & Fils, imprimeurs-éditeurs, 1886.

Daigneault, Gilles. *Artefact 2001: Sculptures Urbaines / Urban Sculptures.* Montréal: Centre de diffusion 3D / Centre d'art public, 2001.

Damasio, Antonio. *The Feeling of What Happens: Body and Emotion in the Making of Consciousness.* New York: Harcourt Brace, 1999.

Darwin, Charles. *The Origin of Species by Means of Natural Selection and The Descent of Man and Selection in Relation to Sex*. New York: The Modern Library, n.d.

Davis, Mike. "The Political Economy of Late-Imperial America." *New Left Review* 143 (1984): 6–38.

– *Late Victorian Holocausts: El Niño Famines and the Making of the Third World*. London and New York: Verso, 2001.

Davis, Oliver. *Jacques Rancière*. Cambridge, Polity, 2010.

De Landa, Manuel. *Intensive Science and Virtual Philosophy*. New York: Continuum, 2002.

Debord, Guy and Asger Jorn. *The Naked City: Illustration de l'hypothése des plaques tournantes en psychogeographique* [sic]. Map and screenprint. First exhibited in the *Première exposition de psychogéographie*, Paris, 1957.

– "Introduction to a Critique of Urban Geography." *Les Lèvres Nues* 6 (September 1955). Translated by Ken Knabb. *Situationist International Online*. http://www.cddc.vt.edu/sionline/ presitu/geography.html. Accessed 21 April 2012.

Deleuze, Gilles. *Difference and Repetition*. Translated by Paul Patton. New York: Columbia University Press, 1994.

– *Logic of Sense*. Translated by Charles Stivale. Edited by Constantin V. Boundas. New York: Columbia University Press, 1990.

– *Nietzsche and Philosophy*. New York: Columbia University Press, 2002.

Deleuze, Gilles, and Félix Guattari. *Anti-Oedipus: Capitalism and Schizophrenia*. Translated by Robert Hurley, Mark Seem, and Helen. R. Lane. Minneapolis: University of Minnesota Press, 1983.

– *A Thousand Plateaus*. 1987. Translated by Brian Massumi. Minneapolis: University of Minnesota Press, 2005.

Deleuze, Gilles, and Claire Parnet. "The Actual and the Virtual." In *Dialogues II*, translated by Eliot Albert Ross, 112–15. New York: Columbia University Press, 2002.

Derrida, Jacques. *Specters of Marx: The State of the Debt, the Work of Mourning, and the New International*. New York: Routledge, 1994.

– "The Future of the Profession, or the Unconditional University (Thanks to the 'Humanities': What *Could Take Place* Tomorrow)." In *Jacques Derrida and the Humanities: A Critical Reader*, edited by Tom Cohen. Cambridge: Cambridge University Press, 2008: 24–57.

Descartes, René. *The Philosophical Works of Descartes*. Translated by Elizabeth Haldane and George Ross. London, Cambridge: Cambridge University Press, 1912.

Descola, Phillipe, and Gísli Palsson, eds. *Nature and Society: Anthropological Perspectives*. London, New York: Routledge, 1996.

Desloges, Yvon. "Behind the Scene of the Lachine Canal Landscape." *Journal of the Society for Industrial Archeology* 29, no. 1 (2003).

Desloges, Yvon, and Alain Gelly. *The Lachine Canal: Riding the Waves of Industrial and Urban Development, 1860–1950*. Sillery, Quebec: Septentrion, 2002.

Dickie, Phil, and Brown, Susan. *The Rise and Rise of Cubbie Station*. Australia: Melaleuca Media, 2007. http://www.melaleucamedia.com.au/default.asp.

*Digital Natives project*. http://digitalnatives.othersights.ca/public-language-trouble. Accessed 8 June 2010.

Diprose, Rosalyn. "What is (Feminist) Philosophy?" *Hypatia* 15, no. 2 (2000): 115–33.

Dobson, Andrew. *Citizenship and the Environment*. Oxford: Oxford University Press, 2003.

Dolar, Mladen. *A Voice and Nothing More*. Cambridge, Massachusetts: MIT Press, 2006.

Dolman, Sarah, Mark Simmonds, and Lindy Weilgart (eds). *Oceans of Noise: A Whale and Dolphin Conservation Society Science Report*. www.swcs.org, 2004. http://www.wdcs.org/submissions_bin/OceansofNoise.pdf.

Dorcey, Tony, Achim Steiner, Michael Acreman, and Brett Orlando, eds. *Large Dams: Learning From the Past, Looking at the Future*. Gland, Switzerland and Cambridge, UK: The World Bank and IUCN, 1997.

Doss, Natalie. "An Iron Ore Rush Above the Arctic Circle." *Businessweek.com*. 27 January 2011. http://www.businessweek.com/magazine/content/11_06/b4214020680025.htm.

Douglas, Mary. *Purity and Danger: An Analysis of Concepts of Pollution and Taboo*. London: Routledge & Kegan Paul, 1966. Reprint, 3rd printing, 1970.

Dowling, William C. *Jameson, Althusser, Marx: An Introduction to The Political Unconscious*. Ithaca: Cornell University Press, 1984.

*Downstream*. http://www.downstream.ecuad.ca.

Dunaway, Finis. *Natural Visions: The Power of Images in American Environmental Reform*. Chicago: University of Chicago Press, 2005.

Durkheim, Emile. *The Elementary Forms of the Religious Life*. New York: Collier Books, 1961.

Earle, Sylvia. "Foreword." In *World Ocean Census: A Global Survey of Marine Life*, edited by Darlene Trewe Crist, Gail Scowcroft, and James M. Harding, Jr, 11–13. Buffalo: Firefly Books, 2009.

Earthjustice. "Planned Operations in the Beaufort and Chukchi Seas Challenged." *Earthjustice*. Juneau, Alaska. 5 May 2008. http://earthjustice.org/news/press/2008/planned-oil-operations-in-beaufort-and-chukchi-seas-challenged.

– "Shell Oil's Arctic Offshore Drilling Plan Illegal Says Federal Appeals Court." *Earthjustice*. San Francisco. 20 November 2008. http://earthjustice.org/news/press/2008/shell-oil-s-arctic-offshore-drilling-plan-illegal-says-federal-appeals-court.

Edu-factory Collective, eds. *Toward a Global Autonomous University: Cognitive Labor, The Production of Knowledge, and Exodus from the Education Factory*. New York: Autonomedia, 2009.

Edwards, Paul. "Noise, Communication and Cognition." *The Closed World: Computers and the Politics of Discourse in Cold War America*, 209–37. Cambridge: MIT Press, 1996.

Edwardson, Rachel Naninaaq, Dir. *History of the Inupiat 1968: The Duck-In*. North Slope Borough School District, 2005.

Eggertson, Laura." Investigative Report: 1,766 boil-water advisories now in place across Canada." *Canadian Medical Association Journal* 178, no. 10 (2008): 1261–3.

Ellen, Roy. "What Black Elk left unsaid: on the illusory images of Green primitivism." *Anthropology Today* 2 no. 6 (1986): 8–13.

Ellen, Roy, and Katsuyoshi Fukui. *Redefining Nature: Ecology, Culture and Domestication.* Oxford, Washington: Berg, 1996.

Emond, Andrew. "Following Rivière St. Pierre under Lachine." *Spacing Montreal: Understanding the Urban Landscape.* http://spacingmontreal.ca/2009/03/23/following-riviere-st-pierre-underground-through-lachine/.

Environment Canada. Interactive map portal. *Geoinformation on the Environment, Integration and Exploration (GENIE).* Date modified, 27 May 2010. http://www.ec.gc.ca/stl/default.asp?lang=En&n=74CE97B8-1. Accessed 30 July 2012.

– "St. Lawrence River." Accessed 30 July 2012. http://www.ec.gc.ca/stl/default.asp?Lang=En&n=F46CF5F8-1.

– "Water & the Canadian Identity." http://www.ec.gc.ca/eau-water/default.asp?lang=En&n=5593BDE0-1. Accessed 18 December 2012.

Environment Canada, and Quebec Department of the Environment. "Critères intérimaires pour l'évaluation de la qualité des sédiments du Saint-Laurent." Ottawa: Environment Canada, 1992.

Environment Victoria. http://environmentvictoria.org.au/content/murray-darling-basin-plan-%e2%80%93-what%e2%80%99s-it-all-about.

Escobar, Arturo. "After Nature: Steps to an Anti-essentialist Political Ecology." *Current Anthropology* 40, no. 1 (1999): 1–16.

– "Constructing Nature: Elements for a Poststructural Political Ecology." In *Liberation Ecologies: Environment, Development and Social Movements*, edited by Richard Peet and Michael Watts, 46–68. London, New York: Routledge, 1996.

"Eskimo's Map of Driftwood." *Popular Science Monthly* 123, no. 3 (September 1933): 44. http://books.google.ca/books?id=_CcDAAAAMBAJ&lpg=PP1&pg=PA44&redir_esc=y#v=onepage&q&f=false. Accessed 29 July 2012.

Esser, Jennifer. "Being Caribou: An Interview with Karsten Heuer." *Alberta Views* (July–August 2005): 38–43.

Evernden, Neil. *The Natural Alien: Humankind and Environment.* Toronto: University of Toronto Press, 1985.

*Excursions de pêche Montréal* website. "La pêche." http://www.excursionsdepechemontreal.com/peche.php. Accessed 31 July 2012.

Fahim, Hussein M. *Dams, People, and Development: The Aswan High Dam Case.* New York: Pergamon Press, 1981.

*False Creek Watershed Society.* http://www.falsecreekwatershed.org/. Accessed 8 October 2010.

Fee, Margery, and Jane Flick. "Coyote Pedagogy: Knowing Where the Borders Are in Thomas King's *Green Grass, Running Water.*" *Canadian Literature* 161/162 (1999): 131–9.

Fielding, Helen. "'The Sum of What She Is Saying': Bringing Essentials Back to the Body." In *Resistance, Flight, Creation: Feminist Enactments of French Philosophy*, edited by Dorothea Olkowski, 124–37. Ithaca: Cornell University Press, 2000.

Finlay, Marike. *The Potential of Modern Discourse: Musil, Peirce, and Perturbation.* Bloomington: Indiana University Press, 1990.

Finley, K.J., G.W. Miller, R.A. Davis, and C.R. Greene. "Reactions of belugas, *Delphinapterus leucas,* and narwhals, *Monodon monoceros,* to ice-breaking ships in the Canadian high arctic." *Canadian Bulletin of Fisheries and Aquatic Science* 224 (1990): 97–117.

Finn, Kathy. "Two years after BP oil spill, tourists back in U.S. Gulf." *Reuters.* 27 May 2012. http://www.reuters.com/article/2012/05/27/usa-bpspill-tourism-idUSL1E8GP15X20120527. Accessed 29 May 2012.

Fitterman, Lisa. "Lachine Canal: Succes or Excess?" *The Gazette,* Sunday, 1 June 2003.

Fortin, Gilles. *Guide des rivières sportives au Québec.* "Le Saint-Laurent – Les Rapides de Lachine," 120–7. La Prairie: Editions Broquet, 1980.

Fortun, Kim. *Advocacy after Bhopal: Environmentalism, Disaster, New Global Orders.* Chicago: University of Chicago Press, 2001.

Foucault, Michel. "Des Espaces Autres (1967), Hétérotopies (Conférence au Cercle d'études architecturales, 14 mars 1967)." In *Dits Et Écrits, 1984; Architecture, Mouvement, Continuité, 5 Octobre 1984,* 46–49, 1984. [See reference below for English translation.]

– "Michel Foucault. Of Other Spaces (1967), Heterotopias." *Foucault.info.* Translated by Jay Miskowiec. http://foucault.info/documents/heteroTopia/foucault.heteroTopia.en.html.

Fournier, Suzanne. "B.C.'s killer whales, at-risk species score victory in landmark court case." *The Province.* Vancouver: 7 December 2010.

Freeman, Victoria. *Distant Relations: How My Ancestors Colonized North America.* Toronto: McClelland & Stewart, 2000.

Freud, Sigmund. *Three Essays on the Theory of Sexuality.* Edited by James Strachey. New York: Basic Books, 2007.

Froschauer, Karl. *White Gold: Hydroelectric Power in Canada.* Vancouver: University of British Columbia Press, 1999.

Frye, Northrop. "The Cultural Development of Canada." In *Northrop Frye On Canada,* edited by Jean O'Grady and David Staines, 665–72. Toronto: University of Toronto Press, 2003.

Galvez-Cloutier, Rosa, and Jean-Sébastien Dubé. "An Evaluation of Fresh Water Sediments Contamination: The Lachine Canal Sediments Case, Montreal, Canada. Part I: Quality Assessment." *Water, Air, and Soil Pollution* 102, no. 3/4 (1998): 259–79.

– "An Evaluation of Fresh Water Sediments Contamination: The Lachine Canal Sediments Case, Montreal, Canada. Part II: Heavy Metal Particulate Speciation Study." *Water, Air, and Soil Pollution* 102, no. 3/4 (1998): 281–302.

Gandy, Matthew. "Part I: Water, Space, and Power." In *Concrete and Clay: Reworking Nature in New York City.* 19–70. Cambridge: MIT Press, 2002.

Garcia, Martha N. "Flow Rate Technical Group estimate of oil for June 20, 2010." *US Geological Survey.* http://www.usgs.gov/foia/FRTG_emails/06-20-2010..Re-%20FRTG%20estimates%20of%20oil%20for%20June%2020,%202010.pdf

Gedeon, Julie. "History's Floodgate: The Lachine Canal Reopens." *The Beaver* 82, no. 4 (2002): 38–42.

Giroux, Henry A. *Against the Terror of Neoliberalism: Politics Beyond the Age of Greed*. Boulder, Colorado: Paradigm, 2008.

Glenn, Jack. *Once Upon an Oldman: Special Interest Politics and the Oldman River Dam*. Vancouver: University of British Columbia Press, 1999.

Glover, Adrian. "Worms Who Eat Whales." *Times Literary Supplement*. March 21, 2008: 11–12.

Goldman, Marlene. "Mapping and Dreaming: Native Resistance in *Green Grass, Running Water*." *Canadian Literature* 161/162 (1999): 18–41.

Goldsmith, Edward, and Nicholas Hildyard. *The Social and Environmental Effects of Large Dams*. San Francisco: Sierra Club Books, 1986.

Government of Canada. "Canada's Extended Continental Shelf." http://www.international.gc.ca/continental/index.aspx?lang=eng&menu_id=7&menu=R.

– "Signature Project: Dahla Dam and Irrigation System," *Canada's Engagement in Afghanistan*. http://www.afghanistan.gc.ca/canada-afghanistan/projects-projets/dam-barrage.aspx.

– *Statement on Canada's Arctic Foreign Policy: Exercising Sovereignty and Promoting Canada's Northern Strategy Abroad*. Ottawa: 20 August 2010. http://www.international.gc.ca/polar polaire/assets/pdfs/CAFP_booklet-PECA_livret-eng.pdf.

Governments of Canada, Denmark, Norway, the Russian Federation, and the United States of America. *Illulissat Declaration*. Ilulissat: 29 May 2008. http://www.oceanlaw.org/downloads/arctic/Ilulissat_Declaration.pdf.

Gowell, Elizabeth. *Amazing Jellies: Jewels of the Sea*. Piermont: New England Aquarium, 2004.

Graeber, David. *Toward an Anthropological Theory of Value: The False Coin of our Own Dreams*. New York: Palgrave, 2001.

Gramsci, Antonio. *Selections from the Prison Notebooks*. Edited and translated by Quintin Hoare and Geoffrey Nowell-Smith. New York: International Publishers, 1971.

Grant, George. *Lament for a Nation: The Defeat of Canadian Nationalism*. (1965). Ottawa: Carleton University Press, 1980.

"The Great Dam of Assuan," *Times of London* (1902).

Greenland Inuit. Carved wooden coastal chart. (n.d.) Nuuk, Greenland: Greenland National Museum and Archives.

Griffin, Susan. *Women and Nature: The Roaring Inside Her*. New York: Harper and Row. 2000.

Grossman, Elizabeth. "Noise Reduces Ocean Habitat for Whales." *scientificamerican.com*. 22 October 2010. http://www.scientificamerican.com/article.cfm?id=noise-reduces-ocean-habitat-for-whales.

– *High Tech Trash: Digital Devices, Hidden Toxics, and Human Health*. Washington: Island Press, 2006.

– *Watershed: The Undamming of America*. New York: Counterpoint, 2002.

Grosz, Elizabeth. *Architecture from the Outside: Essays on Virtual and Real Space*. Cambridge: MIT Press, 2001.

– *The Nick of Time*. Durham, North Carolina: Duke University Press, 2004.

Guattari, Félix. *Three Ecologies*. Translated by Ian Pindar and Paul Sutton. New Brunswick, New Jersey: Athlone, 2000.

Gumbel, Andrew. "Death valley: Two weeks ago on a retreat with new age guru James Arthur Ray, three people died in a sweat lodge. What went wrong?" *The Guardian*. 22 October 2009. http://www.guardian.co.uk/world/2009/oct/22/james-ray-sweat-lodge-death?INTCMP=ILC NETTXT3487. Accessed 10 October 2010.

Gunster, Shane. *Capitalizing on Culture: Critical Theory for Cultural Studies*. Toronto: University of Toronto Press, 2004.

Haddock, Steven H.D. "A Golden Age of Gelata: Past and Future Research on Planktonic Ctenophores and Cnidarians." *Hydrobiologia* 530/531 (2004): 549–56.

Haeckel, Ernst. *Art Forms in Nature: The Prints of Ernst Haeckel*. Munich: Prestel Publishers, 1998.

Hamilton, Graeme. "Boat at Your Own Risk on Fetid Former Sewer." *National Post*, Thursday, 4 July, 2002.

Hanna, Bridget, Ward Morehouse, and Sarangi, Satinath. *The Bhopal Reader: Remembering Twenty Years of the World's Worst Industrial Disaster*. New York: Apex Press, 2005.

Haraway, Donna J. "The Promises of Monsters: A Regenerative Politics for Inappropriate/d Others." In *The Haraway Reader*, 63–124. New York and London: Routledge, 2004.

– *The Companion Species Manifesto: Dogs, People, and Significant Otherness*. Chicago: Prickly Paradigm Press, 2003.

– *Primate Visions: Gender, Race, and Nature in the World of Modern Science*. New York: Routledge, 1989.

– *When Species Meet*. Minneapolis: University of Minnesota Press, 2008.

Harley, J.B. "Rereading the Maps of the Columbian Encounter." *Annals of the Association of American Geographers* 82, no. 3 (1992): 522–42.

Hartmann, Thomas. *The Last Hours of Ancient Sunlight*. New York: Three Rivers Press, 2004.

Harvey, David. *A Brief History of Neoliberalism*. Oxford: Oxford University Press, 2005.

– *The Condition of Postmodernity*. Cambridge Massachusetts and Oxford: Blackwell, 1990.

Heffern, Rich. "Thomas Berry, environmentalist-priest dies." *National Catholic Reporter*. 1 June 2009. Retrieved 9 October 2010. http://ncronline.org/news/ecology/thomas-berry-environmentalist-priest-dies.

Hegel, Georg. *The Phenomenology of Spirit*. Translated by A.V. Miller. Oxford: Oxford University Press, 1979.

Heidegger, Martin. "Building, Dwelling, Thinking." In David Krell, ed., *Martin Heidegger, Basic Writings*, 319–39. New York: Harper and Row, 1977.

– "The Question Concerning Technology." In *The Question Concerning Technology and Other Essays*, 3-35. Translated and with an introduction by William Lovitt. New York: Harper & Row, 1977.

– *Poetry, Language, Thought*. Translated by Albert Hofstadter. New York: Harper & Row, 1971.

Hess, Bill. *Gift of the Whale: The Inupiat Bowhead Hunt, A Sacred Tradition*. Hong Kong: Sasquatch Books, 1999.

Heuer, Karsten. *Being Caribou*. Toronto: McClelland & Stewart, 2006.

Hiatt, Les. "Traditional Attitudes to Land Resources." In *Aboriginal Sites, Rights and Resource Development*, edited by Ronald Berndt, 13–26. Perth: University of Western Australia Press, 1982.

Hird, Myra J. "The Corporeal Generosity of Maternity." *Body and Society* 13, no. 1 (2007): 1–20.

Holden, Sara. *Planet Ocean: Photo Stories from the "Defending Our Oceans" Voyage*. Oxford: New Internationalist, 2007.

Holloway, John. *Change the World Without Taking Power*. New Edition. London and Ann Arbor: Pluto, 2005.

Horkheimer, Max. "Traditional and Critical Theory." In *Critical Theory: Selected Essays*, 188–243. New York: Herder & Herder, 1972.

– and Theodor Adorno. *Dialectic of Enlightenment*. 1944. Translated by John Cumming. New York: Continuum, 2002.

Hornborg, Alf. "Money and the Semiotics of Ecosystem Dissolution." *Journal of Material Culture* 4 (1999): 143–62.

Howes, David. *Empire of the Senses: A Sensual Culture Reader*. Oxford, New York: Berg, 2005.

Huyssen, Andreas. "Present Pasts." *Public Culture* 12, no. 1 (winter 2000): 21–38.

Illich, Ivan. *H2O and the Waters of Forgetfulness*. London: Marion Boyars Publishers, 1986.

Ingold, Tim. "Building, Dwelling, Living." In *Shifting Contexts: Transformations in Anthropological Knowledge*, edited by Marilyn Strathern, 57–80. London, New York: Routledge, 1995.

– *Being Alive: Essays on Movement, Knowledge and Description*. London and New York: Routledge, 2011.

– *The Perception of the Environment: Essays in Livelihood, Dwelling and Skill*. London, New York: Routledge, 2000.

Innis, Harold. *The Fur Trade in Canada: An Introduction to Canadian Economic History*. Toronto: University of Toronto Press, 1930.

*International Rivers website*. http://www.internationalrivers.org/.

Inuit Circumpolar Council. "Inuit Expect to be Invited to *Oceans Five* Foreign Affairs Ministers' Summit on Arctic Sovereignty." Ottawa: 12 February 2010. http://www.inuitcircumpolar.com/files/uploads/iccfiles/oceansfivesummitonarcticsovereignty_feb_12_2010.pdf.

– *A Circumpolar Inuit Declaration on Sovereignty in the Arctic*. Tromso: 28 April 2009. http://inuitcircumpolar.com/files/uploads/icc-files/PR-2009-04-28-Signed-Inuit-Sovereignty-Declaration-11x17.pdf.

Irigaray, Luce. *Marine Lover of Friedrich Nietzche*. Translated by Gillian Gill. New York: Columbia University Press, 1991.

– *Speculum of the Other Woman*. Translated by Gillian Gill. Ithaca: Cornell University Press, 1985.

Irland, Basia. *Water Library*. Albuquerque: University of New Mexico Press, 2007.

Ivakhiv, Adrian. "Ecocultural Theory and Ecocultural Studies: Contexts and Research Directions." *Cultures and Environments: On Cultural Environmental Studies*. On-Line Conference. American Studies Program, Washington State University, 20–22 June 1997. http://www.uvm.edu/~aivakhiv/eco_cult.htm. Accessed 22 June 2011.

Jack, Douglas. "History Map 10.4: First Nations' Place Names" *West Island Project Website.* cbed (Community Based Environmental Decisions), McGill University, Department of Geography, ca 2001. Accessed 21 October 2010. http://cbed.geog.mcgill.ca/atlasPages/history/hires4.htm.

Jack, Douglas, and Roy Wright. "Tiohtiake: place where rivers and people unite and divide." October 13, 2010. vav Gallery, Concordia, Montréal. Workshop curated by Katie Earle and Sarah Nesbitt. Part of the exhibit *Home on the Range*, October 4–15, 2010.

Jameson, Fredric. "Notes on Globalization as a Philosophical Issue." In *The Cultures of Globalization*, edited by Fredric Jameson and Masao Miyoshi, 54–77. Durham, North Carolina: Duke University Press, 1998.

– "Postmodernism, or The Cultural Logic of Late Capitalism." *New Left Review* 146 (1984): 53–92.

– "The End of Temporality." *Critical Inquiry* 29 (summer 2003): 695–718.

– *Archaeologies of the Future: The Desire Called Utopia and Other Science Fictions.* New York: Verso, 2005.

– *Postmodernism, or, The Cultural Logic of Late Capitalism.* Durham, North Carolina: Duke University Press, 1991.

– *The Political Unconscious.* Ithaca: Cornell University Press, 1981.

"Jellyfish Gone Wild." *National Science Foundation.* Educational Multi-Media. http://www.nsf.gov/news/special_reports/jellyfish/textonly/intro.jsp. Accessed 1 October, 2010.

Jensen, Doreen. "Metamorphosis." In catalogue, *Topographies: Aspects of Recent B.C. Art.* The Centre for Contemporary Canadian Art: The Canadian Art Database: Canadian Writers Files, 1997. http://ccca.concordia.ca/c/writing/j/jensen/jen001.html.

Jentsch, Ernst. "Document: 'On the Psychology of the Uncanny,'" (1906). Reprinted in *Uncanny Modernity: Cultural Theories, Modern Anxieties*, edited by Jo Collins and John Jervis, 216–28. New York: Palgrave MacMillan, 2008.

Johnson, Sapna, Ramakant Sahu, Nimisha Jadon, and Clara Duca. *Contamination of Soil and Water Inside and Outside the Union Carbide India Limited, Bhopal.* New Delhi: Centre for Science and Environment, 2009.

Josephson, Paul. *Industrialized Nature: Brute Force Technology and the Transformation of the Natural World.* Washington: Island Press / Shearwater Books, 2002.

Jung, Carl. *The Archetypes and the Collective Unconscious.* London: Routledge, 1990.

*Jupiter Foundation.* www.jupiterfoundation.org.

Kaika, Maria. *City of Flows: Modernity, Nature, and the City.* New York: Routledge, 2005.

Kaika, Maria and Erik Swyngedouw. "Fetishizing the Modern City: The Phantasmagoria of Urban Technological Networks." *International Journal of Urban and Regional Research* 24, no. 1 (March 2000): 120–38.

Kalland, Arne, and Frank Sejersen. *Marine Mammals and Northern Cultures.* Edmonton: Canadian Circumpolar Institute Press, 2005.

Keefer, Thomas Coltrin (1821–1915). Map. "A sketch of Lachine Rapids and Channels to

Montreal Dec 1850." 1 map, coloured manuscript, 14.5 cm x 30 cm. Library and Archives Canada, Mikan no. 4130243, Local class no. H1/312/1850, NMC 10957.

Kelley, Robin D.G. "A Poetics of Anticolonialism." Introduction to *Discourse on Colonialism*, by Aimé Césaire, 7–28. New York: Monthly Review Press, 2001.

Kepler, Johannes. *The Harmony of the World*. 1619. Translated by Charles Glen Wallis. Chicago: Encyclopedia Britannica, 1952.

Khagram, Sanjeev. *Dams and Development: Transnational Struggles for Water and Power*. Ithaca and London: Cornell University Press, 2004.

King, Thomas. *Green Grass, Running Water*. Toronto: Harper Perennial Canada, 1999.

Kirby, Vicki. *Telling Flesh: The Substance of the Corporeal*. New York: Routledge, 1997.

Klaver, Irene J. "Reconnecting Visible and Invisible Water Infrastructures with Water Bodies." Paper presented at Thinking With Water workshop, Concordia University, Montreal, 21–23 June 2010.

Knight, Lindsay. "The Right to Water." edited by Gregory Hartl. France: World Health Organization (WHO), 2003.

Knowlton, Nancy. *Citizens of the Sea: Wondrous Creatures from the Census of Marine Life*. Washington D.C.: National Geographic, 2010.

Koivurova, Timo and Erik J. Molenaar. *International Governance and Regulation of the Marine Arctic*. Oslo: WWF International Arctic Programme, 2010.

Krech, Shepard. *The Ecological Indian: myth and history*. New York, London: W.W. Norton, 1999.

Kroll, Gary. *America's Ocean Wilderness: A Cultural History of Twentieth-Century Exploration*. Lawrence: University Press of Kansas, 2008.

Krupar, Shiloh. "Alien Still Life: Distilling the Toxic Logics of the Rocky Flats National Wildlife Refuge," *Environment and Planning D: Society and Space* 29, no. 2 (2011): 268–90.

KSF. Map. "Rapides Lachine." http://ksf.ca/infos/rapides-lachine/. Accessed 30 July 2012.

Kulchyski, Peter. *È-nakàskàkowaàhk (A Step Back): Nisichawayasihk Cree Nation and the Wuskwatim Project*. Winnipeg: Canadian Centre for Policy Alternatives (Manitoba), May 2004. http://www.policyalternatives.ca/sites/default/files/uploads/publications/Manitoba_Pubs/step_back.pdf.

Kumar, Shiv S. *Bergson and the Stream of Consciousness Novel*. New York: New York University Press, 1963.

Kunzig, Robert. *Mapping the Deep: The Extraordinary Story of Ocean Science*. New York: W.W. Norton, 2000.

Labelle, Brandon. "Seeking Ursound: Hildegaard Westerkamp, Steve Peters, and the Soundscape." *Background Noise: Perspectives on Sound Art*, 201–17. New York: Continuum, 2006.

Labunska, I., A. Stephenson, K. Brigden, R. Stringer, D. Santillo, and P.A. Johnston. *The Bhopal Legacy: Toxic Contaminants at the Former Union Carbide Factory Site, Bhopal, India: 15 years after the Bhopal Accident*. Exeter: Greenpeace Research Laboratories, 1999.

Lacan, Jacques. "The Mirror Stage as Formative Function of the I." In *Ecrits: A Selection*, translated by Alan Sheridan, 1–8. London and New York: Routledge, 1977.

Lai, Larissa. "Radioactive Time: A Politics and Poetics of Asian/Indigenous Relation." Paper presented at the Cultures of Sustainability Workshop, University of British Columbia, 10 July 2010.

Lakoff, George, and Mark Johnson. *Metaphors We Live By*. Chicago, London: University of Chicago Press, 1980.

Lalonde, Michelle. "Old-Timers Recall Glory Days." *The Gazette*, Saturday, 10 April 1999, A10.

*Langara Wetland Project website*. http://iweb.langara.bc.ca/wetland/wetland-project.html. Accessed 8 October 2010.

Langton, Marcia. "The 'Wild,' the Market, and the Native: Indigenous People Face New Forms of Global Colonization." In *Globalization, Globalism, Environments, and Environmentalism. Consciousness Of Connections*, edited by Steven Vertovec and Darryl Posey, 141–67. The Linacre Lectures. Oxford: Oxford University Press, 2003.

Lasserre, Frédéric. "Drawers of Water: Water Diversions in Canada and Beyond." In *Eau Canada: The Future of Canada's Water*, edited by Karen Bakker, 143–62. Vancouver: UBC Press, 2007.

Latour, Bruno. *Politics of Nature: How to Bring the Sciences into Democracy*. Translated by Catherine Porter. Cambridge, Massachusetts: Harvard University Press, 2004.

– *Reassembling the Social: An Introduction to Actor Network Theory*. Oxford: Oxford University Press, 2005.

– *We Have Never Been Modern*. Translated by Catherine Porter. Cambridge, Massachusetts: Harvard University Press, 1993.

Lazarus, Sarah. *Troubled Waters: The Changing Fortunes of Whales and Dolphins*. London: Natural History Museum, 2006.

Lee, David S., and George W. Wenzel. "Narwhal hunting by Pond Inlet Inuit: An analysis of foraging mode in the floe-edge environment." *Études/Inuit/Studies* 28, no. 2 (2004): 133–57.

Lee, SKY. Keynote speech (and unpublished paper) presented at "Imagining Asian and Native Women: Deconstructing from Contact to Modern Times" Conference, Bellingham, Western Washington University, 9 March 2002.

Lefebvre, Henri. *Critique of Everyday Life*, vol. 1. Translated by John Moore. New York and London: Verso, 2008.

Leiss, William. "Modern Science, Enlightenment, and the Domination of Nature: No Exit?" In *Critical Ecologies: The Frankfurt School and Contemporary Environmental Crises*, edited by Andrew Biro, 23–42. Toronto: University of Toronto Press, 2011.

Lejtenyi, Patrick. "Affluence, Boats and Condos." *Montreal Mirror*, 2 May 2002.

Leslie, Jacques. *Deep Water: The Epic Struggle over Dams, Displaced People, and the Environment*. New York: Picador, 2006.

Lesser Knowns. Review. Amazon.com. http://www.amazon.com/Art-Nature-Jellies-Jellyfish-Aquarium/dp/B000JJ5GE2/ref=sr_1_1?ie=UTF8&s=dvd&qid= 1272738866&sr=1-1. Accessed 1 May 2010.

Lévinas, Emmanuel. *Otherwise than Being: Or Beyond Essence*. Pittsburgh: Duquesne University Press, 1981.

Lincoln, Bruce. "Waters of Memory, Waters of Forgetfulness." *Fabula* 23, no.1 (2009): 19–34.

Lingis, Alphonso. "The Murmur of the World." In *The Community of Those Who Have Nothing in Common*, 69–105. Bloomington: Indiana University Press, 1994.

Linton, Jamie. *What Is Water? The History of a Modern Abstraction*. Vancouver: UBC Press, 2010.

LiPuma, Edward, and Benjamin Lee. *Financial Derivatives and the Globalization of Risk*. Durham, North Carolina, and London: Duke University Press, 2004.

Lockwood, Annea. "What is a River?" *Soundscape: The Journal of Acoustic Ecology* 7, no. 1, "Art, Science, Environment, Activism" (fall/winter 2007): 43–4.

Loftus, Alex. "Reification and the Dictatorship of the Water Meter." *Antipode* 38, no. 5 (2006): 1023–45.

*Lord of the Rings: The Two Towers*. Peter Jackson, dir. United States: New Line Cinema, 2002. Film, 179 min.

Lorraine, Tamsin. *Irigaray and Deleuze: Experiments in Visceral Philosophy*. Ithaca: Cornell University Press, 1999.

Lousley, Cheryl. "'Hosanna Da, Our Home on Natives' Land': Environmental Justice and Democracy in Thomas King's *Green Grass, Running Water*." *Essays on Canadian Writing* 81 (2004): 17–44.

Lovelock, James. *Gaia: A New Look at Life on Earth*. Oxford: Oxford University Press, 2000.

Lucky, Matt. "Global Hydropower Installed Capacity and Use Increase." *Vital Signs (World Watch Institute)*, 17 January 2012. http://vitalsigns.worldwatch.org/vs-trend/global-hydro power-installed-capacity-and-use-increase. Accessed 5 December 2012.

McCarthy, Shawn. "U.S. panel warns on Arctic drilling." *Globe and Mail*. Toronto: 11 January 2011. http://www.theglobeandmail.com/report-on-business/industry-news/energy-and-resources/us-panel-warns-on-arctic-drilling/article1865544/.

McCartney, Andra. "Soundwalking Blue Montreal." *Soundscape: The Journal of Acoustic Ecology* 1, no. 2, "Silence, Noise, and the Public Domain" (winter 2000): 28–9.

MacCormack, Carol, and Marilyn Strathern, eds. *Nature, Culture and Gender*. Cambridge: Cambridge University Press, 1980.

McCully, Patrick. *Silenced Rivers: The Ecology and Politics of Large Dams*. London: Zed Books, 1996.

McGregor, Deborah. "Honouring Our Relations: An Anishnaabe Perspective on Environmental Justice." In *Speaking for Ourselves: Environmental Justice in Canada*, edited by Julian Agyeman, Peter Cole, Randolph Haluza-Delay, and Pat O'Riley, 27–41. Vancouver: UBC Press, 2009.

McIntire, Gabrielle. *Modernism, Memory, and Desire: T.S. Eliot and Virginia Woolf*. Cambridge: Cambridge University Press, 2008.

McKay, Don. *Vis à Vis: Field Notes on Poetry and Wilderness*. Wolfville, Nova Scotia: Gaspereau Press, 2001.

McKibben, Bill. *Eaarth: Making a Life on a Tough New Planet*. New York: Times Books, 2010.

McMenamin, Dianna and Mark McMenamin. *Hypersea*. New York: Columbia University Press, 1994.

Madin, Laurence. "Gelatinous but Voracious Predators." In Claire Nouvian, *The Deep: The Extraordinary Creatures of the Abyss*, 103–4. Chicago: University of Chicago Press, 2007.

Mahoney, Jill. "Canadians rank Arctic sovereignty as top foreign-policy priority." *Globe and Mail*. Toronto: 24 January 2011. http://www.theglobeandmail.com/news/politics/canadians-rank-arcticsovereignty-as-top-foreign-policy-priority/article1881287/.

Mail Foreign Service "Sweat lodge deaths: Guru James Arthur Ray charged with manslaughter of three who died during New Age ceremony." *Daily Mail Online*. 5 February 2010. http://www.dailymail.co.uk/news/worldnews/article-1248426/Guru-James-Arthur-Ray-charged-die-sweat-lodge-ceremony.html#ixzz1KVVmpLcq. Accessed 10 October 2010.

Mallin, Samuel. *Merleau-Ponty's Phenomenology*. New Haven: Yale University Press, 1979.

Mallon, Thomas. "Do Jellyfish Rule the World?" *Discover* 28, no. 9 (September 2007): 42–7.

Maniates, Michael, and John M. Meyer, eds. *The Environmental Politics of Sacrifice*. Cambridge, Massachusetts: MIT Press, 2010.

Mann, Thomas. *Joseph and His Brothers*. Translated by John E. Woods. New York: Knopf, 1948.

Manning, Erin. "I Am Canadian: Identity, Territory, and the Canadian National Landscape." *Theory & Event* 4, no. 4 (2000).

Maracle, Lee. "Goodbye, Snauq." In *Our Story: Aboriginal Voices on Canada's Past*. Toronto: Dominion Institute and Anchor Canada, 201–19.

Marcoux, M. "Social behaviour, vocalization and conservation of narwhals." *Arctic* 61 (2008): 456–60.

Margulis, Lynn, and Dorion Sagan. *Dazzle Gradually: Reflections on the Nature of Nature*. White River Junction: Chelsea Green, 2007.

*Marine Photobank: Advancing Ocean Conservation Through Imagery*. http://www.marine photobank.org/home.php. Accessed 27 March 2011.

Massey, Doreen. *For Space*. London: Sage Publications, 2005.

Massumi, Brian. "Strange Horizon: Buildings, Biograms, and the Body Topologic." In *Parables for the Virtual: Movement, Affect, Sensation*, 177–207. Durham, North Carolina: Duke University Press, 2002.

Mato, Daniel. "All Industries Are Cultural." Translated by Emeshe Jahász-Mininberg. *Cultural Studies* 23, no. 1 (2009): 70–87.

Merleau-Ponty, Maurice. *Phenomenology of Perception*. Translated by Colin Smith. New York: Routledge, 1962.

Miller, Vincent. "The Unmappable: Vagueness and Spatial Experience." *Space and Culture* 9 (2006): 453–67.

Milton, Kay. *Environmentalism and Cultural Theory: Exploring the Role of Anthropology in Environmental Discourse*. London: Routledge, 1996.

– *Loving Nature: Towards an Ecology of Emotion*. London, New York: Routledge, 2002.

Minh-ha, Trinh T. *Framer Framed*. New York: Routledge, 1992.

– *Woman, Native, Other: Writing Postcoloniality and Feminism*. Bloomington: Indiana University Press, 1989.

Minnegal, Monica, and Peter Dwyer. "Appropriating Fish, Appropriating Fishermen: Tradable Permits, Natural Resources and Uncertainty." In *Ownership and Appropriation*, edited by Veronica Strang and Mark Busse, 197–215. Oxford, New York: Berg, 2011.

Mitchell, Alanna. *Sea Sick: The Global Ocean in Crisis.* Toronto: McClelland & Stewart, 2009.

Mittelstaedt, Martin. "What amount of nature should nations preserve?" *Globe and Mail.* Toronto: 24 November 2008.

Montreal Engineering Company, Limited. "The Importance and Potential of the Lachine Canal." Montreal: Canadian Manufacturers Association, 1970.

Montreal Flood Commission. *A Series of 38 Plans Relating to the Flood Conditions of the St. Lawrence.* Department of Public Works, Canada, 1887. Library and Archives Canada, B/312/1887, Record no. 5935.

Moore, Michael. "Whither the North Atlantic Right Whale? Scientists explore many facets of whales' lives to help a species on the edge of extinction." *Oceanus:* the online magazine of the Woods Hole Oceanographic Institution. http://www.whoi.edu/cms/files/dfino/2005/4/v43n2-moore_2386.pdf.

Morehouse, Ward, and M. Arun Subramaniam. *The Bhopal Tragedy: What Really Happened and What It Means for American Workers and Communities at Risk.* New York: Council on International Public Affairs, 1986.

Morello, Lauren. "U.S. Pushes for Law of the Sea Ratification as New Arctic Mapping Project Begins." *New York Times.* New York: 29 July 2009. http://www.nytimes.com/cwire/2009/07/29/29climatewire-us-pushes-for-law-of-the-sea-ratification-as-89174.html.

Morgan, Colleen. "Tactile Maps and Imaginary Geographies." *Middle Savagery.* Blog post: 1 March 2008. http://middlesavagery.wordpress.com/2008/03/01/tactile-maps-and-imaginary-geographies/.

Morin, Pierre-Louis (1811–1886). Map. "Plate 1: Figurative Map, Sketch of the Sault St. Louis, Kahnawake, And part of the south shore of the island of Montreal, Washed by left side of the St. Lawrence, made by Champlain in 1611." In *Le vieux Montréal, 1611–1803, Dessins de P.-L. Morin,* Montreal: H. Beaugrand, 1884. 1 plan, 37 cm x 62 cm. Library and Archives Canada, Amicus no. 5272309, LC Class no. FC2947.39, NMC 16357.

Morphy Howard, and Frances Morphy. "Tasting the Waters: Discriminating Identities in the Waters of Blue Mud Bay." *Journal of Material Culture* 11, no. 1/2 (2006): 67–85.

Mortimer-Sandilands, Catriona. "Nature Matters." *TOPIA* 21 (spring 2009): 5–8.

Moss, Lenny, and Vida Pavesich. "Science, Normativity, and Skill: Reviewing and Renewing the Anthropological Basis of Critical Theory." *Philosophy and Social Criticism* 37, no. 2 (2011): 139–65.

*Mother Earth Water Walk.* http://motherearthwaterwalk.com

Mukherjee, Suroopa. *Surviving Bhopal: Dancing Bodies, Written Texts, and Oral Testimonials of Women in the Wake of an Industrial Disaster.* New York: Palgrave Macmillan, 2010.

Murray-Darling Basin Authority. *Basin Plan 2011.* Canberra: Australian Government. 2011.

– *The Basin Plan.* Canberra: Australian Government, 2010.

Musil, Robert. *The Man Without Qualities.* Translated by Eithne Wilkins and Ernst Kaiser, London: Picador-Pan Books, 1979.

*Musqueam Ecosystem Conservation Society website.* http://www.mecsweb.org. Accessed 8 October 2010. [This website no longer exists. See also: http://vancouverpublicspace.ca/

index.php?mact=News,cntnto1,print,0&cntnto1articleid=130&cntnto1showtemplate=false&
cntnto1returnid=18; and http://www.thinksalmon.com/fswp_project/item/musqueam_creek_
wild_salmon_stewardship_habitat_restoration_project.]

Myosis. "St-Laurent, Rapides de Lachine." *Myosis.ca.* http://www.myosis.ca/fi_st_laurent_
rapides_lachine.htm. Accessed 5 February 2009. [This site is now defunct.]

Nagel, Thomas. "What Is It Like to Be a Bat?" *Philosophical Review* 83.4 (1974): 435–50.

Nakata, Martin. "Australian Indigenous Studies: A Question of Discipline." *Australian Journal
of Anthropology* 17, no. 3 (2006): 265–75.

– "Indigenous Knowledge and the Cultural Interface: Underlying Issues at the Intersection of
Knowledge and Information Systems." *International Federation of Library Associations
Journal* 28, nos. 5–6 (2002): 281–91.

– "Introduction: Special Supplementary Issue on Indigenous Studies and Indigenous Knowledge."
*Australian Journal of Indigenous Education* (Supplement) 37 (2008): 1–4.

– "The Cultural Interface." *Australian Journal of Indigenous Education* (Supplement) 36 (2007):
7–14.

– *Disciplining the Savages: Savaging the Disciplines.* Canberra, Australia: Aboriginal Studies
Press, 2007.

Nancy, Jean-Luc. *The Inoperative Community.* Minneapolis: University of Minnesota Press, 1991.

National Ocean Service. "U.S. Extended Continental Shelf Project." http://continentalshelf.gov/.

National Oceanic and Atmospheric Administration. *Final Report: Shipping noise and marine
mammals: a forum for science, technology, and management.* Washington D.C.: 2005.

"Native Protesters Blockade Manitoba Dam Project." *CBC website.* 14 August 2009.
http://www.cbc.ca/canada/manitoba/story/2009/08/14/manitoba-hydro-blockade.html.

Natural Resources Canada, "Government of Canada Welcomes New Mapping Data on Canada's
North." Ottawa: 8 August 2008. http://www.nrcan.gc.ca/media/newcom/2008/200856-
eng.php.

– "Groundwater Geoscience Program – 2009–2014." Date modified 7 March 2011.
http://www.nrcan.gc.ca/earth-sciences/about/current-program/groundwater-geoscience/4106.
Accessed 4 August 2012.

Neimanis, Astrida. "Bodies of Water, Human Rights and the Hydrocommons." *TOPIA* 21 (2009):
161–82.

– "Bodies of Water." PhD diss. Toronto: York University, 2008.

– "Feminist Subjectivity, Watered." *Feminist Review* 103 (2013): 23–41.

– "'Strange Kinship' and Ascidian Life: Thirteen Repetitions." *Journal of Critical Animal Studies,*
Vol. 9, no. 1/2 (2011), 117–43.

– "Water and Planetarity: Epistemologies of Unknowability." *Downstream: Reimagining Water.*
Emily Carr University of Art and Design, Vancouver, B.C., 22–24 March 2012.

Nelles, H.V. *The Politics of Development: Forests, Mines & Hydro-Electric Power in Ontario,
1849–1941.* 2nd ed. Montreal: McGill-Queen's University Press, 2005.

Nikiforuk, Andrew. *Tar Sands: Dirty Oil and the Future of a Continent.* Vancouver: Greystone
Books, 2008.

Noongwook, George, the Native Village of Savoonga, the Native Village of Gambell, Henry P. Huntington, and John C. Georges. "Traditional Knowledge of the Bowhead Whale (*Balaena mysticetus*) around St. Lawrence Island, Alaska." *Arctic* 60, no. 1 (March 2007): 47–54.

Norwegian Polar Institute. *Report Series 129: Best Practices in Ecosystem-Based Oceans Management in the Arctic*. Tromso: Norsk Polarinstitutt, April 2009.

Nouvian, Claire. *The Deep: The Extraordinary Creatures of the Abyss*. Chicago: University of Chicago Press, 2007.

Nuttall, Mark. *Arctic Homeland: Kinship, Community and Development in Northwest Greenland*. Toronto: University of Toronto Press, 1992.

O'Rourke, Ronald. *Changes in the Arctic: Background and Issues for Congress*. Washington: Congressional Research Service (7-5700), October 2010.

"Ocean Explorer." *NOAA. National Oceanic and Atmospheric Administration* (United States.) http://oceanexplorer.noaa.gov/gallery/livingocean/livingocean_inverts.html#jellyfish

Okeanos Foundation. "Report of the Workshop on Alternative Technologies to Seismic Airgun Surveys for Oil and Gas Exploration and their Potential for Reducing Impacts on Marine Mammals." Monterey, California: Okeanos-Foundation for the Sea, September 2009.

Oyama, Susan. *The Ontogeny of Information: Developmental Systems and Evolution*. Durham, North Carolina: Duke University Press, 2000.

Pagé, Jean. "Vraie pêche en ville ... à Montréal." *Chasse et Pêche*, *RDS.ca*. 14 June 2009. http://www.rds.ca/chasse/chroniques/276273.html. Accessed 31 July 2012.

Paine, Stefani. *The World of the Arctic Whales: Belugas, Bowheads, and Narwhals*. San Francisco: Sierra Club Books, 1995.

Pamboris, Xanthe. "Sonar and Seismic Exploration: A Major Headache for Whales." *Vancouver Aquarium Website*. http://www.vanaqua.org/aquanews/features/sonar.html.

Panayotakis, Costas. *Remaking Scarcity: From Capitalist Inefficiency to Economic Democracy*. London: Pluto Press, 2011.

Parks Canada. "Environmental Assessment: Lachine Canal Decontamination Project, Information Supplement." Ottawa: Parks Canada, 1995.

– "Project to Reopen the Lachine Canal to Through Navigation. Lachine Canal Historic Site." Quebec: Parks Canada, 1998.

Parr, Joy, Jon van der Veen, and Jessica van Horssen. *The Megaprojects New Media series*. http://megaprojects.uwo.ca/

Patterson, Brent. "Canadian groundwater mapping taking too long." *Council of Canadian website*. 7 August 2009. [Also published in the *Chronicle Herald*.] http://canadians.org/blog/?p=1460. Accessed 4 August 2012.

– "Harper's public service cuts will hurt water protection." *Council of Canadians website*. 18 June 2011. [Also published at www.canada.com.] http://canadians.org/blog/?p=9428. Accessed 4 August 2012.

Pauly, Daniel, William Graham, Simone Libralato, Lyne Morissette, and M.L. Deng Palomares. "Jellyfish in Ecosystems, Online Databases, and Ecosystem Models." *Hydrobiologia* 616 (2009): 67–85.

Payne, Roger. *Among Whales*. New York: Scribner, 1995.

PBS. "Gulf Still Grapples with Massive BP Oil Leak Two Years Later." http://www.pbs.org/news hour/bb/science/jan-june12/gulfspill_04-20.html. Accessed 29 May 2012.

Pearce, Fred. *The Dammed: Rivers, Dams and the Coming World Water Crisis*. London: Bodley Head, 1992.

Pearson, Noel. *Our Right to Take Responsibility*. Victoria: Institute of Public Administration, 2003.

Peet, Richard, and Michael Watts, eds. *Liberation Ecology: Environment, Development and Social Movements*. London, New York: Routledge, 1996.

Perkins, John. *Confessions of an Economic Hitman*. New York: Berret-Koehler, 2004.

Peterson, Nic, and John Taylor. "The Modernising of the Indigenous Domestic Moral Economy: Kinship, Accumulation and Household Composition." *The Asia Pacific Journal of Anthropology* 4 nos. 1&2 (2003): 105–22.

Pezzulo, Phaedra. "The Most Complicated Word." *Cultural Studies* 22, nos. 3–4 (May–July 2008): 361–8.

Phelan, Peggy. *Unmarked: The Politics of Performance*. London & New York: Routledge, 1993.

Phillips, Stephanie K. "The Kahnawake Mohawks and the St. Lawrence Seaway." Master's thesis, Department of Anthropology, McGill University, 2000.

"Photographing Gelatinous Zooplankton." *The Jellies Zone*. http://jellieszone.com/photography. htm. Accessed 17 April 2010.

"Plan shewing the St. Louis Hydraulic Scheme." Montreal: Burland Lithographic Company, [date uncertain, likely circa 1890s]. Scale 1500 feet: 1 inch, photolithograph. [Based on plan submitted by Charles Legge (1829–1881) to the General Government, 14 October 1867. "Plan shewing proposed hydraulic improvements at the Lachine rapids made under the instructions of the St. Louis Hydraulic company." Library and Archives Canada, Item no. 204, RG11M 923004, Findca3599, Mikan no. 2124238.]

"Planned Oil Operations in Beaufort and Chukchi Seas Challenged." *www.earthjustice.org*. http://earthjustice.org/news/press/2008/planned-oil-operations-in-beaufort-and-chukchi-seas-challenged.

Plumwood, Val. *Feminism and the Mastery of Nature*. London, New York: Routledge, 1993.

Polanyi, Karl. *The Great Transformation: The Economic and Social Origins of Our Time*. New York: Farrar & Rinehart, 1944.

Porter, Roy, ed. *The Medical History of Waters and Spas*. London: Medical History Supplement No. 10, 1990.

Potter, Mitch. "Security standoff stalls Canadian dam project in Kandahar." *Toronto Star*. 9 June 2010. http://www.thestar.com/news/canada/afghanmission/article/820752—security-standoff-stalls-canadian-dam-project-in-kandahar.

Prashad, Vijay. *The Darker Nations: A People's History of the Third World*. New York, London: New Press, 2008.

Princen, Thomas. "Distancing: Consumption and the Severing of Feedback." In *Confronting*

*Consumption*, edited by Thomas Princen, Michael Maniates, and Ken Conca. Cambridge, 103–31. Massachusetts: MIT Press, 2002.

Princen, Thomas. *The Logic of Sufficiency*. Cambridge, Massachusetts: MIT Press, 2005.

Protevi, John. "Water." *Rhizomes* 15 (winter 2007). http://www.rhizomes.net/issue15/ protevi.html. Accessed 5 May 2008.

Proust, Marcel. *Swann's Way*. 1913. Translated by C.K. Scott Moncrieff. New York: Penguin Books, 1999.

Qing, Dai, John G. Thibodeau, and Philip B. Williams, eds. *The River Dragon Has Come! The Three Gorges Dam and the Fate of China's Yangtze River and Its People*. Translated by Ming Yi. New York: Probe International and the International Rivers Network, 1998.

Quebec Department of the Environment. "Politique de Réhabilitation des Terrains Contaminés." Quebec: Department of the Environment, 1988.

*Québec Kayak*. "Débit des rivières par Québec Whitewater." [Scroll down to "Montréal" to link to information on individual standing waves: "Big Joe," "Gaetan," "Pyramide," "Vague à Guy," and the big and small waves at "Habitat 67."] http://www.quebeckayak.qc.ca/kayak-de-riviere/info-debit/quebec-whitewater. Accessed 30 July 2012.

Ramanujan, Krishna. "Sound maps reveal whales and noise pollution." *physorg.com*. 23 February 2010. http://www.physorg.com/news186136916.html.

Ramsden, John. *The Dam Busters: A British Film Guide*. London and New York: I.B. Tauris, 2003.

Rancière, Jacques. *Dissensus: On Politics and Aesthetics*. Edited and translated by Steven Corcoran. London: Continuum, 2010.

– *The Politics of Aesthetics: The Distribution of the Sensible*. Translated with an introduction by Gabriel Rockhill. London: Continuum, 2004.

– "Afterword: The Method of Equality: An Answer to Some Questions." In *Jacques Rancière: History, Politics, Aesthetics*, edited by Gabriel Rockhill and Philip Watts, 273–88. Durham, North Carolina: Duke University Press, 2009.

– "The Thinking of Dissensus: Politics and Aesthetics." In *Reading Rancière*, edited by Paul Bowman and Richard Stamp, 1–18. London: Continuum, 2011.

Ranjan, N., S. Sarangi, V.T. Padmanabhan, S. Holleran, R. Ramakrishnan, and D. Varma. "Methyl Isocyanate Exposure and Growth Patterns of Adolescents in Bhopal." *Journal of the American Medical Association (JAMA)* 290, no. 14 (2003): 1856–7.

*RAVEN (Respecting Aboriginal Values and Environmental Needs)*. http://www.raventrust.com/ fishlaketeztanbiny.html

"Reading Maps." In "Historical Thinking Skills Interactives," *America's History in the Making* online course, *Annenberg Learner* website. Accessed 30 July 2012. http://www.learner.org/ courses/amerhistory/interactives/cartographic/index.html

Reason, David. "Reflections of Wilderness and Pike Lake Pond." In *United States Department of Agriculture, Personal, Societal, and Ecological Values of Wilderness: Congress and Proceedings on Research, Management, and Allocation, Volume 1*. 85–9. Forest Service Proceedings, Fort Collins, Colorado: Rocky Mountain Research Station, RMRS-P-4, 1998.

"Record low water levels in Quebec." André Cantin (Environment Canada), Peter Yeomans (International Seaway Board of Control), David Speak (Beaconsfield Yacht Club), and Denis Lefaivre (Canadian Hydrographic Service) interviewed by Bernard St-Laurent. *Radio Noon Montreal*. CBC Radio. 12 July 2012. Online audio, 22:23. http://www.cbc.ca/player/Radio/Local+Shows/Quebec/ID/2255582552/?page=7. Accessed 24 July 2012.

Renan, Ernest. "What is a Nation." [1882].http://www.cooper.edu/humanities/core/hss3/e_renan.html

*Renewables 2011: Global Status Report*. Paris: REN21 Secretariat, 2011. http://www.ren21.net/Portals/97/documents/GSR/REN21_GSR2011.pdf. Accessed 5 December 2012.

Revkin, Andrew C. "Peeling Back Pavement to Expose Watery Heavens." *New York Times*. 16 July 2009. http://www.nytimes.com/2009/07/17/world/asia/17daylight.html?scp=1&sq=peeling+back+pavement&st=nyt. Accessed 8 October 2010.

Rice, Brian. *Seeing the World with Aboriginal Eyes: A Four-Directional Perspective on Human and non-Human Values, Cultures, and Relationships on Turtle Island*. Winnipeg: Aboriginal Issues Press, 2005.

Rice, James. "Ecological Unequal Exchange: Consumption, Equity, and Unsustainable Structural Relationships within the Global Economy." *International Journal of Comparative Sociology* 48, no. 1 (2007): 43–72.

Richardson, Anthony J., Andrew Bakun, Graeme C. Hays, and Mark J. Gibbons. "The Jellyfish Joyride: Causes, Consequences and Management Responses to a More Gelatinous Future." *Trends in Ecology and Evolution* 24, no. 6 (2009): 312–22.

Richardson, Boyce. *Strangers Devour the Land*. 2nd ed. White River Junction, Vermont: Chelsea Green, 1991.

Rimbaud, Arthur. *Illuminations and Other Prose Poems*. Translated by Louise Varèse. Rev. ed. New York: New Directions, 1957.

Roburn, Shirley. "Literacy and the Underdevelopment of Knowledge." *Mediatribe: Concordia University's Undergraduate Journal of Communication Studies* 4, no. 1 (1994): n.p. http://epe.lac-bac.gc.ca/100/202/300/mediatribe/mtribe94/native_knowledge.html.

Rockhill, Gabriel, and Philip Watts, eds. *Jacques Rancière: History Politics, Aesthetics*. Durham: Duke University Press, 2009.

Roman, Joe. *Whale*. London: Reaktion Books, 2006.

Ross, Andrew. *Bird on Fire: Lessons from the World's Least Sustainable City*. New York: Oxford University Press, 2011.

Roth, Ethan H., and Val Schmidt. "U.S. Geological Survey Coastal and Marine Geology Report on Cooperative Agreement G09AC00352: Noise levels generated by research icebreakers and marine seismic sources in the deep-water, Arctic Ocean." Marine Physical Laboratory of the Scripps Institution of Oceanography, University of California San Diego, March 2010.

Rothenberg, David. *Thousand-Mile Song: Whale Music in a Sea of Sound*. New York: Basic Books, 2008.

Roy, Arundhati. "The Greater Common Good." *Friends of River Narmada*, 1999. http://www.narmada.org/gcg/gcg.html.

– *The God of Small Things*. Toronto: Vintage Canada, 1997.

Ruffo, Armand Garnet. "Ethic." In *Regreen: New Canadian Ecological Poetry*, edited by Madhur Anand and Adam Dickinson. Sudbury, Ontario: Your Scrivener Press, 2009. See also: http://www.library.utoronto.ca/canpoetry/ruffo/poem1.htm.

Runaway Moon Theatre. "What's On: Right Now." http://www.runawaymoon.org/current.php. Accessed 12 April 2011.

Sadler, Simon. *The Situationist City*. Cambridge, Massachusetts: MIT Press, 1998.

Sahlins, Marshall. *Stone Age Economics*. Hawthorne, New York: Aldine, 1972.

Said, Edward W. "Invention, Memory and Place." *Critical Inquiry* 26, no. 2 (2000): 175–92.

Salmon, Enrique. "Kincentric Ecology: Indigenous Perception of the Human-Nature Relationship." *Ecological Applications* 10, no. 5 (2000): 1327–32.

Samson, Colin. *A Way of Life that Does Not Exist: Canada and the Extinguishment of the Innu*. London: Verso, 2003.

Sandilands, Catriona. "Acts of Nature: Literature, Excess and Environmental Politics." In *Transcanada Three: Literature, Institutions, Citizenship*, edited by Smaro Kamboureli and Christl Verduyn. Waterloo: Wilfrid Laurier University Press, forthcoming.

Sarangi, Satinath. *The Hindu*. New Delhi, April 22 (2008): p. 9.

– "The Thiosulphate Scandal." *International Campaign for Justice in Bhopal*. http://bhopal.net/the-thiosulphate-scandal/

Sawicki, Marianne. *Crossing Galilee: Architectures of Contact in the Occupied Land of Jesus*. New York: Continuum International Publishing Group, 2000.

Schafer, R. Murray. "Introduction," "Listening," and "The Acoustic Community." In *The Soundscape: Our Sonic Environment and the Tuning of the World*, 2–12, 205–25. 1977. Rpt. Rochester: Destiny Books, 1994.

Schama, Simon. *Landscape and Memory*. New York: Vintage Books, 1995.

Schrope, Mark. "Marine Ecology: Attack of the Blobs." *Nature*. 1 February 2012. http://www.nature.com/news/marine-ecology-attack-of-the-blobs-1.9929

Schumacher, E.F. *Small Is Beautiful: Economics as if People Mattered*. London: Blond & Briggs, 1973.

Scott, James. *The Art of Not Being Governed: An Anarchist History of Upland Southeast Asia*. New Haven, London: Yale University Press, 2009.

Scudder, Thayer. *The Future of Large Dams: Dealing with Social, Environmental, Institutional, and Political Costs*. London and Sterling Virginia: Earthscan, 2005.

*Scyphozoa Photogallery World Registry of Marine Species*. http://www.marinespecies.org/photogallery.php?album=676.

Secrétariat Archipel. Plan. "Planche 22. Aménagement Hydroélectrique: Agencement Général et Perspective." In *Projet Archipel: Rapport de Faisabilité: Volume 3: L'aménagement hydroélectrique des rapides de Lachine*. Gouvernement du Québec, Ministère des Affaires municipales, avril 1986.

Serres, Michel. *Angels: A Modern Myth*. Translated by Francis Cowper. Paris: Flammarion, 1995.

– *The Natural Contract*. Translated by Elizabeth MacArthur and William Paulson. Ann Arbor: University of Michigan Press, 1995.

"Shell Oil's Arctic Offshore Drilling Plan Illegal Says Federal Appeals Court." *www.earthjustice. org*. 20 November 2008. http://www.earthjustice.org/news/press/2008/shell-oil-s-arctic-off shore-drilling-plan-illegal-says-federal-appeals-court.html.

Shildrick, Margrit. *Leaky Bodies and Boundaries: Feminism, Postmodernism and (Bio)Ethics*. New York: Routledge, 1997.

Shiva, Vandana. *Monocultures of the Mind: Perspectives on Biodiversity and Biotechnology*. London: Zed Books, 1993.

– *Water Wars: Privatization, Pollution, and Profit*. Toronto: Between the Lines, 2002.

Shove, Elizabeth. *Comfort, Cleanliness and Convenience: The Social Organization of Normality*. Oxford, New York: Berg, 2003.

Shubin, Neil. *Your Inner Fish: A Journey into the 3.5 Billion-Year History of the Human Body*. New York: Vintage, 2009.

Simard, Yvan, Natalie Roy, and Cedric Gervaise. "Passive acoustic detection and localization of whales: Effects of shipping noise in Saguenay-St. Lawrence Marine Park." *Journal of the Acoustical Society of America* 123, no. 6 (June 2008): 4109–17.

Simms, Eva Marie. "Eating One's Mother: Female Embodiment in a Toxic World." *Environmental Ethics* 31 (2009): 263–77.

Sims, Daniel. "Ware's Waldo: Hydroelectric Development and the Creation of the Other in British Columbia." Paper presented at "Cross-Pollination: Seeding the Ground for Environmental Thought and Activism Across the Arts and Humanities" Workshop, University of Alberta, 24–27 March 2011.

Singh, Madhur. "Bhopal and the BP Oil Spill: A Tale of Two Disasters." *Time*, 8 June 2010 http://www.time.com/time/world/article/0,8599,1995029,00.html.

"Siphonophores." http://www.siphonophores.org/SiphCollecting.php. Accessed 7 April 2010.

Slack, Jennifer Daryl. "Resisting Ecocultural Studies." *Cultural Studies* 22, nos. 3–4 (May–July 2008): 477–97.

Sneddon, Chris, Laila Harris, Radoslav Dimitrov, and Uygar Özesmi. "Contested Waters: Conflict, Scale, and Sustainability in Aquatic Socioecological Systems." *Society and Natural Resources* 15 (2002): 663–75.

Sorenson, John. "Monsters: The Case of Marineland." In *Animal Subjects: An Ethical Reader in a Posthuman World*, edited by Jodey Castricano, 195–221. Waterloo: Wilfrid Laurier University Press, 2008.

Southall, B., J. Berkson, D. Bowen, R. Brake, J. Eckman, J. Field, et al. *Addressing the Effects of Human-Generated Sound on Marine Life: An Integrated Research Plan for U.S. Federal Agencies*. Interagency Task Force on Anthropogenic Sound and the Marine Environment of the Joint Subcommittee on Ocean Science and Technology. Washington, D.C., 2009.

Spivak, Gayatri. *Death of a Discipline*. New York: Columbia University Press, 2003.

Steeves, Peter H., ed. *Animal Others: On Ethics, Ontology, and Animal Life*. Buffalo: SUNY Press, 1999.

Stein, Max. *Montreal Sound Map*. Last updated 8 June 2012. http://www.montrealsound
map.com/.

Steingraber, Sandra. *Update on the Environmental Health Impacts of Polyvinyl Chloride (PVC)
as a Building Material: Evidence from 2000–2004*. Healthy Building Network, 2004.

Sterne, Jonathan. *The Audible Past: Cultural Origins of Sound Reproduction*. Durham, North
Carolina: Duke University Press, 2003.

Stevens, Joseph. *Hoover Dam: An American Adventure*. Norman, Oklahoma: University of
Oklahoma Press, 1990.

Stevens, Stanley Smith, and Fred Warshofsky. "The Machinery of Hearing," "The Route to the
Brain," and "The Mind's Influence." In *Sound and Hearing*, 30–84. New York: Time Incorporated, 1965.

Stocker, Michael. *Now Hear This: An evaluation of the impacts of specific anthropogenic noise
types on cetaceans*. Greenpeace USA, May 2008. http://www.greenpeace.org/usa/press-center/
reports4/now-hear-this.

Stoekl, Allan. *Bataille's Peak: Energy, Religion, and Postsustainability*. Minneapolis, London:
University of Minnesota Press, 2007.

Stoller, Paul. *The Taste of Ethnographic Things: The Senses in Anthropology*. Philadelphia:
University of Pennsylvania Press, 1989.

Stone, Alison. "The Sex of Nature: A Reinterpretation of Irigaray's Metaphysics and Political
Thought." *Hypatia* 18, no. 3 (2003): 60–84.

Strang, Veronica. "Fluid Forms: Owning Water in Australia." In *Ownership and Appropriation*,
edited by Veronica Strang and Mark Busse, 171–95. ASA Monograph. Oxford, New York:
Berg, 2010.

– "Knowing Me, Knowing You: Aboriginal and Euro-Australian Concepts of Nature as Self and
Other." *Worldviews* 9, no. 1 (2005): 25–56.

– "Life Down Under: Water and Identity in an Aboriginal Cultural Landscape." *Goldsmiths
College Anthropology Research Papers*. No. 7. London: Goldsmiths College, 2002.

– *Gardening the World: Agency, Identity, and the Ownership of Water*. Oxford, New York:
Berghahn Publishers, 2009.

– "A Happy Coincidence? Symbiosis and Synthesis in Anthropological and Indigenous
Knowledges." *Current Anthropology* 47, no. 6 (2006): 981–1008.

– *The Meaning of Water*. Oxford and New York: Berg, 2004.

– *Uncommon Ground: Cultural Landscapes and Environmental Values*. Oxford, New York:
Berg, 1997.

*Superman*. Richard Donner, dir. United States: Warner Bros Pictures, 1978. Film, 143 min.

Swyngedouw, Erik. "Modernity and the Production of the Spanish Waterscape, 1890–1930."
In *Geographical Political Ecology*, edited by Thomas Bassett and Karl Zimmerer, 94–112.
New York: Guilford, 2003.

– *Social Power and the Urbanization of Water: Flows of Power*. Oxford: Oxford University Press,
2004.

Taylor, Phil. "Shell Cancels 2011 Arctic Drilling Plans." *New York Times*. 3 February 2011.

http://www.nytimes.com/gwire/2011/02/03/03greenwire-shell-cancels-2011-arctic-drilling-plans-18881.html.

Tempest Williams, Terry. "Foreword: Sun and Moons in Motion." In Connor and Deans, *Jellies: Living Art*, 9–13.

Terdiman, Richard. *Present Past: Modernity and the Memory Crisis*. Cornell University Press, 1993.

Tetzan Biny (Fish Lake). http://teztanbiny.ca/

Than, Ker. "'Immortal' Jellyfish Swarm World's Oceans." *National Geographic News*. 29 January 2009. http://news.nationalgeographic.com/news/2009/01/090130-immortal-jellyfish-swarm.html. Accessed 30 April 2010.

Thompson, Elizabeth. "Toxic Sites Worth Billions: Task Force." *Montreal Gazette*, Tuesday, February 11, 2003.

Thorpe, Doug. "Living Waters: Israel/Palestine and the War with Literalism." Paper presented at the Association for the Study of Literature and Environment Conference. University of Victoria, June 2009. An unpublished draft of this conference paper is referred to in this chapter, as sent to Rita Wong in summer 2009.]

Treasury Board of Canada. "Federal Contaminated Sites Inventory: What Is a Contaminated Site?" http://www.tbs-sct.gc.ca/fcsi-rscf/home-accueil.aspx.

Truax, Barry. *Acoustic Communication, 2nd Edition*. Westport: Ablex Publishing, 2001.

Tsing, Anna. *Friction: An Ethnography of Global Connections*. Princeton: Princeton University Press, 2004.

Tuan, Yi-Fu. *The Hydrologic Cycle and the Wisdom of God: A Theme in Geoteleology*. Toronto: University of Toronto Press, 1968.

Tuana, Nancy. "Viscous Porosity." In *Material Feminisms*, edited by Stacy Alaimo and Susan Hekman, 188–213. Bloomington: Indiana University Press, 2008.

Tyack, Peter L. "Implications for Marine Mammals of Large-Scale Changes in the Marine Acoustic Environment." *Journal of Mammalogy* 89, no. 3 (2008): 549–58.

Tyler, Tom. "Like Water in Water," *Journal for Cultural Research* 9.3 (July 2005): 265–79.

– and Manuela Rossini, eds. *Animal Encounters*. Leiden: Brill, 2009.

U.S. Bureau of Land Management. *Northeast National Petroleum Reserve – Alaska. Amended Integrated Activity Plan/Environmental Impact Statement*, Vols. 1–3. Washington, 2005.

– *Northeast National Petroleum Reserve – Alaska. Final Supplemental Amended Integrated Activity Plan/Environmental Impact Statement*. Washington, 2008.

Ulmer, Gregory L. *Heuretics: The Logic of Invention*. Baltimore: Johns Hopkins University Press, 1994.

UNEP (United Nations Environment Programme). "Environmental Assessement of Ogoniland." 2011. http://www.unep.org/Nigeria/ and http://postconflict.unep.ch/publications/OEA/UNEP_OEA.pdf

United Nations General Assembly. GA/10967. "General Assembly adopts resolution recognizing access to clean water, sanitation as human right, by recorded vote of 122 in favour, none against, 41 abstentions." 28 July 2010: http://www.un.org/News/Press/docs/2010/ga10967.doc.htm.

*Up the Yangtze*. Yung Chang, dir. Canada: Eye Steel Film; National Film Board of Canada, 2007. Film 93 mm.

*Upstream Battle*. Ben Kempas, dir. Klamath River, U.S.: Preview Production GbR, 2008. Film, 97 min. http://www.upstreambattle.com.

van Wyck, Peter C. "Footbridge at Atwater: A (Partial) Inventory of Effects." In *Journées Sonores, Canal de Lachine, Une Installation Interactive*, edited by Andra McCartney. Lachine, Quebec, 2003.

– *Primitives in the Wilderness: Deep Ecology and the Missing Human Subject*. Albany: SUNY Press, 1997.

– *The Highway of the Atom*. Montreal: McGill-Queen's University Press, 2010.

Vernadsky, Vladimir. *The Biosphere*. Santa Fe, New Mexico: Synergetic Press, 1986.

Verry, E.S., C.A. Dolloff, and M.E. Manning. "Riparian Ecotone: A Functional Definition and Delineation for Resource Assessment." *Water, Air, and Soil Pollution: Focus* 4 (2004): 67–94.

*Victorian Farmers Federation*. "VFF Submission to the Murray-Darling Basin Authority." http://www.vff.org.au/newsite/policy_issues/murray_darling_basin_plan.php.

"Victory in the Arctic!" *pacificenvironment.org*. 13 September 2007. http://www.pacificenviron ment.org/article.php?id=2568.

"Victory! Shell Drops 2011 Arctic Drilling Plans." *Oceana.org*. 4 February 2011. http://na.oceana.org/en/blog/2011/02/victory-shell-drops-2011-arctic-drilling-plans.

Vidal, John. "Outrage at UN decision to exonerate Shell for oil pollution in Niger delta." *Guardian*, 22 August 2010. http://www.guardian.co.uk/environment/2010/aug/22/shell-niger-delta-un-investigation. Accessed 25 March 2012.

Vidler, Anthony. *The Architectural Uncanny: Essays in the Modern Unhomely*. Cambridge, Massachusetts: MIT Press, 1992.

von Uexküll, Jakob. *A Foray into the Worlds of Animals and Humans*. Minneapolis: University of Minnesota Press, 2010.

– "A Stroll through the Worlds of Animals and Men: A Picture Book of Invisible Worlds." *Semiotica* 89, no. 4 (1992): 319–91.

Walkem, Ardith. "The Land Is Dry: Indigenous Peoples, Water and Environmental Justice." In *Eau Canada: The Future of Canada's Water*, edited by Karen Bakker, 303–19. Vancouver: University of British Columbia Press, 2007.

Walker, Matt. "Strange Jellies of the Icy Depths." *BBC Earth News*. 1 September 2009. http://news.bbc.co.uk/earth/hi/earth_news/newsid_8231000/8231367.stm. Accesssed 1 October 2010.

Walter, E.V. "Placeways: A Theory of the Human Environment." In *Placeways: A Theory of the Human Environment*. Chapel Hill: University of North Carolina Press, 1988, 1–43.

Warner, Michael. "Public and Private." In *Publics and Counterpublics*, 21–63. New York: Zone Books, 2005.

Warshall, Peter. "Watershed Governance." In *Writing on Water*, edited by David Rothenberg and Marta Ulvaeus, 40–57. Cambridge, Massachusetts: MIT Press, 2001.

"Water Depletion." Tar Sands Watch. Polaris Institute's Energy Watch Program http://www.tarsandswatch.org/water-depletion. Accessed 18 November 2012.

*Waterlife website*. Online interactive film and map. http://waterlife.nfb.ca/. See also *Waterlife*.

*Waterlife*. Kevin McMahon, dir. Canada: Primitive Entertainment with the National Film Board of Canada, 2009, 109 min.

WCD (World Commission on Dams). *Dams and Development: A New Framework for Decision-Making: The Report of the World Commission on Dams*. London: Earthscan, 2000.

Weilgart, L.S. "The impacts of anthropogenic ocean noise on cetaceans and implications for management." *Canadian Journal of Zoology* 85, no. 11 (Nov. 2007): 1091–1116.

Weiss, Gail. *Body Images: Embodiment as Intercorporeality*. New York: Routledge, 1999.

Weissmann, Ann. Curator. "Ernst Haeckel: Art Forms in Nature." Marine Biology Laboratory. http://www.mblwhoilibrary.org/exhibits/haeckel/index.html. Accessed 30 April 2010.

Wellburn, Kate. "'Not The Way I Heard It': Enderby and District Community Play, May 1999." Originally published in *The Enderby Commoner*. Now on the Enderby & District Museum Society website. http://www.enderbymuseum.ca/thepast/enter/theatre/communityplay.htm. Accessed 12 April 2011.

Welling, Bart. "Ecoporn: On the Limits of Visualizing the Nonhuman." In *Ecosee: Image, Rhetoric, Nature*. Ed. Sidney I. Dobrin and Sean Morey. Albany: SUNY Press, 2009: 53–77.

Whitehead, H. "How might we study culture? A perspective from the ocean." In *The Question of Animal Culture*, edited by B. Galef and K.L. Laland, 125–52. Cambridge: Harvard University Press, 2009.

Whitford, Margaret. *Luce Irigaray: Philosophy in the Feminine*. London: Routledge, 1991.

Whitridge, Peter. "Landscapes, Houses, Bodies, Things: 'Place' and the Archaeology of Inuit Imaginaries." *Journal of Archaeological Method and Theory* 11, no. 2 (2004): 213–50.

Williams, Raymond. *Marxism and Literature*. Oxford: Oxford University Press, 1977.

Wilson, E.O. *The Future of Life*. New York: Vintage, 2003.

Wilson, Elizabeth A. "Gut Feminism." *Differences* 15, no. 3 (2004): 66–94.

Wittfogel, Karl. *Oriental Despotism: A Comparative Study of Total Power*. New Haven: Yale University Press, 1957. Reprinted by Vintage, 1981.

Wolfe, Cary. *Animal Rites: American Culture, the Discourse of Species, and Posthumanist Theory*. Chicago: University of Chicago Press, 2003.

– *What is Posthumanism?* Minneapolis: University of Minnesota Press, 2010.

Woolf, Virginia. *The Voyage Out*. (1915). Oxford: Oxford University Press, 1992.

– *Mrs. Dalloway*. (1925). London: Penguin Books, 2000.

– *To the Lighthouse*. (1927). Oxford: Oxford University Press, 2006.

Wong, Rita. "Watersheds." *Canadian Literature* 204 (Spring 2010): 115–17.

*World Ocean Council: The International Business Alliance for Corporate Ocean Responsibility*. "Frequently Asked Questions." http://www.oceancouncil.org/site/faq.php. Accessed 31 May 2011.

*World Wildlife Fund*. "Our Solutions: Marine Protected Areas." http://www.panda.org/about_wwf/what_we_do/marine/our_solutions/protected_areas/index.cfm.

Worm, Janette, Jan Maarten Dros, and Jan Willem van Gelder. "Policies and Practices in Financing Large Dams." Research Paper II prepared for WWF International – Living Waters Programme: AIDEvironment and Profundo, April 2003.

WORMS. *World Registry of Marine Species.* http://www.marinespecies.org/about.php. Accessed 18 April 2010.

Worster, Donald. *Nature's Economy: A History of Ecological Ideas.* Cambridge: Cambridge University Press, 1994.

– *Rivers of Empire: Water, Aridity, and the Growth of the American West.* New York: Pantheon, 1985.

Wright, Roy. "Le Plan Vincent et la toponymie historique des Hurons-Wendats." In *A Passion for the Past: Papers in Honour of James F. Pendergast*, edited by James V. Wright and Jean-Luc Pilon, 205–40. Ottawa: Canadian Museum of Civilization, 2004.

Wright, Tamara, Peter Hughes, and Alison Ainley. "The Paradox of Morality: An Interview with Emmanuel Levinas." In *The Provocation of Levinas: Rethinking the Other*, edited by Robert Bernasconi and David Wood, translated by Andrew Benjamin and Tamara Wright, 168–80. London: Routledge, 1988.

Yan, Katy. "Canada's Hydro Partnerships No Panacea for First Nations." *International Rivers.* 9 June 2010. http://www.internationalrivers.org/resources/canada's-hydro-partnerships-no-panacea-for-first-nations-1713

Yes Men. *The Yes Men Fix the World,* 2009.

Zandberg, Bryan. "Reviving a Native Tongue: Can a UBC program bring back to life the Musqueam dialect?" *The Ubyssey.* 23 March 2007. Reprinted in *The Tyee.* http://thetyee.ca/News/2007/03/23/RevivingANativeTongue/. Accessed 8 June 2010.

Zhao, Xiaolan. *Reflections of the Moon on Water.* Toronto: Random House, 2006.

Žižek, Slavoj. *Living in the End Times.* New York: Verso Press, 2010.

– and Glyn Daly. *Conversations with Žižek (Conversations).* Cambridge: Polity, 2003.

# Contributors

ÆLAB. Gisèle Trudel and Stéphane Claude are artists. In 1996 they co-founded the artist research unit Ælab. Gisèle Trudel is a professor at the École des arts visuels et médiatiques, Université du Québec à Montréal and acting director of Hexagram-UQAM, the Centre for Research/Creation in Media Arts and Technologies. Stéphane Claude is an electronic composer, audio mastering engineer, and head of research of the Audio sector at Oboro's new media lab. Ælab's commitment to collaboration, creative dissemination, and innovative technologies enables ways of thinking and doing that strive to bridge the arts and sciences. Their process-oriented investigations creatively engage art, nature and technology, as intertwined ecologies. Their work is presented regularly on the international art scene.
www.aelab.com
www.hexagram.uqam.ca
www.grupmuv.ca

STACY ALAIMO is professor of English and Distinguished Teaching Professor at the University of Texas at Arlington. She has published widely in the environmental humanities, science studies, and feminist theory, on such diverse subjects as environmental literature and film, environmental art and architecture, environmental pedagogy, performance art, gender and climate change, "queer" animals, the campus sustainability movement, and ocean conservation. She currently serves on the MLA Division of Literature and Science and edits the "Critical Ecologies" stream of the Electronic Book Review. At UTA she worked as the academic co-chair for the University Sustainability Committee and as the coordinator for the interdisciplinary Environmental and Sustainability Studies Minor. Her publications include *Undomesticated Ground: Recasting Nature as Feminist Space* (Cornell 2000); *Material Feminisms* (edited with Susan J. Hekman); and *Bodily Natures: Science, Environment, and the Material Self* (Indiana 2010). *Bodily Natures* won the ASLE Award for Ecocriticism in 2011. She is writing a book tentatively titled *Sea Creatures and the Limits of Animal Studies: Science, Aesthetics, Ethics.*

JEANNETTE ARMSTRONG is Syilx Okanagan, a fluent speaker of nsyilxcen and a traditional knowledge keeper within her nation. She has a PhD in Environmental Ethics and Syilx Indigenous Literatures. Awarded the 2003 EcoTrust Buffett Award for Indigenous Leadership, she is the executive director of En'owkin Centre, the cultural research and education facility of the Okanagan Nation as well as being on faculty in Indigenous Studies at the University of British Columbia Okanagan. She has been instrumental in the research and implementation of a successful nsyilxcen adult language fluency and revitalization program. She is distinguished with honorary doctorates from the University of St Thomas, the University of British Columbia Okanagan and the Queen's University and holds the Okanagan College Lifetime Fellow award. She is an author and Indigenous activist whose published works include literary titles and academic writing on a wide variety of Indigenous issues. She serves on Environment Canada's Traditional Knowledge Subcommittee.

ANDREW BIRO is an associate professor in the Department of Politics at Acadia University. He also teaches in Acadia's Environmental and Sustainability Studies program and in the graduate program in Social and Political Thought. He is the author of *Denaturalizing Ecological Politics*, and editor of *Critical Ecologies: The Frankfurt School and Contemporary Environmental Crises*. His research focuses on the social construction of scarcity, at the intersections of environmental politics, cultural studies, and political philosophy.

MIELLE CHANDLER is a gypsy scholar stationed in Toronto cobbling together contracts at York University en route to the Peruvian Amazon. She has a PhD in Social and Political Thought and is pursuing an LLM at Osgoode Hall Law School. Motivated to bring to the fore the violence bound up in desacralizing the material world, her current writing project asks what the plant spirits might say to Law. Such an unorthodox project is made possible by a liberation from academic disciplinary propriety that accompanies throwing the goal of a tenure track job to the wind. Growing up in East Africa and Southeast Asia with an ecologist father and an anthropologist mother significantly shaped Mielle's thinking. As did grappling with the experience of profound meaning and love on the one hand, and social stigma and economic poverty on the other, which she found upon becoming a mother at an early age. Her thought has been further shaped by the reverence of matter she cultivated in Art School, and the de-privileging of matter woven through the philosophical canon she studied in graduate school. An increasing phenomenological attention to the significance of embodied awareness in a plural world guides her most recent thought.

CECILIA CHEN is an architect working with L'OEUF s.e.n.c. and a doctoral candidate in communications with Concordia University in Montreal. As one part of the evolving entity of a city, she is interested in how we collectively imagine, negotiate, and build urban and watery places in relationship with more-than-human environments. With the majority of humans now living in urban contexts even as the climate changes, the thoughtful design of cities and their complex relations with water are increasingly important. Her current dissertation project proposes that how we come to know, understand and represent water – particularly through mapping – is of radical importance to the quality of our relations with water.

DOROTHY CHRISTIAN is a writer, video artist, and producer/director of documentaries. She is of the Okanagan-Secwepemc Nations of the interior of British Columbia, and has written over seventy-five mini-documentaries for Vision TV. Her most recent work, an experimental film called *"a spiritual land claim,"* has been screened at many festivals. Dorothy is currently completing doctoral studies at the University of British Columbia, where she is researching the Visual Sovereignty of Fourth World Cinema, and Indigenous Pedagogy. She co-organized a public forum called "Protect Our Sacred Waters" with Denise Nadeau in 2007.

ADAM DICKINSON is a writer, researcher, and teacher. His poems have appeared in literary journals in Canada and internationally, as well as in anthologies such as *Breathing Fire 2: Canada's New Poets* and *The Shape of Content: Creative Writing in Mathematics and Science*. His book of poetry *Cartography and Walking* (Brick Books) was short listed for an Alberta Book Award. His collection *Kingdom, Phylum* (Brick Books) was a finalist for the Trillium Book Award for Poetry. His next book, *The Polymers* (House of Anansi), was published in the spring of 2013. He teaches at Brock University in St Catharines, Ontario.

MAX HAIVEN is an assistant professor in the Department of Art History and Critical Studies at the Nova Scotia College of Art and Design in Halifax. His research focuses on the cultural dimensions of finance capitalism and on contemporary social movements. He is the author of the forthcoming books *Cultures of Financialization* (Palgrave Macmillan 2014), *Crises of Imagination, Crises of Power* (Zed 2014), and (with Alex Khasnabish) *The Radical Imagination* (Zed 2014). Max's academic work has appeared in journals including *Social Text, Cultural Studies, and Cultural Critique*, and his political and cultural commentaries have appeared in venues including *Truth-Out, Art Threat*, and *Dissident Voice*. More information can be found at www.maxhaiven.com.

DAPHNE MARLATT's poetry titles include *Steveston, This Tremor Love Is*, and *The Given*, which received the 2009 Dorothy Livesay Poetry Award. She has written three novels, *Zócalo, Ana Historic*, and *Taken*. The 2006 production by Pangaea Arts of her contemporary Canadian Noh play, *The Gull*, received the international Uchimura Naoya Prize. In 2012 she was awarded the George Woodcock Lifetime Achievement

Award. She lives in Vancouver's Strathcona neighbourhood, which used to lie between Burrard Inlet and False Creek. Her most recent title, *Liquidities: Vancouver Poems Then and Now*, a double series of her poems about the city, appears from Talonbooks in 2013.

JANINE MACLEOD is a PhD candidate in the Faculty of Environmental Studies at York University. Her work considers water's capacity to carry memory between diverse bodies, habitats, and landscapes of the imagination. In her doctoral research, she examines the roles of memory and affect within political and commercial discourses on water, and explores potential points of seepage through which alternative meanings and histories might animate public life. She has published magazine articles and book chapters on water, environmental politics, and chemical toxicity. MacLeod is currently completing a book manuscript on water and memory, in which she further considers the relationships between vital watercourses, emotional life, and everyday understandings.

DON MCKAY has published numerous books of poetry and several books of essays. The poetry has been recognized by a number of awards, including two Governor General's Literary awards and the Griffin Poetry Prize. His most recent book of essays, *The Shell of the Tortoise*, received the Winterset Prize for Excellence in Newfoundland and Labrador Writing for 2011. *Paradoxides*, his most recent book of poems, includes meditations on geology and deep time, and pursues ongoing obsessions with birds and tools. He lives in St John's, Newfoundland.

EMILY ROSE MICHAUD is an artist, educator, and organizer who works at the intersections of community development, civic participation, and urban ecology and urban development. Her courses, images, installations, performances, events, and land art favour experimental, participatory, and socially driven approaches to creativity. Based in Montreal for over twelve years, she has collaborated with community groups, architects, botanists, journalists, and artists. She is a founding member of Les Amis du Champ des Possibles, a citizen-run non-profit that demonstrates and advocates for the cultural, ecological, and social importance of wild urban spaces.

ASTRIDA NEIMANIS is a feminist writer, teacher, and affiliated researcher with the Gender Studies unit at Linköping University. She has taught gender studies at the London School of Economics (LSE), Brock University, and McMaster University. Her work has been published in numerous feminist, philosophical, and cultural studies journals and books, including *Alphabet City*, TOPIA, *Janus Head*, *Feminist Review*, and an edited collection of new feminist theory entitled *Undutiful Daughters* (Palgrave, 2012). She has also collaborated with visual artists, designers, and playwrights, and her creative non-fiction has been published in *Descant*.

SARAH T. RENSHAW received her BFA in painting and MFA in Digital+Media from the Rhode Island School of Design. She is an artist, designer, and arts writer currently based in New York City. www.textarttech.com

SHIRLEY ROBURN is a PhD candidate in the Joint Program in Communication Studies at Concordia, UQAM, and the University of Montreal. Her research, inspired by living in northern Canada, concerns the "public stories" that First Nations communities and environmental groups tell about climate change and food security in northwestern North America, and asks whether these stories are effective in garnering public support and influencing global, national, and regional policy. Roburn is a long-time community activist and has served as an employee, volunteer, and organizer for many environmental justice and human rights organizations, ranging in scope from Amnesty International to the Yukon Conservation Society, from CoCo (a Montreal umbrella organization that builds capacity in the allophone and anglophone community sector) to SPEC, the community group that spawned Greenpeace. Roburn has also worked as a journalist, editor, creative writer, and media producer in areas concerning environmental justice.

MELANIE SIEBERT's first collection, *Deepwater Vee* (McClelland & Stewart, 2010), was a finalist for Canada's Governor General's Award for poetry. Siebert completed her MFA at the University of Victoria, where she received the Lieutenant Governor's Silver Medal for her master's thesis. She has worked as a wilderness guide on rivers in the Northwest Territories, Nunavut, and Alaska.

JENNIFER BETH SPIEGEL is a postdoctoral fellow in the Department of Art History and Communications at McGill University. Her research focuses on performance and performativity in contemporary social movements. In 2006–07 she worked with the Sambhavna Clinic and Documentation Centre in Bhopal, India, to raise awareness of the ongoing state of water contamination. She also became involved with the International Campaign for Justice for Bhopal. In 2011 Spiegel completed a doctorate in Cultural Studies at Goldsmiths College, University of London, entitled *Staging Ecologies: The Politics of Theatricality and the Production of Subjectivity*. She also teaches courses at McGill and Concordia universities on the history and theory of modern and contemporary theatre and performance.

RAE STASESON is an associate professor, and chair of the Department of Communication Studies at Concordia University. She is a media artist, and her work has been screened and exhibited both nationally and internationally. Staseson's videos have been curated into exhibitions at such venues as the National Gallery of Canada, the Walker Art Center (Minneapolis), and the Museum of Contemporary Art (Los Angeles). Her work has been collected by numerous institutions both public and private, including the National Gallery of Canada and the Saskatchewan Arts Board. Staseson's landscape work traces themes of home, site/place, and memory, and for the last seven years she has been working on the project *Between Sand and Snow*, which includes the installation *Water Drawing*. She also curates and programs exhibitions for the Media Gallery at Concordia University.

VERONICA STRANG is a professor of Anthropology at Durham University and the executive director of the university's Institute of Advanced Study. Prior to studying anthropology, Veronica worked as a writer and researcher on environmental issues, and contributed to *The Brundtland Report* (1987). She received her DPhil (studying diverse environmental values in northern Australia) at the University of Oxford in 1995. She has previously held positions at the University of Oxford, the University of Wales, Goldsmiths University, and the University of Auckland. In 2000 she was awarded a Royal Anthropological Institute Urgent Anthropology Fellowship, and in 2007 she was named as one of UNESCO's, *Les Lumières de L'Eau* [Water's Leading Lights]. She has conducted research in Australia, the UK, and New Zealand. Her work focuses on human-environmental relations, cultural landscapes and, in particular, societies' engagements with water. Key publications include *The Meaning of Water* (Berg, 2004); *Gardening the World: Agency, Identity and the Ownership of Water* (Berghahn Books, 2009) and (with Mark Busse) *Ownership and Appropriation* (Berg, 2010).

PETER C. VAN WYCK is professor of Communication Studies at Concordia University in Montreal, where he is also the director of the MA in Media Studies graduate program. He is an interdisciplinary scholar and writer with an abiding interest in the theoretical and practical relations between culture, nature, environment, landscape, and memory. His most recent book, *The Highway of the Atom* (McGill-Queen's University Press, 2010) – winner of the 2011 Gertrude J. Robinson book award from the Canadian Communication Association – is a theoretical and archival investigation concerning the material and cultural history of uranium production in the North of Canada. Other writings include *Signs of Danger: Waste, Trauma, and Nuclear Threat* (University of Minnesota Press, 2005), and *Primitives in the Wilderness: Deep Ecology and the Missing Human Subject* (State University of New York Press, 1997). He is now working on a new book project concerning nuclear media, apology, justice, and the future.

RITA WONG is the author of three books of poetry: *sybil unrest* (co-written with Larissa Lai), *forage* (winner of Canada Reads Poetry 2011 and the 2008 Dorothy Livesay Prize), and *monkeypuzzle* (for which she received the Asian Canadian Writers Workshop Emerging Writer Award). Wong is an associate professor in the Faculty of

Culture and Community at Emily Carr University of Art and Design. With the support of a fellowship from the Center for Contemplative Mind in Society, she has developed a humanities course focused on water. She is researching the poetics of water in the Downstream Project, with the support of an SSHRC Research/Creation grant.

# Index